If You Ain't a Pilot…

By

Ray Wright

Dedication:

To Ben, Jackson, and Wesley

Acknowledgements

"Write your book," Rachel Wright, 2008.

> Thank you, Rachel. Without your support, encouragement, patience, and love, I would never have gotten this far.

"Send me the galleys," Michael Dolan, 2011.

> Thank you, Doley. Without your feedback, I would still be focused on a different aim point.

"You have to include that story," Malia Spranger, 2012.

> Thank you, Malia. Without your blessing, I would not have included that story. In fact, I probably never would have mentioned it again. Ever.

"There are way too many characters," Catherine Michele Adams, Inkslinger Editing, 2014.

> Thank you, Catherine. Without your guidance, coaching, and direction, I would still have a mess on my hands.

"My head is not that big," Kurt Spranger, 2014.

> Dude, c'mon.

To my motivator, my co-conspirator, my conscience, my visionary, and my hero:

> You were right. I needed to hear this.

Table of Contents

Author's Note

In the pages that follow, I've used some real names to tell some real stories. I've used some made-up names to tell some other stories.

I've combined and condensed both people and events to simplify the chaos of Undergraduate Pilot Training for those who have not shared in this experience.

Some of my classmates may remember things differently.

This is my version.

Enjoy.

"Thermodynamics is a funny subject. The first time you go through the subject, you don't understand it at all. The second time you go through it, you think you understand it, except for one or two small points. The third time you go through it, you know you don't understand it, but by that time you are so used to the subject, it doesn't bother you anymore."[1]

Attributed to Arnold Sommerfeld, German theoretical physicist, 1868–1951

---

[1] Stanley W. Angrist and Loren G. Helper, *Order and Chaos – Laws of Energy and Entropy* (New York: Basic Books, 1967), 215.

Chapter 1 — "All Fun and Games"

You can't fart with impunity while a ceiling fan spins overhead. It's the same concept as getting caught in the jetwash. If you pushed the power on your engines up too high when taxiing around on the ground, the wind and fumes from your tailpipes, the jetwash, could knock over a crew chief standing in your blast cone. Two summers earlier, in the big hit *Top Gun,* when Maverick flew into Ice Man's jetwash, he slipped into a flat spin and went out to sea. Maverick and Goose had to punch out. And Goose died, because he smashed his head on the canopy. But I wasn't thinking about that. All I could think about was that my insides were growling almost as loudly as the bedroom ceiling fan above me was rattling.

We started flight school the summer after *Top Gun.* At the beginning of our training—now ten months past—our aerospace physiology lessons stressed the importance of equalizing pressures inside the body during climbs and descents to keep up with changes in atmospheric pressure outside the body. Anticipate the changes. Stay ahead of them.

I definitely had pressure built up inside my stomach as I descended from the alcohol-induced high of the previous night. My stomach was gurgling and rumbling out of control. I couldn't keep up with the changing pressures. For ear pressure, you yawned and stretched the Eustachian tube in your inner ear to deal with trapped gases inside your head. Upon descent from altitude, as the pressures around your body increased, you performed the Valsalva maneuver by plugging your nose and attempting to blow through blocked nostrils until your ears popped.

For gastrointestinal pressure, which hit during the climb to altitude, student pilots learned the Air Force's unofficial pressure equalization technique: the One Cheek Sneak. Without drawing attention to yourself, dig one cheek into your seat, lean, and lift the other cheek ever so slightly to spread the two out wide. Release the gas slowly with control, and most importantly, pretend like you're not doing anything. Polite, discreet, necessary, and very effective.

I knew I'd never get back to sleep if I didn't equalize the pressure in my stomach with the bedroom atmospheric pressure. The only thing that concerned me was being so loud my roommates heard. Slowly and silently, I initiated the diffusive process with a flawless execution of the One Cheek Sneak.

Much better.

Relief was instant, but almost as instantly, my jetwash blew back into my face, courtesy of the ceiling fan. Wind, hot fumes, and a flat spin, the consequences were inescapable.

Instead of jet exhaust, however, these fumes reeked of tequila. I had forgotten I drank tequila, which explained why my mouth and throat were so dry. It also explained my buzzing headache.

As I lay on my bed, having closed my eyes again, the room spun faster than the ceiling fan. I didn't know which one spun left and which one spun right, but I did know I was about to get sick. And for the first time since I woke up, I noticed there was no cool air. It was hot. Wicked hot. The air conditioner had broken again. I was starting to think I had to punch out of bed.

Nothing worked right in our house from the time we first moved in. Kenny and I had been renting it for just about the full year of flight school, which started two months after graduating from the Academy. Doley only lived with us since February. Month in and month out, something needed to be fixed. This month, it was the air conditioning, and this was maybe the third time the AC had broken down—not a good thing in Mississippi in the middle of June, when every day is ninety degrees or hotter.

Yesterday, I bet it was a hundred!

Even after the sun went down, it stayed hot. I'd never lived anywhere hotter. Growing up in Rhode Island, we probably had three days each summer over ninety degrees. At the Academy in Colorado, where I studied as a cadet, you might get to ninety degrees for about a week in the summer, but after the sun went down behind the mountains, the nights were always cool. Sometimes even cold. But in Columbus, Mississippi, I regularly saw temperatures over a hundred on the local Chevy dealer's time, temp, and message sign. Once, I even saw a hundred and twelve!

Above my bed, the ceiling fan wasn't aligned correctly. As the fan blades spun and the light fixture hula'ed around its y-axis, the beaded metal pull-chain circled and scraped the glass fixture upon each revolution with a tiny *clink*. Every fourth rotation, the wooden knob at the bottom of the pull-chain rotated fast enough to swing up and knock the lamp, making a much louder CLINK!

The beat reminded me of a marching cadence back at the Academy.

Clink. Clink. Clink. CLINK!

HuP. TooP. ThreeP. FOURP!

When you called out a marching cadence, you were supposed to add the "P" sound to your numbers to emphasize the point in each step when marchers' heels were supposed to dig into the ground. Supposedly, the extra "P" sound made the calls extra sharP and crisP.

As much as I appreciated a good marching call, this clink was wicked annoying. And as a second lieutenant, I wasn't a cadet anymore. Without AC, though, what other choice did I have besides the fan?

Maybe outside?

I didn't know.

I sorted through chaotic images of this insane party the night before. The white poster board taped to the side of the beer truck announced forty-seven kegs downed so far—though that might have covered Friday night, too. The drummer from the band had the tequila — *that*, I remembered. He came through the dancing crowd with two bottles and poured shots into people's mouths. The band called it their *crazy set*. They'd come back from their second break wearing cat makeup, which was weird. But they were loud, and the party was good. They were just having fun.

I remembered Lieutenant Holtzmann, a T-37 instructor pilot, tumbling down the long, wooden flight of stairs from the upper deck of the restaurant's porch all the way to the sand at the bottom. Proffitt's Porch restaurant sat at the edge of the beach near Officers' Lake. You'd get your food inside from Mr. Proffitt or some member of his family and take it out on the porch overlooking the lake. Lieutenants Holtzmann and Hartlaub, another T-37 instructor, sang and acted out the lyrics to "Swing Low, Sweet Chariot" at the top of the stairs during one of the band's breaks. It appeared to be some kind of tradition of theirs, because they had coordinated all their moves. A lot of people watched. Their fellow instructors sang along. After they finished, I don't know if Lieutenant Holtzmann fell or if he was pushed, but his long fall down the steps was funnier than their routine.

At the bottom of the stairs, he staggered and stumbled and almost fell again, getting to his feet. I couldn't tell if he was hurt or just drunk. Then, Lieutenant Holtzmann dropped to his hands and knees in the sand and began to crawl. I quickly made my way over to check on him — as if I were in any condition to help.

As I pushed through the crowd, he started looking for something, presumably something he'd lost in the sand as he tumbled down the long flight of wooden steps.

Yup, just confused!

I figured he'd lost his teeth.

Lieutenant Holtzmann normally wore a bridge of false teeth, fitted like retainers teenagers wear after they've had their braces removed. He'd lost his real teeth in a car wreck years earlier. As he stumbled and crawled around, mumbling to himself in a familiar Rhode Island dialect that sounded like baby talk while nobody else paid any attention, I laughed.

He was okay. And because I was a student, and he was an instructor, I didn't offer help.

In Undergraduate Pilot Training, students pilots and instructors pilots didn't mix. Though officially equal as Air Force officers, that didn't matter. Lieutenant Holtzmann and I might both be Rhode Islanders, with even some of the same friends in high school—but students and instructors didn't mix. So I left him sifting in the sand on his hands and knees. Babbling his Rho Diland baby talk. He'd find his own teeth…eventually.

I sneaked back into the woods to urinate because I figured the trees didn't stink as badly as the port-o-potties, and the line looked a lot shorter. Instead of a private place to pee, however, I discovered a few guys from a class behind mine, the idiots known as the Nightmares, in a small clearing.

The Nightmares spent too much time in flight school trying to garner favor from the leaders of Columbus Air Force Base with their stupid spirit missions. But their pranks always turned out to be jokes at the expense of other classes. So, most classes on the base couldn't stand the Nightmares.

They'd stretched the biggest slingshot I'd ever seen between two trees about fifteen feet apart. The ringleader was all business, inspecting their stockpile of water balloons for proper size and knotting techniques, planning his targets, calling out adjustments to launch angles to correct for wind, and giving the orders to fire.

His classmates were using the slingshot to launch water balloons up to the edge of the stratosphere so that they'd descend on their targets from above without giving away the position of the launch site. After launching about a dozen projectiles in different directions, the Nightmares unhooked the tubing from the trees, cleaned up any evidence that might have pointed to their having been there, and moved to a new position to establish another discreet launch location.

I concluded a quiet pee.

Jerks.

I remembered I ate dessert inside the restaurant with Doley very late into the night. Mr. Proffitt's chocolate chess pie. I had to eat.

I remembered I puked. At least once. I had to puke. That happened before the dessert.

I remembered I drove Kenny and Doley home.

Very stupid!

I shouldn't have done that.

My head really hurt.

I was thirsty.

I knew that I wouldn't get back to sleep in my room. It was way too hot. The clinking grew louder. The spinning spun faster. I thought maybe in the backyard I could lie in Kenny's hammock and sleep in the shade. Maybe, there would be a cool breeze. Maybe, it would be quiet. Maybe, the images from the party would stop racing through my head.

So I got up and sloshed barefooted across the swampy shag carpet to the bathroom. The water from the AC unit that had pooled up in the rug oozed between my toes as I stepped across the hall. When I stepped onto the bathroom linoleum with my wet feet, I just about slipped and fell.

I used the toilet and washed my hands. I tried to drink cold water from the faucet to help myself feel less sick. It didn't work. When I bent down and stuck my head under the tap, I got dizzy, lost my balance, and almost fell again.

I could have used a good teeth-brushing, but I hadn't picked up a new toothbrush since I'd visited the Dental Hobby Shop last August. The bristles on my old brush had gotten so mashed down and hard that brushing my teeth with a Lego would have been softer. So, I just squeezed some toothpaste onto my finger and rubbed and swished and spit. It helped.

I'd slept in my bathing suit and my favorite pink flamingo tank top that I'd worn to the party. Filthy, I stunk of sweat, bug spray, and sunscreen. I never did go swimming in Officers' Lake, because as hot as it was, the cloudy, dark, and stagnant lake water was just disgusting.

Imagine swimming in hot chocolate — the kind made with water, not milk. Instead of sand beneath your feet, imagine warm muck. Throw in floating tree branches and aggressive water moccasins. That's Officers' Lake! I didn't find this refreshing, but it didn't stop people from swimming or throwing others into the lake.

I waded back through the shagmire in the hallway, past the air conditioner that spit on my ankles, as if to spite me. The pooling water stunk. Already thirsty again just five steps from the bathroom, I checked the fridge for something else to drink on my way outside. But inside our orange 1950s refrigerator, we had nothing but the condiments we bought when we first moved in — a bottle of runny ketchup and a jar of watery mustard.

I should have worn my flip-flops outside. We didn't have a lot of grass in the backyard — not like our next-door neighbors, Diane and Dennis. An older, retired couple with no children that we knew of, they worked on their beautifully landscaped and manicured piece of property lawn all the time. Our yard was an eyesore. We had dirt, lots of roots, and spiky pine cone-like balls that had dropped from the trees. We never raked. We never watered. We almost never mowed. We had fire ants. Lots of fire ants.

My feet weren't very tough, so I tried to pick my spots and step on grass only, as I made my way to the hammock. Next door, Diane and Dennis had already changed out of their church clothes and were diligently working on their lawn and shrubs, as they did every Sunday. I waved and smiled a hello.

They were nice people—older than my parents. They had a nice lawn. Nice grass, nice bushes, nice trees, and a nice house. Always nicely dressed. We probably gave them nightmares with our unkempt yard and late-night parties. I'm sure they prayed for us.

As I climbed into the hammock and stretched out my wet, dirt-covered feet and toes, I realized it was way hotter outside than inside. But it was too late. I'd already committed to the hammock; there was no going back. I'd made my bad decision, and I was going to stick with it. Like an idiot.

The sun was too bright. The air was too thick. My mouth was too dry. My headache was too strong. The images in my mind were too loud. There would be no sleep. There was no going back. So I fidgeted uncomfortably, closed my eyes, and tried to catch up with the racing images of the party from the night before.

Ten months spent in Columbus, Mississippi. Seven weeks from graduation. Six days until Assignment Night. So close to getting my first Air Force assignment and so close to becoming a real pilot...yet I still didn't feel comfortable partying with instructors. We were supposed to keep our distance. But at the FAIP Mafia Party, rules didn't apply.

The FAIP Mafia was the unofficial name of an anonymous and, officially, non-existent fraternity of young instructor pilots who kept the training squadrons running in spite of the questionable leadership and management skills of the senior officers assigned with such tasks at the base. The Lost Weekend, a trilogy of back-to-back-to-back parties: Friday, Saturday, and Sunday, served to help the entire base blow off the intensifying pressure as our year of flight school drew to a close.

According to the tradition, the Friday night component of the party was held at the Officer's Club. I didn't hang out at the O-Club much, so I didn't go. My guess was that Friday's party was a diversionary tactic so that when senior officers on base heard talk about a party, they'd assume that it was the Friday night gathering at the O-Club, where many senior officers went on Friday nights. The second and third days of the party moved off base to the remotely located Officers' Lake, a little swimming hole with a sandy beachfront and a great family-owned restaurant called Proffitt's Porch at the backside of the lake's beach area. You could only get there by dirt roads or by parachute.

Lying in the hammock with my eyes closed, my mind still racing, and the world still spinning, I heard the back door open, and I looked over to see whom I'd woken. It was Kenny. Dressed only in tighty-whitey underwear, a sleeveless white undershirt, and his dark-lensed eyeglasses with a wrap-around strap, Kenny twirled his lacrosse stick as he stepped out onto the back patio. He had been the goalie on the Air Force lacrosse team. As the kitchen door closed, Kenny stopped, gave an imaginary opponent a couple fakes, and threw his lacrosse ball off the brick wall on the kitchen side of the patio. As it bounced back, he scooped it with the net of his stick. Then, he threw a couple more fakes at his opponent.

Satisfied that he'd juked a defender, Kenny grabbed a lawn chair from the patio and dragged it behind him in his right hand as he continued to shake his lacrosse stick back and forth in his left. Clearly, his bare feet were no tougher than mine, because he hobbled across the spiky pine cone balls and roots in the yard.

The closer Kenny got, the harder I had to fight to keep from laughing. I might have been in bad shape, but Kenny looked like a cartoon character that just had a stick of dynamite explode in his hand. His face was dirty, he had no clothes, and his normally gelled and spiked hair blasted out in every direction. I spotted a huge black and purple bruise on his leg, like one you might get from playing tackle football without pads. And then, there was the wax on his neck and shoulders. Oh yeah, I remembered that.

Kenny didn't stop until he got a little too deep into my comfort zone for a guy lying in a hammock talking to another guy in a pair of tighty-whiteys.

"Aaay! What happened?" he asked.

"You drank wax."

"What?" he asked, like he had no recollection of drinking wax.

"You drank wax. All around the party, there were little metal buckets that burned orange candles that supposedly keep mosquitoes away. As the candles burned, the wax turned to liquid, and you'd pick up the bucket, and drink it. Then you'd cough up a wax ball from your throat back into your hand, and once the cud cooled, you'd throw it at somebody. Usually me, you bastid," I said.

"No wonder why my throat tastes like shit," Kenny coughed. "Aaay! That stuff almost tastes like tequila."

"You drank that, too."

"Who had the tequila?" Kenny asked.

"The drummer," I said. "He walked around the crowd and poured tequila down people's throats. He had a bottle in each hand. That was during the band's crazy set."

"Aaay, that whole party was crazy," Kenny said. He pulled his lawn chair around to the tree at the end of the hammock where my feet were. Thank goodness. But then he put his right foot, which was his outside foot, up against the tree. Not a good pose for a guy in his underwear. Still holding his lacrosse stick in his left hand, Kenny rubbed around the giant black and purple bruise on the inside of his thigh.

"What happened to your leg?"

"Fuckin' water balloon!" he said incredulously.

"What?" I pretended I had no idea how a water balloon could travel fast enough to leave such a mark.

"Aaay, I was takin' a piss near the woods. I hear a *snap!* like someone shot a giant elastic band, and then it feels like I get hit in the leg with a lacrosse ball. The water balloon was like an ice ball. I think it had ice in it, and it was goin' a hundrit miles an hour. It hurt like a bastid!" Kenny cried out.

"Good thing it didn't hit you in the eye. You know, it's all fun and games until someone loses their PQ." I quoted a universal Air Force Academy truth about the importance of being PQ: Pilot Qualified.

"Good thing it didn't hit me in the eye?!" Kenny screamed. "Good thing it didn't hit me in the fuckin' balls!" And with that, he opened up his legs even wider, dropped his lacrosse stick, and pointed at his balls with both hands.

"Dude! I don't need to see that." I closed my eyes and looked away.

Kenny's operating envelope, to use pilot terms to describe the parameters of one's behavioral comfort levels, had taken a lot of getting use to over the past year. If the graph plotted *Things You Comfortably Say* on one axis and *Things You Comfortably Do* on the other, our values for the things we'd comfortably say would be close. But I wouldn't even measure up on the same scale as Kenny for things that I'd comfortably do.

Like me, Kenny was out of place in Mississippi. I was Rhode Island, and he was Long Island, and neither of us assimilated into the ways of the South over the past year. But this would be over soon. We were less than two months from UPT graduation and our first flying jobs in the Real Air Force…unless, of course, our first assignment was to be FAIPs — First Assignment Instructor Pilots. We'd find out at our class's Assignment Night. Friday night. Less than a week away.

The back door from the kitchen opened again, and both of us turned to see Doley, another misplaced Northerner — Massachusetts — coming out to join us. While Kenny and I were clearly suffering physical pain and looking like we'd just walked away from a Class A Mishap, Doley was showered and clean shaven. His *Top Gun* flat top was perfectly coiffed, as usual, and dressed in khaki shorts and an Izod shirt, he looked as if he might be headed to church.

"What a great pahty!" Doley proclaimed in a thick Boston accent and smiled.

"Doley, I can barely open my eyes; I'm so hungover. How are you even standing right now?" I asked. "You were worse off than I was last night."

"Ray, I've always said, *A little vitamin B and two glasses of water before bed...and no hangover in the morning.* I feel great." Doley smiled again and jogged back to the patio to grab a lawn chair.

"Bastid," Kenny shot back at him and gave him a couple of fakes with his lacrosse stick.

Doley carried his chair back over to the side of the hammock and took a seat with Kenny and me. "There is one thing I can't figure out, though," Doley began. "I don't know if this was real or if it was paht of a nightmare I had last night."

"What?" I asked.

"Well, this is gonna sound nuts, but I have this image in my mind of Lieutenant Hahtlaub starin' me in the face with his mouth wide open, and he had three rows of teeth...like a shahk!" Doley made a shark face for us. "It was the freakiest thing."

"What?!" Kenny shook his head, laughing in disbelief.

"That was real," I told them, having seen the other images of Lieutenant Holtzmann flash through my head earlier in the morning. "Hartlaub was wearing Holtzmann's teeth!"

"What?!" Kenny shook and laughed in disbelief again.

"After the band finished their first set," I explained, "Hartlaub and Holtzmann sang 'Swing Low, Sweet Chariot' with a bunch of crude gestures. Right after they finished, Holtzmann took an Aunt Bunny fall down the steps of the deck. I found him on his hands and knees, combing through the sand, because he couldn't find his bridge of false teeth. I bet Hartlaub tried to yank them out of Holtzmann's mouth at the top of the steps after their song, and in their fight over the teeth, Hartlaub won and pushed Holtzmann down the steps. Hartlaub must have worn the teeth around the party for the rest of the night while Holtzmann gummed his beer." At least, that's how I figured events had taken place.

"I didn't see Lieutenant Hartlaub with the teeth," I finished telling them, "but I saw the rest of it. That's how I know it was real."

"That's just bizzah." Doley smiled. "So, how'd we get home?"

Kenny just looked over at me and shook his head.

"I drove," I confessed.

"You dumb bastid," Doley shot back.

"I know. That was stupid," I agreed. "You guys remember? I made Kenny hook up the radar detector before we started back, so we'd know if a cop was around."

"So, what...?" Doley began to laugh now, too. "So, if the radah detecta went off, you'd know to drive more soba? Or were you gonna use the faw wheel drive abilities of the Isuzu P'Up —"

"Winner of the Baja 1,000," I interjected.

"Winnah of the Baja 1,000," Doley conceded with a head nod and hand roll. "Were you gonna go off-road and evade the cops because they wouldn't be able to see you, the only cah around for miles, crunching through the bramble with your headlights on the whole time?"

While keeping two hands on an imaginary steering wheel, Doley got up from his lawn chair and started in on me.

"Beep-beep. Beep-beep. Radah detecta! It's the cops!" Doley slurred loudly. Then, he hit me one more time with: "You dumb bastid."

"Yeah," I agreed. "That was stupid."

I could have killed someone. I could have killed all three of us. It's all fun and games until somebody loses his PQ. Or his top row of teeth. Or takes a life.

Seven weeks from graduation. Six days from Assignment Night. About to find out the first flying assignments of our Air Force careers. What cool jets would we get to fly? What exciting roles would we play in fighting the Cold War? In defending our country? In supporting freedom and liberty around the world? What fun and exotic locations would we be stationed at? What country? What city? What mountain? What beach?

"You know what really sucks about that pahty last night?" Doley asked, making sure he had looked both Kenny and me in the face before providing the answer. "In three years, we'll be runnin' it."

FAIPs.

Nobody said a word.

We sat there and thought about this possibility.

Upon completing flight school, some student pilots would be selected to remain at their training base to become instructors for the next classes of student pilots. No one ever told us this at the Academy.

As cadets, we all thought that when you finished UPT, Undergraduate Pilot Training, you moved on to an F-15, F-16, or a bomber, tanker, or cargo plane, a life of travel and big adventure in the Real Air Force on your way to becoming an astronaut or a test pilot.

Or so I thought.

What you learned soon after arriving at Columbus, however, was that a lot of us would probably have to wait for a life of travel and big adventure. In an average year, 20–25 percent of graduating student pilots were chosen to be instructors and remain at the base where they trained, except for the special training base in Texas, where everyone who graduated would be assigned to fly fighters.

No next great adventure beyond Columbus, Mississippi.

No flying jets around the world.

No fighting communists.

Assignment Night was Friday. We had no idea what fate and the Air Force Personnel Center might have in store for us. What aircraft? What mission? What continent? What base?

Mountain or beach?

Or would we even get out of Columbus? Were we doomed to repeat UPT over and over again, class after class, because we'd come back as instructors?

I closed my eyes and sucked in a deep breath of hot, wet Mississippi air. I was worrying too much about my next assignment. I needed to focus on getting ready for my upcoming checkride. If I couldn't pass it, I might not even graduate.

Chapter 2 — "If You Ain't a Pilot"

"I'd like to welcome y'all to Columbus. My name is Lieutenant Sims, and I'll be y'all's class commander. Y'all look to y'all's left," he said and waited for a moment, "and now look to y'all's right." He paused again. "One of the people y'all just looked at won't graduate from this program." He smiled and looked around the room.

If he was expecting a laugh, I didn't find this very funny. I wasn't about to laugh.

The first instructor introduced on day one at Columbus Air Force Base, Lieutenant Sims wore a pilot's olive green flight suit and stored his dark blue flight cap in the unzipped pocket at the bottom of his right leg. We were all dressed in our blues — dark blue pants with light blue short-sleeved shirts. We didn't have flight suits yet. The silver bar on each shoulder of Lieutenant Sims's flight suit meant that he was a first lieutenant, so he was probably only two or three years older than most of us, assuming he was commissioned right after college. A rectangular object that looked to be about the size and shape of a pack of cigarettes poked at the zipper of the pocket on the front left side of his chest. Neither a tall man nor a thin man, maybe smoking had stunted Lieutenant Sims's growth, but it didn't appear to have curbed his appetite.

On a pilot's flight suit, there are about seven or eight zippered pockets and two adjustable strips of Velcro that go around either side of the waist. While I never really figured out the function of these Velcro strips, they kind of act like a belt — even though you don't need a belt with a flight suit, because it's just a one-piece, flame-retardant jump suit that you step in and out of through one long zipper down the front.

I noticed these Velcro strips because Lieutenant Sims wore his peeled back as far as possible, so that the grippy side of the

Velcro, the side with the little hooks, barely reached the soft side that it was designed to grip onto. Before him, I had never seen a pilot with a gut! His look didn't project the *Top Gun* image, and I made up my mind on the spot that my goal in the Air Force was to never become so fat that I had to move my Velcro strips back on my flight suit. Maybe it wasn't a very lofty goal, but at least I'd set one.

"I'm a T-37 FAIP, and I'm assigned here to the 14th Student Squadron. We call it the Stu-ron. At any one time during y'all's next year here, there might be between eight and twelve classes of students, and all student pilots on the base are assigned to the Stu-ron," he said.

I had read this in the welcome package I picked up when checking into the base, assigned to live in a barren room at the Unaccompanied Officers' Quarters. We'd get our academic instruction in the Student Squadron for the whole year, but we'd report to the flight line for our flying training. For training in the T-37, the Air Force's smaller, primary trainer jet, the instructor pilots of the 37th Flying Training Squadron would teach us to fly during the first half of the year. Then, we'd transition to the 50th Flying Training Squadron, where a new set of instructor pilots would teach us to fly the T-38, the Air Force's advanced jet trainer, for our second half of the year.

We'd have two sets of academic instructors over the course of our training year...one for T-37s and one for T-38s. We'd even have two class commanders, but for the next six months, we were going to get to know Lieutenant Sims.

"I grew up in Starkvul, Mis'sippi, which is about twenty-five miles west of here. I went to Mis'sippi State University. So, I'm a Bulldog not a Rebel. Mis'sippi State's in Starkvul. For y'all Yankees, it's pronounced *Starkvul*, not *Stark-ville*. Y'all have to say *Starkvul* while y'all're here." When Lieutenant Sims said *Starkvul*, it was almost like he was swallowing a gulp of air as he spoke the second half of the word, *-vul*.

I would not be saying *Starkvul.* In fact, I might even be invoking the New England accent I'd suppressed my last four years in Colorado to say, *Stahk-ville.* Maybe even add an *S* and call it *Stahks-ville.*

"People are very friendly here in the South," Lieutenant Sims went on. "Any of y'all Yankees?" I raised my hand, as did several others. "We don't call y'all *Damn Yankees,* for example. That's only for Yankees that stay in the South. That's the definition of a Damn Yankee. As long as y'all leave, y'all're just Yankees, not Damn Yankees." I couldn't tell if he was trying to be funny or not.

I also couldn't tell what his first name was. In our welcome package, Lieutenant Sims had written, *My name is Mike Sims,* but in closing the letter, he signed it, *Billy M. Sims.* Not that I'd call my class commander by his first name, but was he Billy or Mike?

"I know a lot of y'all—especially y'all who are Yankees—have some preconceived ideas about the South and about Mis'sippi, especially when it comes to blacks and whites. Let me just assure y'all that despite what y'all may have heard, there are no race problems here. The blacks stay in their part of town, and the whites stay in their part of town, and when the two do come together, there are no problems." Lieutenant Sims then silently looked around our all-white class, as if inviting anyone in the room to refute his proclamation that race relations in the South were anything less than perfectly harmonious.

I think most of us were too stunned to reply. Also, since this was day one, and he was the class commander, this wasn't the time to have a debate. In matters of rank or ignorance, sometimes it was best just to shut up.

"As an Academy class, y'all became officers and showed up here in Columbus all at the same time," Lieutenant Sims said, referring to the fact that most of the forty-eight students in our class had just graduated from the Air Force Academy two months earlier. "The result is that y'all's class is twice as big as the other classes on the base, and we need to split y'all in half. The flight rooms on the flight line only hold about twenty-five students apiece. Since it looks like the room is pretty much balanced, left side and right side of the room, I'm going to split the class down this here center aisle. Those of y'all sitting on my left will be assigned to the Warhawk flight for T-37 training and Scorpio Flight for T-38 training. Those of y'all on my right will be Dagger flight for T-37s and Eagle flight for T-38s."

I was sitting on the Dagger/Eagle side.

"Before we go on," Lieutenant Sims continued, "we might need to make a couple of changes here to make sure y'all's classes are really even." He counted each side of the room before he started up again.

"First of all, how many of y'all are married?" A few hands went up, including the giant hand of my friend Kurt. Kurt got married right after graduation to a woman who was on the gymnastics team at the Academy. Fortunately for Kurt and his wife Malia, they both were assigned to Columbus. Malia was going to have to do some training initially at Keesler Air Force Base in Biloxi, Mississippi, some four and a half hours south of us, but afterwards, she'd be assigned to Columbus, where she'd work in the personnel office.

Lieutenant Sims kept rolling on, "We've got a few married folks. Y'all will have to live in base housing," he proclaimed. "It's good that y'all's class has a few wives, too, because once y'all get y'all's class patch designed and produced, the class wives are going to have to sew y'all's patches and y'all's rank onto y'all's flight suits."

What?!

With the exception of Kurt, these guy's wives weren't in the Air Force. What made it their job to sew patches on uniforms? Did that mean that if the women in the class were married, the class husbands would have to take out the class garbage? Was this 1987 or 1957?

"Y'all have y'all's blues on right now, but y'all will want to be in flight suits as quick as y'all can. Out on the flight line, it gets to be one hundred and twenty degrees here on some days. Even though y'all won't be on the flight line for another month or so, it gets pretty hot around the base walking around in y'all's blues," Lieutenant Sims said.

"To differentiate the students from the instructors once y'all do get into flight suits, students wear cloth rank and cloth nametags." Lieutenant Sims then tapped the silver bar on his shoulder. "Instructors wear metal rank and leather nametags. That's how we differentiate between the students and the instructors with their uniforms."

This came across to me as a little strange, as well. Didn't the word *uniform* mean that everyone wore the same thing? Weren't we all officers? Did we not swear the same oath to support and defend the Constitution? I may only have been a stupid student, but one would think you'd be able to tell the instructors from the students by the bright set of silver wings on the billboard-sized nametag Velcro-ed to the front of a pilot's chest. Pilots had silver wings, and students did not. There was already a rank-system in place. Did we need to have a caste system, too?

At the Academy, the freshmen, who were actually treated like a sub-class of people, wore the same uniforms as the upperclassmen—except for the prop-and-wings insignia that upperclassmen wore on their flight caps, but this was because the freshmen hadn't earned the prop-and-wings insignia yet. Made sense to me. Why wouldn't student pilots, who were all Air Force officers, wear the same uniforms as pilots without the silver wings insignia, because they hadn't earned their silver wings yet?

"How many of y'all are coming to Columbus from active duty?" Lieutenant Sims asked. The two first lieutenants in our class each put up a hand. They had been navigators for pilots on active duty, like Goose was for Maverick. I had noticed the silver navigator wings pinned onto their blue shirts when I first walked into the room. While a navigator's silver wings are about the same size as a pilot's silver wings, the shield in the middle of the wings is different. Pilot wings have the America shield in the middle, which looks like a cool front grill of a classic car. I don't know what the shield is called on navigator wings, but to me, it looked like a Hanukkah lamp floating above a castle wall.

The rest of us in the classroom were second lieutenants, and the Academy grads had been second lieutenants for all of about sixty days. I wasn't sure about how long the handful of non-grads had been second lieutenants. It really didn't matter now, though, because we were all here to learn how to fly.

"For y'all two coming from active duty," Lieutenant Sims picked up where he'd left off, "UPT is especially special, because y'all know, if you ain't a pilot, you ain't shit."

Lieutenant Sims smiled and blew a little laugh through his nose, as if he had just made a great joke, but again, I wasn't finding what he said as either funny or even clever.

"How many of y'all are Academy graduates?" Lieutenant Sims asked. Nearly everybody on both sides of the room raised their hands. "Alright, put y'all's hands down. Let's try this again.... How many of y'all are from the National Guard or Reserve?" Five hands went up. Only one on my half of the class.

Lieutenant Sims looked puzzled. "This isn't going to work," he suggested and shook his head. "We've got three girls and one Guard guy sitting on the Dagger side of the room, and on the Warhawk side, we've got one girl, who is going to a Guard unit, and three Guard guys. That's four Guard and Reserves in Warhawk and only one Guard and Reserves in Dagger. That's not balanced. The classes have to be balanced. One of y'all three Academy girls is going to have to move to the other side of the room and be over in Warhawk so we can balance the two flights."

Nobody moved.

"Sir, do you really think that moving one woman will make a big difference in the training we receive?" one woman called out, making a very good point.

I recognized her...Chuck, short for Charlene. She lived in the hallway right next to mine for three years at the Academy. I spent my sophomore, junior, and senior years in 21st Squadron, and Chuck was in 22nd Squadron. We shared a common hallway in our dormitory, and I saw her a lot during the school year. Because every uniform you wear at the Academy has a nametag on it, you learn to match just about everybody's face with a last name, even if you don't really know them. And because women made up only about 10 percent of the cadet wing, you eventually knew just about every woman in your class by full name.

"The three of us got here a few days early, and we've already signed a lease to rent an apartment together for a full year," Chuck said as she motioned to the two women sitting next to her: Sandy Benning, who'd gotten her hair permed since we'd graduated, and Marcia Fuller, the most prolific athlete in our class at the Academy, winning about a dozen varsity letters for tennis, volleyball, and I forget what other sport...maybe rugby.

"We've heard that you should live with people from your class, because it makes studying and commuting to the base easier." Chuck spoke confidently, as if she were telling Lieutenant Sims something he should have already known. She'd been on the debate team as a cadet, too. If this showdown was going to be a battle of wits, Lieutenant Sims was probably outgunned.

Our new class commander sat quietly for a moment, trying to think up a comeback. I don't think that addressing this question was part of his prepared remarks. I don't know if his view of the world had ever been challenged before this morning.

"Do y'all have to live together?" he finally asked.

"Yes, sir," Chuck replied confidently. "We've already signed a lease," she repeated.

Lieutenant Sims scratched his head, and Chuck looked content to let him scratch. I think she was ready to sit there and wait for as long as it was going to take him to respond. The rest of us waited, too.

Finally, he formed a thought. "Well, I've got to balance these classes off as evenly as possible." He stopped scratching while he spoke and put his hand to the rectangular object zipped in the pocket on the front left side of his chest, just to check and see that it was there, like he was reaching for his security blanket. The rest of the room remained quiet to see who'd blink first, and after more than a moment of caressing the rectangular object in his pocket, the head scratching started all over again. Lieutenant Sims considered his next move.

Some guy behind me, one of the self-identified Yankees from a few moments before and someone that I genuinely didn't know by either face or nametag, threw his hand up and offered a suggestion to Lieutenant Sims without being called on to speak. "Sir, how's about you have one of these Academy girls on this side of the room get married to one of the Guahd guys on the otha side of the room?"

Everyone laughed. The proposal seemed to be made even funnier by the guy's wicked Boston accent. But my fellow Yankee wasn't done yet. "Then, not only would they be in the same class," he continued, "they could also get a base house togetha, and the classes would be even!" The room was roaring with laughter at this solution, which was absolutely brilliant in its stupidity!

I recognized that a marriage would also address another problem, so I quickly shouted before Lieutenant Sims had a chance to speak again, "And after they get married, there would be another wife in the class, which means there'd be one more person to sew on our patches. We could go from blues to flight suits that much more quickly."

"Lieutenant Sims," my fellow Yankee continued, "as class commanda, you can puhform the ceremony. Does anybody have a ring?"

"Don't we need to be on a ship?" I asked.

Before anyone could take this line of logic to its next level of stupidity, our class commander made a command decision. "Okay, fine!" he raised his voice over the laughter and snickering. "Y'all stay where y'all are! These will be the classes." He waved his hands through the air as if performing magic. "This side is Warhawk in T-37s and Scorpio in T-38s. This other side is Dagger in T-37s and Eagle in T-38s." I don't know why, but we all applauded.

"We're fixin' to break for a few minutes while I go check on the wing commander," Lieutenant Sims announced as his hand rubbed the rectangular object that looked like a pack of cigarettes in his chest pocket again. "Y'all can go out in the hall, use the latrines, but y'all be back in y'all's seats in five minutes. Don't change sides of the room. This is Warhawk. This is Dagger."

During the break, I shook hands with most of the guys I knew from school and hadn't seen in the last sixty days. I had been in various classes over the years with nearly everyone. In a class of only about a thousand, there aren't too many faces or nametags you don't recognize after four years, and even for those of us who didn't know each other, we had common friends, common teachers, and all of us had the last four years at the Academy as a common experience. Well, those of us who were Academy grads. Of course, a few people I knew very well.

"Kurtie!" I shouted and gave my giant buddy a hug when I finally caught up with him. Kurt and I had played baseball together at the Academy. We'd been friends since we were freshmen.

"Ray-bonus!" Big Kurt shouted back, wrapped me in a bear hug and just about cracked a rib when he tightened his grip. Kurt stood six-four or six-five and had hands so big that his fingers barely fit inside a baseball glove. His equally gigantically proportioned head was topped with thick, wavy, orange hair. Kurt played catcher in baseball. I don't think the equipment ever fit him.

"Can't breathe!" I gasped, pretending that Kurt had squeezed all the air out of me.

When he finally stopped crushing me, I had to ask, "How's married life, big buddy?"

"Fuckin' awesome, man!" Kurt smiled happily. Then, he gabbed all about his wedding and a little too much about his honeymoon, which was typical of Kurt.

Back in the room with our new class, Mark Jellicot, one of the two navigators from active service, came over to us. As a first lieutenant and the highest-ranking officer in our flight, this guy would be our class leader. "I flew F-4s in the Philippines. I was a back-seater," Mark Jellicot stated proudly after we'd gotten our introductions out of the way.

I looked from Mark to Kurt and back to Mark's navigator wings just above the nametag of his blue shirt. Since I've never been as gifted a conversationalist as my friend Kurt, I applied what I'd just learned. "You ain't shit." Then, I smiled and blew a fake laugh out through my nostrils, so Mark Jellicot would know I was joking. But I don't think he thought being a pilot was anything to joke about.

"Lieutenant Sims is right," Mark confirmed for us very matter-of-factly, completely not offended by my crude remark. "If you ain't a pilot, you ain't shit," and he nodded his head, so that I would be sure to know that he wasn't joking. "I flew F-4s in the Philippines as a back-seater. That's just the way it is."

Neither Kurt nor I challenged him on this point. We just kind of looked at each other. Sometimes, it's best just to shut up.

Everybody filtered back into the room. We all knew that you didn't walk in late when the wing commander was scheduled to speak. Rank had its privileges, and the privileges of being wing commander included students sitting in their seats, waiting for you to enter a room, and snapping to attention when you walked through a door.

The wing commander was responsible for our training, our instructors, our support personnel, and our safety. He oversaw the upkeep of the jets in which we'd be flying. We hadn't even met him, but by his position alone, he deserved our respect.

"Kurt, I'm actually kind of excited," I admitted. "Do you think his welcome speech will be as motivating as a scene out of *Top Gun?*"

"No." Kurt shook his giant head and smiled widely, gazing toward a distant vision that I couldn't see. "Way better."

Lieutenant Sims hustled through the doorway and snapped to the position of attention.

"ROOM! TEN HUT!" he commanded.

In unison, our class jumped up from our seats and snapped to attention, too. The wing commander bolted through the door, blowing past Lieutenant Sims as if he never saw him. No students moved or spoke. We all stood firm, looking straight ahead, as if Academy freshmen all over again. We all knew the first impression our class made ought to be a good one.

The wing commander, a full colonel, was wearing an olive green flight suit like Lieutenant Sims. He was wearing his flight cap when he walked in the room. At the Academy, I learned that the only time you wore your hat indoors was when you were *under arms,* which means carrying a rifle or a sword. But this was his base, and maybe this was how things were done in the Real Air Force, and at this moment, my adventure in the Real Air Force was about to begin.

"Take your seats!" the wing commander ordered us as he stood in the front of the classroom and paced back and forth while we settled into our chairs. Show time! This was going to be good, one to remember.

"Welcome to Columbus Air Force Base and Undergraduate Pilot Training," he barked rather gruffly, as if slightly annoyed that he had to be here at all. The wing commander was tall and thin. As he paced quickly to the far side of the room, I noticed the Velcro strips on the side of his flight suit didn't need to be pulled back or loosened at all. Underneath the flight cap that he hadn't removed, he sported a thick, buzzed crew cut of fiery orange hair—more orange than Kurt's, but unlike Kurt, the wing commander had one of those classic, red-head complexions where his hair, skin, and freckles all seemed to shine with the same fair brightness of orange. He spoke with a distinct Texas twang. In his left hand, he carried a black walkie-talkie. Still looking annoyed, he pivoted right before he got to the wall and quickly paced back to the side of the room where he entered.

"In the Air Force, if you ain't a pilot, you ain't shit," he declared. Then, he looked us over for a moment, pivoted, and paced back to the far side of the room.

"Look to your left," he continued. "Now look to your right. Either you or one of the people you just looked at won't be here when this class graduates next July." He reversed his direction again.

"At Columbus Air Force Base, we have what I call Columbus Class," he went on, drawling out the word *class*.

"While you're assigned to this base, you need to conduct yourselves with Columbus Class." He pivoted again, but this time, he stopped right in the middle of the room.

"A DUI is not Columbus Class," he barked angrily. "If any of you assholes get a DUI, I'll cut off your foreskin." The wing commander was getting madder. He stared us down for a moment or two, looking the room over from one side to the other.

"Seems like every class," he continued, now using the antenna of his walkie-talkie to point at people in the classroom seats, "there's some asshole that gets a DUI. Four days ago, some asshole got a DUI. A DUI is not Columbus Class."

When his walkie-talkie antenna pointed my way, his steely eyes locked onto my face and drilled a hole straight through my own eyes—all the way to the back of my head. Maybe the antenna could help him read my thoughts to see if I was going to be the next asshole to get a DUI.

After checking to see if I was the asshole, he paced, pivoted, and pointed his antenna a few more times to drill through the eyes and read the minds of the rest of the class. Then, the wing commander stopped again in the center of the room to conclude his pep talk with one last motivational and inspirational cliché.

"Mark my words," he warned, "anybody who gets a DUI, if you're lucky enough to graduate from this program, you will not be flying a fighter when you leave my base." Then, he turned and bolted toward the door and his next appointment where he would, no doubt, motivate more troops and spread the good word of Columbus Class. Before the toe of his highly polished boot crossed the threshold of the classroom door, Lieutenant Sims called the room to attention. We all snapped up, straight and tall. And just like that, the wing commander and any enthusiasm I had about the start of Undergraduate Pilot Training were gone.

Lieutenant Sims followed the colonel outside. I noticed his hand reaching up to his front left pocket, so I figured we were going to have a short break before our next agenda item. I turned to Kurt and asked the obvious question, "What if you get a DUI, but you're already circumcised?"

Kenny Wessels was sitting on the other side of Kurt. Even though I didn't really know Kenny, I knew who he was because his locker for lacrosse was in the same row as my locker for baseball in the cadet gymnasium back at the Academy.

Kenny quickly posed a question of his own: "Aaay! What if one of the chicks gets a DUI? What happens to them?"

I had to think about that for a moment. "Well," I replied, "I suppose they really don't have any consequences—they don't have foreskin, and they aren't allowed to fly fighters." This was true: Women were not allowed to fly fighters. So, with no fighters and no foreskin, there was only one logical conclusion I could draw....

"I guess this means that the chicks are the all-time designated drivers," I reasoned. "Even if they're drunk and get a DUI, what's the worst thing that could happen? No foreskin. No fighters. No problem. Somebody just has to make sure the sign at the front of the base that counts the DUI-free days gets reset back to zero."

This must have made sense to Kenny, who laughed and nodded.

Just then, Lieutenant Sims came back through the classroom door. Mark Jellicot called the room to attention.

"Y'all take y'all's seats." Lieutenant Sims directed. "I've got a lot of things to cover today. I think the wing commander was pretty clear about DUIs. A lot of what I'm going to cover in this session isn't in y'all's packets, so the section leaders for each flight might want to take some notes.

"First, y'all are going to need to design a class patch. Y'all may have seen some patches on display on the walls of the Stu-ron, and y'all may have noticed that some are a little more dirty than others." I hadn't seen any patches yet, but I could kind of guess where he was going with this.

"There are a few rules for y'all's class patch," Lieutenant Sims warned, the corners of his mouth slowly pulling back and curling up.

"The first rule is *no hidden meanings*. If y'all get caught with a hidden meaning on y'all's class patch, y'all are gonna have big troubles. That means no sex words or cuss words. No nekkid parts. Nothing that the wing commander's wife or a base chaplain is going to look at one day and get upset about. Y'all know what I'm talking about." Lieutenant Sims had started out sternly, but by the time he'd finished, he was looking around the room and smiling and almost laughing, which was strange. Was he trying to tell us that we really did need to try to slip in a hidden meaning on the class patch? Or maybe we shouldn't? I was confused.

"If y'all don't know what I'm talking about," Lieutenant Sims smiled even wider, "y'all go have a look at some of the class patches from the past that are up on the wall." Now, I actually thought that he was telling us that, even though he was saying not to have a hidden meaning, we were being challenged to slip in a hidden meaning.

"The second rule is that y'all can have any aircraft that y'all want on y'all's class patch," Lieutenant Sims continued. "But if y'all have a T-38, then y'all have to also have a T-37. Y'all are going to be flying T-37s with T-37 instructor pilots for y'all's first six months of training, and y'all can't be wearing a T-38 on y'all's sleeves without a T-37. I'm not saying that there's any type of competition between the T-37 and T-38 instructor pilots or that the T-38 is any better than the T-37. I fly the T-37. I'm just saying that if y'all have a T-38 on y'all's class patch, y'all also have to have a T-37." Somehow, I don't think that was all he was saying.

"The third rule is that y'all's class patches have to have *14 STUS* on them for the 14th Student Squadron," he said. "Y'all are assigned to the 14th Student Squadron. The T-37 instructors have their own squadron. The T-38 instructors have their own squadron. When y'all will train in those jets, y'all'll be reporting to flight rooms in those two squadrons, but y'all are students, so y'all are assigned to the Stu-ron. That's why y'all's class patches have to have *14 STUS* on them." This was kind of confusing, but we really didn't need to figure it out just yet. All we really needed to know for now was that our patches needed to have *14 STUS* on them.

"That's it for the class patches. That should be pretty clear." Lieutenant Sims nodded and looked to the first lieutenants to ensure they had taken sufficient notes and were ready to move on. "But there's something else about y'all's class patches, too," he suddenly remembered, which was good, I guess, because it certainly wasn't in our information packets.

"Y'all will need to buy scarves that match y'all's class patches for when y'all wear flight suits." He tugged on the dark blue scarf with little yellow airplane silhouettes on it from under his flight suit and around his neck to show us an example. "So, y'all ought to pick some good colors for y'all's patch, so y'all can have some scarves with some good colors. Y'all also need to paint y'all's class patch onto a large, wooden plaque to give to give the wing headquarters for when y'all are the senior class. Y'all need to give one to the Stu-ron and one to the O-Club, too. Y'all need to buy and paint three, altogether. Y'all also get to paint the dunk tank with y'all's class patch and class colors when y'all solo, so try to pick some colors that will look good out on the flight line when they're painted on the dunk tank." The first lieutenants were writing quickly, because Lieutenant Sims seemed to have left a lot out of our all's information packets.

"Next is Officers' Club. Membership at the Officers' Club is officially voluntary, but y'all all need to go over to the Officers' Club and sign up for membership and get y'all's club cards. It costs sixteen dollars a month, and y'all can set up y'all's account to have the money taken right out of y'all's paychecks. I'd like y'all to have that done before Monday," he said.

I couldn't let this one go by without a little clarification. I didn't care all that much about whether or not a class patch had boobs or pubes, but now he was tapping into my spending money. Putting my hand up, I called out, "Lieutenant Sims!"

"What?" he looked up, annoyed that I interrupted him when he had so many things to get through that weren't in our packets.

"Sir, if membership to the Officers' Club is voluntary, do we *all* need to sign up by Monday, or do just those people who want to join the Officers' Club need to sign up by Monday?" I didn't know if I wanted to join the O-Club, and even though I was now pulling in about nine hundred a month as a second lieutenant, I had maxed out my credit card to its $2,000 limit over the summer, which I needed to start paying down, and I knew I'd need money for rent, gas, clothes, food, and parties.

"Look, y'all are officers now," Lieutenant Sims replied. "This isn't the Air Force Academy, and y'all aren't going to be spoon-fed and spoiled here at Columbus Air Force Base. The Officers' Club is called the Officers' Club because officers belong to the club, and y'all are officers." I think I'd struck a little bit of a nerve here, because Lieutenant Sims's tone became a little more serious, and the "y'all's" were starting to fly fast and furious.

"The wing commander is proud of our Officers' Club here at Columbus. Look, we have a nice, new ten thousand-dollar chandelier in the lobby, and the wing commander says that we all need to support the O-Club by being members. He gets a report every month that tells him what percentage of officers are members of the O-Club. If y'all would like y'all's names on the list of officers that haven't joined...well, I suppose that's y'all's choice, but as y'all's class commander, I'm not going to be on the list of class commanders whose classes have less than 100 percent participation, if y'all follow what I'm tellin' y'all. So, it's really not a choice. Y'all need to get this done before Monday," Lieutenant Sims said.

"Yes, sir. Thank you," I acknowledged. Sometimes, it was best just to shut up.

Lieutenant Sims made sure nobody else was going to challenge him before he continued with his list of things that weren't in our packets. Fondling the rectangular object in his front left pocket, he picked up where he'd left off before I had interrupted.

"Alright, y'all also need to assign some people to some additional duties. Even though y'all're in training, y'all have things to do that need to get done like Snacko, box scheduler, a PT officer, O-Club officer...all kinds of things that need to get that keep the base running smooth."

Okay, this sucked. First, I thought this was pilot training—learning to fly, not dealing with administrative issues! Second, because most of us were commissioned as second lieutenants on the same day, and my last name begins with W-R, I was technically the lowest ranking person in the class, which meant that I'd either be told I was going to get the crap job, or I'd have last pick and end up with the crap job, which in my mind was Snacko, the guy who schedules people to work the snack bar. I hated that kind of stuff!

The only additional duty Lieutenant Sims had mentioned that had any appeal to me was the PT officer. In the summer of my junior year at the Academy, I was assigned to be the group staff athletic sergeant for basic cadet training for the incoming class of 1989. To the basic cadets that summer, I was the expert demonstrator, performing the morning's calisthenics on top of the observation tower to the cadet parade field while my boss, a football player known affectionately as Horse-Head, counted into a loudspeaker: "One-Two-Three-ONE! One-Two-Three-TWO!" Except for the time Horse-Head announced that I would pump out seventy push-ups in sixty seconds, it was the easiest job I ever had at the Academy!

By the time Lieutenant Sims needed to take another break, I had made up my mind that I'd preemptively volunteer my services to Mark Jellicot, section leader.

"Mark, I'd like to volunteer to be the PT officer. I really enjoy exercising, and I think I can really make PT fun and productive. I have some experience as..."

"Okay," Mark said without much interest in hearing about my vast three weeks' worth of experience as the expert demonstrator. "Wright. PT officer. Thanks." He scribbled what looked like a word that began with a capital W next to a scribble that looked like PT in his notebook. I took that as a good sign.

"What we really need to get done," Mark Jellicot started to say after he'd finished his scribble, "is come up with a cool class patch, and I think we should have an F-4 Phantom on it. I flew F-4s in the Philippines. We were the Fiends. It's a hot jet with a hot mission. It will look really sweet on our class patch."

Kenny Wessels had walked up behind us. I thought maybe that because his name began with *W-E*, and I was the only one he outranked, he might be thinking the same thing I was. But he wasn't.

"Aaay! An F-4?" Kenny asked, reaching up to grab Kurt by the back of the neck. "Where's the hidden meaning in that? I don't get it." He tried to shake Kurt, but Kurt was too big. Kenny couldn't budge him.

"Aaay, c'mon out in the hall," Kenny directed Kurt with a thick New York accent that sounded like it had been influenced by both the Fonz and Nick from *Family Ties*. "Let's go find some patches and their hidden meanings." The two of them walked out of the room, laughing it up, with Kenny asking Kurt about the benefits of married life, and Kurt all too happy to share.

Kurt and Kenny were both preppies, which meant that they went to the Air Force Academy Prep School before getting into the Academy. So, Kenny had been friends with Kurt longer than I had. If the Academy was the fishbowl of the Air Force, a very sterile environment nicely set out and perfectly maintained for all passers-by to look inside without being able to get in or even to tap on the glass, the prep school was the Air Force's holding tank, tucked away behind the fishbowl. For no one to see.

The prep school gave people who wanted to go to the Academy an extra year to either work on their SAT scores or to wait for an open appointment slot from one of their senators or their local representative to Congress. For young men and women who joined the Air Force right out of high school and needed to ease their way back into studying before drinking from the academic fire hose at the Academy, the prep school helped them build their study habits and knowledge base that maybe they hadn't built in high school. Hidden somewhere on the Academy campus, the prep school's cadet candidates all wore military uniforms, learned the Air Force ways, and earned more money than Academy cadets.

Kurt had enlisted in the Air Force after high school and had worked as a crew chief on F-16s. He'd learned about the Academy while on active duty, and his commander recommended that he go. When the Academy baseball coach saw him at the prep school, Kurt instantly became a recruited athlete. While I knew Kenny Wessels played lacrosse, I didn't know enough about him to tell if he was a guy who had to wait for a congressional appointment slot to open up or if he was a guy who needed to work on his SAT scores, though I suspected the latter.

After more shaking of hands, I chased down Kurt and Kenny in the hallway to find displays of class patches from the Stu-ron's past classes. It didn't take long before we'd found our first example of a class patch that the wing commander's wife or a base chaplain might not find acceptable because a bunch of guys were hanging out around a display case on the wall, pointing and giggling. The patch was from a class a few years before ours. Its picture and caption gave a little double entendre to region of Mississippi where Columbus Air Force Base was located, the three town area of Columbus, Starkville, and West Point, Mississippi. The picture on the class patch gave what might be described as an obstetrician's eye view of an unclothed woman. A T-38 had been positioned in front of her stomach so that the orange-yellow flames from its afterburners were either pubes or labia majora. The caption read, *Operating in the Golden Triangle*. There was no hidden meaning here; it was all pretty much out in the open.

Other patch mottoes from recent classes included *Hot Sticks, Stick Envy, Better Penetration,* and *It's Best on Top* with either the T-38 or the control stick as a phallic symbol. Every now and then, one of the class patches would have both T-37s and T-38s, but most of them just had T-38s. In design, content, and intent, most were pretty much what Lieutenant Sims had said they ought not to be, which left me even more confused. Was that what he wanted?

As one of the last ones to walk back into the classroom after the break, I seemed to have been missing out on some fun. At the front of the classroom, my fellow Yankee who had suggested that an Academy girl marry a Guard guy to even out the classes was entertaining the troops. With a quick glance at his nametag, I identified him as Dolan. And right now, Dolan was pacing back and forth around a central spot in front of the classroom, wearing sunglasses and his flight cap, just like the wing commander.

With a pretty good Texas twang, Dolan was asking the people in the class as he pointed at them, "What does your daddy do?"

"My dad's a teacher," I heard somebody shout back.

"A teacher?" Dolan repeated in his wing commander voice. "He ain't shit." Everyone was laughing.

I wanted to play, too, so I rushed into the front and sat down right in the front row. Wing Commander Dolan stuck his finger in my face and challenged, "You, what does your daddy do?"

"When my daddy isn't caring for orphans and the hungry —" I turned sideways in my chair so that I could address the back of the classroom, too — "he works on the cure for cancer." Of course, that was totally made up; my dad was a teacher.

Wing Commander Dolan paused momentarily and stared back at me through his mirrored sunglasses. He was fighting back a little laugh. I could tell. I thought for a moment he might break character, but he didn't.

"Orphans, hunger, and cancer cure?" Dolan repeated, still twanging away as the wing commander and pausing again — this time for effect. "He ain't shit!"

Everybody laughed. Except Dolan. Still in pacing and pointing, he waited for the noise to die down so he could keep the joke going. Before he could ask anyone else, however, I gift-wrapped him a line to see where he might take it.

"Before my dad did that, sir," I said, being sure again to broadcast my dad's occupation to the entire room, "my dad cleaned septic tanks." I stared into Dolan's mirrored sunglasses, unable to see his eyes.

"Septic tanks!" Dolan repeated, paused, and stopped again while the wheels spun in his head. "Your daddy might have pumped shit, but he ain't shit!" *Very quick,* I thought, while the rest of the class laughed again. Dolan resumed his pacing, feeding on the class's laughter.

Then, Dolan turned back, and he threw it right back to me. "What about your daddy's daddy? What did he do?"

Oooh! A challenge! I accepted. "My daddy's daddy," I served up, "was a fertilizer salesman."

"A fertilizer salesman!" Dolan successfully fought back a smile again while the rest of the class just kept enjoying the show. "He might have peddled shit, but he ain't shit!" This guy was pretty quick.

I scrambled to think of another line to feed Wing Commander Dolan.

"Where's Billy Mike?!" Wing Commander Dolan barked, referring to the two different first names our class commander had used in his welcome letter. He'd caught that, too! "I'm a-wasting my time with students!"

"I have an Uncle—" I started, but just then I was interrupted.

"ROOM! A-TEN-SHUN!" was shouted by someone who was obviously not an Academy grad, because a grad would have shortened this to *Room, Ten Hut.* But no matter, everybody snapped to the standing position of attention, including Dolan, who with his back turned to the door of the room, whipped off his mirrored sunglasses and flight cap.

False alarm! The officer was only Mark Jellicot.

"Guys," Mark shook his head, "I'm in your class. Please don't call the room to attention when I come in or go out of a room."

Mark Jellicot came over to me. "Lieutenant Wright," he started, "I've assigned you to be PT officer for Dagger."

"Thanks, Mark." I replied. "We'll have…"

"ROOM! A-TEN-SHUN!" the same guy shouted again.

Who was this guy?!

Turbiglio, I read his nametag. He was the one Guard guy in our Dagger/Eagle flight. Strangely, he had been carrying his wallet all morning, like it was a woman's purse.

"Y'all take y'all's seats." Lieutenant Sims was back. "I've got y'all's schedules for next week. Dagger flight, y'all have y'all's first PT session on Monday morning, so y'all need to have a PT officer before Monday."

Mark Jellicot was quick to respond, "Lieutenant Sims, I've assigned Lieutenant Wright to be our PT officer."

"Who's Wright?" Lieutenant Sims asked.

"Sir, I am," I said, standing up again, because I had just taken my seat.

"Y'all need to make sure that y'all are there on time and that y'all do the exercises as they're written in your packets. PT gets monitored a lot, and when y'all have it in the morning, every officer on this Arr Base is going to drive by the base gym, and they'll know if y'all are doing y'all's exercises right or not," our class commander told me.

"Yes, sir," I said, still standing. "We'll do all our exercises just like they're typed up in the packet." I sat right back down so that Lieutenant Sims could get on with his business.

Lieutenant Sims checked his watch and smiled. Then, he fondled the rectangular-shaped object in his front left pocket and smiled even wider. "Y'all're done with me for today," he announced happily. "Y'all have just about twenty minutes before y'all need to report to base chapel for the chaplain's in-briefing. Do y'all know where the base chapel is?"

"No, sir," just about everybody replied. So, Lieutenant Sims gave us directions. Go out of the parking lot. Turn right at the base exchange. The base chapel was on the left—just past the base gym.

Chapter 3 — "Head Games"

If an air pocket existed between a pilot's head and the foam shell liner of his helmet, the higher the pilot climbed into the atmosphere, the more the air trapped in between these two barriers would try to expand. Because neither a pilot's head nor the foam shell liner would change shape during flight, the pocket of expanding gas between the two would heat up, and this tiny thermodynamic system would result in both heat and pressure on a pilot's head, causing a great deal of discomfort and pain. The Air Force had determined this condition to be unacceptable. A pilot's helmet needed to fit so precisely to a pilot's head that no air pockets could exist between the skull and the foam shell liner. No air pockets. None.

Our Section Leader Mark Jellicot had convinced Class Commander Lieutenant Billy Mike Sims that since the helmets took about fifteen minutes to make and that the helmet-making guys could only make a couple of helmets at a time, the whole class didn't need to show up all at once. Mark assigned us staggered report times throughout the morning, and of course, he did so by alphabetical order. This was good for me because I was able to get to the gym for a workout in the morning. I was surprised, however, when I showed up and saw my friend Kurt Spranger there because he should have been done and long gone. Kurt's scheduled time had been at least an hour ahead of mine.

I watched as the helmet-making guys, a couple of enlisted men about the same age as most of us in the UPT class, screwed a giant, metal, semi-spherical, mushroom cap contraption against the sides of my classmates' faces and heads. Once this metal mushroom cap was clamped down, the helmet-making guys would mix some chemicals together that would react, grow like the Blob, heat up, and harden over the course of about ten minutes. This hardened foam would serve as the firm-but-absorbing cushion between the skull and the shiny white outer shell of the flight helmet. Because it had been molded to the shape of each person's head, there would be no air spaces between the firm form-fitting foam and the skull.

Because it was Saturday, and because the process had the potential to ruin an Air Force uniform, we were permitted to wear civilian clothes for this event. The enlisted guys making our helmets wore green Air Force fatigues. Even though Lieutenant Sims warned us the procedure could be messy, the helmet-making guys were very good at what they did, and I didn't see any signs that they had so much as spilled a drop of helmet-making goop all day. In addition to the big metal mushroom cap contraption used for the mold on most heads, they did have a slightly smaller contraption for the women and the pinheads in our class. What these helmet-makers didn't count on, however, was someone whose head was bigger than that of the Underdog balloon at the Macy's Thanksgiving Day parade in New York City—someone like my giant friend Kurt, which was why he was still there when I arrived.

Apparently, try as they may, the helmet-making guys couldn't unscrew the screws of the inner part of the metal mushroom cap far enough back to slide the contraption over Kurt's giant, over-sized head. After they'd tried in vain for all of Kurt's allotted time in their shop, they asked him to hang around until the rest of the class was done, and they were going to try to come up with a plan.

I guess Kurt didn't mind that much. His wife was still down in Biloxi for her training, and Kurt would always rather talk with people than not. Knowing him, he probably wanted to learn everything about the helmet-makers' job and how they did things. Prior to going to the Academy—and even before he went to the Academy Prep School—Kurt was an enlisted guy. The helmet-making guys were his people.

Kenny Wessels was finishing his turn in the helmet-makers chair when I arrived. With the metal mushroom cap on his head and a giant bib draped over his clothes, he looked like a beauty salon patron sitting under an old-style hair dryer. Once the helmet-makers determined that the foam molding had properly conformed and dried in the shape of Kenny's head, they lifted off the metal mushroom cap, removed Kenny's bib, and let him out of his seat. Kenny tried to fix his normally spiked-up hair, which had been matted down.

"That didn't look very comfortable," I said to him as I took my place in the seat.

"Aaay, it sucked," he acknowledged, "but I'm okay."

"I guess it's better dealing with it here than upside-down at twenty thousand feet," I replied.

"Aaay," Kenny nodded.

"Kenny, stick around," Kurt said. "Ray looks a little scared. He might need our help to get through this."

"Aaay," Kenny agreed.

"Thanks, guys," I said. "I'll stay for you when I'm done, Kurtie."

After putting a light cloth on my head about the size of a small hand towel, the helmet-maker enlisted guys lowered the metal mushroom cap contraption onto the top half of my skull. Then, as they tightened the screws of the metal mushroom cap right up against the sides of my face and head, they began talking over me, like the way barbers at a barber shop talk to one another while they cut guys' hair, brainstorming about possible ways to create a mold on Kurt's head.

"We could pull out the bottom section of the mold, re-cut it to make the hole in the middle bigger, and then just throw the whole thing out and order a new mold after we finish with the big guy," the helmet-maker on my left suggested, cranking the screws into my temples. "We won't need to make helmets again until the next class shows up in a month."

"Naw," said the helmet-maker on my right, cranking the screws on the other side of my head into my skull just behind my right ear. "The Air Force is fixin' to do away with these big white helmets. Just the students get 'em now anyway. The IPs get them new gray helmets. We won't be able to get a new molder, and if we can't get a new molder, we're screwed."

Just as he said, "We're screwed," he cranked down on the screw up by my right temple.

"Maybe the weather shop can give us one of their old satellite dishes, and we can cut that up into a molder that will fit," the guy on my left suggested.

"Naw," the other guy shot back again. "Ain't big enough. I think we need somethin' like a radar dish that's out by the side of the runway." They both laughed. I wanted to laugh, too. I loved teasing Kurt about the size of his head, but the screws pushing into my head were killing me, and I didn't want to move my jaw, because doing so might give them more room around my temples to tighten the screws even further. It was all I could do not to cry at that point.

When I thought they were done screwing around—both literally and figuratively—they cranked all of the screws around the circumference of my head down another quarter of a turn each, and the helmet-maker on my right picked up a couple of milkshake cups to mix the helmet-making goop.

Now that Kurt had seen how uncomfortable the metal mushroom cap contraption was, I guess he figured he was going to give me a hard time. "Hey, Ray, how's that thing feeling right about now?" Kurt called my way.

Since the helmet-makers had stepped away to mix their goop, I thought I could get away with a quick *Back to the Future* joke. I jumped up out of my chair and spun around to face Kurt with the metal contraption screwed tightly against my skull, like when Doc first met Marty, and yelled, "So tell me, future boy, who's President of the United States in 1985?"

The helmet-makers were all over me for jumping out of the chair. Kurt, Kenny, and I thought my joke was funny, but the helmet-makers weren't laughing. They respectfully helped me to sit back down in the chair, and then they checked the tightness of all the screws, squeezing my skull all over again. I think they thought that was funny.

Once they were satisfied that the metal contraption was still snugly secured in the correct position and with the correct tightness, they resumed their work and their discussion about Kurt's oversized problem.

"Once we do make a molder that fits," the guy on my left started up again, "are we gonna have enough goop left to mix up and pour into it? We're gonna need a least a double batch for the big guy's helmet. Maybe a little more...."

"That's for sure," the helmet-maker on the right agreed.

I wished I could have looked back at Kurt, but I didn't want to have the helmet-making guys have to speak to me a second time for moving around while I was supposed to be still, and by this time, these guys had poured the helmet-making goop into the metal mushroom cap screwed into my skull. They had told me not to move or even try to look around so that the goop could be evenly distributed throughout the mold.

"Sir," the helmet-maker on my right leaned in and said, "you don't have to say nothin' with all that mess on your head and all, but we forgot to mention that when we mix them chemicals together to make our expandin' and hardenin' goop, they combine in what you call an exothermic reaction. That means it's fixin' to get a little bit hot on the top of your head."

Thanks, dude.

I had already realized that the goop was heating up. How come they never showed this part of flying in *Top Gun?*

After that, I can't remember what was said or done or how long it took. All I know was that I just put up with the most uncomfortable, painful, and forgettable ten minutes I ever wanted to volunteer for again, and I was ready to get out of helmet-makers' lair. Except that I had to hang around and see how they figured out how to make a helmet for Kurt.

In the end, the helmet-making guys decided that to make Kurt's helmet, they needed to totally dismantle their metal mushroom cap contraption without cutting it apart and damaging it. They didn't cut into the base of their semi-sphere; they just unscrewed the whole thing and took all the pieces of the cap apart. They separated the base that ran through the diameter and took that apart, too. Then, they pulled out a drawer of screws and metal parts that looked like an ERECTOR Set and re-built the base of the contraption around Kurt's head as he sat in their helmet-making chair. They'd screw in one part...unscrew it. Screw in another. Try again. And they repeated this process until they'd built a ring around his head—like the planet Saturn, only with the ring pressing right up against Kurt's head instead of out in orbit around it. At least they didn't have to screw these parts into his neck, because if they did, he'd look way too much like Herman Munster, and he'd never hear the end of it.

Once they'd put together a metal band that circumnavigated Kurt's head, they created some spokes by connecting some long, skinny ERECTOR Set beams to the ring. They probably attached seven or eight of these things every few inches, and it didn't look like any two of them were the same length. Now it was my turn to have a little fun with Kurt.

"Kurt, the Statue of Liberty just called. She'd like her hat back," I said.

Kenny and I laughed, but I couldn't see Kurt's reaction.

The helmet-makers had already closed in around him and started to position flat, metal plates around this new ring-and-spoke thing to form a new base plate. They locked the plates together with electrical tape, figuring that this thing only had to work one time. Once the base was secure, they lowered the makeshift metal mushroom cap part down over Kurt's head and centered it as best they could to complete their improvised molder.

Satisfied that the modified metal mushroom cap contraption was ready and that they could make Kurt a helmet without air pockets, the helmet-makers mixed up a double-batch of helmet-making goop and poured the mixture through the hole at the top of the thing on Kurt's head to work its exothermic magic. Because their new molder didn't exactly fit together properly and because the double-batch of helmet-making goop was a lot more than the helmet-makers really needed, expanding foam just kept pushing out of the hole in the top of the molder and through the cracks in the sides that hadn't been fitted together with a perfect seal. The helmet-makers tried to shave off the expanding foam as fast as they could, but the exothermic Blob kept growing and growing through the cracks in the contraption on Kurt's head, like a Play-Doh toy I played with as a kid.

Kenny and I laughed as we watched, and at one point, when the helmet-makers found themselves a little too slow to shave off the expanding foam, I found myself inspired enough by the whole episode to burst out in song...

> *Brother needs a little off the top*
> *At the Fuzzy Pumper Barber Shop.*
> *We'll make mommy's hair just so.*
> *You can make it with Play-Doh!*

Kenny joined me in song for the last line of the classic commercial. As we finished singing, the Play-Doh-like foam stopping pushing through the shell on Kurt's head. The helmet-makers finished shaving off the snake-like strands that had wiggled and grown through the cracks of the makeshift molder, and we all waited for the foam to harden to see if their invention and this process had worked.

Fifteen minutes later, we learned that apparently it had. The foam had hardened nicely and would fit perfectly into the shell of an extra-large helmet.

A week later, our helmet-makers would have our helmets put together for a custom fitting, complete with oxygen masks. A week after that, we'd be able to pick up our fitted helmets and bring them home. In two weeks, we'd need them for the altitude chamber, my first major test in UPT.

As easy as a ride in the altitude chamber might sound, I had a fair amount of anxiety about it. I had flown in the altitude chamber twice as a cadet, but I had successfully completed the mission only once. I knew that if I couldn't get through the training, UPT was going to be over for me before it ever even started.

*

Only a handful of classmates were still around by the time I got to the base bowling alley. I didn't have any food in my fridge in my assigned room, but because I'd worn casual civilian clothes for my helmet fitting, I didn't think I was dressed appropriately for lunch at the Officer's Club or the snack bar on the flight line. I didn't feel like bowling, but they probably had a griddle and a fryolator for greasy food, like grilled cheese sandwiches and fries, a couple of my favorites.

A bunch of the guys were bowling, seeming to have a good time in lanes seven and eight, but Chuck and Sandy, two of the three women in our half of the class, and Dolan, my fellow Yankee who had entertained the troops as the wing commander, were sitting around one of the tables reserved for eating in the area between the pinball machines and bowling lanes. After ordering a patty melt, curly fries, and a Coke, I asked if I could join them.

"Sure, Ray, have a seat," Chuck said.

"Thanks, Chuck," I said, pulling up a chair and putting my receipt with my order number on the table.

"Where's Marcia?" I asked. "I thought you girls had to travel together."

"That's only when they go to the bathroom," my fellow Yankee said.

"Ray, do you know Mike Dolan?" Sandy asked, waving an open hand his way.

"Actually, no. We never met at school," I admitted, but I had heard enough of his shtick already to appreciate his humor.

We both stood up and offered each other a handshake.

"Call me Doley," he said.

"I'm Ray," I answered.

Sitting back down, I double-checked the order number at the top of my receipt. I wanted to be sure to get my food as soon as it was ready.

"This base is pretty small, isn't it?" I threw out to the table, thinking that in comparison to the Air Force Academy, Columbus kind of sucked.

"It's just got one main road that's less than a mile long," Sandy agreed.

"Simler Boulevard," Chuck pointed out the name of the main street down the center of the base.

"Gen'ral Simla bought the fahm doin' a vic'try roll in a T-38," Doley said.

Bought the farm was an Air Force euphemism for someone who died in a crash—but the rest? "What's a victory roll?" I asked.

"Isn't it just an aileron roll?" Sandy asked.

"It's an aileron roll right after takeoff," Chuck clarified.

"It's an aileron roll with attitude," Doley corrected.

"Forty-nine!" the guy behind the bowling alley cash register yelled.

"That's me!" I said, grabbing my receipt and getting up to get my food. "Excuse me, please. I'll be right back."

"That's okay," Chuck said. "I was about to go to the ladies' room."

"Wait up, Chuck," Sandy said, gulping down the last of her drink. "I'll go with you." Sandy glanced sideways at Doley as she stood up to join Chuck to see if he'd offer some kind of wisecrack.

He didn't.

Until Chuck, Sandy, and I walked away from the table.

"Nothing further, your honor," Doley called out to no one in particular.

*

I didn't have a silver dollar for the security guard who saluted me as I rolled up to the main gate of Columbus Air Force Base, the entryway to Simler Boulevard, for the very first time. According to US military tradition, a newly commissioned officer is supposed to give a silver dollar to the first enlisted person that salutes him. This gate guard guy was my first real salute from an enlisted person. Unfortunately, the closest thing I had to a silver dollar was a bicentennial quarter in my ashtray, and I couldn't give him that because I needed my change for emergency Taco Bell runs. So much for military tradition.

I didn't have a whole lot of flight experience as a pilot other than two flying programs at the Academy. All freshmen cadets had to solo in a sailplane, which required a week of instruction in a motor-glider, followed by a week in real glider. In my senior year, I had to pass the flight-screening program in the T-41, a single-engine, wing-high Cessna, which required about twenty-five hours of flying time. That was about it for my flight experience.

The first time I even stepped foot onto an airplane was at age eighteen, when I flew to the Academy for basic training a few weeks after graduating from high school. After saying good-bye to my mom and dad at the airport in Providence, my concerned mom ran back to the terminal and had the airline ticket agent call ahead to O'Hare Airport to see if a representative from the airline could meet me and help me change planes in Chicago.

"Well, how old is your little boy?" my mom was asked.

"He's only eighteen!" she cried.

The main gate at Columbus was flanked by large brick walls. The walls weren't really part of a fence that could keep anybody out, however. They were more like walls you might see on the obstacle course at the Academy or on ABC's *The Superstars* that used to come on TV right before *Wide World of Sports*. Inside the confines of the base, behind each brick wall, there was a full-sized jet-on-a-stick. To the right side of the inbound road, there was a T-37, mounted on its stick and pointed as if it were flying into the base. Over to the left, on the far side of the gate guard guy's hut, just beyond the outbound side of the road, there was a T-38, pointed as if it were flying off the base.

Columbus Air Force Base had an interesting welcome sign near the T-37-on-a-stick. It was just a small, chocolate brown rectangle with three rows of slots to hold sliding white letters. The message wasn't very warm or welcoming. It read:

WELCOME TO COLUMBUS AIR FORCE BASE
DAYS SINCE LAST DUI: 3
COLUMBUS CLASS

Why did I pick Columbus again?

Just like everything else at the Academy, the order by which you got to pick your base and your start date was a result of how you were ranked against your peers.

Everything was a competition at the Academy. For the Class of '87, about seven hundred out of around a thousand graduating seniors would be going to flight school or "Undergraduate Pilot Training." UPT for short.

To determine a cadet's rank for choosing a UPT base and start date, the Academy kept two lists. The first one ordered students by grade point average, which didn't help me too much. My first two years of school, I was playing in the baseball program, and I didn't have good study habits. My GPA was about a 2.5, and I even spent a semester on academic probation. After I hung up my glove and spikes, I averaged a 3.5 for my last two years and made the Dean's List every semester, but my overall average was slightly less than a 3.0 for all four years combined—2.96 for those keeping score, and the Academy always kept score.

The second list the Academy kept was one that ranked us by MPA or military performance average, which also worked on a 4-point scale—just like GPA. While I never was too crazy about all of the rules and regulations, I found that it didn't take too much trouble to keep my room clean and my shoes shined. I never was one to go out and get myself into trouble, and standard cadet punishments like marching back and forth on the tour pad with my rifle for an hour and sitting in my room in uniform on the weekends to serve confinements were sufficient deterrents for me to ensure that I would not go out of my way to do stupid things. So for the most part, I stayed out of trouble and did what I was told.

Without really trying, I had always been on the Commandant's List for MPA, which meant my average scores from my commanding officer, teachers, and cadet chain-of-command were over a 3.0 each semester. When you were on both the Dean's List and the Comm's List, you were named to the Superintendent's List. So for my last four semesters, I was actually on the Sup's List (pronounced *Soup's List*). Being on the Comm's List or the Sup's List usually meant a couple extra weekend passes each month and an extra hard time from my friends at school who didn't get to leave the campus as often as I did. What I didn't know, however, was that after four years at the Academy, there was a pay-off. I was ranked ninth in my class for MPA, and until it came time to pick where and when we wanted to go to flight school, I had no idea that such a ranking even existed.

A month or two before graduation, the way the draft was run, the top pilot qualified student for GPA picked his UPT choice of bases first. The top student for MPA picked second. Then GPA. Then MPA. Using this method, I got to pick eighteenth out of the seven hundred in the class who were headed to flight training. Not too bad for a sub-3.0 GPA!

The Air Force had five UPT bases from which to choose. In addition to Columbus, there was a base in Enid, Oklahoma, two in Texas—actually, three in Texas, but Sheppard Air Force Base in Wichita Falls was reserved for guys who scored highest in the T-41 flight screening program, and that wasn't an option for me. The fifth was Williams Air Force Base in Phoenix, Arizona.

There were about forty slots for each base where you could have sixty days of leave before starting UPT. Then, there were another forty slots for each base where you could have sixty days of leave and then thirty days at a desk job before starting UPT. After that, there were another forty slots that only got thirty days of leave.

I had made up my mind that I was going to choose Columbus. First, my two best friends at school were going to select Columbus. One was from Prattville, Alabama, and the other was from Ocala, Florida, and Columbus wasn't too far from either of their homes. Next, Columbus was the only pilot training base east of the Mississippi, which meant it was the closest to my home in Rhode Island. Finally, the inside word on Columbus was that because the weather was so rainy and cloudy, it was the best place to learn how to fly using just your cockpit instruments. Besides, even if the town wasn't the greatest, I'd only be there for a year, which wasn't a very long time—especially, compared to the four I had just spent at the Academy.

As one might imagine, the most sought after assignment was Williams AFB, *Willie,* in Phoenix with sixty days of leave. In fact, all but one of the seventeen guys who chose ahead of me chose Willie with sixty days of leave. When I announced Columbus and a 31 July start date, the room filled with seven hundred of my classmates gave me a standing ovation. I had freed up a Willie spot for somebody else a little farther down the list.

I had no idea if I'd made the right choice, but at the time, it seemed like the right choice for me. Besides, no matter what UPT base I chose, if I couldn't clear my ears in the altitude chamber, I couldn't be a pilot. I'd wash out and be sent to some other Air Force base. And I wouldn't be shit.

Chapter 4 — "Warm Beer"

Like all new classes in UPT, we wouldn't meet our first set of instructor pilots for primary jet training in the T-37 until about a month into the program. As the new students, we had a lot to learn and do before we hit the flight line. In addition to a couple of academic classes, we had ejection seat training, parachute training, aerospace physiology training, ground safety training, and a new program called CAI for computer-aided instruction. Although our helmets were finished and ready to be picked up, we needed to come up with class patches and scarves, and we needed our rank insignia, nametags, and all of the proper patches sewn onto our flight suits. Once all that was done, my half of our double-sized class would report to Dagger flight in the T-37 squadron for the first six months of our training program, and the other half the class would report to Warhawk flight.

Our class commander, however, had his own priorities, and at the top of that list was keeping his name off the wing commander's bad boy report for classes not having 100 percent membership to the Officers' Club. Lieutenant Sims had ordered all of us to voluntarily stop by the O-Club and sign up to become members, and I was one of the last ones to do this.

"This place is dead." I heard Doley's voice behind me as I looked around the plain and empty lobby of the Columbus Air Force Base Officer's Club.

"Do you think that chandelier's worth ten thousand dollars?" I asked him, pointing up to the gaudy, overly large, out-of-place lighting fixture in the center of the lobby.

"I don't think this whole building's worth that much," he replied dismissively. "Where do we go to sign up for ah cahds?"

I pointed to the O-Club business office, where the club manager was sitting behind his desk and speaking on the phone. He waved for the two of us to have a seat outside his office.

As we settled on the cushioned bench, I took an oblique glance at this guy I didn't know much about. As freshmen at the Air Force Academy, besides the misery of the first-year experience, childhood TV was about the only thing you had in common with classmates coming from every state in the country. With limited talking privileges and no television privileges, one way to get to know someone quickly was to drop references to your favorite shows or movies. You could have a full conversation this way in a matter of moments. Not only did this game help you see if your classmates liked what you liked, but a quick reference under your breath to a well-known scene lessened the chances of getting caught by an upperclassman when talking in a place where freshmen were supposed to be silent.

Without having established any commonality on which to build a conversation with Doley, I figured that we might have watched some of the same TV channels growing up in southern New England. So I launched into local shows.

"Were you ever on *Community Auditions?*" I asked. *Community Auditions* was a cheesy, talent show on Channel 4 out of Boston.

"'Sta'rof the day!'" Doley knew the show, obviously. "From Woo-bun, Mass, singing 'You Light Up My Life,' *Community Audition* numbah five: Michael Dolan." Doley smiled and slid back on the bench to lean against the wall. "No, I was neva'ron that show."

"What was better, *Duckpins for Dollars* or *Candlepins for Cash?*" I stuck with the local TV show theme for the conversation.

"Duckpins are Suck-pins," he replied, twisting a favorite cadet saying, "The O-Course is a Blow-Course," about the cadet obstacle course.

I kept quizzing Doley on his local TV viewing preferences. Major Mudd or Rex Trailer? UHF Channel 38 or 56? *Speed Racer* or *Kimba*? *Kung Fu Theater* or *Creature Double Feature*? He certainly was entertaining with his quick wit, and if he didn't have a reference or didn't give evidence to support the shows, personalities, or channels he liked, he would unmercifully bash what he didn't like. Even though I had no idea where Woburn was, I grew confident that he would understand just about any obscure reference that I might be inclined to drop.

After being issued our optional Officers' Club membership cards, Doley and I decided to exercise our new membership privileges at the O-Club bar. A great big room at the back of the building with a long bar, maybe a dozen round tables, a jukebox, and a pool table, which wasn't so much used for pool as it was for a popular pilots' bar game called Crud, the O-Club bar, like the O-Club lobby, was dead. The place must have made more money collecting monthly dues from student pilots than from any business it did during the week.

A middle-aged woman in the official O-Club uniform of dark pants, a white shirt, and a dark vest was washing glasses behind the bar, wiping them off, and hanging them upside-down to dry. She didn't seem to notice the two of us. There was one guy in a flight suit at the far end of the bar, drinking by himself. Since Doley and I were still in blues, we bellied up to the bar well away from the guy in the flight suit. I put my dark blue flight cap up on the bar as I climbed onto a stool near the bartender, who continued to wash, dry, and hang glasses. As soon as I had let go of my flight cap, without ever having looked up at Doley and me, she stopped what she was doing and rang a bell on the wall behind the bar three times.

"Hat on the bar!" she called out to no one in particular. I looked over at Doley.

"Hat on the bah," he stated, like he knew what it meant.

"What about it?" I asked.

At the sound of the bell and the bartender's announcement, the guy in the flight suit at the other end of the bar got up from his stool and came toward us.

"Gentlemen, you might know what that bell means. You might not. But that bell means that someone has placed his hat on the bar as a sign that he is volunteering to buy a round of beer for the house," said the guy as he approached. He was a tall, dark-haired man. He wore metal captain's bars on the shoulders of his flight suit, so he wasn't a student, and as a captain, he was maybe four or five years older than Doley and I. On the shoulder closest to us, he wore the patch of the 37th FTS (Flying Training Squadron). The dark blue scarf with yellow planes on it under his flight suit confirmed for us that he was a T-37 instructor. His black nametag with silver pilot's wings on it told us his name: CAPT DAVE WRIGHT.

Like our class commander, the Velcro on the sides of Captain Wright's flight suit had been adjusted back quite a ways—probably the result of too many evenings like tonight in the bar of the O-Club. But Captain Wright was about a foot taller than Lieutenant Sims, so his gut didn't look as large. He had a big smile on his face, as if he was happy to see us, but the pronounced creases at the edges of his mouth ran down the sides of his jaw to make it look like he might be frowning, but he was definitely smiling.

"Captain Wright," I greeted him excitedly—like I knew him—as I stood up from my stool, grabbing my flight cap off the bar with my left hand in case anyone else walked in. We shook hands. "I'm Lieutenant Wright. No relation. It's a pleasure to meet you, because I've always wanted to be CAPTAIN WRIIIIIGHT!" I dragged out *Captain Wright,* called it out loudly in my best TV announcer voice, and stuck a heroic pose with my feet spread widely, my hands on my hips, and a slight turn of my head to project a heroic profile.

"Captain Wright, I'm Michael Dolan. Nice to meet you." Doley introduced himself with a handshake — much less dramatically.

"Sir, this round's on me," I owned up. "What would you like to drink?"

"My favorite beer is cold beer," Captain Wright told us. Then, he looked over at the bartender and told her, "I'll have the coldest beer you have back there."

"Make that two, please," Doley said.

"Three, please," I added.

The bartender pulled the last three mugs she'd hung upside-down back down to the bar, set them right-side up, filled them with beer from the tap, and handed one to each of us. As we raised our glasses to one another, Captain Wright offered a toast, "To cold beer," he said, and we drank.

"Gentlemen, there's no finer beer than cold beer," Captain Wright continued after his first gulp. "You might think free beer is better than cold beer. You might not. I thank you for the free beer, but sometimes free beer can be warm beer, and I'm not a fan of warm beer. The only time I'd drink warm beer is if it were free beer." He paused for another gulp.

"Don't get me wrong, if any beer is free beer, then even if it's warm beer, I won't turn it away. When someone offers to pour me a beer from a pitcher of beer that's been sitting on a table for a long time, I won't say no, because it's free. But I know from the Zeroth Law of Thermodynamics that a warm pitcher in a warm room means warm beer. If I'm warm, the pitcher's warm, and the room's warm, I know that warm beer will taste great, but it's not refreshing." He gulped again.

"This glass is actually a little warm," he directed the bartender's way, but she didn't look up and just kept washing glasses.

"But when free beer is cold beer," Captain Wright continued, "like this beer I'm enjoying right now, it's all the more enjoyable, and it's preferred." His head swept back and forth between Doley and me like a radar dish, scanning the sky as he spoke, only pausing from his scan to have another swig from his mug.

GIVEN: *Captain Wright does not like warm beer.*
PROOF: *Cold beer is better than free beer.*

Captain Wright had proved his theorem by invoking the concept of thermal equilibrium. Even as a humanities major at the Academy, I had to study aerodynamics, astrodynamics, and thermodynamics in school. I never mastered any of these subjects, but I passed, and I always thought it was funny that the Zeroth Law was so named because it's an assumption that needed to be made in order to support the First, Second, and Third Laws of Thermodynamics, but nobody came up with it until after the other laws had been numbered. Maybe if I'd applied thermodynamics to beer, like Captain Wright, I would have been a better student.

"Cold beer, by definition, is always cold, even though it's not always free. Free beer, while always free, is not always cold. Because I prefer cold beer to warm beer, you can see why I say that cold beer is always better than free beer." He scanned back and forth between Doley and me one more time, and then he downed the rest of his cold, free beer.

"Are you two here for UPT?" he asked.

"Yes, sir," Doley replied first. "We're in the newest class."

"Eighty-eight-oh-seven?" Captain Wright asked. Our projected graduation date was July — the seventh month — 1988.

"Yes, sir," I jumped in. "Does that mean you've heard of us?"

Captain Wright smiled as Doley suggested other possibilities: "Ray, did you stop to think he just may have added one to the last class, 88-06? Or maybe he read one of the twelve signs around the base that says *Welcome, Class 88-07*?"

"No," I responded with a puzzled look. "Good points."

"Do you know yet if you'll be going to Dagger flight or Warhawk flight?" Captain Wright asked.

"Sir, we're assigned to Dagger," I answered.

"We'll be going into Dagger flight at the end of August," Doley added.

"Oh? What have you heard about Dagger flight?" Captain Wright followed up.

I hadn't heard anything about Dagger flight. I looked over at Doley to see if he could answer Captain Wright's question, and his look told me he hadn't heard anything either. Not knowing Captain Wright and what his job was, I certainly didn't want to respond in a way that might sound negative.

"Sir, we've really just arrived at Columbus. I don't know much about the different flights, but I have heard that Columbus is the best pilot training base because you really learn how to fly in the weather." I thought I gave a pretty diplomatic answer.

"Lieutenant Wright," Captain Wright smiled and got up from the bar, "that is a true statement." He pulled his own flight cap out from the pocket at the bottom of his right leg, zipped the pocket closed, and thanked us for the free, cold beer.

When he stood up, Doley and I both stood, too.

"Captain Wright, will we see you when we get to the flight line?" I asked, knowing from his pilot wings, scarf, and squadron patch on his sleeve that he was an instructor, but I just didn't know enough about the flight line to know what his role might be.

Captain Wright spun around so that Doley and I could see the patch sewn on the sleeve of his other shoulder for the first time. A thin yellow border outlined a circle of dark blue, and in the circle a red blade flanked by yellow-feathered wings spread majestically above the wingspan of a white T-37. Underneath the circular part of the patch in a small, dark blue arc, also outlined in yellow, the name of his flight in capital letters was stitched in red. He reached across his body to touch it: DAGGER.

"Maybe you might." He grinned widely, deepening the creases that ran from the corners of his mouth. "I'm the Dagger flight commander."

*

The altitude chamber re-created the classic Mr. Wizard experiment where Mr. Wizard sucked the air out of a metal gas can with a vacuum cleaner until the can collapsed under the pressure of the air around it. The Air Force threw a twist into its version of the experiment, as the trainees were inside the gas can while the air got sucked out, which made for all kinds of fun.

To demonstrate the effect that pressure changes have on the trapped gas in your body, a rubber glove dangled from the ceiling inside the chamber by a string that also tied off the opening of the glove. As the air was removed from the chamber, the rubber glove would inflate like a balloon because the air pressure inside the glove became greater than the air pressure outside the glove. It was interesting to watch but uncomfortable to experience.

While the air pressure inside the glove grew greater and greater, relative to the pressure in the chamber, the same thing happened to the pockets of air inside your body. The expanding air trapped in a sinus cavity might result in a headache or a pain underneath the eyes. On commercial airline flights, little kids often cry in the descent to landing because they can't equalize the air pressure in their inner ears.

Depending on what you may have eaten the night before, you also had the potential to fart like a tuba player trying to hold a note for as long as possible during the climb to altitude. If you didn't take steps to equalize the pressure that built up in your body by yawning, farting, wiggling your jaw, or by a move called the Valsalva, the pressure could get kind of painful. My first time in the chamber, it got worse than painful—it got absolutely humiliating.

I don't know if I had a cold that first time, which blocked up my inner airways so that I couldn't possibly clear my ears and sinuses, but I do know that I had no clue how to do a proper Valsalva maneuver. Imagine blowing your nose as hard as you can while pinching your nostrils so that you cause your ears to actually pop! That's the proper way to perform a Valsalva, which should be done when moving into an environment of greater outside pressure. Scuba divers do it as they swim deeper down into the ocean. Pilots (and passengers) should do it while descending from areas of higher altitude to lower altitude. My first time in the chamber, I didn't know how to do it, and what a mess that was.

During our sophomore year at the Academy, the twenty or so of my classmates and I in 21st Squadron got bused to Peterson Air Force Base in Colorado Springs for our first altitude chamber ride. One of the summer programs cadets took between their sophomore and junior years was a program called Operation Air Force, where you'd deploy to a Real Air Force base for three weeks. About half of the class would get to go overseas, and nearly everyone could expect to get some kind of incentive flight in an Air Force jet, which was why we had to go through the chamber training.

I remember the training went smoothly on our simulated climb. I yawned, wiggled my jaw, blasted some bench-vibrating farts, and watched the rubber glove expand to the size of a small beach ball. On the way down, however, a railroad spike-sized pain pierced both sides of my head, stabbing into my ears, and underneath my eyes. The more we descended, the worse it got until finally, I had to ask the chamber controller take us back up to a higher altitude to make the distress go away.

I shook off the pain, and we started to descend again. But the lower we dropped, the stronger the pain got. I yawned. I wiggled my jaw. I pinched my nose and blew, but nothing helped. I called for the controller to suck the air out of the room and climb back up a second time, as my asymptomatic classmates grew concerned. The controller climbed, but because I'd hit the buzzer for a second time, he also sent in the medics, a couple of guys with a large cup of water and two turkey basters.

"Take your helmet and mask off, Cadet Wright," I heard, and I did, while everyone else waited and watched. "Here's what we're going to do: You're going to drink this cup of water, and we're going to stick these squirters in your nose. On the count of three, we're going to squeeze them. When we do, you keep drinking the water. You'll feel a rush of fluid in your head, and there may be a little more pain at first, but that will be what clears your ears. Got it?"

I got it.

The controller started increasing the atmospheric pressure for a third time, and I could feel the pain growing stronger and stronger. I drank the water, as instructed, and on the count of three, the medic guys squeezed the turkey basters they'd stuck up my nose to blast water through my sinus cavity. The inside of my head completely exploded. Water squealed and gushed behind my ears, under my eyes, and around my eyebrows. The pressure built even more, and then my eardrums burst just like the rubber glove would have, if it had been stuck with a pin and popped when fully inflated. The BANG inside my head was so loud, I went deaf for a day and a half, and my ears rang for nearly a week.

I had a physics test the next day in school that I flunked — and that was what landed me on academic probation for the rest of the semester.

Before this morning's training in UPT, I had practiced my Valsalva, but I had no idea if it would work. And that was bothering me as I followed the other guys into the chamber. The altitude chamber was not much bigger than a baseball dugout and not much more elaborate. Benches lined the walls of the room on the inside, but the positions where we sat were numbered. As trainees, we wore our newly completed helmets and oxygen masks in the chamber, and we had to sit in certain spots in order to plug our oxygen hoses and communication jacks into the system. Numbered seating also helped the trainers interact with the trainees, because they could address us by the numbers on the wall above each student.

Two trainers were assigned to us. Both were enlisted guys, young airmen who got to wear flight suits rather than blues or fatigues—unlike most of the other enlisted personnel we'd met to that point. One sat on the outside of the altitude chamber at an elevated instrument panel, where he could watch and wave to us through a glass window at one end of the chamber. He was the guy who would suck out the air, take us through our training exercises, and then pump the air back into the room. He wore a radio headset with a microphone, but he didn't need to wear a helmet or oxygen mask. The other guy sat with us on the inside of the chamber. He would be flying the mission with us, and he would probably be the guy to stick the turkey baster in my nose if I couldn't clear my ears on the way down.

As instructed, we all filed into the altitude chamber and assumed a numbered position on the benches inside the room. Kenny Wessels sat on my left, and Turbiglio, the wallet-carrying Pennsylvania Guard or Reserves guy who didn't go to the Academy, sat on my right. His first name was Al. Kurt and Doley were across from me on the other side of the room.

I put my helmet on and plugged into the communication and oxygen systems through the hose and audio jack at my seat, which was position number eight. I left the chinstrap on my helmet to dangle like in *Top Gun,* and kept my tinted visor slid up.

Once everyone got settled into a spot on the bench, the controller on the outside got started. "All right, Class 88-07, welcome to the altitude chamber. Please make sure you connect your chinstraps and oxygen masks." Everyone snapped and buckled up. This wasn't *Top Gun.*

"Before we begin our climb to 25,000 feet, we've got to have you breathe pure oxygen for thirty minutes," he continued. "Once you've secured your mask to your face, please reach down to your regulator, and set your oxygen switch to the 100 percent pure oxygen setting." We all complied.

"I'd like each of you to make sure your mask is properly tightened and secured to your helmet," the young controller went on. He directed us to observe the airman on the inside of the chamber with us. "To tighten your mask, you can push the metal slider on either side of your helmet back toward your face until it clicks. To loosen your mask, push the other side of your metal slider away from your face." The airman on the inside of the chamber made sure all of us could see how he fastened and loosened his mask.

"In spite of what you may have seen in the movies, your mask is worn securely up against your face at all times. It does not dangle from one side of your helmet until you are ready to dogfight. A dangling mask that you are constantly connecting, disconnecting, and reconnecting makes for an unnecessary distraction in the cockpit, so your mask should be worn up against your face at all times. Having your mask securely fastened at all times will also help to prevent the insidious onset of hypoxia, which you'll get to experience firsthand today," he said.

"I'd like everyone now to reach down to where your oxygen hose plugs into the chamber hose, and please check to see that the oxygen hoses are properly connected. The metal ends should fit snugly together, and there should not be any hissing or leaks." While the controller spoke, the airman on the inside of the chamber demonstrated the connections, like a flight attendant showing passengers how the metal end of the seat belt fastens into the buckle for a secure fit across your lap.

The altitude chamber was cool and comfortable, which felt good compared to the August steam bath of Mississippi summer air outside the building. We sat for a while, a little bored, and breathed in our pure, canned oxygen. To me, just as an aircraft's canned air is only slightly different from ambient air—mostly in its smell—100 percent pure, canned oxygen was only slightly different from canned air. While it really didn't smell or taste any different, it did seem a little bit thicker. It certainly wasn't any fresher.

It did sound different. Inside our oxygen masks was a small, circular microphone about the size of a quarter. The oxygen we breathed through our hoses hit the microphone from both sides, which resulted in a Darth Vader–like breathing sound in the headset inside our helmets. Others must have been thinking the same thing because they slid their tinted sun visors down for the full Darth Vader effect.

The young airman on the inside of the chamber reminded us through our headsets to keep our visors up. He needed to see our faces in case anyone had any trouble.

Like me.

"We've got a number of required elements to our training today," the outside guy told us. "I'll brief you on the specifics during this period of oxygen saturation, and again as we begin to climb to our cruising altitude of 25,000 feet. First of all, let me tell you about your communication system in the chamber. I'm speaking over an intercom system to you, so all of you can hear me at the same time. Your intercom system, however, has been disabled. If you want to speak, you'll need to press the red button on your comm-jack, which activates your microphone. Just like the radio system in the aircraft, only one microphone in the altitude chamber can be active at any time, so please be careful not to step on each other's transmissions.

"Let's go around the room with a comm-check," the outside guy continued. "Number 1, how do you hear me?"

"Loud and clear," replied Number 1. "How me?"

"Loud and clear, sir," said the airman. "Number 2, how do you hear me?"

"Loud and clear," replied Number 2, whose voice I recognized as Chuck's. "How me?"

"Loud and clear, ma'am."

The controller on the outside went all around the room to ensure everyone knew how to use their microphones. With our masks up and everyone's voice piped right to the speakers inside my helmet, the only way I knew who was talking was when I could recognize the voice, like Chuck's, or when the controller identified the person's seat number.

"All right," the airman continued, "everyone's comm system seems to be working fine."

After a half-hour of pure oxygen and pure boredom, we were told to switch regulators back to the normal oxygen setting, and we began our ascent.

As we climbed, the airman on the outside continued narrating our flight through the altitudes and asking us questions based on the material we had covered in the classroom. The guy on the inside didn't say much of anything at all; he just demonstrated things and pointed to the slowly expanding rubber glove every once in a while.

"We're passing 3,000 feet in a nice, slow climb," he said. "Number 1, at 3,000 feet, how should your oxygen regulator be set?"

"On-Normal-Normal," Number 1 answered.

"Yes, sir. That's correct," said the airman. "Everyone, please ensure at this time that your regulators are set to On-Normal-Normal." The inside guy made some flight attendant-like hand waves around his regulator panel.

"Number 4," the controller asked, "above what altitude is supplemental oxygen required?"

"Ten thousand feet," replied Number 4.

"Correct, sir," said the controller, who continued with his instructions.

The controller briefed us on all the objectives of our mission. We'd be climbing up to 25,000 feet, where the rubber glove and our internal gas pockets would be fully inflated. At our cruising altitude, we'd be taking off our oxygen masks so that we could experience the effects of hypoxia first hand. Along with this exercise, we'd practice the proper hypoxia recovery procedures. We'd discuss the proper way to report a physiological incident to the controller over the radio. Then, we'd be subjected to a rapid loss of cabin pressure from 25,000 feet to 43,000 feet, so that we could learn what to do in the event that this might happen in the jet. Only at the end, when we were nearly all the way down to local atmospheric pressure, would I learn if I had figured out how to clear my ears.

"We're continuing our climb through 8,000 feet. As you pass through a certain altitude, you should check your oxygen system to ensure that it is working properly. Number 7—" the controller called on Al Turbiglio, who was sitting just to my right—"passing through what altitude should you check to ensure that your oxygen system is working properly?"

"Twenty-five thousand feet!" The reply came very quickly. But the voice wasn't Al's.

Al shook his helmet back-and-forth, as if to say, "It wasn't me!" but no sound came through my headset.

Then, I figured it out. It was Doley. Doley had surmised that with our masks up, the controller was just as unaware as we were as to who was talking.

"No, sir, I'm afraid that's not correct. Number 8, do you know?" the airman asked me.

"Ten thousand feet," I said quickly, before Doley answered incorrectly for me.

"Yes, sir. Ten thousand feet is the correct answer," the controller said.

Al threw his hands up, and then, he slapped his leg in anger. Looking around at people's eyes and eyebrows, I could tell that a lot of them were laughing. And I could tell Al was mad. Doley sat very innocently on the bench on the other side of the chamber. Al hadn't figured out who stepped on his radio call to make him look bad and continued to look around for the culprit.

"Let's all perform an oxygen check now as we pass through 10,000 feet," the controller directed. "There should be no air leaking from any part of your mask."

Here's where my mask posed a problem—or rather, my nose posed a problem. Because the bridge of my nose had become slightly askew over the years thanks to collisions with basketball players' elbows, one guy's forehead, and a badminton racquet, I could not get a good seal on my mask. When I gangloaded my regulator, not only did I get a blast of air in my mask, the air blew up into my right eye in a steady, cool stream, which also meant that I couldn't get my blinker to turn a solid color. Was this going to be a problem? I wasn't going to say anything.

"In the aircraft," the controller went on, "you'll be using your checklist as you perform this check, which is part of your climb check and your level-off check. This check requires both a *challenge* and a *response* from each crew member upon its completion, at which time you return the regulator to the On-Normal-Normal position," he said.

"Assuming that your oxygen system is functioning properly, you would say, *My oxygen system is On-Normal-Normal, good pressure, good blinker. How about you?*"

The airman on the inside answered the controller's challenge. "My oxygen is On-Normal-Normal, good pressure, good blinker."

As the controller went around the room again with another round of questions—on our climb to 25,000 feet—nobody had the nerve to duplicate Doley's joke—except Doley. Of course, he waited until the question came back to Al.

"Number 7," the controller said to Al. I was watching Doley, who had his eyes focused on the thumb Al held over his red radio button. "What are some common signs of hypoxia?"

"Coughing, sneezing, and a terrible itch," Doley interjected again.

"No, sir, I'm sorry. That's not right," the disappointed controller responded.

"I didn't say that!" Al protested over the radio.

"Yes, I did," Doley quickly added, still pretending to be Al. "I mean...I don't know the answer, so I made that up."

Al threw his hands up in the air again and looked around for someone to back up his story, but by this time, everyone was shaking with laughter and nobody could talk. I held out my hands to show Al that it wasn't me, and just like a game of Indian Chief, everyone else held out their hands, too. Al couldn't figure out who was the chief.

Our big, white, foam-lined flight helmets weren't totally soundproof. Over the sounds of our own breathing and the muffling effect the masks had on our voices, you could actually hear people laughing. As we climbed higher and the rubber glove grew fatter, I heard the farting begin. It started out as one here and one there, but the higher we flew, the louder and longer the farting got. There was an impromptu game of fart tennis, which developed into an impromptu contest for the longest fart blast.

The bench on which we sat served a dual purpose as both a seat and a fart-seismograph. You could actually measure the strength and duration of each fart by the bench's vibrations, even if you couldn't hear it, and after experiencing a number of quakes, tremors, and aftershocks, you could approximate the epicenter of each. By this point in the ride, I was glad we had to keep our oxygen masks on at all times.

I held my own gas in as long as I could, but eventually, the pain in my stomach was just too strong. I needed to get some relief. Enter the One Cheek Sneak.

When we leveled off at 25,000 feet, we performed the level-off check and received our instructions for the hypoxia portion of the training. At the controller's command, we would take off our oxygen masks in order to breathe the thin, oxygen-deficient air of 25,000 feet. Under our seats were clipboards, on which we'd find a short quiz to complete as best we could. Within a couple of minutes, we were told, we would begin to feel our personal symptoms of hypoxia. For most, these symptoms would include a headache, tingling sensations in the limbs, and loss of concentration. Once we had a chance to experience these symptoms, we were to gangload our regulators, put our masks back up to our faces, and find a picture of a circle on the wall to look at while we did so.

Since nobody had any questions, we were instructed to take off our masks and begin our quiz. I unfastened my mask and let it dangle to breathe in the thin chamber air. With our masks down, it was easier to talk with each other, but I wasn't sure if academic integrity was to be in place for this quiz, so I wasn't going to say anything. I was thankful that the farting had seemed to subside, and most of the smells had dissipated.

I grabbed the clipboard from under my seat and began.

1. *Above what altitude is supplemental oxygen required?*

That was an easy one — 10,000 feet.

2. *What is the highest altitude at which you can fly in a non-pressurized cockpit?*

I was pretty sure the answer was 25,000 feet.

3. *Under normal conditions, how should the switches on your regulator be set?*

Another easy one.

"How easy is this?!" Doley called out. "I'm almost done."

I was still on number three.

"On-Normal-Normal," I wrote very slowly. For some reason, I was writing my letters like I was in first grade. I started to giggle.

4. What is your favorite sports team?

This question didn't seem like it belonged on the quiz. I couldn't decide between the Celtics and the Red Sox. I had a Celtics bumper sticker on the back of the Isuzu P'up, Winner of the Baja 1,000. I wrote down *Red Sox.* I also drew the *B* in the style that it is on the hat, and I drew the two socks side by side. I thought this would show the physiology guys how much of a Red Sox fan I was. I think I was giggling a little more, too.

"The Red Sox suck," Kenny shouted from my left.

So much for academic integrity.

"The Red Sox do not suck!" Doley shouted back from the other side of the chamber.

"Aaay! They couldn't even beat the Mets!" Kenny came back even louder, pointing at Doley.

All of a sudden, this discussion became more important than the quiz. I couldn't do the stupid quiz anyway! Everybody was talking. My fingers were tingling. I felt a little dizzy, and everything I thought about was making me giggle. I had to tell Kenny that my favorite team didn't suck.

How did the Red Sox blow Game 6? How did they blow the World Series?

I was sitting in my cadet room—still in my cadet uniform, watching the game on my little black-and-white TV with its four-inch screen. The Red Sox had the lead in the game and the Series. I don't remember where I got a cigar, but I had a cigar in my cadet room, unwrapped and ready to be lit with the match I held in my other hand. They were one strike away from being world champions. Then, everything fell apart. They blew it, and they lost.

I couldn't do the stupid quiz anymore! I couldn't even understand the next few questions even though I could still kind of read them. My fingers were tingling. I had a headache, and the Red Sox argument had frustrated me. I didn't feel like giggling anymore.

I was starting to feel sick, and I realized I had become hypoxic. Looking around the chamber, nobody else had gone back on oxygen yet, but I needed to. I needed something to make me feel better.

I put down my clipboard, gangloaded my regulator, and put my mask back up to my face. I found the picture of the gray-shaded circle on the wall across the chamber in front of me Black lines cut through its center, dividing it into eight equal parts, like a pizza.

Almost as soon as the oxygen hit my face, the gray pizza slices in the circle turned into a beautiful wheel of vividly bright colors. Each slice was a different color than the others. I felt like Dorothy opening the door of her black-and-white house after crash-landing in Munchkin Land to a world of wonderful colors. The picture hadn't really changed colors; the colors were always there, but my brain couldn't see them without the help of oxygenated air.

With the cool rush of pure oxygen blowing in my face, my headache and lightheadedness went away, as did the tingling in my fingers. I reviewed my quiz as most of the rest of the class started to put their masks back up to their faces. I hadn't even made it through half of the questions, and they were very easy questions. With each answer I'd written, my printing got worse and worse. At the bottom of the page, I had just scribbled a whole bunch of disjointed lines.

"Done!" Doley announced, and he fastened his mask back to his helmet. Kenny and Al were back on oxygen on either side of me. Soon, everyone had put their masks back up — except Kurt.

Kurt sat at position number 19 on the wall to my right. The controller was right behind him, watching all of us through a thick, glass window in the wall.

"Did you finish your quiz, Number 19?" the controller asked. He could only see the top of Kurt's giant helmet through the window.

"Yes, I finished my quiz," Kurt said through his radio while his mask still hung from the side of his helmet. He held up the thumbs up sign.

"How do you feel right now, sir?" the controller wanted to know.

"I feel fine. Do you have any more tests, or is this one all you've got?" Kurt asked him.

"As a matter of fact, we do have another test for you." After the controller said this, the airman in the chamber with us reached under his seat and slid out a box. He pulled out Kurt's next test and handed it over to him.

The test was the half-red, half-blue plastic Tupperware ball that every baby has in his or her playpen. It's the one with ten yellow shapes that have to be pushed through the right holes in the ball, and when the ball is filled with the shapes, you pull the little handles to split the ball apart, and the ten yellow shapes spill back out.

"I love this toy," Kurt said, pulling the sides apart, and he quickly put the shapes back into their holes in no time at all. Everybody clapped and cheered for Kurt.

"Nice work, Number 19," the controller complimented Kurt. Not wanting to miss a teaching moment, he asked, "Can you do the puzzle again for us? This time, as you put the puzzle back together, please tell us if you are feeling any symptoms of hypoxia."

"Okay," Kurt responded, dumping the puzzle pieces back into his lap. "I do feel a little light-headed, but I don't have a headache." This time, I could hear Kurt's voice across the room. He wasn't transmitting over his microphone anymore—just talking loudly. He started to fit the yellow shapes back into the ball. "My fingers and toes are fine. As far as my concentration goes, I'm still doing okay."

Kurt talked as he worked on the puzzle, and in no time, he had put it together for a second time. He held up the ball to show the airman through the window. Again, we all applauded and cheered for Kurt.

"The record in the altitude chamber for that puzzle is three times, Number 19. Do you want to go for it?" the controller challenged Kurt. As we all cheered, Kurt held up the ball and moved it from left to right, as if he were showing his fans the championship trophy. Then, he dumped the pieces into his lap for a third time.

"*Here we go,*" sang Kurt, and this time, he gave us a play-by-play as he began the puzzle for the third time. "The circle piece goes into the circle hole. Here it is. Mr. Circle."

Kurt pinched another piece between his giant thumb and index finger for all of us to see, but he didn't take his eyes off of the Tupperware ball. "Mr. Oval looks like Mr. Circle, but he's a little longer. Got it!" The tone of his voice had changed, and Kurt sounded like a preschool teacher talking to a playpen full of babies.

"*The plus sign…*the plus sign is one of the few pieces that can go in either on its side or vertically." Kurt was starting to sound a little silly, and for a moment, he stopped talking so he could think.

"How are you feeling, Number 19? Are you ready to put your mask back on?" the controller checked in with Kurt, who didn't answer for a moment. "Number 19?" the controller checked in again.

"I'm fine!" Kurt yelled, fitting another piece back into its hole, "but Mr. Square can't find his hole." Kurt held the square piece at the top of the ball and slowly rotated the ball around while he tapped the square piece at the top of it.

"*Where's Mr. Square?*" Kurt started to sing in a high-pitched, preschool teacher voice. Tap, tap, tap. "*Here comes Mr. Square.*" Tap, tap, tap. "*Where are you, Mr. Square?*" Tap, tap, tap. He sang and spun the ball and tapped the square on the surface of the ball. Everyone was laughing. We were all rooting for Kurt to set the record.

"Number 19, are you doing okay? Are you ready to put your mask back up?" called the controller through our headsets.

"Not until I help Mr. Square find his hole!" Kurt told him. He was not going to give up. "And here it is! Good-bye, Mr. Square." Kurt finished the puzzle for a third time. He held up the plastic ball to a round of applause and cheering muffled by oxygen masks and aircrew helmets.

"Congratulations, Number 19. Please reconnect your oxygen mask to your helmet, and gangload your regulator." Kurt looked up to the color wheel on the wall and complied with the controller's instructions.

As Kurt focused on the wall, watching for the gray pizza slices to explode with color, the rest of us focused on him. Not only were we in awe of his record-setting performance...we wanted to hear more about Mr. Circle, Mr. Oval, and Mr. Square, but the airman inside the chamber took back the plastic ball with Kurt's geometric friends and slid it under the bench.

After a few minutes, we were all instructed to switch back to the normal oxygen setting. The next part of our training, the rapid loss of cabin pressure, went smoothly. The purpose was to simulate a loss of the jet's canopy at altitude. There was a loud *POP!* when it happened, and the rubber glove that hung from the ceiling doubled in size instantaneously. I could feel my ears bubble, but I didn't experience any pain. Going up, however, was never my problem.

Because you don't perform the Valsalva maneuver in a climb, I yawned several times, stretched my neck, and pointed one ear to the ceiling, followed by the other, to make the bubbling go away. The controller reviewed the proper steps to take in the event of a rapid loss of cabin pressure. After he did, it was time to start back down. And this was when anxiety flooded me.

I don't remember much of the instruction given on the descent. I had one thing on my mind: Keep my ears clear. I pinched my nose through the top of my oxygen mask and blew every couple of minutes—but I couldn't make my ears pop.

The balloon-like rubber glove hanging from the ceiling started to shrink in size as the chamber slowly filled back with air, and the atmospheric pressure increased. The controller called out our simulated altitudes on the descent. Thirty thousand feet. Twenty-five thousand feet. Twenty thousand feet. I felt the pressure start to build. First, underneath my eyes. Then, inside my ears. Unlike the rubber glove, the spaces in my head that had trapped expanded gas weren't deflating. I needed to force them to clear, and if I couldn't clear my ears, my flying career would end before it ever even began.

I stretched my neck to one side and wiggled my jaw.

No relief.

Fifteen thousand feet.

I tilted my head to the other side and yawned to try to get my ears to pop.

Nothing.

Not only was the pressure growing inside my sinuses and ears, but a feeling of angst was growing in my stomach.

I saw Kenny pinch the top of his oxygen mask and lean his head forward.

"I see some of you are performing the Valsalva maneuver," the controller said. "That's good. Stay ahead of the pressure changes."

Ten thousand feet.

My yawns and jaw wiggles weren't working. I'd pinched my nose a couple of times and tried to blow, but I still couldn't clear my head. Not quite to the point of panic, I breathed in to fill my lungs with as much air as they could possibly hold. I reached up and pinched the top of my rubber oxygen mask, squeezed my nostrils closed, and forcefully honked the air from my lungs up against the fingers pinching my nose as hard as I possibly could for the king of all Valsalva maneuvers.

I heard it happen in my head before I felt it. A very quiet *pa-pop*. First in my right ear and then in my left ear. The sounds were followed by immediate relief.

I did it!

I actually felt my ears pop! The relief felt great. The Valsalva didn't hurt at all — not like two streams of water shot up my nose. I could hear clearly. I had no pain. Once I heard and felt the air trapped inside my ears blow from the inside out, I realized that I had never fully understood how to correctly perform the Valsalva. And I had no problem with my ears or sinuses the rest of the descent.

"Aaay, Kurt!" Kenny said as we filed out of the chamber at the end of the training session. "Awesome job wit' dat puzzle!"

"Yeah, Kurt, if I didn't know better, I'd think that you'd practiced it," I added.

"Ray, ah you saying Kurt plays with baby toys?" Doley joked.

"Well, Doley, funny you should say that." Kurt stopped to address Doley's remark. He reached out to put one giant hand on Kenny's shoulder and the other on mine and pulled us in closer. "Malia and I have recently started a collection of baby toys."

"What choo talkin' 'bout, Kurtis?" I asked, flashing a cheeky Arnold Drummond pout.

"Malia's pregnant," Kurt said.

"Aaay! Congrats!" Kenny offered. "Let's hit the O-Club and celebrate with a couple beers."

"The O-Club is a Blow-Club," Doley said.

Chapter 5 — "Behavioral Disorder"

"We are not ready for the flight line," Mark Jellicot declared at a rare joint session of our entire class. Just like we'd been divided on day one of UPT, those of us soon to report to Dagger flight sat on one side of the center aisle in Room 12 of the Student Squadron building, and the half of the class soon to report to Warhawk flight sat on the opposite side.

As class leader, Mark ran our meetings when none of our instructors were around. The other first lieutenant in our class, Val Martelli, joined Mark at the front of the room, because he was the section leader for the other half of our class. Like Mark, Val had been a navigator in the backseat of an F-4 fighter jet, but I don't know if he'd been stationed in the Philippines.

"There's a lot that we have to do outside of our regular twelve-hour days to get ready," Mark said, holding out a notebook in front him. "Lieutenant Sims gave me a list, and I'll run through it for you. We need to design a class patch and have it made. We need to design a class scarf for under our flight suits and have them made. We need to have all our patches sewn onto our flight suits before we can get out of these blues. We need to all write a one-page, personal essay for the flight line instructors no later than a week before we hit the flight line. We need to start memorizing our **BOLDFACE**."

At that point, Mark seemed to have lost his train of thought. He looked over to his left, where Val and the rest of his section were sitting. "Was there something else we talked about?" he asked.

"Call signs," Val reminded him.

"Call signs!" Mark repeated excitedly. "We need call signs! When I flew F-4s in the Philippines, our jet's call sign was Fiend, and I'm a University of Florida Gator. So, my call sign is either going to be Gator or Fiend."

Mark and Val had apparently envisioned recreating the *Top Gun* world of fighter pilots in the backwoods training base of Columbus, Mississippi.

"Lieutenant Sims suggested patches first," Val reminded Mark before he got too excited.

"Thanks, Val. That's right," Mark acknowledged. "We need to come up with a concept for a class patch. We've got about twenty minutes here before our two sections split up to get to our first events of the day. Let's take care of this right now while we're all together. The other things can be done individually or within each flight."

Mark flipped through the pages of his notebook, obviously looking for a certain page.

"Remember, if we have a T-38 in our design, we also have to put a T-37 in it, too," he said, referring to his notes. "Having two jets on our patch might make it a little crowded. Now, I flew F-4s in the Philippines, and I'd like to fly the F-15 when I graduate, so I think we should either have an F-4 or an F-15 on our patch. Remember, it also has to say *14 STUS* for the Stu-Ron."

Mark had apparently spent some time envisioning *Top Gun*-styled patches, too.

"There's a tailor shop right outside of the base where I was stationed in the Philippines." Mark went on. "They can print up our patches and sew them on our uniforms real quick!"

"Hold on!" Kurt threw one of his giant hands into the air in protest. "Real men fly jets with only one engine." When Kurt was enlisted before his Academy days, he had worked on the one-engine F-16. "The F-4 is on its way out, and F-16s are way cooler than F-15s."

"Yeah!" a bunch of other guys agreed with Kurt, and an argument began.

F-15!

F-16!

Less filling!

Tastes great!

With the room now in total chaos and half of our allotted time gone, the class patch planning session didn't look like it would result in any agreement on aircraft, themes, or even hidden meanings. Looking around the classroom, I could see least a half-dozen different little pockets of bickering or joking.

"I got it!" I yelled above all the noise. I stood up at my seat, and when everyone was quiet, I made my pitch. "Lieutenant Sims didn't say that we *had* to have any jets on our class patch. He only said that if we *had* a T-38, then we had to have a T-37." I looked around to see if anybody was following where I was going with this. "So how about no jets? How about just a picture of a beach? On the beach, there's a pink flamingo. Under the picture of the pink flamingo on the beach, the patch just says, *Columbus Beach Club.*"

At first, nobody said much of anything, but as I scanned the room, I could see I had more than a few people seeing the anti-establishment genius in my stupidity. After four years at the Academy, almost everyone in the room was used to having rules shoved down their throats on a daily basis — what to say, what to wear, where to be, how to make your bed, and even how to fold your underwear into 3-by-5 inch rectangles subject to measurement with a ruler during a Saturday morning inspection. By cadet wing regulation, we could only display three items of memorabilia in our cadet dormitory rooms! It wasn't that often that we'd been given a chance to get creative.

"In order to match the pink flamingos on our class patches," I continued, "our scarves would be hot pink, and if we ever wanted to run any spirit missions around the base, we could stick pink lawn flamingos into the grass in front of any building or anyone's base housing unit." Now the eyes were starting to light up around the room, and I could tell I was winning over the crowd.

"What about the hidden meaning?" somebody challenged me.

"Aaaaah! That's the best part," I said. "The hidden meaning is that there is no hidden meaning. No class has ever had a class patch that's had nothing to do with flying, and I bet it's safe to say that no class has ever worn hot pink scarves under their flight suits as part of their uniforms. Looking into our patch for a hidden meaning will drive the leadership crazy, because they'll think there must be a hidden meaning, but in fact, there is no hidden meaning, and we can keep that hidden. Think about it!"

I don't think that anybody knew quite what to say.

Mark Jellicot finally broke the silence. "No, we have to have a hot jet. A pink flamingo on a beach? That makes no sense! C'mon. Where do we put *14 STUS?*"

I thought for a moment about a pink flamingo on a beach and tried to imagine where I could hide the one mandatory component of the class patch....

"On the surfboard!" I shot back. And by the cheers and applause that followed, it was decided that our class patch and class theme would be the pink flamingos of Columbus Beach Club with no jets, no hidden meanings, nothing really to do with flying at all, and hot pink scarves to wear with our flight suits.

*

The academic instructor for our class in T-37 Operations, Captain Van Dorn, gave us a ten-minute break in between lessons. In the back hallway of the Student Squadron building, several of us were getting to know the other non-Academy guy besides Mark Jellicot in Dagger—wallet-carrying Al.

Al Turbiglio had attended the University of Pittsburgh, and after he graduated, Al had attended Officer Training School in San Antonio, Texas. OTS was a six-week program for civilian college graduates that resulted in the same rank, uniform, and pay as those of us who had spent our last four years—or five for the preppies like Kurt, Kenny, and Chuck—isolated from civilization on the side of a mountain in Colorado at the Academy.

Al had dark, thick, black hair that was all combed backwards and moussed down into place. In the front, his spiky widow's peak clung together in a thick point, like Eddie Munster—except Al was grown, married, and a little heavier than Eddie Munster and a little heavier than the rest of the class. Al also had his private pilot's license, and apparently, he had a lot of flying experience.

Unlike the rest of the students in our Dagger section, Al already knew what aircraft he'd be flying after graduating from UPT. Al would be flying the C-130 Hercules cargo plane as an officer with the Pennsylvania Air Force Reserves. The rest of us were competing against one another for an unknown assignment at an unknown base with the assumption that those who finished at the top of the class would get to fly fighter jets in exotic places, and those who finished at the bottom of the class would be flying tankers and bombers in the middle of nowhere.

"Aaay, Al," Kenny approached our new classmate, "how come you always carry your wallet? Why don't you just put it in your pocket?"

"I can't," Al answered. "My training instructor at OTS said that it's unprofessional to carry items in your pockets."

"What about your car keys?" Kenny was trying to understand. "Where do you put your car keys?"

"I just carry one key, and I put it in my wallet," Al told him.

"Aaay, what about a pen? You can't put a pen in your wallet. Can you put a pen in your pocket or what? Where do you put dat...in your hat?" Kenny wanted to know. In the military, you always wear a hat outside. So, unless you're at home or in a building with a special room for hats, you are always carrying your hat with you when you're inside.

"No," Al told the group of us matter-of-factly. "I don't put anything in my pockets. I can't put anything in my pockets now, anyway, because the training instructor at OTS said it would be more professional if we sewed our pockets shut; so I had all of my pockets sewn shut. If I need a pen, I'll just carry it around — like my wallet." Al seemed happy to share this helpful hint with everybody within earshot.

"Aaay, the way I see it," Kenny said, "is that if we weren't supposed to use our pockets, we wouldn't have pockets. I hope it's not unprofessional to use your fly...what if you gotta take a leak? Haaaa!" Kenny laughed as he walked off towards the men's room.

Even though Kenny had walked away, Al was eager to share with the rest of us standing in the hall what else we could do to be more professional.

"You know, I'm noticing that not all of your shoes are as shiny as they could be," he said.

Really, dude?

"At OTS," Al continued, "our training instructor showed us this stuff that you can put on the sides of your shoes and boots... around the soles. It's called edge dressing, and it makes your shoes look really professional."

This was too good to be true. Around the room, eyes rolled — as if we didn't know all about edge dressing. Even though our new friend Al was only trying to help, he had violated a key Academy lesson learned either in POW training or through their one's stupidity: *Don't volunteer information.* Sometimes, it's best just to shut up.

"Hey, I'm just trying to help everyone look more professional," Al offered.

Al would be learning through his own stupidity. I turned to Doley, whom I assumed was familiar with *Highlights* magazine.

"Second Lieutenant Goofus unprofessionally carries his lip balm in his pants pockets," I said. "Second Lieutenant Gallant challenges his classmates to look their very best at all times while showing them his *toe-shine.*"

As soon as I threw out *toe-shine,* Doley was all over it.

"A toe-shine is no shine," he recited automatically. Then he got up in my face to issue a contest of his own.

"Ray," Doley smiled, "I have a *challenge* for you."

"Yowsa! Yowsa! Yowsa!" I shouted, flashing back to a dance challenge on *Happy Days.* "A Challenge Dance. Yowsa! Yowsa! Yowsa! What is it? The jitterbug?"

"No," Doley smiled. "As long as we're going to have to put up with people saying stupid things ev'ry once in a while, in this next ow'a of class, I *challenge* you to ask a stupidah question than I do."

"Yowsa! Yowsa!" I started, but in keeping with the *Happy Days* theme, Doley gave me a thumbs down, just as the Fonz had done to Richie when he got sick of hearing Richie repeating "Yowsa!"

"Lieutenant Dolan," I nodded, "I accept your challenge."

Chuck had been watching. "You guys know you're complete idiots, don't you?" She laughed as she said it.

"Chuck, we're stuck in Columbus for a whole year," I said. "Why not have fun with a little orchestrated entropy?"

*

Captain Van Dorn was undoubtedly the most oddly-shaped instructor we'd met at Columbus. He was almost as tall as Kurt, but about five-and-a-half feet of him was legs and ass. He had no shoulders, and his fat legs and rearend that started just below his armpits expanded backwards unlike any human backside I'd ever seen. He was also one of the loudest officers on the base.

"Yo! Tur-BIG-lio!" Captain Van Dorn shouted at Al, who sat in the front row. "What's your acronym for figuring out if you've dialed in the right VORTAC?"

"Sir, it's *Tune, Identify, and Monitor,*" Al answered.

"That's right, Tur-BIG-lio!" Captain Van Dorn shouted.

Game on, Doley.

"Captain Van Dorn." I threw my hand up.

"What is it, Wright?" Captain Van Dorn wanted to keep going with the lesson.

"Sir, *Tune, Identify, and Monitor* is actually not an acronym," I said. "It's a mnemonic device. Could we refer to *Tune, Identify, and Monitor* as a mnemonic device rather than an acronym?"

"Wright! What in the hell are you talking about?" Captain Van Dorn screamed at me, using the formal Southern phrasing *What in thee hell...*, as opposed to the Yankee *What the hell....*

"Sir, acronyms are words formed from the first letter of other words, like RADAR," I said. "So TIM might be a good acronym for *Tune, Identify, and Monitor,* but if we're going to use the whole words of *Tune, Identify, and –* "

"Wright! Shut the hell up," Captain Van Dorn screamed.

Across the room, Chuck waved her pen in the air as if to say, "Watch this," to Doley and me. Placing it on the table in front of her, she turned the point of her pen my way, declaring that I had taken the early lead in Doley's contest.

"Yo! Tur-BIG-lio!" Captain Van Dorn shouted at Al again. "How come we don't wear hats on the flight line?"

"Sir, we don't wear hats on the flight line because hats are FOD!" Al knew right away. He was a private pilot, after all.

"That's right, Tur-BIG-lio! Hats are FOD! And FOD is what, Wright?" Captain Van Dorn asked me.

"Foreign Object Damage, sir," I answered.

"No, Wright! You're wrong! It's an acronym. Ha!" Captain Van Dorn was pleased with himself. "It's an acronym that *stands for* Foreign Object Damage. Isn't that right, Wright?"

"Yes, sir," I acknowledged.

"Captain Van Dorn," Doley interjected with his hand up, not waiting any longer to jump into the contest.

"What is it, Dolan?" Captain Van Dorn asked, still enjoying the fact that he'd just put me in my place.

"Sir, if an object is picked up b'faw causing damage," Doley began, "isn't it FO?"

"Dolan, what in *thee* hell are you talking about?" Captain Van Dorn screamed at Doley.

"Sir, since there's no damage, it's not FOD...it's FO. Picking up FO prevents FOD," Doley explained. "Shouldn't we call FOD *FO?*"

"Dolan, shut *thee* hell up! It's FOD!" Captain Van Dorn screamed.

Chuck spun her pen back to point toward Doley, now in the lead.

"Enough review!" Captain Van Dorn clucked. He flipped on the overhead projector at the front of the room and placed a transparent sheet onto the flat, illuminated surface. A diagram of a T-37 cockpit filled the screen at the front of the classroom.

"In the T-37, the student and the instructor sit side by side." Captain Van Dorn used a dry-erase marker to write *SP* under the student's seat on the left and *IP* under the instructor's seat on the right. "The throttles on the left are for the student, and the throttles in between the two seats are for the IP. Each position has a stick that moves the ailerons and elevator. The sticks are stuck together, so it's very important that only one pilot fly the aircraft at a time."

Captain Van Dorn moved away from the overhead projector to walk down the aisle in the center of the room. "Many crashes have occurred in the T-37 and T-38 when both pilots fight each other for control. You never want a situation where both pilots are trying to fly at the same time. The transfer of aircraft control is critical, and there's a very specific procedure to do it by. Remember this...*mnemonic device:* The Shaker is the Taker."

He paused and stopped right in front of me before continuing. "Did I get that right, Wright? Mnemonic device? You happy?"

"Yes, sir," I happily agreed. "Good memory."

Captain Van Dorn then acted out the procedure by which to transfer aircraft control. "Three steps!" he clucked. "The pilot assuming control of the aircraft shakes the stick and says, *I have the aircraft*. The pilot giving up control of the aircraft shows that his hands are off the stick and says, *Roger, you have the aircraft,* and the pilot assuming control shakes the stick and confirms, *I have the aircraft."*

"Sir, is that procedure or technique?" Al wanted to know. This was a favorite question of Al's because we had been told that any procedure was fair game for testing but lessons offered as helpful techniques could not be graded. Al took page after page of notes during class, and any time an instructor offered an example or a side story, Al would ask if it was procedure or technique.

"Yo! Tur-BIG-lio! That is procedure!" Captain Van Dorn shouted, and Al feverishly filled up his workbook with notes.

"Captain Van Dorn?" I raised my left hand, purposely holding my pen in it to show that I had been taking notes. "Sir, I'm left-handed. How do the cockpits in the left-handed jets differ from the cockpits in the right-handed jets?" I stared at him innocently and waited for an answer while the class laughed.

"Wright, I hate to be the one to break this to you," Captain Van Dorn replied, "but there are no left-handed jets! You're just going to have to suck it up and learn to fly with your right hand like the rest of us!"

I looked over towards Doley and Chuck after Captain Van Dorn turned back around to his projector. Chuck's pen was once again pointing in my direction. I had retaken the lead.

"Page fifteen! Starting procedure! Here are the starter and ignition switches!" Captain Van Dorn clucked and circled the starter and ignition switches on the overhead transparency with his marker.

"Yo! Jellicot! Read the Starting Engines checklist," he ordered.

Mark read the checklist out loud.

> *Starter – Ground and Hold*
> *Ignition – On at 5% RPM*
> *Throttle – Idle at 8% RPM*
> *Ignition – Off at rapid EGT rise*
> *Starter – Off at 25% RPM*

Mark stopped when he was done reading and waited for Captain Van Dorn to shout, which he did right away.

"That's good, Jellicot. Everyone needs to memorize that checklist! Y'all still need to exercise good checklist discipline, and run the checklist step by step, but memorizing this checklist will help you keep up with the steps while you crank your engines," Captain Van Dorn explained.

"Sir, I've invented an acronym," Al volunteered. "It's SIT-IS."

I looked over at Doley, who threw his hands into the air.

"Sir, would you say SIT-IS is procedure or technique?" Al asked.

I threw my hands up, too.

Chuck pointed her pen towards Al. Without even being a contestant, he was the clear winner.

Chapter 6 — "Prereqs"

"I want to fly the Air Force's most powerful, most maneuverable air-to-air combat aircraft, the F-15 Eagle, when I graduate from UPT..."

Mark Jellicot read from his personal essay in front of our class. We had been assigned to write a one- to two-page personal essay for the flight line instructors we would meet at the end of the week in Dagger. I thought the paper wasn't due for a couple more days. I hadn't even started thinking about mine, but Mark apparently couldn't wait to get his done.

"I flew the F-4 Phantom as a back-seater in the Philippines and have grown to love the air-to-air mission. But the F-4 is being phased out of service, and I'd like to test my skills in the world's hottest fighter, the F-15 Eagle."

I could identify the F-15 Eagle. I knew what it looked like. I knew it had two engines and two vertical stabilizers on its tail, and I had to memorize a bunch of stuff about it as a freshman at the Academy so that I wouldn't get yelled at by upperclassmen, but I had no idea about what missions it flew.

I knew that A was for Attack, B was for Bomber, C was for Cargo, F was for Fighter, R was for Reconnaissance, and T was for Trainer, but I didn't really know much more than that. I just knew that I wanted to get stationed at a base near a beach. After living in Colorado Springs for the last four years, I didn't really care what I was going to fly as much as I cared where I was going to live and how much I was going to get to travel around the world.

As Mark continued to bore everyone with his clichéd essay about the air-to-air combat mission, Vietnam-era F-4s, Fiends, and the Philippines, I looked around the room and wondered who in this room didn't want to fly the newest and coolest jets? Who didn't want to fly an F-15 or an F-16 or an FB-111, the most advanced high-performance aircraft that man had ever built? And even if somebody didn't want to fly these jets, who would admit it?

Watching Mark proudly drone on about his paper to the class in his new flight suit, I thought that our Columbus Beach Club patches were looking pretty good. In the foreground of the beach scene on our patches, a pink flamingo stood on one leg on a surfboard with *14 STUS* printed on its centerline. Everything was encircled by a hot pink border, and on the top, the words COLUMBUS BEACH CLUB were printed in black letters on a hot pink arc. Our class number, 88-07, was stitched in black numbers at the bottom of the beach scene.

The colors of the patch were bright and vibrant, and our patches and matching electric-pink scarves really popped off our drab, olive green flight suits, and grabbed the eyes' attention.

Mark Jellicot looked up excitedly from his paper after he finished reading. "That's how we need to write our essays. Let's show the Dagger flight IPs how motivated we are to fly jets. I need to get all our essays to Dagger the day after tomorrow, so everyone needs to get theirs to me by tomorrow."

I couldn't see my essay sounding anything like Mark's.

"One more thing…" Mark announced before we headed off to our next class. "I've got Room 12 reserved at 1700 hours. After we finished with our computer-aided instruction today, we're all going to meet there for about an hour for a naming ceremony."

*

I finished up my CAI session a little ahead of schedule at the end of the day—thanks to Chuck. Maybe the smartest student in our class, Chuck would usually finish these lessons well before anyone else. Definitely the most selfless of students, Chuck would take such good notes on what she'd learned and on what was tested that someone with access to her supplemental study material, like me, wouldn't even have to read what was shown on the computer in order to answer the questions correctly. As Air Force Academy classmates, we all tried to help each other out when we could, and Chuck's help greatly reduced the amount of time the rest of us had to spend in the computer lab.

Since I had a little extra time at the end of the day before the naming ceremony — again, thanks to Chuck — I figured I'd swing by the flight line snack bar and pick up a deliciously filling Hostess snack cake, which for some strange reason had been on my mind most of the day. Besides, I had no idea how long Mark's naming ceremony would actually take, and I was starving.

I hadn't ventured to the flight line snack bar yet because I didn't feel comfortable walking around in blues when everyone else was wearing green flight suits. But now that we were in flight suits, too, even though we hadn't reported to the flight line, this snack bar was a lot closer than having to drive to the bowling alley.

A quick walk from the back door of the Student Squadron building, where we had our academic lessons, the flight line building was a long, skinny, one-level, flat-roofed, brick building that paralleled the three runways behind it. The center doors opened to a foyer in the middle of a hallway that ran the entire length of the building. Standing in the foyer, a left turn led to the briefing rooms for Dagger, Warhawk, six other T-37 flights, and the snack bar; a right turn down the long hall would lead to the T-38 side of the building, which our class wouldn't see for another six months.

Turning left to the T-37 side, the snack bar was the first room on the left side of the long, center hallway, where I found Kurt with a handful of snacks and talking to a few guys from the Academy who had reported to Columbus a month ahead of us.

"Kurt, have you thought about what you're going to write on your essay?" I asked after our Academy friends checked out.

"F-16 Fighting Falcon all the way, brother!" Kurt shot back immediately. "Real men fly jets with one engine."

"Aren't you worried how they're called lawn darts for the way they drop to the ground when the engine goes out?" I asked.

"That's why you wear a parachute, Ray-bonus," he said. "What about you? What are you going to write?"

"I don't know," I said honestly, grabbing a delicious-looking, cream-filled snack cake. I didn't have my sights set on any particular aircraft. For me, it was more about *where*.

I supposed that if there was still a chance I could be an astronaut, flying a fighter might be the best way to get into the space program, which had always been my dream. But we hadn't sent anyone to the moon in over a decade, and the shuttle hadn't flown since the Challenger blew up over a year ago. The space program was on indefinite hold.

If I were assigned to a fighter jet, I guess I'd take it, but it wouldn't be because I wanted to be a fighter pilot. You pretty much had to take what the Air Force gave you. That was part of the deal.

*

"Aaay! What's a naming ceremony?" Kenny Wessels asked as our classmates filed into Room 12 of the Student Squadron.

"In fighter squadrons, everybody has a nickname or a call sign. The guys in *Top Gun* were Maverick, Iceman, and Goose. Everyone needs a call sign. I went to the University of Florida, so I'm a Gator, and in the Philippines, our call sign in the F-4 was Fiend. My call sign is either going to be Gator or Fiend," Mark Jellicot said...again!

I was a little bothered by the concept of a formal — and sober — naming ceremony. Was this really how nicknames were given in the Philippines? It seemed like we were just checking a box. A naming ceremony needed to happen at the O-Club bar after a couple pitchers of beer.

"My nickname will be King Dolan, Lord of the Sky. I will not allow abbreviated versions of this," Doley proclaimed loudly—mocking Mark.

"Nicknames *cannot* be chosen," I declared in frustration. "They are earned through acts of great stupidity or embarrassment. The better the story…the better the nickname."

"Now, a good play on words is appropriate, too," Doley stated. "Don't you agree, 'Dogleg' Wright?"

"That's not bad," I nodded, "but how about 'Nuclear' Wessels? No, wait…we're in the South…. 'Nucular' Wessels!"

"Aaay!" Kenny seemed to like it. Chuck did, too, because she pulled out her judge's pen and pointed it my way.

"I'm just gonna throw this out there…." Doley looked over to Chuck to make sure he had her attention. "'Foghawn' Van Dawn!"

Oh! This was the perfect name for our large-mouthed, large-assed academic instructor.

Chuck immediately pointed her pen at Doley and threw her free hand up in the air, declaring him this round's winner.

"Hey! Everybody, be quiet!" Mark Jellicot yelled over the laughter, annoyed that we weren't showing more reverence for the ceremony. "In fighter squadrons, everybody has a call sign. I went to the University of Florida, so I'm a Gator, and in the Philippines, our call sign in the F-4 was Fiend, so my call sign is either going to be Gator or Fiend."

"Shouldn't we do this at a party or at the O-Club bar rather than in a classroom?" I challenged.

"Yeah, c'mon. Let's go to the O-Club," someone said.

"No," Mark objected. "We're doing this now. We can all go to the O-Club for dinner as a class tonight, if you want, and we can use our new call signs later at the O-Club bar." He was the class leader. He was going to lead.

"Let's vote," he ordered. "What should my nickname be: Gator or Fiend?"

I couldn't let this go on, but I also knew that I couldn't stop it. I didn't like the setting for the naming ceremony — way too sober and way too contrived. Everyone seemed a little on edge, and after a day in the classroom with an essay to write, this wasn't any fun.

"How many say Gator?" Mark pushed the issue, holding up his own hand to vote.

"Wait a second! Wait a second!" I interrupted. "I have a suggestion." Suddenly, I was hit by a bolt of inspiration, brought about by the soft and doughy manner in which Mark filled out his flight suit, as if he were a human-sized snack cake.

"I propose an alternative," I stood and said loudly. "I propose that your nickname should be...Ho Ho!" I shouted.

The class exploded with cheers. People jumped out of their seats, arms were waving, and fists were pumping like the Cosby kids did when a member of the Fat Albert gang got in a good insult on Rudy. Then, the class broke into a spontaneous chant of: "Ho Ho! Ho Ho! Ho Ho! Ho Ho!" Mark just stood there without saying a word while the rest of us chanted. And when the chanting stopped, it was decided. Mark Jellicot's new aviator call sign was neither Gator nor Fiend. It was Ho Ho. Mission accomplished.

From that point on, Mark's naming ceremony pretty much turned into an insult ceremony. There was little imagination and no real creativity. Short of using swear words for nicknames, nothing was off limits. Personal defects were the motivational sources for most of the call signs. Any skin impurity, appendage abnormality, or other such sample of ugly that a person might have had on his or her face became nickname fodder. As Mark introduced each person for naming consideration, shouts of *Mole-Cheek* and *Zits* and *Ear-Hair* flew back and forth across the room.

Once all deformities and their synonyms had been used, the name game became even cruder. We had strayed a long way from Maverick, Iceman, and Goose with names like *Sack, Stain,* and *Scrotum*. Kenny Wessels was cracking up. I didn't keep track of who made what suggestions, but I saw that if Kenny heard a name he liked, and it didn't win the vote, he'd say it over and over again as each new person was introduced until the label finally stuck to someone. As for Kenny...Nucular? No. His Air Force lacrosse nickname, Weasel? No. Kenny was dubbed Queef. I don't know that anyone ever called him that after the naming ceremony.

Only a few of us escaped without being named for a body part, a body sound, or a bodily excretion. I was one of the few. Because of my last name, Mark Jellicot insisted that my nickname had to be either Orville or Wilbur, both of which I thought were totally devoid of creativity. But no. Ho Ho was mad because he wasn't Gator or Fiend, so my nickname, my UPT pilot nickname, which may have been used a total of one time after the naming ceremony, was Wilbur.

Kurt didn't get a good nickname, either. Ho Ho wanted Kurt's name to be Frankenstein or Herman, for Herman Munster, and truth be told, Kurt was two bolts in his neck away from being either one of those characters. With Frankenstein and Herman being the only two choices the class could come up with for Kurt, in his characteristically good-natured way, he stood in the front of the room and laughed a perfect Herman Munster–like laugh— right down to the mannerisms, and Herman won out easily.

In the end, the event had been too contrived, the environment was too sterile, and we were all way too sober. We didn't really know each other well enough yet. We hadn't faced any adversity together. We hadn't even had a class party. But those would be soon to come.

*

The next morning when I walked into our classroom, Kurt was standing in front of a dozen classmates who were listening politely to his personal essay and dream of flying F-16s after UPT.

Just like the NCAA had a rule that you couldn't be older than twenty-five and still compete as a college athlete except for athletes at BYU, the Air Force had a rule that you couldn't be older than twenty-seven and still compete to fly fighter jets. For most of us in the class, who were twenty-two years old after graduating from college, this wasn't anything we needed to think about, and even for guys like Kenny, who spent a year at Prep after high school, this wasn't any big deal, because even if we didn't get fighters right out of UPT, there was enough time to serve a full tour of duty somewhere and still be young enough to be considered for fighters a few years down the road.

For those in the class, however, who followed less of a straight line to flight school, like Mark Jellicot and my friend Kurt, UPT was probably their one-and-only shot to get into the fighter community. Prior to UPT, Mark had been flying F-4s as a back-seater in the Philippines. Prior to Prep School and the Academy, Kurt had worked on F-16s as an enlisted guy. Between the Real Air Force, the Prep School, and the Academy, Kurt had spent six or seven years of his life in an Air Force uniform and been through basic training three times already to get where most of the rest of us were in four years and one basic training.

Of course, Al Turbiglio took just six weeks in OTS—so how stupid were the rest of us?

If any one of us had demonstrated commitment to a goal and deserved what he most wanted, in my mind it was Kurt. But unless Brigham Young himself could apply his persuasive powers on Uncle Sam to raise the upper age limit for new fighter pilots and rig the system for Kurt like the NCAA was rigged for BYU, he would probably never be assigned to fly a fighter if he didn't get one when he finished UPT.

When Kurt wrapped up his personal essay, he wasted no time in calling me to the front of the room. I assumed that the others in the room had already shared their essays about their desire to fly the two-engine F-15 Eagle or the single-engine F-16

Fighting Falcon. Maybe there was an occasional FB-111 fighter-bomber that some said they wanted to fly.

Only about half of our section had shown up so far. I looked up at the clock to see if it might be possible to stall long enough that our academic instructor would arrive and start class, but there was too much time still left before report time. What did I care what these guys thought of my essay? Maybe I'd get the same kind of reaction from my classmates that I was hoping to get from the IPs. This might be a good test. So why not? My essay *was* about fighters...just not the kind you fly. I walked up to the front of the class, personal essay in hand, and began to read out loud:

> If I were a professional wrestler, I would be a bad guy — like Jake "The Snake" Roberts. Bad guys win a lot more matches when they first break into the professional ranks and climb the rankings much faster than good guys. Bad guys have typically perfected a signature move or submission hold that serves to both demonstrate their strength and define their character, like Jake the Snake's DDT —

"Ray, wait a second," Mark interrupted me before I'd finished my first paragraph. "What does this have to do with flying?"

"Absolutely nothing," I answered and picked up my reading from the point where I'd been interrupted.

After I'd finished, I stood silently in front of the room. I knew from the laughs and enthusiastic applause from my classmates that they'd approved. I smiled and nodded thankfully, avoiding eye contact with Mark as I threaded my way to a desk. UPT was as much a competition as it was a training environment. My classmates liked my essay not only because it was ridiculous but also because, by not saying I wanted to fly a fighter, I was improving their odds of getting one.

As the room filled up, I picked out only a handful of people who might not write about flying fighters in their essays. Al, already committed to a C-130 with the Pennsylvania Air Force Reserves, wouldn't write about fighters. Why would he want a report to go back home to his sponsoring unit that he didn't want to fly the aircraft they were holding for him? Women were not allowed to fly fighters, so I didn't think Chuck, Sandy, or Marcia would mention fighters in their essays. What would be the point? Unless, they wanted to make a point.

I wanted to be a good pilot, and I wanted to do well in flight school, but I never had been hell-bent on flying a fighter. If I had written, *My dream is to fly a cargo plane in Charleston,* what kind of message would that be sending to my prospective new instructors, many of whom wanted to fly fighters, themselves?

So, my personal essay didn't contain a single word about flying. I took a risk that 99 percent of the other essays would start out something like *When I graduate from UPT, I want to fly a fighter jet.* I was banking on most of the instructors tuning out as essay after essay seemed to be saying the same thing. Then, when mine was finally pulled from the pile, some instructor with a sense of humor would tune back in and say, "I'll take that idiot." And just maybe, UPT might be fun.

Mark Jellicot took our essays over to Dagger flight about fifteen minutes before academics with Foghorn Van Dorn was supposed to start. Finally, after a month of preparation, we were about to hit the flight line. We'd flown in the altitude chamber to simulate the stresses that changes in atmospheric pressures would put on our bodies and minds. We'd learned the proper ejection, parachute, and parachute-landing procedures, and we'd even been flown like kites on a four hundred-foot rope off the back of a pick-up truck to simulate emergencies in which our jets would no longer be airworthy, and the only way to survive would be to light a rocket under our seat and hope that we'd have enough time to deploy the 40-pound parachute strapped to our backs so that we'd get one good swing under a canopy full of air before we'd impact the ground.

We'd finished our first round of academic exams. We'd designed our class patch, been given nicknames, and written our personal essays. Thanks to Kurt, I'd chewed my first stick of Beeman's gum, Chuck Yeager's favorite, and ordered some really cool pilot sunglasses like the guys wore in *Top Gun*. We'd checked all the boxes that needed to be checked to hit the flight line. But I had no idea what was about to come next.

"I just met with Captain Wright and handed in our personal essays," Mark Jellicot reported to us upon his return from delivering our essays. "Captain Wright told me that no Dagger class has ever passed its **BOLDFACE** test on the first attempt."

Of course, we were determined to be the first Dagger class to pass the **BOLDFACE** test on our first attempt. Already as a group, we had taken the **BOLDFACE** test and passed it with everyone scoring 100 percent three times. Everybody was all smiles, including Mark: "I told Captain Wright that Class 88-07, the Pink Flamingos, would be the first class in Dagger flight history to pass its **BOLDFACE**, and I felt so confident about it, I bet him a keg of beer that we'd pass the test on our first try."

I had been writing and reciting my **BOLDFACE** procedures every night in my Q room before I went to sleep after I'd learned that everybody had to make 100 percent on **BOLDFACE** tests every time. No misspelled words. No missed punctuation marks. No mistakes. I was confident that I could do this, but I just wasn't so sure about everybody.

Say nothing, and we all pass...then, we look good. Say nothing, and we don't...we're no different from the rest. Bet we pass, and we don't...we look bad.

What was Ho Ho thinking?

Chapter 7 — "Dollar Rides"

"You might know about Dagger flight. You might not. You know that Columbus Air Force Base trains the world's best pilots. Well, Dagger flight trains the best pilots in Columbus. That means Dagger flight trains the best pilots in the world."

Dagger Flight Commander Captain Wright stood at the front of the flight room and scanned back and forth from one side of the room to the other, having presented his proof that Dagger flight trains the world's best pilots with the same chain of logic that he used to prove cold beer is better than free beer to Doley and me in the O-Club on the night we first met him.

"You might be wondering how you performed on your **BOLDFACE** exam, your first opportunity to excel as a class. You might not," Captain Wright said, knowing we all wanted to know. Because creases ran down from the corners of his mouth to his jawline, like a ventriloquist's puppet, I couldn't tell if he was smiling or frowning. "I told you before your test last night that no class had ever passed its **BOLDFACE** exam on its first try. Well, that is still a true statement. Your class did not pass its **BOLDFACE** exam, and so, you will have another opportunity to excel at the end of the day today before we dismiss."

Everybody was bummed. I could feel it, even though nobody showed it. Nobody spoke, and nobody moved. Captain Wright had instructed us to sit at a position of attention during the morning's formal report, which might last anywhere from a half hour to an hour, so we all sat perfectly still with our eyes locked on him as he talked. Captain Wright stood at the front of the room, scanning his gaze from left to right and back again. He didn't stray too far from his podium, but after every couple of scans of the room, he'd shift his weight from one side to the other, as if striking a new pose for each new line of thought.

I was sitting in the back of the room, looking directly at my new flight commander. When I had arrived about twenty minutes earlier, the rectangular room was set up so that the desks of the instructor pilots formed the shape of the letter *U* along the two long walls and the short back wall. Three desks lined each of the parallel long walls, and two desks ran along the short wall at the back of the room. Eight personalized table-desks for eight instructor pilots. At one of those along the back, I found a black binder with my name on it at the desk of Lieutenant Wilson. Kenny Wessels also had a book with his name on it at this same desk; so we sat together.

For formal reports and formal releases, our chairs were to be turned around to face the center of the room, and all eyes needed to be focused on the speaker. When you were working with your assigned instructor, your chair would be turned to face your instructor at his desk. I hadn't yet seen my instructor because the IPs came into the room while we were standing at attention, and my assigned instructor, Lieutenant Wilson, had sat down behind me. I didn't dare turn around during the formal report.

"**BOLDFACE** is a non-negotiable. Every word, every letter, every punctuation mark must be 100 percent correct every time you say a **BOLDFACE** or write **BOLDFACE**, or it is incorrect. Any time you recite **BOLDFACE** or write a **BOLDFACE** procedure incorrectly, you will not fly that day, because if you do not correctly perform your **BOLDFACE** actions in the jet when an emergency situation calls for it, you will die," Captain Wright said and paused again to scan and shift his weight. The scan pattern, I noticed, seemed to follow along with his sentence pattern. At the beginning of a sentence, he'd be looking at one side of the room, and at the end of the sentence, he'd have scanned to the other side of the room.

"You might remember I said that Columbus trains the world's best pilots. You might not. One record our base is very proud of is that there has never been a Class-A mishap involving a T-37 at Columbus. One of the reasons that Dagger trains the best pilots in the world is because we treat **BOLDFACE** as non-negotiable. Next week, you'll all have your dollar rides, which means the real fun is about to start. It also means that you need to be prepared to fly every time you strap on a jet. If you cannot properly write or recite your **BOLDFACE**," Captain Wright said, "you are not prepared to strap on a jet, and any time you are not prepared to strap on a jet, you will not fly."

Another proof: Safety is important for flying. **BOLDFACE** is important to safety. Therefore, if you cannot pass your **BOLDFACE**, you cannot be safe, and if you cannot be safe, you cannot fly. Made sense to me.

Captain Wright paused, scanned the room, and shifted his weight back to his other side again before continuing.

"You might think that learning to fly is hard. You might not," he began again. "Well, there's a lot to learn, and there are a lot of rules, but when we can, we try to keep the rules as simple as possible. There are three basic rules of flying that I want all of you to remember:

"One. Have a good time.

"Two. Don't panic.

"Three. Always sound cool on the radio."

Yes! My kind of rules!

"First, have a good time. You're not digging a foxhole and sitting in the cold ground waiting for something to happen like they do in the Army. You're not drifting out at sea on a boat in the ocean for months at a time, waiting for the day you get back to dry land like they do in the Navy. You're not doing whatever it is Marines do," Captain Wright paused to shift his weight and scan the room.

"I appreciate the work Marines do, but I don't really know what they do," he wondered out loud, "even though I know they do what they do like Marines are supposed to do." Captain Wright shifted and scanned again.

"All of these are important jobs, but in your job, you get to strap a jet aircraft onto your back every day and burn holes in the sky—upside-down, right-side-up, over-the-top, and back again. And you do this in order to defend the United States of America from Ivan and his comrades, and this keeps our country free and our families safe. It's important, it's fun, and you should have fun doing it."

After Captain Wright's scanning eyes passed by me, I stole a quick gaze around the room. While I had been bummed out to learn that we hadn't passed our **BOLDFACE** exam, I was getting pumped up listening to our new flight commander talk about flying jets.

"The second rule is don't panic. Your missions might go just as you plan them, but sometimes, they might not. Your aircraft might perform exactly as it's supposed to, but sometimes, it might not. When things go wrong, don't panic. Your priorities are to aviate, navigate, communicate—in that order. Aviate. Navigate. Communicate. We're going to practice this over and over. Every day. Every morning. Every mission. Every ride," he said.

"Some of you might have done some civilian flying. Some of you might not have done much of any flying other than what you needed to get here. Military flying is different from civilian flying in that we will drill into you the importance of checklist discipline. Your checklist is not optional. It is procedure, which means it is mandatory. It is your guide, and it will save your life when you find yourself in a situation where entropy runs wild, and everything that can go wrong does go wrong.

"Airplanes don't just fall out of the sky when there are problems. Wings don't just fall off airframes. Air doesn't stop flowing under your wings. When things don't go as planned, a downward spiraling chain of events is set in motion, and if you do not recognize that downward spiraling chain of events and take the appropriate action to break that downward spiraling chain of events, then order turns to disorder. And if you don't restore order, that's where you will get into trouble and find yourself in a smoking hole in the ground. So, don't panic."

Captain Wright shifted his weight again and swung his arms to strike a new pose from which to speak.

"The third rule of flying is always sound cool on the radio," he continued.

"It doesn't matter if the sky is crumbling around you or flames are shooting out of both engines. Every time you cue up your microphone button, you are broadcasting a signal that can be heard by anyone with a UHF radio, and most likely, what you say is being recorded as you say it and can be played over and over and over again for the Accident Investigation Board and maybe even someone you know. Even if you know that you cannot break the chain of events that may result in you making a smoking hole in the ground, remember that you are a military pilot, and when the Accident Investigation Board plays your radio transmissions over and over and over again to determine what might have gone wrong and caused you to auger in, the one conclusion that they have to make after listening to your radio calls is *Whoa! This was one cool pilot.*"

We hadn't been in the Dagger flight room for an hour, and Captain Wright already had my vote for wing commander. For sure, he gave a way better speech.

At the conclusion of the morning's formal report, Mark Jellicot called the room to attention, saluted Captain Wright, and reported, "Sir, Class 88-oh-7 is ready to sim."

Immediately, the rest of us sounded off with a loud and thunderous shout of: "DAGGER!"

*

After our inaugural loud and thunderous shout of "DAGGER!" that first morning, everybody relaxed. Kenny and I turned our seats around and met our assigned instructor, First Lieutenant Tim Wilson.

Without ever having met Lieutenant Wilson, I knew him as soon as I saw him. His younger brother was a great guy and friend of mine from our class at the Academy, and the two of them looked just alike—except his brother's hair was curly brown while Lieutenant Wilson's hair was straight black and parted slightly left of center. Our new instructor's eyes were also slightly closer together than his brother's, but other than the hair, eyes, and his being two years older, the Wilson brothers could have been twins.

"Have a seat," Lieutenant Wilson ordered after we shook hands. Kenny and I sat, eager to begin learning.

"We need to go over some important business before we start briefing up this morning's missions," our IP said. "First thing—" Lieutenant Wilson pointed the red end of his dual-tipped, red-on-one-end, blue-on-the-other pencil across the room at our classmate Tom "PePé" LaPierre. "What's up with that guy's face?"

Named in honor of the great PePé Le Pew, PePé had one of the few naming ceremony nicknames that actually got some use. I had noticed when we filed into the room that morning that PePé's face was red, swollen, and all scratched up, like he'd been stung by a swarm of bees armed with electric sanders, but I didn't have time to say anything.

"Aaay, dis is sick, but he got a roach problem in his Q room. Last night, he woke up to a bunch of roaches munchin' on his face," Kenny filled us in.

"I gotta get outta the Qs," I said, cringing—Pepé's room was just a few doors down from mine.

"I do believe that's an *intrusion*," Lieutenant Wilson stated. Then, he mumbled out of the corner of his mouth, "The Terminix guy comes out to the house once a month and teaches me all about roaches while he treats the property."

Having covered his first important order of business, Lieutenant Wilson reached for a piece of paper and starting drawing upside-down with the blue end of his red and blue pencil.

"Do y'all know what this is?" Lieutenant Wilson asked, finishing. He just slid his picture across the clear plastic sheet on top of his desk. His crude drawing reminded me of a ZOOM doodle from the old PBS show ZOOM. In the middle of his drawing was a circle, topped by a smaller semicircle. On each side of the smaller semicircle, it had what looked like wings with multiple engines sticking out from the trailing edge of each wing. I was going to think about this for a minute. I let Kenny guess first.

"Aaay, is it a B-52?" Kenny guessed, shaking his head. Pretty good, I thought.

"No, that's not it. You got a guess?" Lieutenant Wilson asked me before I felt I had a chance to run through all of the possibilities.

"Sir, it kind of reminds me of Bullwinkle. Is it Bullwinkle?" I asked. Though it did look kind of like a B-52 and kind of like the silver wings a pilot wears on his chest, it actually looked more like Bullwinkle to me.

"Yeah, it's a moose head," Lieutenant Wilson nodded. "Do y'all know what this means?" he asked, making five parallel, vertical lines that were cut by a transversal, the way you'd make the tally marks for the number five—only he'd made six total tally marks.

"Aaay, dat's a bunch of moose," Kenny said.

"I do believe that would be a herd," I stated.

"Actually, it's a six-pack," Lieutenant Wilson corrected me. "See, Moosehead is my favorite beer. This is my way to ensure that you keep good track of your gradebooks. Every time I find a mistake in your gradebooks, I make a tally on this sheet, which represents one Moosehead beer that you owe me. This here," he said, pointing to the five vertical tally lines with the sixth transversal line running through them, "is a six-pack. Four of these six-packs make a case. You pay me by the case...every twenty-four gradebook mistakes. Fair enough?"

Lieutenant Wilson looked up from his paper to see if we had any questions. Other than wondering if this stuff was really the most important business we needed to cover, I didn't have any questions.

"This next one is Captain Wright's big thing," Lieutenant Wilson began. "I don't mind if you have food or drinks at my desk, but make sure your trash gets in the garbage when you're done. Captain Wright wants us to keep our desk areas clean, and he likes to tell the other flight commanders that Dagger maintains the cleanest flight room in the squadron.

"Questions?" Lieutenant Wilson asked.

I didn't have a question on what we'd just discussed, but having had a chance to glance over Lieutenant Wilson's shoulder at the Dagger scheduling board on the wall behind him while he was covering his important business, I did have a question.

"Sir, I see that you and Kenny are scheduled for a sim ride this morning, but I don't see that you and I have a ride together today," I stated as a preface.

"No," Lieutenant Wilson answered. "Wessels is with me at the end of first period. Wright, you're with Major Lawson during second period. We only have ten IPs in the flight, and y'all have more than twenty students. We need to rely on instructors from outside of Dagger to fill all our assigned missions. We call them guest help. Major Lawson is one of our assigned guest helpers. He works in the sim building. I'll tell you how to find him before you need to go over there and brief up your mission."

"Yes, sir," I said, trying not to show my disappointment at not getting to do my first mission with my newly assigned instructor.

"Alright, Wessels and I need to start briefing up our sim an hour before our scheduled start time," Lieutenant Wilson said. "That gives you almost an hour before we need to begin. Wright, you should listen in, too, because you'll be flying the same mission with Major Lawson."

"Yes, sir," I said again.

"I've got a couple things I've got to do between now and then. Y'all should go practice your checklists in the CFTs," Lieutenant Wilson suggested.

Kenny and I stood when Lieutenant Wilson got up, but we didn't go right away to the CFTs, the cockpit familiarization trainers. First, we had to discuss our new IP and the items on his table-desk.

The desktop was an off-white color upon which a large piece of clear plastic — or maybe acrylic — had been placed in order to protect the desktop from damage. In between the clear plastic and the desktop itself, Lieutenant Wilson had placed a bunch of pictures of aircraft and other printed materials, as could be said of most of the other IPs' desks in Dagger flight.

Several pictures were of the A-10, Thunderbolt II, affectionately known in the Air Force as the Warthog. I figured that must have been the aircraft he'd written about in his personal essay when he went through UPT. He had a pocket-sized card with the poem "High Flight" by John Gillespie Magee, Jr., printed on it. I had memorized the poem as part of my freshman fourth-class knowledge from a pocket-sized book called *Contrails* at the Academy, as had everyone else in the Dagger flight section of our class — except for Al and Mark Jellicot. Until I'd seen it on this particular pocket-sized card, however, I never realized that it was a sonnet. A-B-A-B-C-D-C-D E-F-E-G-F-G.

How had I missed that?

The Moosehead tally sheet had been slid under the clear plastic on Lieutenant Wilson's side, too. There were also several dollar bills...dollar bills that had been written on and decorated with pictures that had been cut out of magazines. The custom was that a student pilot would present his instructor with a dollar after his first ride in a particular jet, but rather than a silver dollar, the student would give his IP a dollar bill that had been decorated on the front. During training, we would do this twice — once for our first flight in the T-37 and then the second time for our first flight in the T-38.

On the front of the dollars displayed on Lieutenant Wilson's desk, some had pictures of F-15s on them, and some had pictures of F-16s on them. All of them had the names and class numbers of the student pilots with whom Lieutenant Wilson had flown these dollar rides.

"Aaay! I wonder if anything's on the back of these dollars," Kenny said, lifting up the big, clear plastic desk protector. I hadn't thought about this, but it made sense to me. If the students decorated the front of the dollars, maybe they'd decorated the back of them, too. Kenny pulled the dollars out from under the plastic and flipped them over. On the back of each were pictures of naked women cut out of magazines.

Pointing to one on which a naked woman was making a face like she was committing a sex act, I said to Kenny, "No hidden meaning there."

"Aaay, maybe we should ask Billy Bob about that," Kenny whispered back and tilted his head toward the doorway as Lieutenant Sims waddled in. Some of us had started calling our class commander *Billy Mike* behind his back, but Kenny called him *Billy Bob*.

"Where's Lieutenant Jellicot?" Lieutenant Sims called out to no one in particular as he waddled to a stop in the center of the room.

"Sir, he's over at the CFTs," said our classmate Stan Melton, who was serving as the Duty Dog for the morning. The Duty Dog was the poor idiot who got stuck answering the telephone, taking messages, and calling the room to attention for big wigs at the desk next to the doorway to the Dagger flight room. Whenever our class was assigned to the flight line during work hours, we had to have a student assigned to be the Duty Dog to answer the phone, take messages, and call the room to attention if someone important walked through the double doors. Stan had been stuck with the first shift.

"Would you like me to give him a message, Lieutenant Sims?" Stan politely asked.

"Yeah, Melton, but part of it applies to all y'all." Lieutenant Sims raised his voice so that all of us could hear him. "Let Jellicot know I need to speak with him when he gets back here. I'll be over in the Stu-Ron in my office. And y'all can tell everyone that the rest of y'all's class has been authorized to move out of the Qs. That means y'all can all move off base if y'all want, but when y'all do, I need to know."

Thank you, Billy Mike!

Kenny and I put Lieutenant Wilson's dollars back underneath the protective sheet of clear plastic on his desk, grabbed our flight caps and flying checklists out of our new lockers in the hallway of the training squadron, and walked over to the Stu-ron together to familiarize ourselves with the cockpit familiarization trainers.

"Kenny?" I asked as we stepped from the cool inside air of the training squadron building to the oppressive brightness and thick, humid, JP-4 exhaust-filled air of late August in the Deep South.

"Aaay!" He turned his head my way in time for me to see his prescription glasses darken automatically as we moved from inside to outside. His eyes disappeared behind his lenses.

While I still didn't know him well, he had provided some good laughs throughout our first month of training, something I appreciated. "Did you have any plans to live off base and rent a house with anyone?" I asked.

"No, why? You wanna rent a house together?" he asked me.

"Yeah," I smiled back.

"Cool," Kenny nodded. "Let's find a place this weekend."

*

"Major Lawson, Lieutenant Wright, reporting as ordered," I said as I held my salute, standing in front of Major Lawson's desk in his office deep in the bowels of the sim building.

He gave me a casual, hey-howya-doin' kind of salute back from his seat behind his desk, smiled widely, and smacked his gum a couple times before saying, "Well, hey now. That's a mighty fine salute," as a grown-up might comment on a child's performance at a pre-school event.

I held out my hand and introduced myself, "Hi, sir, I'm Ray Wright. Nice to meet you."

"Ray Wright. Mighty fine, mighty fine. Nice to meet you, too. Please, have a seat. I'm Richard Lawson. A lot of people call me Hal."

Whereas Lieutenant Wilson had a couple of years on me, Major Lawson looked like he had a couple of decades. He might even have been pushing fifty. Though he didn't have any gray hairs, his face had seen a lot of days in the sun, and judging from his belly, his eyes had seen the bottom of many an empty beer glass. He didn't look old enough to be as old as my dad, but he certainly looked old enough to be my dad.

Sitting in the chair facing Major Lawson's desk, I noticed that his office was filled with thick, three-ring binders labeled with subjects of interest to both military and civilian aviation. I wondered if he might be some kind of liaison from Columbus Air Force Base to the local civilian airports and FAA controllers. He had books on FAA flight regulations, civilian airliners, and even some kind of giant FAA study guide. In between FAA books, his shelves were packed with Tennessee Volunteers football memorabilia.

"Major Lawson, what is it that you do here in the sim building?" I asked, looking at all the books and materials and Vols stuff in his office. None of us student pilots had ever met Major Lawson, and he didn't seem to be assigned to either the Student Squadron or the flight line.

"Ray," he smiled widely, "I do as little as possible." Then he had a good laugh at his own joke. "You see, I'm fixin' to retire from the Air Force in less than a year. I've enjoyed a good, long career, and now, I'm ready to move on. So, I hide out here in the sim building. It's quiet. It's nice and cool, and nobody bothers me. That's how I like it."

"Sir, what are you planning to do when you retire?" I asked.

"Well, Ray," he said sitting back, and as he did, I could see him drift away, out of the room and into his vision of his world after the Air Force. "I've got a tobacco farm up in Knoxville that I need to take care of, and I need to be able to watch the Vols on Saturdays; so I'd like to get me a job flying for one of the major airlines. That'd be mighty fine."

"Sir, what kind of aircraft have you flown in the Air Force?" I asked, finding it kind of refreshing to be talking about something other than my first sim mission.

"Well now, back when I started, I flew helicopters in 'Nam. After two tours, I decided that I just got sick of bein' shot at. I wanted to play *offense* rather than *defense*. So I came back to the States, got my fixed wing rating, and headed back over to 'Nam in the mighty BUFF-a-saurus."

The mighty BUFF-a-saurus: Major Lawson had flown the B-52 bomber. BUFF is the Air Force acronym for the B-52 because it is a Big Ugly Fat Fellow of an aircraft.

Eventually, we got around to briefing up our mission. Then, we went and flew it in the sim.

After we'd filled out my first grade-sheet together—a *Good* for the ride overall, though he gave all of my maneuvers a grade of *U* for *Unsatisfactory*—I reported out by standing and saluting Major Lawson again. Then, I headed back to the Dagger flight room. The hour and fifteen minutes in the sim with Major Lawson went by pretty quickly.

Back in the Dagger flight room, Lieutenant Wilson finished his debriefing with Kenny. "So, how'd it go with Major Lawson?"

"Sir, it went pretty well, I guess," I answered. In truth, he was a good teacher, and while I didn't have much of a clue as to what I was doing, it felt like I did things better as the ride went on. Even though he held the rank of major, which is considered a senior officer, I found him easy to relate to, certainly a likable guy. "He graded me *Unsatisfactory* for all of my maneuvers, but I got a *Good* for the ride overall. So, a *Good* is good, I suppose."

"For your first sim ride, a *U* is all that's required for each maneuver; so, yeah, *Good* is good," Lieutenant Wilson agreed.

"Aaay, you got a fav'rit dollar?" Kenny asked Lieutenant Wilson out of the blue, checking out the decorated dollar bills under the plastic again.

Lieutenant Wilson reached across the desk with the blue-tipped end of his pencil to point to one. "Yeah, I'm kind of partial to this one here because it's got A-10s on it. The back side is pretty good, too."

Kenny and I grinned. The one he noted was the one with the naked woman on the back, making a face like she was participating in a sex act. "You know, if you all want to put any pictures of aircraft..." and then, looking at me, added, "or wrestlers under the plastic on your side of the desk, feel free to do so."

"Sir, are you saying that you're a wrestling fan?" I quickly asked.

Lieutenant Wilson shook his head. "No. It's fake."

He tapped the dollar again. "I wanted to fly A-10s out of UPT, but I got FAIP'ed instead. I was in a double-sized Academy class, just like you guys, and there always seems to be higher percentage of FAIPs from Academy classes. Y'all are going to be lucky to get out of Columbus."

"Sir, what do you mean, *get out of Columbus?*" I wanted to know. We were all still at the point of naivety about life after training. Like everyone else, I had been thinking all along that UPT was a year-long deal, then off to fly around the world.

But before Lieutenant Wilson could respond, Captain Wright walked out of the door of the IP room, which was in the back, left-hand corner of the Dagger flight room.

"Let's finish up our debriefs and prepare for the **BOLDFACE** exam," Captain Wright announced, his head and eyes scanning back and forth as he spoke. Meanwhile, in my head, I ran through the colleges of the Dagger IPs. A disproportionate number were Academy grads.

Captain Wright had us turn our chairs around so that we all faced the center of the room. He had a few things to say prior to re-taking the exam.

"You might have heard of the three most useless things to a pilot. You might not. So, let me tell you the three most useless things to a pilot. The three most useless things to a pilot are altitude above you, runway behind you, and an empty pitcher of beer. As a result of your class's first **BOLDFACE** exam, the Dagger flight IPs will have plenty of beer this weekend. Thank you for the free keg of beer. We'll make sure that it's cold before we drink it, because the only beer that's better than free beer is cold beer." Most of the class laughed nervously at this point.

The pressure was starting to build up around our **BOLDFACE** re-take. Captain Wright, however, veered in another direction.

"Besides being the best training flight in the world, you might have heard what else Dagger flight is known for. Then again, you might not." He scanned the room slowly from left to right and back to the left.

"I tell the flight commander of your sister flight at the other end of the hall, the Chickenhawks, that Dagger flight maintains the cleanest flight room in the squadron. I know the sign outside of their flight room says Warhawks, but I call them the Chickenhawks, and until they can say that their flight room is cleaner than ours, I'll continue to call them the Chickenhawks," Captain Wright boasted.

"As I look around the room, I see some Styrofoam cups on the desktops behind you, and some gradebooks have been left out on the desks, as well. If Dagger flight is to remain the cleanest flight room in the squadron, we can't leave Styrofoam cups on the desktops," Captain Wright said. "Your gradebooks need to go back on the bookshelf in the corner of the room after you're done with them, and Styrofoam cups need to either go in your lockers or in the trash. That's how we continue to have the cleanest flight room in the squadron. Right, Lieutenant Wright?"

I stood up to answer Captain Wright, "Yes, sir."

"Excellent, Lieutenant Wright," Captain Wright complimented me. "So with that in mind, let's all take a moment to clean up the flight room, and then, I'd like everyone to find an open seat, because you all have another opportunity to excel as a class by filling out a **BOLDFACE** exam."

This time, we all passed.

*

That Saturday morning, Kenny and I signed a rental agreement on the first house we went to see. At twelve hundred dollars a month plus a twelve hundred dollar security deposit, it was pricier than what most of our friends had said they were paying, which was more like nine hundred a month. Most guys also lived three-to-a-house, but Kenny and I didn't have a third person, meaning rent would eat up about half of my monthly paycheck. If we were late with the rent, we'd have to pay a 20 percent penalty. This probably wasn't the most financially sound decision on our parts, but it was a big house in a nice neighborhood at the end of a long cul-de-sac downtown behind the local Chevy dealership with the sign that showed the time and temperature, and we figured that we could have some good parties in the place with plenty of room for parking in the driveway, the garage, and the cul-de-sac.

Since the house wasn't furnished and we had no furniture, we spent the rest of the morning shopping.

"Aaaay! Check out dat!" Kenny pointed across my face as we hauled my new, very soft and comfortable brown velour sectional sofa-love-seat-and-corner-table thing back up Highway 45 North in the bed of the Isuzu P'Up, Winner of the Baja 1,000.

"What—*Ninety-six degrees* or *Free gun rack with truck purchase?*" I asked, reading the messages on the sign at the Chevy dealership at the top of our street. I wasn't sure what he was pointing to.

"No! Over there! Gary's Pawn and Gun. Pull over. I bet we can get some good deals in there. Let's go," Kenny insisted. I wouldn't have thought to ever stop at a pawn shop, and I'd never been in a gun shop before, but now that I was out of money and credit, Kenny's idea seemed like it might be a pretty good one.

It was. We bought a touch-tone phone with a built-in answering machine, a microwave, and a toaster all for twenty-five dollars.

After scoring big at Gary's Pawn and Gun, there were a couple more stops Kenny wanted to make on our way back down our new road, Azalea Drive.

"Aaaay, let's stop at a couple of these yard sales," Kenny suggested, referring to some of the signs we'd seen that morning in our new neighborhood. "We'll get to know our new neighbors."

So, we did, and in getting to know our new neighbors, we picked up a fridge from the 1950s, a Pepsi machine from the 1960s, a pinball machine from the 1970s, and a set of patio furniture: four chairs, a table, and an umbrella for our kitchen table from the

1980s — and dropped another $240. I told Kenny that I'd have to write him a check for my half next week when we got paid, and he was cool with that.

But we weren't done yet. We still had to make our dollars for our dollar rides.

"Here," Kenny said later that evening, handing me a twenty-dollar bill. "We need scissors, glue, and porno mags. Get some good ones. Did you notice that he liked the dollar where the chick was rolling her eyes back? We need to make some good dollars."

Then, Kenny burst into song as he went for his car keys.

"*Now your mom threw away your best porno mag,*" he sang.

"*Now your mom threw away your best porno mag,*" he sang again and laughed.

"*Now your mom threw away your best porno mag.*" This was the only line of the song I think that Kenny knew, but it did seem to fit the moment pretty well. Then, he laughed again and headed out to pick up our dinner.

For me, the day had been a day of firsts: I rented my first house. I bought my first bed. I bought my first very soft and comfortable brown-velour sectional sofa-love-seat-and-corner-table thing. I went into a gun store for the first time. I bought my first pawned merchandise. Now, at the age of twenty-two, I was on my way to make my first porno mag purchase. On the other hand, the biggest first was still yet to come in the next week, and that was that I'd be taking my first jet flight toward becoming an Air Force pilot. In that context, all these other things really weren't very big deals at all.

Since I happened to have a pair of scissors with my stuff from school, all I really needed to pick up was glue and porn. I figured that any Skank Store — my brother and sister coined the phrase Skank Store when we were kids because they'd always see our neighbors, the Skanks, at the corner convenience store — would have glue and porn, and I found both in the first one I stopped at. The glue was easy to find in the aisle, but they kept the porn behind the counter with the cigarettes and snuff, and I was going to have to ask the guy working at the cashier to pick it out for me. Buying porn wasn't like buying comic books, where you could read a little bit of the story at the magazine rack first.

When I put the glue up on the counter, I knew the guy would ask me what else I'd want. Skanks go to Skank Stores to buy the behind-the-counter stuff: cigarettes, snuff, scratch tickets, and/or porn. Cashiers at Skank Stores know that they need to ask their customers what else they might want, because skanks always want something that's behind-the-counter. If the cashiers at Skank Stores didn't ask what else their customers might want, they'd miss out on a lot of sales.

Sure enough, the guy asked me, "What else do you need, sir?"

I couldn't really think of any discreet way to ask for porn, so I just owned up to it.

"Sir, may I please have ten dollars worth of the filthiest pornography?" I asked.

"Yes, sir. I hear you." The cashier smiled a discolored and crooked-toothed smile, reached back, and pulled something off the porno rack from the shelf behind *Playboy* and *Penthouse*.

He'd picked out something in a sealed black plastic wrapper, and when he handed it to me, I saw that it wasn't just one magazine but a three-pack of porn, a trifecta of filth that offered a savings of 20 percent off the regular price as a bonus. I couldn't open them in the store, but I figured these would be ideal for making the dollars for our dollar rides with Lieutenant Wilson.

*

"Ray, I think you missed the point of the dollah," Doley said to me as a bunch of guys from our class compared the dollars we'd decorated for our IPs at the tables in the middle of Dagger flight room. Doley kept spinning the back of the dollar I had decorated for Lieutenant Wilson around and around and around, studying my work. Then he continued with his thought, "The dollah is supposed to be about your first time flying a jet, and on the back, you compare that experience to the experience of your first time with a woman. That is supposed to be the essence of the dollah—not a scene from *Caligula.*"

Doley may have been right. On Saturday night, when Kenny and I made our dollars for our first flights with Lieutenant Wilson, we each drank a six-pack of the beer that we'd loaded into our new, vintage 1960s Pepsi machine while we watched *The Jerk* and *The Man with Two Brains.* We got a little silly that night, and we may have gotten a little carried away with our dollars.

My dollar wasn't just my name, our class number, and an aircraft on the front with a scantily clad or naked woman on the back. The later we stayed up, the more we drank, and the more Steve Martin we watched that night, the more we cut, glued, compared, and laughed. We used our Academy-issued textbook *U.S. War Machine* as our source for our aircraft pictures. Because we needed images small enough to fit on the back of a dollar, the cutting got more and more difficult the more we drank, and I'd accidentally cut off the skinnier pieces of the pictures, like the end of a woman's arm, the tip of a missile, or the end of a pitot tube that extends from the nose of many aircraft. By the end of the second movie, the back side of my dollar had become a bacchanalian orgy of naked women intertwined and interlocked with very phallic, military aircraft and weaponry, and I managed to figure out a way to cover up all of the cutting mistakes that I'd made.

Kenny and I had pretty much cut every picture out of the three-pack of porn I'd bought at the Skank Store earlier that day and used them in our dollars, thinking that if Lieutenant Wilson liked the expression on the face of the naked woman on the back of his favorite dollar, he'd really get a kick out of something a little more over-the-top...and on top...and perhaps some of the other points-of-view that we had included with our work. Just about the only visible part of the original backside of my dollar was the eyeball on top of the pyramid, which appeared in a very peculiar spot on a picture of a woman that I'd cut out from the packet of porn.

"Okay, Doley, my bad. I didn't make that connection. I just thought the dollar was supposed to have porno on the back, but I think Lieutenant Wilson will get a good laugh out of it. Don't you think?" I asked.

"Well, I guess you'll find out at the end of the day," Doley said with a nod toward the scheduling board.

The scheduling board was a white, dry erase, magnetic board on the wall behind the desks of the head scheduler, Lieutenant Prince, and the assistant scheduler, my instructor Lieutenant Wilson, at the back of the Dagger flight room. There, the daily flying schedule would be posted. A typical day on the flight line consisted of either two or three flying periods of four hours each. Students and instructors were required to begin briefing up their missions at least one hour prior to their scheduled takeoff times, the flights and simulator missions would last about an hour and fifteen minutes, and the debrief after the mission would last about an hour.

If you were flying or were assigned to the simulator, you wouldn't get much down time during the four-hour period. If you weren't flying or assigned to the simulator, you might be assigned to the duty desk or the snack bar, practice checklists and flying procedures in the CFTs, or stay in the flight room and study. Normally our flight-line day would consist of just two flying periods and an academic class or a physical training session would make up the rest of our 12-hour day, but for our dollar rides, Captain Wright wanted us all to get them done as soon as possible. So, on whatever day it was around the end of August that first day we flew, the schedulers planned for three flying periods.

While Doley had been critiquing my dollar, a third of the students from Dagger flight were already burning holes in the sky. Lieutenant Wilson was airborne with our buddy PePé. Kenny would be flying with Lieutenant Wilson second period after serving as Snacko first period. Then, I'd fly my dollar ride with Lieutenant Wilson during third period.

Every element of the flying mission would be graded each time we flew: ground operations, takeoff, departure, level off, etc. In learning to fly, we'd plan for each of these elements, perform each element, be graded on our performance of each element, and receive instruction on how to better perform each element next time. This is why each training period required four hours, and this procedure at UPT wasn't very different from how we were trained at the Academy in the T-41, the single-engine Cessna propeller plane used in the Academy's flight-screening program.

When a sweaty PePé returned from his dollar ride, I sat at Lieutenant Wilson's desk with him to listen to his debriefing. Only, it wasn't so much of a debriefing as it was a debarfing. Apparently, PePé had been sick the whole ride, and Lieutenant Wilson was trying to help him figure out if he had eaten too much, too little, or just something that didn't agree with him. Was he dehydrated? Was it too hot outside? Had he had the same feelings in his stomach during his flight-screening program at the Academy? How many times had he puked? Dry heaves or chunks? The exchange sounded more like a doctor's visit than anything else.

Lieutenant Wilson pushed his chair away from his desk and told PePé he'd be back in a couple of minutes to continue their debrief. He walked back into the IP room through the doorway behind his desk.

"You okay?" I asked PePé, who still sat hunched over at the desk, staring down at the desktop without really looking at anything in particular. "I'm going to go grab a cup of water from the snack bar. Do you want one?" I asked, getting up from my seat.

PePé nodded his head enough for me to see. So, I headed over to the snack bar to grab some water. Kenny was doing in his first shift as Snacko.

"Hey, man. I don't think PePé's ride went too well," I told Kenny.

"What happened?" he shot back.

"I think he may have gotten pretty airsick. His face looked worse than the time it was eaten by roaches." I thought back to a cadet trip to MacDill Air Force Base in Tampa. "When I had an F-16 ride at MacDill, I puked three times during the flight," I told Kenny. "I remember that as I got more and more queasy, I thought that if I just puked, I'd feel better."

"Like when you're really drunk?" Kenny asked.

"Yeah," I agreed. "It helps you feel alright for a few minutes, and then, you just feel like puking again."

"Aaay! Everyone that's coming in here after their rides is totally soaked in sweat," Kenny told me. I had observed that, too. "Make sure you drink a lot of water," Kenny advised. "Remember what that guy said in the physiology class about drinking enough water?"

"Yeah, if you're 2 percent dehydrated, you lose 50 percent of your G-tolerance, and you feel thirsty when you're 3 percent dehydrated. So by the time you're thirsty, it's already too late." I had found that pretty interesting.

"Aaay, nice!" Kenny was impressed. "All I was going to say is that your piss needs to be clear — not yellow. That's what I remember."

"Well, that's why I'm here...to get some water. I need to hydrate, and I need to re-hydrate PePé," I said.

As I grabbed two Styrofoam cups, our large buddy Kurt raced into the snack bar.

"Ray-bonus! Lieutenant Wilson is looking for you. You're flying this period," Kurt said hastily.

"Kurtus Interruptus, I'm flying with Lieutenant Wilson third period," I corrected my oversized friend. "Kenny's flying with him second period, but he needs someone to take over as Snacko before he goes back to the flight room."

"You've just been switched on the schedule to a second-period ride with Major Lawson, and he's in the flight room waiting on you. Get over there, right now!"

"Aaay! We'll be on our dollar rides at the same time," Kenny said excitedly.

"This sucks!" I wasn't as excited as Kenny. "I gotta give a major who's old enough to be my dad a totally triple-X-rated dollar." This did suck. "What if Major Lawson gets offended? I could get in some real trouble. What do I do?"

"Aaay! Just give him the dollar," Kenny said.

"Just get your ass across the hall, and worry about that later," Kurt said sternly. "They're all looking for you!"

Great! I hadn't even left the ground yet, and my flying career was off to a ridiculous start.

*

"You ready for this, old buddy?" Major Lawson asked over the intercom of the T-37.

"Yes, sir," I answered confidently, even though I was sure I wasn't.

"Mighty fine," Major Lawson acknowledged, organizing his side of the cockpit.

Even though he was sitting next to me, I couldn't see his face. Inside the helmet, my face and eyes dripped with sweat, my sun visor clouding up with the steam. I fidgeted with the pages of the checklist Velcro-ed to my thigh, and I fumbled to find and flip the appropriate dials and switches to prep the jet for takeoff. I'm sure that Major Lawson knew well enough that even though I said I was ready, I wasn't. In fact, I had no idea what I was in for.

Brave man. He was going to let me perform my first takeoff in the T-37, nicknamed the "Tweet" for the shrill, screeching whistle of its twin engines.

Once we were cleared for takeoff on Sunfish, the smallest of the three parallel runways at Columbus Air Force Base, I turned the jet to the centerline of the runway. In position, I recited my checklist as if I knew what I was talking about: "Three green, no red, no amber, point-on-point, line-on-line, squawking normal."

I released the brakes, and off we went…straight off to the right side of the runway. This was not a good thing. I kicked the left rudder pedal, and because I was still squeezing down on the nose wheel steering button, we cut sharply back to the left, heading for the grass across the centerline of the runway. But I recognized this, too, so I kicked the right rudder pedal and zigged back to the right. Only, once again, I cut across the centerline of the runway. But knowing that I'd screwed up again, I kicked the left rudder pedal even harder and zagged back to the left—even harder and sharper than my other cutbacks.

By this time, the Tweet had picked up a little speed, and the faster we rolled back and forth down the runway, the bigger and sharper my zigs and zags got. I was totally out of control; we were about to end up in the grass. I kicked the right rudder pedal in hard, and the jet jolted like it was about to roll up on two wheels like a car driven by Joie Chitwood on *ABC's Wide World of Sports,* but at least it was heading back to the center of the runway…until I crossed over it and headed toward the grass on the right-hand side once again.

"I have the aircraft," Major Lawson said calmly, shaking the stick to let me know he was taking control of the aircraft away from me.

"You have the aircraft, sir," I said, throwing both hand up in front of me.

Thank you!

"Roger, I have the aircraft," he said, shaking the stick, and immediately he righted the jet's direction, smoothly rotated the nose back, and the jet took off right down the center of the runway, avoiding a dollar-ride disaster.

Just after ten AM by the time we took off, the temperature that day was already above ninety degrees, and this being Mississippi, it was a wet heat—like being inside a sauna while wearing a flame-retardant body suit, a ten-pound foam helmet, gloves, a rubber face mask, and a forty-pound parachute. Throw in the feelings of panic and failure, and I was totally soaked in sweat by the time the wheels retracted into the belly of the jet. Short of crashing, the ride couldn't have started off any worse, but there was still plenty of time and fuel to burn.

With the landing gear and the flaps up, Major Lawson gave control of the aircraft back to me so I could fly the rest of the departure. A couple of miles past the end of the runway, I banked up the jet to the left to fly the departure route as published in the in-flight guide fastened to my right leg by a green Velcro strap. As soon as I broke wings level, I realized my seat was definitely not locked like the checklist required.

Wham! My seat slid right down whatever rail it was sitting on and dropped me to the floor of the jet.

Instead of having my head at the same level as Major Lawson, I was looking up at him, like a kid at the grown-ups' table. Scared to readjust it for fear of triggering the ejection sequence, I wouldn't be able to use the center of my windscreen or my proper references for level flight while we were in the air.

My takeoff sucked, my departure sucked, and if the air traffic controllers were watching my blip jump around on their radar scopes, I'm sure my signal looked more like a rodeo cowboy on a bucking bronco than a pilot in a jet at level flight, and that sucked. The more I pitched up and down, chasing what I thought would get me back to level flight, the more queasy my stomach felt, and even before we had established ourselves in our assigned slice of military operating airspace, I really felt like I needed to puke. But I fought it. And I fought it. And for the rest of the ride, I fought it. And I didn't puke.

*

Major Lawson earned every penny of his dollar that morning. I gave it to him when we climbed into the crew bus that drove us back from the jet to the parachute shop. He looked at it quickly and stuck it in one of the pockets on his chest. He wasn't nearly as tired or sweaty as I was, but he'd had a pretty good workout.

Major Lawson sat in Lieutenant Wilson's chair, and I sat in my regular seat for the debrief. Kenny and Lieutenant Wilson hadn't come back to the Dagger flight room yet.

"Ground ops...U," Major Lawson began. "You need to keep practicing your pre-flight checklists so you can finish them in about two minutes. Did you notice how hot it was out there, old buddy?"

I nodded, keeping my eye on that U. The grading options on our grade-sheets were as follows:

> NG for *No Grade*—to be used if a maneuver was demonstrated by the instructor but not flown by the student
>
> U for *Unsatisfactory*—to be used if the student could not properly execute a maneuver or was unsafe in executing a maneuver
>
> F for *Fair*—to be used if the maneuver was completed safely with deviations that did not compromise safety
>
> G for *Good*—to be used when a maneuver was completed competently with minor deviations

              E for *Excellent*—to be used when a maneuver was
              completed successfully without deviating
              from proper parameters

"You also need to make sure your seat locks into place after you adjust it. Otherwise, you could have problems with your visual references for the rest of the ride. That wouldn't be too good, would it now?" Major Lawson smiled; he knew what had happened.

"Takeoff...*U*. Barely. What were you doing?" Major Lawson asked and waited for me to respond.

"Sir, I didn't straighten out the nose wheel when I rolled out onto the runway," I said. "When I let go of the brakes, we headed off to the right. I tried—"

"All right, I know. I was there. I just wanted to hear you say that you weren't tryin' to kill me, because if you said you were tryin' to kill me, I might not want to fly with you again." He stopped and stared at me, letting me know that I needed to do better.

Major Lawson drew a sine wave that grew in amplitude each time it crossed a horizontal axis to represent what I'd been doing. "Recognize this situation, pick a point in the distance where you want the jet to go, and point the jet in that direction. That's how I kept us from joy-riding through the grass on the side of the runway."

That made perfect sense to me. I got it.

"The same thing goes for level flight," Major Lawson continued his instruction. "Set the pitch. Set the power. Trim, trim, trim." While not exactly like cruise control in a car, the trim button, operated by the thumb on the control stick of the T-37, reduced the pressure on the stick needed to maintain the desired pitch angle for the nose of the aircraft.

Rather than trying to control the aircraft by chasing the performance instruments, Major Lawson wanted me to set the control instruments to put the aircraft in the position I wanted it, and the performance instruments, like the airspeed indicator and altimeter, tell you how the aircraft is responding to your inputs. Of course, if I couldn't get my seat to stay locked in the proper position, and I wasn't able to see half-ground and half-sky through my windscreen, then I wouldn't be able to set the proper pitch, and I'd never be able to control the aircraft.

"Yo! Tur-BIG-lio! I thought you said you were a pilot. What in *thee* hell was that? I need to fly with Jellicot. Where are the schedulers? Put me on the schedule with Jellicot."

Captain Van Dorn, our Foghorn Leghorn academic instructor, had just flown Al's dollar ride. The two of them came into the Dagger flight room, and Captain Van Dorn sat down at the desk next to Major Lawson as we were wrapping up our debrief. I don't know if he was joking with Al or if Al's ride was as bad as mine, but either way, Captain Van Dorn sure was loud, and it didn't look like Al appreciated the resulting attention.

In spite of all my screw-ups on my dollar ride, Major Lawson gave me a grade of *Good* for the flight overall. I think he may have been about to leave until his "Old Buddy" Captain Van Dorn sat down next to him and kept berating Al for his flying.

Major Lawson laughed without looking up, but then he pulled the dollar I had given him out of his chest pocket.

"Lieutenant Wright, while you bubble in the rest of the circles on your grade-sheet, I'm gonna have me a look here at this dollar." Major Lawson smiled as he examined the G-rated front side of the dollar first. Then, with his voice raised a little louder, as is to grab some attention from Captain Van Dorn, Major Lawson said, "This is mighty fine."

Captain Van Dorn did look over momentarily, but immediately turned his attention back to digging into Al for his flying. It was like listening to a baseball team pepper an opposing pitcher with chatter to try to throw him off his game.

Lieutenant Wilson and Kenny walked in. Kenny took the seat next to me, and Lieutenant Wilson told Major Lawson to take his time at the desk. I introduced Kenny and Major Lawson, and Kenny's eyes lit up when he saw the dollar on the desk.

"Aaay, how do you like that back of that dollar?" Kenny asked Major Lawson.

"Lieutenant Wilson," Captain Van Dorn called out. "You're a scheduler. Put me on tomorrow's schedule with Jellicot."

"There's something on the back?" Major Lawson answered Kenny, projecting loudly enough to drown out Captain Van Dorn. "Let's take a look," and with take, he flipped the dollar over, nodded his head repeatedly, and fought back a smile.

"Well, now...that's mighty fine," Major Lawson announced, and as he got louder and louder, Captain Van Dorn was getting distracted at the desk next to us.

"Yo! Tur-BIG-lio," Captain Van Dorn turned his attention back to Al, but before he could make his point, Major Lawson interrupted him.

"Dana," Major Lawson addressed Captain Van Dorn by his first name. "Do you reckon that's a heat-seeking missile?" he asked, pointing to a particularly crude combination of pictures on the back of the dollar I'd given him.

Captain Van Dorn turned his attention to what Major Lawson was waving in his face and completely lost his train of thought. Major Lawson pulled the dollar back to Lieutenant Wilson's desk to study it some more.

"Tur-BIG-lio! What were you thinking..." but again, before Captain Van Dorn could beat up on Al some more, Major Lawson interrupted.

"Dana, look at this here," Major Lawson leaned over again. "Do you suppose this might be a new way to clean off a pitot tube?"

Captain Van Dorn stopped again, and this time, he spent a little more time looking the back of my dollar. He was catching on to what Major Lawson was doing.

"Now, Dana," Major Lawson pointed to another area on the back of the dollar, "did you ever see a KC-135 involved in this kind of refueling?"

Captain Van Dorn turned to address me. "Yo, Wright! I could tell you were a little strange, but I didn't know you were this sick!"

"Now, Dana, he's not all that bad," Major Lawson defended me, and then dropping the volume back down to normal conversational levels, he added, "Of course, his flying sucked, but I didn't expect too much on the first ride. I gave him a *Good* overall. How'd your boy Turbiglio do? 'Bout the same?"

"Yes, sir," Captain Van Dorn replied and nodded. "'Bout the same. Sounds like they did about the same."

Almost immediately, all signs of stress disappeared from Al's face.

Lieutenant Wilson sat down after Major Lawson got up and left. Then, before he left, Captain Van Dorn leaned over to Lieutenant Wilson—our flight's assistant scheduler—and said quietly, "For tomorrow, put me on the schedule with Jellicot. I'd like a jet around nine-thirty or ten, if you can make that happen."

Chapter 8 — "Funky Chicken"

The DUI tote board that warmly welcomed visitors at the main gate of Columbus Air Force Base reached as high as thirty-four days before some asshole demonstrated that he did not have Columbus Class and got the base's next DUI. I imagined that the wing commander had his new swathe of foreskin on display at wing headquarters, like a Kupaki headhunter might display a shrunken head trophy.

As part of a renewed effort to indoctrinate the base in the undefined tenets of Columbus Class, the morning's ground safety briefing, a once-weekly component of the morning's formal report, was a personal testimonial to the dangers of drunk driving. Our guest speaker was Check Section Pilot Lieutenant Holtzmann, who was sharing a story about the time he was a passenger in a drunk driving accident.

Check Section was the group of instructor pilots that evaluated the students' proficiency at the end of each block of training. Our Dagger flight IPs were our teachers, and the check pilots were our judges. We would have three checkrides in T-37s and three in T-38s, and these six scores would go a long way in determining our class ranking and ultimately our first assignments. Fail three checkrides and odds were you wouldn't graduate from UPT.

Lieutenant Holtzmann's story took us back about a half-dozen years, before he was in the Air Force — before he was even in college. He was in high school...about to graduate. He and some buddies had been drinking. They were speeding down a country road at night....

As I sat listening, I realized that I already was familiar with the details of the story — and tuning into his distinctly Rhode Island accent, I *knew*. I had seen it on the news when I was in high school. The kids were all athletes. One had accepted an appointment to West Point. One had accepted an appointment to Annapolis.

"My friends didn't ansuh me when I called their names. I didn't know if they wuh unconscious aw dead," he told us, recalling what happened after they'd wrapped their car around a tree. "Even though I had been ridin' in the back seat, I was mashed all the way up against the dashbawd of the cah. When I looked down at my legs, I could see that my broken leg bones had poked right through my skin, and my kneecap just flapped ovah backwids and just kinda dangled outside a' my leg."

From my seat at Lieutenant Wilson's desk, I was looking straight ahead at Lieutenant Holtzmann. My position gave peripheral vision on my classmates. Like me, everyone was sitting perfectly still. Everyone except one.

Sandy Benning looked to me like she'd involuntarily twitched a couple of times. I watched her for a moment, and after I saw her twitch for sure, her head started to slowly roll around in small circles.

I kept an eye on Sandy while listening to Lieutenant Holtzmann telling about his injuries, his friends' injuries, and all the blood. Sandy's face had become completely expressionless— and not in a way that was meant to convey military discipline...she was somewhere else. She twitched again and again when Lieutenant Holtzmann told how he could feel his broken teeth in his mouth and taste his own blood on his tongue and in his throat. Something bad was happening—like she was having some kind of seizure, and I didn't know what to do. We had been told that during the formal report, we were not to speak unless addressed, we were not to look around except to look at the person speaking, and we were not to move in our seats until after the formal report.

"Lemme show you just what kinda damage was done to my mouth," Lieutenant Holtzmann said. Opening his mouth, he reached up, yanked out his top row of teeth, and held it out in front of his face while flashing his toothless gums, like the way a Kung Fu fighter might pull out an enemy's heart with the two-finger method and show it to him while it was still beating before the enemy dropped dead.

In front of me, Sandy quivered and shook. Her head snapped backwards, and her shaking body started to roll out of her chair.

In a flash, Kenny sprang forward and dropped to his knees by Sandy's side to keep her from falling and slamming to the ground. While some heads turned, nobody but Kenny moved to help. He caught her, grabbed her hand, and helped her to stay in her chair. Lieutenant Holtzmann stopped his talk. Captain Wright strode forward, joining Kenny in trying to snap Sandy out of her spasmodic, zombie-like state.

When the life came back into her eyes, Kenny and Captain Wright helped Sandy back to the IPs' private room. Lieutenant Holtzmann popped his teeth back into his head, and nobody else moved again until the end of the formal report when Mark Jellicot called the room to attention, saluted Assistant Flight Commander Lieutenant Peena, now filling in for Captain Wright, who was still in the back room with Kenny and Sandy. We sounded off with a loud and thunderous "DAGGER!" to end the formal report.

I caught up with Lieutenant Holtzmann in the snack bar right after that.

"Lieutenant Holtzmann." I got his attention as he was toasting a Pop-Tart. "Sir, are you from Rhode Island?"

"Yeah," he smiled, his fake teeth all back in their proper places. "What gave it away? My accent?"

"No, sir," I said. "Your story. I remember reading about it in the *Providence Journal,* and I remember seeing the report on the news. One guy was going to go to West Point, and one guy was going to go to Annapolis."

"Yeah, I was the unda r'achievah with the Rotsy scholahship to Va'mont," Lieutenant Holtzmann replied, grabbing his Pop-Tart from the toaster and putting it on a paper plate.

"Somebody always passes out when I tell that story," he reflected, referring to Sandy as he grabbed a banana. "Is she gonna be okay?"

"Yes, sir. She's grounded until she gets cleared by the flight surgeon, but she'll be fine."

*

"Kenny," I said, spreading the last of the newspaper pages onto the garage floor. "That was quick thinking."

"Aaay!" he thanked me. "I didn't want her to get hurt."

We each picked up a can of spray paint for our vintage 1950s refrigerator and the metal bread, sugar, and flour containers Kurt and Malia had given us for our kitchen. We picked out caution orange for the color so that no matter how drunk we might happen to be, we'd always be able to find the fridge. Plus, caution orange was the cheapest paint color we could find at the store.

We figured the garage would be the best place to try to paint. If we painted inside, we'd trash the carpet and the walls. If we painted outside, it would be ninety-five degrees by ten in the morning, and the paint would never dry. The garage was the least-bad option.

"Aaay, are we early week or late week next week?" Kenny asked, shaking up his spray can.

"We're on late week again," I told him, shaking my can up, too. The pattern for students on the flight line was two weeks on early week, then two weeks on late week, then back to two weeks on early week, then late week again, and so on. "Didn't you get a schedule yesterday?" We always got the next week's schedule on Fridays.

"Nah, I got one. I just didn't look at it," he said. "I was askin' 'cause a guy from my high school is gonna be on *The*

Tonight Show next week, and I wanted to stay up and watch it." Kenny hit the front of the fridge with a long blast of orange paint, and I blasted the side.

"Did you go to high school in New York or in Atlanta?" I asked, remembering Kenny had told Lieutenant Wilson that his parents lived in Atlanta.

"Massapequa, Lawn G'Island," Kenny told me, shaking up his paint can again. "I never lived in Atlanta. My parents just moved there." He sprayed some more orange onto the bottom of the fridge door. Thank goodness the Pepsi machine would be sitting in the other room; the combination would have been fatal to the eyes. "My dad drove the Coke truck my whole life. When he wanted to retire, he sold his Coke route for a lot of money. Then, my parents sold their house, and overnight, they were like millionaires."

"Good for them! Did your dad plan to retire, or was it the New Coke thing?" I joked. I actually didn't mind New Coke, though I thought it tasted better warm than cold, and in Mississippi, you really need something cold. Captain Wright had convinced me of that.

"Naa, I think he just got tired of drivin' the truck," Kenny supposed.

"Have you told him that you bought a Pepsi machine yet?" I asked.

"Naa, I don't think the Pepsi machine is anything my dad needs to know about," Kenny laughed.

We painted while we talked, and after just a few minutes, we'd nearly finished up the first coat. It wasn't too hard to paint because it wasn't very tall, maybe five feet high. And it only had one door. The freezer section of the appliance was a just tiny compartment that was behind a flimsy, plastic, inner door at the top of the inside of the unit. Though the fridge only cost us sixty bucks, we probably overpaid.

I drained my first can of spray paint and went to pick up another one when another question hit me. Something that didn't quite make sense.

"Hey, Kenny, why don't you just record *The Tonight Show* next week?"

"What do you mean?" Kenny looked at me with a puzzled expression.

"Why don't you just tape *The Tonight Show?*" I repeated. I thought I had been pretty clear the first time.

"Aaay! Whadda ya talkin' about? Are you talkin' about using my VCR? Do you want me to try to record a show onto a movie?" Kenny still wasn't sure what I meant.

"No. No, you could record the show on a blank videotape," I said. "Your VCR can record TV shows. You program it to record. You wouldn't have to stay up late to watch *The Tonight Show*. You could go to sleep, and if your friend is funny, you could watch it over and over again."

"Wait a second! Are you talkin' about using my VCR to record the TV show, like using it like a tape recorder?" I think the light bulb was starting to turn on for Kenny. "I thought it just played movies."

How do you own a VCR and not know that it stands for Video Cassette *Recorder*?

"Hey, I'll tell you what," I said, looking over the fridge for any spots we might have missed with our first coat of caution orange, "I'll buy a blank videotape, and I'll set up your VCR to record *The Tonight Show* every night next week. That way, no matter what night the guy from your high school comes on, you won't miss it. And, if it's okay with you, I have a few shows that I like to watch and don't want to miss. If I buy the videotape and set up your machine to record *The Tonight Show,* do you mind if I record a couple of things, too?"

Kenny thought for a moment and squeezed off a few quick blasts of orange over some rough patches that he'd found in our first coating. "Aaay. I guess that's cool. What do you want to record?" he asked.

"Well, *Pee-wee's Playhouse*," I admitted. "I usually make sure I'm free to watch it, but if I miss it, I'd like to be able to record it. It's coming on in a couple of hours, if you wanna catch an episode with me."

"Ha! I love the Pee-wee Herman movie. I didn't know he had a show. Okay," Kenny said.

The caution-orange fridge and containers looked excellent once back inside the kitchen. No matter how drunk we got, we would always be able to find the fridge—it was that bright. We had already set up the white, plastic yard-sale patio table—maroon umbrella included—and its four white plastic chairs as our kitchen table. We'd stocked the Pepsi machine with bottles of beer from the supermarket and set it up in the big room at the front of the house. We learned all too soon that only long-necked bottles would fit in the Pepsi machine, which was bad news for our friends who drank Colt 45 or any other brand in a stubby bottle. Occasionally, the neck of a bottle might get cracked if you didn't exercise good technique and pulled the bottle out of the Pepsi machine the wrong way. But not wanting to waste any beer, even if a bottle got cracked, we'd drink it anyway. Captain Wright would be proud, I thought.

Kenny and I set up my new, very soft and comfortable brown velour sectional sofa-love-seat-and-corner-table thing in the big room with the Pepsi machine. Kenny's TV, movie-playing VCR, and the pinball machine picked up at a yard sale went in the big room, too. Kenny had a fish tank, which we put on the mantle of the huge stone fireplace. He didn't have any fish, but we could get some. While the house only had one floor, the ceiling in the big room was so high that we could have set up a basketball hoop inside.

Finally, in honor of UPT Class 88-07, we planted a couple of pink plastic lawn flamingos in the front yard. Our rental house was looking pretty good by the time we finished putting everything into place, just in time for *Pee-wee's Playhouse*. Kenny watched it with me. In fact, Kenny enjoyed the show so much, as we watched it, he got more and more motivated to convert our rental house into a UPT-version of *Pee-wee's Playhouse*.

When the show was over, Kenny made me go shopping. Neither one of us had much stuff because at the Academy about the only thing we could have in our cadet dorm rooms besides uniforms, books, and a bulletin board were three pieces of memorabilia.

We blew the next couple of hours and another couple of hundred bucks at the Leigh Mall on a bunch of really stupid things. Certainly stuff we didn't need. Among some of our dumber purchases were a six-foot, hot pink wrist watch/wall clock; a large, inflatable stegosaurus; a giant poster of Jon Bon Jovi; an ant farm (ants not included); and a gumball machine, gumballs, some pink flamingo helium-filled Mylar balloons, and several plastic plants. Kenny also got some goldfish for his aquarium, and I picked up the blank videotapes.

"Aaay!" Kenny declared, inspired by Pee-wee with another idea. "Our first class party is going to be a Tin Foil Ball Party. Everybody needs to bring tin foil, and we'll make a giant ball of foil, like Pee-wee's."

*

I sat at the table in the middle of Dagger, trying to review my flight profile for my first ride with Lieutenant Wilson. Since we'd hit the flight line, I had simmed three times with Major Lawson, flown my dollar ride and my second ride with him, but I hadn't done anything with Lieutenant Wilson, my assigned instructor.

Though pretty psyched, I really wasn't getting much accomplished. While I was chair-flying my mission, Doley sat next to me, working to develop his pen-spinning skills so that he could twirl his pen like Iceman did in *Top Gun*. Every other twirl attempt, his pen would fly across the table and hit me, my checklist, or my maps.

"SMS...I know it's tough," Doley said to Al Turbiglio, who was sitting across from us at the table in the center of the room.

Al didn't know what to say. He had been placed on SMS for stupidly driving up to the main gate without wearing his seat belt. On day one of UPT, Lieutenant Billy Mike had warned us about SMS—special monitoring status. You didn't want to be on it.

"If y'all get into any trouble in UPT, before y'all wash out, y'all'll go on SMS," our class commander had warned us that first day. "There are three kinds of SMS. Flying SMS is for those of y'all who're having trouble flying, and that'll be about a third of y'all. Academic SMS is for those of y'all who might have problems with academics. Military SMS is pretty much for those of y'all stupid enough to get a DUI. Y'all don't really need to worry about flying SMS or academic SMS when it comes to y'all's careers, but y'all don't want to wash out of UPT for military SMS, because that will follow y'all around."

Al's seat belt infraction earned him a thirty-day sentence on military SMS. If he kept his nose clean, he'd be okay. But if he got into any more trouble, he could be on his way out.

Continuing his take on a speech that Iceman had made to get into Maverick's head in *Top Gun*, Doley rolled on, "The Academy rejected you because ya' Duke Tuhbiglio's kid."

Al must have seen *Top Gun*, but I wasn't sure if he realized that Doley was quoting the movie or actually teasing him because he hadn't gone to the Academy. I handed Doley back his pen after he'd flipped it into my local area map yet again. "But it's like ya' flyin' against a ghost," Doley continued, his stare locked onto Al's psyche.

Because of military SMS, I think Al was afraid to say or do anything that might be perceived as being out of line. He didn't need more trouble. He just sat on his side of the table and looked back at Doley, not knowing how to respond...unable to respond.

"It makes me nervous," Doley finished Iceman's lines, unofficially starting an Iceman-versus-Maverick staring contest right as his spinning pen flew from his hand one more time. Despite the pen's clatter on the floor, Doley didn't break from character or his missile-lock stare...until Kenny shouted from the duty desk.

"Hey, Everybody! Val's here!" Kenny yelled as Val Martelli hit the threshold of the Dagger double-doors.

Whenever Kenny got stuck being the Duty Dog, he announced anyone who came to the door, like Mr. Window did for Pee-wee Herman. I wouldn't go as far as to compare the atmosphere at a military training base to that of *Pee-wee's Playhouse,* but I don't think it would be an exaggeration to say that at times, the Dagger flight room could be just as ridiculous.

"Valsalva!" I yelled as the Warhawk student section leader entered, and I pinched my nostrils with my thumb and forefinger, pretending to clear my ears.

"Valsalva!" the rest of the Dagger students yelled and performed mock Valsalva maneuvers.

Upon hearing the commotion, Captain Wright popped his head out the door of the IPs' room. "Lieutenant Martelli, be sure to tell your flight commander how clean the Dagger flight room is when you get back to the Chickenhawk room."

Val had come to tell Mark that because 88-07 was the freshman class on the flight line, we'd been assigned to do a FOD walk on the center runway a week from Saturday.

Kenny and I balked. *Not the morning after our party!*

We'd already told everyone we'd host our first class party, the Tin Foil Ball Party, a week from Friday. Now, in preparation for a visit by General Todd, the leader of Air Training Command, we'd have to clean a 12,000-by-300-foot runway the very next morning. The center runway was so big that when the Space

Shuttle program was up and running, Columbus Air Force Base was an alternate landing site for the 747 that carried the shuttle on its back from California to Florida. Depending on how many foreign objects we found, this FOD walk might take a couple of hours. Not only could we not sleep in that morning, I needed to be sure to set Kenny's VCR to record *Pee-wee*.

*

I rolled out of my last maneuver and lined the jet up over the road between the towns of Guin and Winfield, Alabama, which meant that I was in the center of my assigned airspace. I tried to catch my breath. My heart was pounding, and I was drenched in sweat. I didn't have the same need-to-puke feeling that I'd had on my dollar ride with Major Lawson, but my stomach was a little queasy, and I did have a headache. Even so, I had flown a pretty solid ride—by far, better than either of my first two.

"Is that it for your profile?" Lieutenant Wilson asked. It was. We still had to do recoveries, which meant Lieutenant Wilson would fly the jet into an extreme, nose-high climb or an extreme, nose-low dive and then transfer aircraft control to me, and I would have to recognize the aircraft's unusual attitude, confirm the unusual attitude, and recover from the unusual attitude in order to prevent a stall, spin, or dive into the ground. It was kind of like he'd shuffle the cards, and I'd have to put them back in order.

"Yes, sir," I replied, looking down at the list of maneuvers. I'd flown everything on my list, and we still had plenty of fuel. Maybe Lieutenant Wilson was going to have me practice one more loop, because maybe my loop wasn't really all that good.

"Okay, you got all of the maneuvers, and we still have some extra gas. That's good, because I want to show you something. I have the aircraft," Lieutenant Wilson said, shaking the stick.

"Roger, you have the aircraft," I replied and held up my hands.

"I have the aircraft," he said again, shaking the stick.

Lieutenant Wilson pushed the throttles up to MIL—100 percent power—rolled upside down, and started a dive at the ground to pick up speed.

"Your acro and other maneuvers aren't all that bad," he began, "but you're not very efficient at stringing them together. You waste too much gas." He rolled the aircraft back to right-side-up, still diving and accelerating with the throttles in MIL.

"Instead of performing one move and droning back to the center of the area for the next one, string them all together so that you fly from one right into another...lemme show you what I mean," he said.

With the fluidity of a champion figure skater, Lieutenant Wilson strung together an aerial ballet of acrobatics and traffic pattern stalls without once having to turn the jet around to drive it back to the center of the area or climb or descend to set up the proper altitude and airspeed required to fly his next maneuver. Each maneuver flowed gracefully into the next, setting up the next...perfectly. A barrel roll led into a loop that led into an Immelmann that reversed our direction and set us up for traffic pattern stalls heading back into the center of the area.

"It's all about energy management," he said.

In about a tenth of the time it took me to run through my profile, Lieutenant Wilson flew his, showing me that he'd also only used about a fifth of the gas that I'd used. We still might even have enough for me to even fly one last loop after all. But Lieutenant Wilson was having fun, so he kept the stick a little longer.

"Eight-point aileron roll?" he asked.

"Yes, sir. Sounds good," I said. I had no idea what an eight-point aileron roll was, but this was turning into a fun ride.

Besides, having seen Lieutenant Wilson string together his acro, I felt like a light bulb was turning on in my head.

After pulling the nose up a little, Lieutenant Wilson quickly rolled the aircraft to the left and paused momentarily in increments of 45 degrees as he rolled the aircraft around: 45–90–135–180. Roll. Pause. Roll. Pause. Roll. Pause. As we rolled upside-down, the nose of the jet crossed right through the horizon. Then came 225–270–315 and back to wings-level. He had stopped at every 45 degrees during his aileron roll—8 times at 8 points.

"The team keeps asking for me," he said. "You know, the Thunderbirds."

"Yes, sir," I laughed.

"Hey, look down and make sure your D-ring is where it's supposed to be," Lieutenant Wilson directed.

The D-ring was designed to automatically deploy your parachute upon ejection at low altitude if connected to your lap belt, but it wasn't supposed to be connected at higher altitudes. Since it was tough to see down into my lap while wearing my flight helmet and oxygen mask, I leaned forward and cranked my head as far down as could with my chin turned and flattened against my chest.

Disconnected, just as I thought, I—
WHOOOOAAA!

All of a sudden, G-forces increased the weight of my body, head, and helmet. Because of the way I had turned, my heavy head pinned my chin to my chest. I couldn't move it! About a second after trying to fight off the G's, all of the color in the instrument panel and the small portion of the sky that I could still see through the canopy with my head pinned down on my chest drained from my vision. The world turned gray-and-white.

Lieutenant Wilson pulled up into a loop as I was looking down. I felt like I'd just taken a hit to the jaw while an elephant was stepping on my stomach.

Thinking this had to end soon, it only got worse. My field of vision, already colorless, shrunk down like an old black-and-white TV with a broken picture tube; the vertical and horizontal edges of what I could see simply collapsed into a tunnel vision. Just after this happened, the gray-and-white picture changed to more of a red-and-white picture.

From here, things got even stranger. Without exerting any control over my arms, my hands popped up in front of my face, like a puppet-master somewhere above me had jerked on my strings to make me dance. With elbows and wrists bent, my arms and hands began shaking spastically back and forth.

Shake-shake-shake-shake-shake-shake-shake! Right in front of my face! And I couldn't do anything about it. What was happening?!

Peace. Then came peace. Peace and tranquility. And vivid color. All around me was green grass. I was in a wooded area with birds and other animals around me. Then, in my mind, I was playing tennis on a grass tennis court in the middle of these woods against an IP. There was a black chain-link fence around the grass court so we never had to chase the balls into the woods. I was very relaxed, and even though I'm not that good at tennis, I was playing pretty well. The woodland animals watching us from the bushes around the court seemed to be enjoying both nature and our tennis match.

"Lieutenant Wright! Lieutenant Wright!"

I heard Lieutenant Wilson calling from far away in my head. The tennis match was over.

Feeling like I'd just scraped myself up off of the mat of a boxing ring, I had to shake out the cobwebs before I could answer him. After a few moments, my head finally started to clear. I could answer.

"Did you see that?!" I asked Lieutenant Wilson, realizing I was back in the cockpit with him and flying my training mission. "Did you see that?! Did you see my hands?! And my arms? They went like this." I held up my hands in front of my face and shook them violently. "What was that?"

"Yeah, I saw it. That's called the Funky Chicken. You were unconscious for a few seconds," Lieutenant Wilson said. "You G-LOC'd," he said. G-LOC is an Air Force acronym for gravity-induced loss of consciousness.

I got very anxious all of a sudden.

What good is a pilot who can't stay conscious during a loop?

"You okay now?" Lieutenant Wilson asked. He told me to finish any water I had left in my water bottle. I reached down to get it from the pocket of my flight suit leg, suspiciously, careful not to lower my head as I did.

I dropped my mask to take a few gulps of water, and then, realizing that I hadn't yet answered his question, I said, "Yes, sir. I'm okay. I was playing tennis with one of the Dagger IPs. We were on a grass court."

"Yeah, we can talk about that after we get back. Don't mention this to anybody before we've had a chance to debrief the ride first," he advised. "Do you think you're okay to fly a few patterns when we get back to the base?"

"Yes, sir," I replied. I still had some anxiety, but otherwise, I was feeling okay again after a few sips of water and a little time to get my wits about me.

"I'll get us started on the recovery," Lieutenant Wilson told me. "Take a minute or two, and let me know when you're ready to fly."

"Yes, sir," I acknowledged. Finishing my water, I turned my checklist and in-flight guide to the right pages for a descent from the area and recovery to the T-37 traffic pattern on the inside runway, Sunfish. I looked outside for the river, which I knew would lead me to the base.

After we had landed, we didn't go straight back to the Dagger flight room. Instead, Lieutenant Wilson called me into the Warhawks' empty flight room at the other end of the hallway in the T-37 squadron. Because we were following a late week schedule, the Warhawks were on early week, and they must have already finished their flying ops for the day. Lieutenant Wilson pointed me toward the back of the room. It just so happened to be the hardest desk to see for anyone who might be walking past the door to the flight room.

Sitting on the instructor's side of the desk, Lieutenant Wilson grabbed the black three-ring binder that held the flying manual for the T-37 that pilots called the Dash One.

"Read this," he instructed, spinning the book around so that I could read it. "I'm going to go get a Coke while you do. Do you want a Coke?"

"Yes, sir," I said, reaching for my wallet.

"I got this one," he said, pushing the Dash One over to my side of the desk. He had opened it to the section that stated the procedure to be followed when a student experiences a G-induced loss of consciousness while flying.

The key phrases of the passage he had me read included the following: *immediate change in flight status to Duty Not Including Flying for a period of six months...suspension from Undergraduate Pilot Training...evaluation by a flight surgeon...*and *successful demonstration of the L-1 anti-G straining maneuver required for reinstatement.*

That feeling of anxiety was growing again. It seemed like I had just read that I was about to be removed from UPT only three rides into the program.

Sandy Benning had been automatically grounded the day she passed out during a safety briefing. Was I about to be automatically grounded for six months? Did I have a problem with G-forces that was going to keep me from becoming a pilot?

"If you understand what that section of the Dash One says," Lieutenant Wilson said kind of quietly as he returned from the snack bar with a couple of Cokes, "then you understand why neither one of us is going to mention what happened out there in the area to anyone. You follow?"

"Yes, sir," I acknowledged as he handed me my drink.

"I don't think what happened would have happened if I didn't pull a loop while your head was pinned to your chest," he said. "I set you up, and I probably shouldn't have done that."

I was pretty relieved that I wasn't about to be grounded for six months, but I couldn't shake the anxiety. What if I was prone to G-LOC? What if I G-LOC'd on a solo ride one day, and no one was with me to take control of the jet?

"Get into the habit of doing sit-ups every day," Lieutenant Wilson advised. "The tighter you can squeeze your stomach muscles, the longer you can keep the blood up in your brain." His arm swept across the desk. "C'mon, let's head back to Dagger," he said. "We don't want anyone to wonder what we're doing in the Warhawk room."

As I put the Dash One back behind the desk, I found a half-eaten sandwich and an opened bag of chips on a paper plate. "We could always say that we were checking to see if the Warhawk flight room was as clean as Dagger," I said. "Look at this." I held up the paper plate with the half-eaten sandwich and opened bag of chips.

"Captain Wright would like that," Lieutenant Wilson smiled, and we headed back to Dagger.

I started incorporating a hundred sit-ups into my morning routine before a shower, and although I continued to struggle with G-forces in the Tweet, I didn't G-LOC again. I hadn't puked yet, either, but not puking was getting easier...not G-LOC'ing wasn't.

I tightened up my stomach muscles and fought to keep blood flowing through my brain whenever I felt my body's weight multiplied by high-G maneuvering, but it was always a battle. There had to be others in the class who were having similar challenges, but I didn't want to say anything, because if word got out that I'd G-LOC'ed....

I wouldn't be shit.

*

A couple of rides and several hundred sit-ups later, I faced my next big challenge, a simulator ride designed to test a student's knowledge of the T-37 emergency procedures. The formal nickname for the mission was EP sim. The informal nickname was Dial-a-Death.

Lucky me, mine was scheduled with the Dagger flight commander.

I sat with Kenny at Lieutenant Wilson's desk, waiting to be called back into the IPs' briefing room to brief up our mission.

"Lieutenant Wilson," I said, "I brought something to put under the plastic on our side of your desk. Did you want to check it out first?"

"Sure, what have you got?" Lieutenant Wilson asked.

"Well, sir, just as flying inspired John Gillespie Magee, Jr., to write the 'High Flight' sonnet, my first several UPT rides have inspired me to verse, as well."

As I spoke, Lieutenant Wilson pulled his chair as close as he could get it to his side of the desk, leaning over to get a better look.

"Unlike 'High Flight,' which is a celebration of the beauty and freedom of flight, my poem is more a coming-of-age work...from being the one along for the ride to being the one who actually controls the ride. It's about that moment of epiphany when you find yourself taking charge of things."

Lieutenant Wilson nodded. "Sounds like this might have some potential. Let's hear it."

I unzipped one of the front chest pockets of my flight suit and pulled out a 3-by-5 index card. Then, I recited my work:

"Transfer of Control" by Raymond John Wright

Transfer of control
The shaker is the taker
I have the aircraft

I paused for a moment and reflected on these words before looking up. I looked at Kenny first, who smiled widely. Then I looked across the desk at Lieutenant Wilson, who sat quietly with a puzzled look on his face.

"Sir, would you like me to recite it again?" I asked.

"Is that it? Isn't there more?" Lieutenant Wilson wanted to know, still puzzled. "I'm no poet, but I'm pretty sure 'High Flight' is a little longer than that."

"Sir, that's it. My poem, 'Transfer of Control,' is written in the form of Japanese haiku." I replied, matter-of-factly. "Since 'High Flight' is a sonnet, I chose to write my work using another form of poetry. I didn't want my work to come off as being a rip-off of 'High Flight' so I wrote it as haiku."

"Haiku? That's really a kind of poetry?" Lieutenant Wilson questioned.

"Yes, sir," I answered. "Five syllables in the first line. Seven in the second. Five in the third. It's the imagery—not the words—that tells the story, and I think this is certainly the case with 'Transfer of Control.' I think it's one of my best works. *I have the aircraft.* It's powerful imagery."

"I don't get it," Lieutenant Wilson replied.

"Sir, in 'Transfer of Control,' the taker character is someone who has not been in control. For whatever reason, someone or something else is in control. This is not to say that the taker is necessarily out of control, but clearly, prior to taking control, the taker has not had control. Only when the taker shakes, an action of change, does the taker take control and no longer *not* have control. I think it's as powerful an ending as the last line of 'High Flight.' Don't you agree?"

"Not really," Lieutenant Wilson said.

After a comfortably awkward moment, he pushed his chair back from his desk and stood up to look over the day's schedule one more time. Satisfied that the schedule looked good, he turned back to me, and grinning widely, he threw out one last thought on my poem, "Go ahead and slide your haiku under your side of the plastic," he said. "When you come back as a FAIP, it can be the centerpiece of the things on your desk."

Now, I was the one who didn't quite know what to say. I wanted to fly a C-141 and be based in Charleston, South Carolina. I didn't want to be a FAIP. I couldn't say that to Lieutenant Wilson because he was a FAIP, and it might come across like me saying, "Your job really sucks." That wouldn't be cool. So, I decided it would be best to let my IP have the last laugh.

As I slid in the new classic under the protective plastic on my instructor's desktop, Captain Wright stepped into the doorway behind Lieutenant Wilson's left side.

"Lieutenant Wright, grab your gradebook and a blank **BOLDFACE** sheet, and bring them to my desk in the IP briefing room. It's time to start briefing up your EP sim," the Dagger flight commander ordered.

"Yes, sir," I said, having stood up as soon as he called out my name.

The poems and pictures under the layer of clear plastic on Captain Wright's desk were only slightly different from those on Lieutenant Wilson's desk. Captain Wright had his copy of "High Flight" and the decorated dollars that his students had given him over the years. Instead of pictures of A-10s, though, Captain Wright had pictures of F-15s. He also had a photograph of a woman that looked like it had been taken in a studio.

"Sir, is this Mrs. Captain Wright?" I asked.

"Yes, Lieutenant Wright. That's my wife, Tina. Maybe you'll get to meet her...maybe you won't, but right now, we need to brief up your EP sim." Captain Wright wasn't going to let me distract him from our mission.

Captain Wright had me write out all of the T-37 **BOLDFACE** procedures and fill out all of the operating limits for the aircraft's performance indicators, like oil pressure, hydraulic pressure, exhaust gas temperature, etc. In my EP sim, I would be tested on every type of aircraft malfunction.

In our pre-brief, I was treated to a number of Captain Wright's best soliloquies:

- You might have heard of the three rules of flying. You might not.
- You might have heard the three most useless things to a pilot. You might not.
- You might have done some civilian flying. You might not.

"Remember, Lieutenant Wright," Captain Wright reiterated, "airplanes don't just fall out of the sky when there are problems. The laws of physics do not change, and you must keep air flowing under your wings. Aviate. Navigate. Communicate," he said.

"When things don't go as planned," Captain Wright continued, "you have got to break the downward spiraling chain of events. Maintain aircraft control. Analyze the situation, and take the proper action by executing your **BOLDFACE** procedures and getting into your checklist. If you do not recognize the downward spiral and take the appropriate action to break that chain of events, you will find yourself in a world of trouble and end up in a smoking hole in the ground."

*

"Aaay. How was your EP sim with Captain Wright?" Kenny asked, having showered, thrown on shorts and a t-shirt, and joined me in our playhouse room on the very soft and comfortable brown velour sofa-love-seat sectional.

A bunch of guys from our class were going to the buffet at Quincy's, Home of the Big Fat Yeast Roll. Doley was going to drive over to our house and give us a ride.

"It went fine," I said. "I didn't miss any **BOLDFACE**, and I only did one thing that was pretty stupid."

"Aaay, what?" Kenny was laughing already.

"Well, after we had done about a bunch of takeoff emergencies, like low-speed tire failure and low-speed engine failure, that resulted in my aborting, I aborted a takeoff for a perfectly good aircraft," I admitted.

"Why did you do that?"

"Because when I hit 90 knots on takeoff roll, the aircraft was still on the ground. We should have been airborne, and I thought there was a problem. So, I aborted. Captain Wright laughed for about five minutes before he could even talk," I said. "Then, he told me that in order to make the aircraft fly, I needed to pull back on the stick."

Kenny agreed that that was both stupid and funny.

"Oh, it got even better from there," I confessed, "because I think I've given Captain Wright a new monologue."

I got up from my comfortable section of the sectional. I thought I could get into character better if I were standing up. I half-closed my eyes, turned down the corners of my mouth while trying to smile at the same time, and starting scanning the room back and forth.

"Lieutenant Wright, you might know this...you might not," I mocked, "but when you fly a jet, you have to pull back on the stick to make the houses get smaller."

I don't know which Kenny thought was funnier, my Captain Wright imitation or the fact that I tried to drive a jet like a car and aborted my takeoff when the jet didn't fly.

A few minutes of performing some more Captain Wrightisms for Kenny inspired me to start work on another UPT poem. This one—a rap, using the same rhythm and pace as Run-DMC's "King of Rock."

When Doley came by, we told him the plan. Instead of hitting the Home of the Big Fat Yeast Roll, we stayed in and worked on our rap. Dagger flight would never be the same.

*

The double-doors leading into the flight room were closed. The formal report had begun, and Kenny, Doley, and I were locked out. All part of the plan.

Kenny knocked softly on the single door that led to the Dagger IP briefing room to let Lieutenant Wilson know that we were outside.

"Hey! You guys ready? You're up," Lieutenant Wilson said, in on the plan.

"Good morning," I could hear the Dagger safety officer at the front of the room. "Please join me in welcoming to the Dagger flight room...*Funky Chicken!*"

That was our cue.

Kenny, Doley, and I busted out of the Dagger IP briefing room in our cadet raincoats, berets, and aviator glasses and took our positions at the front of the room. I stood on stage left, Doley on stage right, and Kenny stood in the middle, slightly behind us. We took a moment to pose with our arms folded to let the laughter and applause die down. Then, Kenny lifted the clear desktop plastic off the table at the front of the room, scratched a few "wiki-wiki, wiki-wiki, wiki-wiki-wikis," and the three of us rocked the house...

(Kenny, scratching:) *Wiki-wiki, wiki-wiki, wiki-wiki-wiki*
(Me:) *I'm Captain Wright*
            (Doley:) *from Dagga flight!*
     You might not know me,
                    but maybe you might!
I got a wife
            named Tina.
My assistant

is Peena.
I tell the Warhawks
that my flight room is cleanah.

Wiki-wiki, wiki-wiki, wiki-wiki-wiki
I got three rules of flying
that you should know.
You should take them with you
wherevah you go.
Have fun!
Yes! Yes!
Don't panic!
No! No!
And always sound cool
on the radio!

Wiki-wiki, wiki-wiki, wiki-wiki-wiki
Some say the best things in life
ah free!
But no, you will never hear that
from me.
Don't believe everything
that ya' told.
The best kind of beer's not free...
It's cold!

Wiki-wiki, wiki-wiki, wiki-wiki-wiki
The training in Dagger
is the best in the land,
And all my IPs
ah picked by hand.
I'm Captain Wright
from Dagga flight
You might not know me,
but maybe you might!

When we finished, the three of us folded our arms and posed. We stood still until the laughing and screaming stopped. There was nothing formal left of the morning's formal report. Captain Wright couldn't even stop laughing long enough to direct Mark Jellicot to call the room to attention. Finally, he just pointed at Mark and waved for us to stand.

Mark saluted smartly and exclaimed, "Sir, Class 88-07, ready to fly."

Having spent my night working on a rap instead of studying, I wasn't so sure.

Chapter 9 — "The Dream We All Dream Of"

"Tweet 2-0, closed downwind," Kurt reported his jet's position.

"That's right," Chuck said.

The Friday morning of the Tin Foil Ball Party, we sat in the Dagger flight room, practicing our traffic pattern radio calls around the center table as an afternoon thunderstorm interrupted the flying schedule. Chuck moved the plastic toy model of the T-37 to another point on the table-sized drawing Kurt had made of the Sunfish overhead traffic pattern.

"Kenny, how about here? What's your radio call?" Chuck asked, flying the plastic model Tweet to a stop.

"Tweet 2-0, closed downwind," Kenny said.

"DIS-re-gaaaaaaahd!" Doley called out.

"Doley, shut up!" Kenny quickly shot back.

"Disregahd *Doley, shut up*," Doley rejected Kenny's directive.

Whenever student pilots said the wrong thing on the radio, our instructors would immediately broadcast, "Disregard," to alert those using the frequency to ignore our improper radio call. Some instructors simply stated, "Disregard," followed by the right words, but others interjected varying degrees of disdain into their "Disregard" to reinforce that all-important credo: Students ain't shit.

"Aaay, Kurt's call was right," Kenny said to all of us. "I said what he said."

Chuck moved the plastic model back to where it was moments earlier when she'd asked Kurt. "Kenny, over here is closed downwind." Then, moving the toy Tweet back to the spot about which she'd just asked Kenny: "But here—at the perch point—your radio call is *Tweet 2-0, gear down.*"

The Sunfish overhead traffic pattern had a lot of rules. Not only was it a very busy and crowded place, but because pattern altitude was just one thousand feet above ground level, the environment left very little margin for error. The rules helped keep Sunfish safe, and proper radio calls were a big part of the rules.

"Aaay, my bad," Kenny acknowledged. "Tweet 2-0, gear down."

"You got it," Chuck said.

Kurt's drawing of the Sunfish overhead traffic pattern looked like a giant paper clip with a very wide outer loop. In the pattern, jets flew around the outer loop of the paper clip at an airspeed of 200 knots and used the inner loop of the paper clip to slow down and configure the jet for landing by lowering the landing gear and the wing flaps before making a diving turn to land. At the takeoff end of the runway, jets had the option to turn crosswind and fly around the outer loop or request a closed pattern from the Sunfish controller to proceed directly into the inner loop, saving time and gas and allowing for more touch-and-go attempts.

Chuck moved the model Tweet to the far end of the runway on Kurt's drawing. "Doley, if you've just done a touch-and-go and you don't want to fly all the way around the outer edge of the pattern, what's your call?" she asked.

"Tweet 2-0, request closed," Doley said.

"You got it," Chuck nodded.

If the Sunfish controller said, "Closed approved," you could fly your jet around the inner loop of the paper clip only, bypassing the trip around the larger, outside loop. But if the Sunfish controller said, "Negative closed," you'd have to fly your jet around the outer loop of the paper clip, over the top of the runway, and then make a 180-degree turn over the top of the runway—assuming you were clear to do so—in order to get to your perch point for your final turning dive to a landing.

The job of Sunfish controller was performed in three-hour shifts by instructor pilots who sat in a small, glass box in the grass one thousand feet beyond the approach end of the Sunfish runway. From the Sunfish box, the IP serving as the Sunfish controller observed the Sunfish pattern, monitored the Sunfish radio calls, and enforced the Sunfish rules to ensure safe and orderly Sunfish air traffic. At the center table, Chuck was playing the role of both controller and instructor.

"What if you didn't fly a closed and had to fly all around the pattern, Doley," Chuck began, moving her plastic Tweet around the outer loop of Kurt's drawing until the jet once again lined up with the runway, "and you got to this point. What would be your call?"

"Tweet 2-0, initial," Doley said.

"You got it," Chuck smiled.

"Chuck, you know your stuff," Kurt observed.

"Hey, you guys are getting it, too," she replied.

"Ray, you've just done a touch-and-go," Chuck continued, "and you want to request a closed pattern, because you don't want to fly all the way around the outer loop. You just heard the call Doley made. What do you do?"

"Tweet 2-0, request closed," I answered.

"Dis-REEEE-gaahd!" Doley called out, now emphasizing the middle of the word.

"I am going to disregard that disregard," I said. "Besides, your first one sounded better."

"Ray, you can't request a closed right after somebody reports initial," Chuck reminded me. "You have a conflict, and you have to turn crosswind."

"Then, that was a trick question," I rebutted.

"Dis-re-GAAAAAAAHD!" Doley said again, now dragging out the last syllable. "You gotta know if someone calls initial, you can't request a closed."

"Oh," I said. I didn't really understanding all the Sunfish rules yet.

"Aaay, flying was a lot easier when all we had to say was Barn-with-the-numbers," Kenny remarked in reference to an obscure ground reference used in the T-41 flight-screening program at the Academy.

"I never did see the numbers," I joked. As a cadet, I looked for the numbers painted on the roof of the stupid barn every time I flew over it—not knowing what I didn't know.

"Ray, my T-41 IP was one of the highest-ranking guys at the Academy," Doley said. "Ev'ry ride, I would call, *Falcon Zero-One, Bahn-with-the-numbahs,* when we flew ova Bahn-with-the-numbahs, and ev'ry ride, my IP would say, *We don't have the numbahs.*"

Doley paused and flashed a huge smile.

"*What numbahs?!*" he cried out and threw his hands up in despair.

Saying the phrase *with the numbers* on the radio meant that you already knew certain information that the person on the other end of your radio call might be required to recite if you did not report to him that you had the numbers. The numbers referred to the active runway, the prevailing winds, and the current altimeter setting. If you added the phrase *with the numbers* to your radio call, that told the air traffic controller that he didn't need to provide this information to you. If you didn't say *with the numbers,* the controller would have to recite all the numbers. The problem was, however, that for a lot of cadets in the T-41 program, radio calls were just words you had to say, and sometimes, we learned to say the words before we ever really knew what the words were supposed to mean, like memorizing prayers in church as a kid.

"Ray and Kenny, I can't make your Tin Foil Ball Party tonight," Kurt confessed suddenly.

"*DIS*-re-gaaaaaaaahd!" Doley said.

"That one sounds best," I told Doley.

"Kurt, what the hell?!" Kenny asked.

"Malia is graduating from her training class in Biloxi. I'm going to drive down tonight after dismissal, go to the ceremony, and bring her back home this weekend," Kurt told us.

"Cool!" Chuck said.

"Does that mean you got out of the stupid FOD walk?" I asked.

"Yeah, I don't have to go to the FOD walk tomorrow," Kurt acknowledged.

"*DIS*-re-gaaaaaaaahd!" Doley said.

*

The house was looking pretty good. Our vintage Pepsi machine was fully stocked with long-neck bottles of beer. Our caution-orange vintage refrigerator was fully stocked with ice-cold cans of beer. We displayed the Colt 45 Malt Liquor bottles on the mantle of the fireplace because they wouldn't fit in the Pepsi machine, and they didn't stack as easily as cans stacked in the fridge. They'd have to stay warm for now. We lined up other liquor on the mantle, too.

Mark Jellicot was going to bring over his jam box, through which we could pump the two hours of music videos I'd recorded from the show *Night Tracks* on TBS. Music videos on MTV would have been ideal, but the owners of Columbus TV Cable did not offer MTV in their ten channel line-up because they thought MTV was a bad influence on teenagers. We were in the heart of the Bible Belt after all.

We put all of our pink lawn flamingos on display in our big room. Kenny set the starter ball of foil up on the mantle next to the line of Colt 45 bottles, then fed the ants and the fish before either of us realized that we didn't have any food for our party guests. We would just have to order Domino's.

Just about everybody in our section of the class said they were coming to our party…except Kurt. Some of the guys from the Warhawk section of the class said they might show up, but a few of them said they needed to study. *Really? All we ever did was study.* We also invited our IPs from Dagger and Class Commander Lieutenant Billy Mike Sims. The ticket into the house—everyone had to bring tin foil.

Mark Jellicot was the first to show. He didn't bring his wife, but he did bring his jam box. "I couldn't find any tin foil at the commissary. I hope it's okay that I brought aluminum foil," he said to Kenny, offering him an entire roll of aluminum foil.

Kenny grabbed it and immediately started wrapping it around the tiny piece of foil I had given him from a grilled cheese sandwich I'd bought. "Aaay, 'dis *is* tin foil. Tanks."

"I brought my copy of *Top Gun,* too," Mark added. "I didn't want to leave it outside because it might get too hot in the car, and I don't want my tape to melt. So I brought it in…in case we wanted to watch it."

Fortunately, Doley showed up next with a new cassette that he wanted us to play, Prince's *Sign 'o' the Times.* I knew a couple of the songs from the radio, and I liked the song, "U Got the Look." It happened to be one of the music videos I'd recorded for the party off of *Night Tracks* on TBS. Of course, Doley also brought a roll of tin foil, which Kenny immediately took to add to his now softball-sized foil ball.

Chuck brought her blender, a bottle of tequila, and a carton of eggs for making her special marguerites. She also brought a roll of tin foil. UPT's kindest soul, the once-skinny Stan Melton, apologized for not bringing any tin foil. He had stopped by the commissary at the base on his way home, but apparently they were all out of both tin foil and aluminum foil, so he picked up a few bags of pork rinds for the party, one of which looked as if it had already been opened.

Kenny's foil ball grew pretty quickly until it got to be about volleyball size. Then, it slowed down…a lot! Kenny would add a whole roll at a time, but the foil ball barely looked like it got any bigger, whereas Pee-wee Herman's foil ball was so big, it stood higher than Pee-wee's waist. He couldn't carry it and had to roll it across the playhouse floor.

In no time, the party was packed with people. Except for Stan, who did bring pork rinds, everybody brought a roll of tin foil. Well, the Domino's Pizza delivery guy didn't bring any foil, but he did bring pizza, and he did join us for a shot of rum at Kenny's insistence; Kenny had found out he was from Jamaica.

The cops didn't bring any tin foil either. The first time they came, about ten-thirty, they were responding to complaints from our neighbors that people were urinating in their yards. I invited the cops in and assured them that we neither encouraged nor supported this type of behavior. Even though we'd never mowed our lawn or asked our guests to not to park in front of other peoples' houses in the cul-de-sac, which is where I figured people were peeing, I told the cops that we tried to be good neighbors and that we would speak to our guests about respecting others' properties.

The second time the cops showed up was just after midnight. They had just gotten off duty, and we let them in without any tin foil.

After the fourth bottle, I stopped counting how many cracked long-neck beers I drank for guests that complained their bottles from the Pepsi machine were broken. I had to slow my drinking pace in the middle of the party and eat some pizza and pork rinds, after I made the mistake of yelling, "Goldfish Frenzy!" and reaching into Kenny's tank to scoop out and swallow one of his new goldfish as it swam innocently around the tank on the mantle. Within about fifteen seconds after I'd declared, "Goldfish Frenzy," all of the cute and innocent playhouse goldfish had been scooped out of the tank and eaten alive.

Unexpectedly, the highlight of the party was the new drinking game "Clothesline" that evolved during the viewing of a video on Japanese lady wrestling's greatest grudge matches.

Whenever one lady wrestler was whipped off the ropes of the wrestling ring and then clotheslined and slammed to the mat by an outstretched arm across the neck from her opponent, everyone had to drink. This was a great game—made even better by my *Dana Dana with Fame* cassette blasting through Mark Jellicot's jam box in the background.

I don't know what time the party broke up, but like most parties, when the beer ran out, and the music stopped, the party was over. The fridge was empty, the Pepsi machine was empty, and any coolers people brought with them were empty. The pizza, the pork rinds, and the goldfish were all gone—as was most of the rest of our food. We even drank the warm bottles of Colt 45 Malt Liquor that were up on the mantle. I didn't know if Captain Wright had biased me against warm beer or if Colt 45 just sucked, but drinking them may have been my biggest mistake of the night.

*

To begin our FOD walk, Lieutenant Billy Mike Sims lined up the students from both sections of our class side by side at the northeast end of the 12,000 foot long center runway. He had us spread our arms and fan out sideways so the whole class stretched across the 300 foot wide concrete surface from one edge to the other in one long, human chain. For the most part, the Warhawk students stuck to the left-hand side of the chain, and the Dagger students stayed to the right.

Lieutenant Billy Mike had to inspect the ranks before he'd let us put our arms down. To me, the whole scene looked like we were going for a *Guinness Book of World Records* entry for the world's largest game of Red Rover.

"Red Rover! Red Rover! Send Kurtie right over!" I yelled to the other end of the runway once Lieutenant Billy Mike was out of earshot. I still felt drunk from our Tin Foil Ball Party.

"Aaay." Kenny could picture this, too—Kurt speeding from the other side. I was fingertip to fingertip with Kenny on my left. Doley was on my right.

"Do you think anything could stop Kurt?" I asked my friends.

"Impossible," Doley answered quickly and definitively. "Kurt cannot be stopped."

"I suppose it could happen," I speculated, trying to suppress the urge to purge, "especially if Kurt were to slip in the puddle of liquid FOD that I'm about to hurl onto this runway."

"Colt 45 Malt Liquah," Doley admonished, "I saw you drink it. What the hell were you thinkin'? Liquid headache!"

"I don't think thinking had a whole lot to do with much of anything I did last night," I replied to Doley in a low and scratchy voice.

Suddenly, I remembered that I owed Kenny an apology.

"Kenny, I'm sorry about your goldfish," I told him.

"Aaay," Kenny shrugged. "We weren't dat close."

"I forgot to record Pee-wee, too," I admitted.

"You dumb bastid," Kenny scolded me about that.

Lieutenant Billy Mike gave the order to lower our arms, followed by the order to begin walking forward. Side by side, each about six feet apart, all Dagger and Warhawk student pilots stretched across the three hundred foot wide center runway and slowly walked together for twelve thousand feet, looking to identify objects, O, so that they would not be foreign objects, FO, that might possibly cause damage, FOD, if sucked into a jet engine.

Our Saturday morning FOD walk seemed like one never-ending IP joke.

The IPs had an entire You Ain't a Pilot playbook of practical jokes. Some were funny. Some...not so much. The more memorable jokes included the following.

The Look-Down-While-I-Drain-The-Blood-From-Your-Brain-With-G-Forces Joke: Of course, I had fallen for this classic at the hands of Lieutenant Wilson.

The Call-The-Crew-Bus Joke: Stan Melton, my baby-faced and once-skinny friend from Alabama, had been duped by his IP, Lieutenant Peena, into believing that the audio jack at the helmet cleaning station in the chute shop was actually connected to a live radio frequency that students needed to use to call the flight line van.

At the direction of Lieutenant Peena, Stan stood at the front of the chute shop, wearing his big white helmet, calling into his oxygen mask, "Crew Bus, Crew Bus!" Of course, nobody responded to the radio call because the only personnel who could hear Stan's transmission was Stan and anyone else in the chute shop who either worked there, were coming in from flying, or were heading out to fly. The longer and louder Stan called...the harder the IPs laughed.

The Watch-My-Student-Blow-A-Jet Joke: When checking the pitot tube, the long, protrusion that sticks straight out from the nose of the Tweet, you were supposed to make sure that the canvas cover had been removed and that the pitot tube, itself, wasn't blocked by debris, like dirt or bugs. That's about it. Lieutenant Peena, however, had convinced Stan (again) that he needed to wrap his lips around the pitot tube and blow into it for an extended period of time. This joke was just plain sadistic.

The When-You-Come-Back-As-A-FAIP Joke: I think this was the cruelest joke of them all. Have me transmit a radio call on a radio frequency that doesn't exist. Send me on a snipe hunt for birds or cockpit blindfolds. I didn't really care that much if I was the butt of a good joke — especially if it was funny. I don't think Lieutenant Wilson intended to drain the blood from my head until I passed out the first time we flew together; I think he just wanted to pin my head down with the G's. If I hadn't actually passed out, that joke might have been funny, too. As for the Blow-A-Jet Joke,

I think that said more about the character of the instructor than it said about the student.

The When-You-Come-Back-As-A-FAIP Joke was different from all the rest. The purpose of all the other jokes was to make the students look like total idiots, and when it came to flying, most of us were. As Academy cadets, every one of us except Mark Jellicot and Al Turbiglio had been trained in the fourth-class system, where we were treated like idiots for a year by the upperclassmen. Being students in UPT—with its *If you ain't a pilot...you ain't shit* mentality—wasn't really so different from being Academy freshmen.

We had all been indoctrinated into believing that Air Force officers are officers first and pilots second. But if that were true, why did student officers and IP officers wear different uniforms in UPT? If that were true, why would one officer fool another officer into simulating a sex act on a Tweet?

The purpose of the *When-You-Come-Back-As-A-FAIP Joke* was about more than making students look stupid. It was about denying us our dreams...taking away our aspirations to travel the world and fight Communism...making us feel like UPT was an unwinnable scenario, the Air Force's version of *Star Trek's* Kobayashi Maru.

At the Academy, no one ever mentioned that being an IP was even a possible first flying assignment. The conventional wisdom was that if you did well in UPT, you would fly a fighter, and if you sucked in UPT, you would get stuck with a tanker or a bomber, but you still got to be a pilot and travel around the world. Now, as student pilots, the picture was becoming clearer and clearer about how we would be categorized and what these categories meant for our flying futures, and the clearer the picture got, the longer the odds seemed that I'd get my C-141 on a beach.

Students with a ranking in the top half of class would most likely be tagged as FAR: considered for **F**ighter, **A**ttack, or **R**econnaissance aircraft. The bottom half of the class would be tagged as TTB—assigned to Tanker, Transport, or Bomber aircraft. Most FAR aircraft were single-seat cockpits, and most TTB aircraft required an entire crew to fly. This meant that students at the bottom half of the class would spend time as co-pilots, learning, training, and flying under the guise of experienced first pilots for at least another year before shaking the stick and really taking control of their own aircraft. Put even more plainly, they'd get another year of help learning to fly.

So the math we were all doing in our heads as we combed the runway looking for FOD went like this: If our class followed the statistical norm, roughly thirty-three of the forty-eight of us who started together would graduate. Al and the three Guard guys and the one Guard woman in the Warhawk section already knew their next assignments before they got to UPT, which was true of all Guard and Reserve student pilots at all UPT bases. That is, they would fly whatever aircraft were assigned to their home units in the Air Force Reserves or National Guard. That left twenty-nine of us to compete against one another for the rest of our class's *drop,* the term used to describe the combination of fighter, attack, reconnaissance, trainer, tanker, transport, and bomber aircraft and the bases at which these aircraft were stationed, as deemed to be available by the Air Force Personnel Center, located somewhere in Texas.

We would all learn our Air Force fates on Assignment Night in June, about six weeks before our scheduled graduation in July. I imagined the pre–Assignment Night pep talk that might come from our wing commander. "Look to your left. Now, look to your right," he'd begin in his Texas twang, pointing the antenna of his walkie-talkie at us and drilling his eyes into the backs of our heads to see if we might be the next asshole to get a DUI. "One of the people you just looked at will become a FAIP tonight, and all but four or five of y'all are gonna get screwed."

In exchange for the privilege of wearing the silver wings of Air Force pilots on our chests, we were in a year-long training process. Dreaming what might come after…that was a lot of fun. Beginning to realize what probably would be…this was kind of unnerving. It kind of sucked, actually, and that's why I felt that the *When-You-Come-Back-As-A-FAIP Joke* and its corollary, the *You-Might-As-Well-Buy-A-Boat-Now Joke,* were the cruelest in the IPs' joke book.

*

"Sire 3-3, initial," I radioed as I rolled out of my turn at 200 knots and a little beyond the centerline of Sunfish, the T-37 runway, which on this day was landing to the northeast, opposite to the direction we walked on our FOD walk.

The "Sire" part of my call sign told the Sunfish controller, the IP sitting in the small, glass box in the grass off to the side of the runway, the other Tweets in the pattern, and the Supervisor of Flying back in the building, all of whom were tuned into the Sunfish radio frequency, that I was a solo student. As I made my call, I corrected my course so that I'd fly my jet right over the top of the runway. Aviate. Navigate. Communicate.

I had just taken off a few minutes earlier and made my first full trip around the traffic pattern.

"Winds are 2–7–0 at 10-gust-to-14. Trends are becoming overshooting finals," the Sunfish controller stated.

In ensuring that the traffic pattern ran safely and smoothly, the "trends" part of Sunfish controller's radio call told me that he saw me miscalculate my turn to initial, that there was a strong crosswind, and that students, like me, weren't making the proper wind adjustments to their overhead patterns. *Are becoming* meant he didn't want incriminate his fellow instructors; IPs were not supposed to allow their students to overshoot the runway.

I had just completed a trip around the outer loop of the traffic pattern. Trouble was—the controller had just previously approved a closed pattern for another jet. This meant that as I flew above the runway, looking to turn into the smaller loop of the paper clip, there had to be a jet off to my left that was already there, flying in the opposite direction.

No problem, though, because I knew what to do: Once I spotted my conflict, the jet on inside downwind, I would wait until it was exactly abeam to my position on my left before I initiated my break, the 180-degree turn I would use to dissipate my speed, reverse my direction, and establish my spacing from the runway so that once I lowered my landing gear and flaps, I could roll off the perch, the point at which I'd begin my descent from pattern altitude for my final turn and landing approach. If the jet on inside downwind didn't pass exactly abeam to my position on my left by the time I'd flown three thousand feet down the runway, about halfway down Sunfish, I'd make the radio call, "Breakpoint, straight through." I'd make another trip around the traffic pattern, unless the controller said, "Straight through, you're cleared to break."

As I flew up initial, I spotted my conflict on inside downwind at eleven o'clock on my left, just like I knew he'd be there. Now, if he weren't abeam me by the time I flew halfway down the runway, I'd make the call, "Breakpoint, straight through." I didn't want to get too cocky, but I was feeling like I almost knew what I was doing…almost like a pilot.

I was going to fly a great pattern, and I would plan my break so that I'd get good spacing for my inside downwind leg, and I wouldn't overshoot my final turn.

"Overhead, break departure end. Acknowledge." It was Sunfish, the controller.

Who was he talking to?

I was flying over the box, and there was someone below me who was now at the departure end of the runway on takeoff leg, having just performed a touch-and-go. With me flying up initial, the takeoff leg at the departure end could not request a closed pattern until I'd started my break.

Was he talking to me?

According to the rules of the pattern, I was next into the inner loop, but until the jet on inside downwind passed off to my immediate left, I could not start my break into the inner loop, because the jet on my left had the right of way over me, and he was just now at my ten o'clock. I needed him to be at my nine o'clock.

Was that radio call for me?

I had a conflict, and the pattern had two. Both the takeoff leg and I were going to have to fly all the way around the traffic pattern because the guy on inside downwind had slowed down to drop his landing gear too far away from the perch point, and now, he was jamming up the pattern. But was the controller trying to tell me to initiate my break so that the jet that had just flown the touch-and-go could request a closed pattern? Was he saying, "Overhead, you break, and departure end, you acknowledge," and wait to ask for a closed pattern until I broke? If that was the case, both the touch-and-go and I would be able to squeeze in a pattern and a landing without having to go around the box again, and all of the conflicts would be resolved.

What did that call mean?

I didn't know. I had never heard that radio call before. We hadn't studied it in class, I hadn't practiced it with my friends around the center table, and I had never heard it used before in the pattern.

The guy on inside downwind still wasn't at my nine o'clock or 90 degrees off to my left, even though we were getting closer. Because he already had his landing gear and flaps down, he had to be going a lot slower than my 200 knots. It was taking way too long for our jets to pass one another. I was just about halfway down the length of the runway. I was going to have to call, "Breakpoint, straight through."

"OVERHEAD, BREAK DEPARTURE END, ACKNOWLEDGE," the controller said again only a few seconds after he'd said it the first time.

I still had no idea what this radio call was all about, but since nobody had answered, and I was the only solo student in the traffic pattern (as no one else was using a "Sire" call sign), he had to have been talking to me. I just didn't know what action he wanted.

Maybe he was trying to prevent both of us from flying all the way around the traffic pattern box again without completing a touch-and-go.

"Sire 3-3," I acknowledged. Concluding that I was being directed to initiate my turn, I broke aggressively into my 180-degree power-slide by rolling the jet into about 60 degrees of bank and pulling through my turn to bleed down my airspeed.

In doing so, I was heading right into the configured jet on inside downwind that was still not quite at my nine o'clock.

"Tweet 3-4, inside downwind, breaking out," the aircraft on inside downwind called, and I watched him retract his landing gear and flaps, initiate a climb, and turn toward Old Waverly Manor as I turned toward him and pulled my aircraft directly into the flight path he had been traveling.

"Tweet 2-3, request closed," the aircraft on the departure leg called.

"Closed approved," the controller replied over the Sunfish frequency.

Now that I had initiated my break, Tweet 2-3 could request his closed pattern, and the controller was able to approve it. I figured that the instructor in Tweet 3-4, the jet that had been my conflict on inside downwind, needed to demonstrate a traffic pattern break-out to his student, which was why they had broken out of the inside loop of the pattern, climbed, and pointed toward Old Waverly Manor.

"Tweet 4-1, VFR entry point," someone said.

"Sunfish is landing runway 3-1. Winds are 2-7-0 at 12-gust-to-15. Trends are becoming overshooting finals." The controller stated coolly now that the conflictions in the pattern had been resolved. He stated all the numbers because Tweet 4-1 had not reported "with the numbers" at the VFR entry point. The winds had picked up a little more in the past few minutes. I'd adjust my pattern accordingly.

As I pulled through my 180-degree turn to inside downwind, my airspeed bled off, and by the time I rolled out of my turn, I was flying slowly enough that I could lower my landing gear and flaps without violating the maximum speed restrictions for doing so.

I said my before-landing check out loud from memory and confirmed it with the numbered checklist that was strapped to my leg: "Handle down. Three green (lights). Good (hydraulic) pressure. Flaps are full."

Then, I said it again. "Handle down. Three green. Good pressure. Flaps are full."

"Tweet 2-3, closed downwind." The guy who had done the touch-and-go when I was flying up initial reported that he had completed his climb to the inside downwind position and was now following me on inside downwind.

"Tweet 2-7, closed downwind." I recognized Kenny's voice.

"Disregard. Tweet 2-7, initial." That was Lieutenant Wilson correcting Kenny's radio call. They were flying up initial, where I had just been before my power-slide. Since I was approaching my perch point, I wouldn't be a conflict for Kenny, but the jet behind me, Tweet 2-3, would be.

Sunfish was a busy place. I hadn't even done my first touch-and-go, and my role in maintaining an orderly flow to the traffic pattern had already been put to the test.

"Handle down. Three green. Good pressure. Flaps are full." I ran my before-landing check one more time as I approached the perch, cross-referenced my checklist, and prepared to make my final turn for my first touch-and-go on my solo flight in the traffic pattern that would last about an hour and fifteen minutes before I'd use up all my fuel. My checklist was complete. My spacing on the runway was good. Even though trends were becoming *overshooting finals,* I wasn't going to overshoot. I keyed up my mike button, called, "Sire 3-3, gear down," and rolled off the perch for my first touch-and-go.

"Sire 3-3, make this a full-stop," the Sunfish controller directed.

"Sire 3-3," I replied, "gear down, full stop."

So much for my hour-and-fifteen minute solo.

The winds had been pretty strong, and trends were overshooting finals. The winds must have gone over the limits for solo students, I figured, and I bet the controller didn't want to announce the high winds until after I was safely on the ground.

Handling the growing crosswinds quite well, I thought, I put down a pretty good landing.

*

The T-37 supervisor of flying called me over to his desk across from the chute shop upon my return to the flight line building. He told me to sit in the empty Warhawk flight room with my gradebook and wait for the instructor pilot who had been serving as the Sunfish controller during my solo to return to the squadron. I stood up when First Lieutenant Scowcroft came into the room and asked if I had been Sire 3-3.

Lieutenant Scowcroft wasn't just another IP. The red patch with a white checkmark on his sleeve told me he was assigned to Check Section. Every student's enemy!

I was screwed!

"Do you know why I had you make a full stop?" he asked, taking my gradebook from my hands and sitting down behind a Warhawk IP's desk.

"No, sir," I began as I sat at the desk on the student-side. "I figured that maybe the winds were getting out of limits for a solo student."

"Then you *didn't* see that aircraft on inside downwind!" he snapped back, almost like an attorney making his case while questioning a witness on the stand.

"Yes, sir. I saw him," I said.

"If you saw him, then why did you break into him?" Lieutenant Scowcroft asked, now marking grades on my latest computer printout from my gradebook with the red end of his red and blue pencil. "I even told you not to break into him, and you broke into him."

This hadn't started well. I thought that maybe the controller wanted to see me to tell me that I'd done a good job in a busy pattern with strong winds, but that certainly wasn't where Lieutenant Scowcroft was headed.

"Sir, I was about to call, *Breakpoint, straight through,* because I didn't think I had spacing. Then—"

But he didn't seem too interested in what I was going to say.

"I said, *Overhead, break departure end.* Why didn't you acknowledge the first time when I told you to acknowledge my call, and why—after I told you a second time not to break—did you then acknowledge my call and proceed to break into the aircraft on inside downwind?" Even though Lieutenant Scowcroft wasn't raising his voice, I could tell that he was starting to get mad at me.

Where was this coming from? Why was he getting mad?

"Sir, I didn't think the call was for me at first, which is why I didn't respond. I was going to call, *Breakpoint, straight through,* but then once you made your call, I didn't want to step on the guy you were calling." I tried to answer Lieutenant Scowcroft's questions without any hint of emotion or frustration in my voice, but as his questioning went on, the more difficult this was getting.

"Who did you think I was talking to?" he asked. "Who was *Overhead?*"

"Sir, I was *Overhead*. I knew that part was for me. I thought the other part was for *Departure End.*" I tried to explain.

"What?!" Lieutenant Scowcroft shot back incredulously. "*Overhead, break departure end.* What does that mean? What did I want you to do?"

That's when the light bulb went off for me. I had overcomplicated everything.

"Sir, you wanted me to break at the departure end," I answered.

"Yes, I wanted you to break at the departure end, but you didn't answer. I didn't know what you were going to do; so I called you *again*. Then you *did* answer to let me know that you *would* break at the departure end, but as soon as you answered, you cracked your wings and broke into the jet on inside downwind and created a very unsafe situation. Not only did you break the rules of the pattern, you ignored my specific instructions." He stopped and looked right at me and waited for me to reply.

I understood now. I understood my mistake, and I understood why he was so mad. I thought I knew what I was doing. I thought I knew what he was doing when I thought I knew what I was doing, but when he said, "Overhead, break departure end. Acknowledge," I had no idea what he was doing, and I had no idea what I was supposed to do.

And this whole time, he had no idea what I was going to do, which is why he told me what he wanted me to do, but he didn't know I would do what he wanted me to do until I acknowledged what he told me to do, and when I acknowledged what he told me to do, I did exactly what he didn't want me to do. And it was very unsafe.

He was right.

"Yes, sir. You're right," I said. Lieutenant Scowcroft sat back in his chair when I acknowledged my mistake.

"So, why'd you do it?" he asked me in a completely different tone than he'd had during the rest of our discussion. "Why'd you break into the jet on inside downwind?"

Now that he had rested his case and proven me guilty, it was like he had changed back from a prosecuting attorney to an instructor.

As a freshman at the Academy, you're taught that the only answer to a *Why?* question is "No excuse, sir." For a year, any time an upperclassman asked you a question that included the word *why,* you had to say, "No excuse, sir." Lieutenant Scowcroft had just asked me back-to-back *Why?* questions, and there was no excuse for me not knowing my radio calls, and if he'd asked me these questions in his prosecuting attorney's voice, I probably would have said, "No excuse, sir." But there was a reason why I'd screwed up, and if there was a downward spiraling chain of events, as Captain Wright so often described, that would lead to disaster unless corrective actions were taken, I needed to let Lieutenant Scowcroft know why, so that the next time this situation happened, he'd know what might be going on in the student's mind.

"Sir, I was not familiar with the call *Overhead, break departure end. Acknowledge.*" I admitted. "I actually thought that you wanted me to break and the guy on the departure end to acknowledge so that he wouldn't turn crosswind. I thought you were trying to get both of us sequenced in for touch-and-go landings without having to go around the box. Then, when the jet on departure end didn't answer, and you made the call again, I figured that you wanted me to respond, but I still wasn't really sure what you wanted me to do."

"So, you broke into the oncoming aircraft," he completed my response for me.

"Yes, sir. I broke into the oncoming aircraft," I confirmed.

Lieutenant Scowcroft looked at me for a moment and then silently finished marking up my grade-sheet. When he had finished, he looked up again.

"Lieutenant Wright, this ride is going to be an *Unsat*," Lieutenant Scowcroft stated. "I will make the write-up in your gradebook, and I'll talk to your instructor Lieutenant Wilson. Before you get back into the traffic pattern in the jet, I want you to cover every possible radio call you might hear in the pattern with your instructors and your classmates."

Lieutenant Scowcroft stopped for a moment to think about something. He looked back down at my grade-sheet and made a couple changes to the markings he had made.

"I was going to give you an *Unsat* grade for clearing, but I've changed my mind," he said. "I'm convinced that you saw the jet on inside downwind the whole time. Instead, I am going to give you an *Unsat* for airmanship and another *U* for radio procedures.

"For the airmanship *U*, you never break into another jet in the traffic pattern, and for the radio procedures *U*, what are you supposed to do if you are unsure about a radio call?"

"Sir, I should have queried the controller," I replied automatically. The words had been drilled into my head for test purposes, but just like *Barn-with-the-numbers*, I only knew the words — not what the words meant...until now.

"That's right, you query the controller," Lieutenant Scowcroft repeated softly and calmly in the voice and tone of a teacher, a teacher who had just taught a student a very important lesson.

*

"Lieutenant Wright, what happened?" Lieutenant Wilson asked when he got back from his ride with Kenny.

I told him the story.

Lieutenant Wilson was very cool in that he didn't get mad at me. Some instructors berated their students when they'd had bad rides. I was glad my IP wasn't like that. I was the first student in our class to *Unsat* a solo ride. I already felt bad enough. The way Lieutenant Wilson phrased the situation was actually kind of comical:

"A surface-to-air hook!" he declared.

"Yes, sir," I confirmed. This was kind of funny. "He hooked me from the box...a surface-to-air hook."

We talked about the traffic pattern, and we talked about radio calls. Kenny sat with me the whole time, listening, participating, and supporting. Our IP used the opportunity to teach us, and we used the opportunity to learn. I was ashamed about getting an *Unsat*, and I didn't ever want to get another one.

We reviewed Sunfish traffic procedures for nearly the next hour. Lieutenant Wilson covered every potential radio call an aircraft might hear or make in the pattern. Then, he read me my rights as a student who had just hooked a solo mission.

"Since you're on an *Unsat*, you can't do anything but study for your next ride, which is when we'll try to clear up that *Unsat*. You can't sim. You can't go to the box. You can't work the snack bar. Just study," Lieutenant Wilson said. "Do you understand?"

"Yes, sir. I understand," I acknowledged, but not knowing everything the *Unsat* grade meant, I also asked, "Does this mean I have to go on special monitoring status?"

"No, you're not on SMS. All it really means is that you have to clear up the *Unsat* on your next ride. You can even still get FAR'ed. It's just one ride," Lieutenant Wilson tried to reassure me.

I really didn't care too much about being FAR'ed, of course, because I didn't really want to fly a fighter. I was disappointed in myself, however, because I wanted to do well in flight school. Even though hooking a solo ride didn't mean that I had to go on SMS right away, the pressure was on for the next ride. I didn't want to hook two in a row. That wouldn't be good. Like students who hooked three check rides in the program, students who hooked three rides in a row were on their way out of UPT.

"You need to go back to the gradebook rack, get a red *Unsat* tag, and slide it into the front pocket of your gradebook." Lieutenant Wilson pointed me toward the front, left corner of the room where all of the gradebooks were stored when students weren't briefing or debriefing missions.

While Lieutenant Wilson, Kenny, and I had been reviewing Sunfish pattern procedures, Doley had pulled a chair up to the desk, too. He had probably caught the last ten minutes of our discussion, but he hadn't said anything until I pushed back my chair and got up to get my red *Unsat* tag.

"Walk of shame," Doley whispered.

I don't think anybody heard Doley but me. I didn't say anything. I just gave him a nod. Most Air Force Academy cadets had seen *The Lords of Discipline,* a movie about cadets at the Citadel. Everyone but Mark Jellicot and Al would know about the walk of shame, but I was sure they could figure it out pretty easily.

Back at the gradebook rack, I grabbed a red *Unsat* tag and slid it into the transparent pocket on the front of my thin, black gradebook binder. You could still read my name through the transparent *Unsat* tag, but there was no mistaking the big, red UNSAT now on the cover.

"Walk of shame!" Doley called out loudly enough for everyone in the room to hear.

I pressed the gradebook against my forehead so that the red *Unsat* tag stood out like a shining beacon and started my walk back to my seat. Anyone who wasn't debriefing a ride with an instructor stood up in the position of attention, facing me from their spots around the room. As I approached them with my gradebook and red *Unsat* tag pressed up against my forehead, my classmates shunned me by performing an about face move as I walked in front of them.

As I undertook my walk of shame, Doley paid tribute to my performance by offering a musical tribute. Singing both as Prince and Sheena Easton, he belted out a new take on the song we had heard a couple of times at the Tin Foil Ball Party and three times over the Dagger intercom in the last few hours:

You broke in
He broke out
All because the radio call
Was in doubt, baby
You got that hook

I kept walking back to my seat with my gradebook pressed up against my forehead. My classmates continued to spin around and turn their backs to me as I approached them. Even though it sucked that I had hooked the ride, and nobody thought hooking a ride was funny, everybody was laughing.

You've got the hook
You've got the hook
Put a red Unsat tag in
Your gradebook

By this time, the noise from Doley's singing and the students' laughter was so loud that even Captain Wright and Lieutenant Peena, the flight commander and his assistant, came out of the IP briefing room. I pulled my gradebook down from my forehead and placed it on Lieutenant Wilson's desk. The laughter died down after Captain Wright scanned the room a couple of times.

"Lieutenant Wright, don't worry too much," Captain Wright consoled me. "It's one ride...one solo...and you're still early in the Contact phase of T-37 training. You can still get FAR'ed."

"You might have a hard time finishing at the top of the class, now," Lieutenant Wilson said, doing an about-face on what he'd said minutes before. "A fighter might be out of reach, but you could still come back as an IP."

"Hey, Wright, I'm coming up for an assignment in about six months," Lieutenant Peena added. "Would you like to buy my boat?"

Chapter 10 — "Two Bonks"

"Guys, how many hits to put this nail into that board?" Kurt asked Kenny and me, waving a long nail in front of our faces.

"I bet I could do it in six or seven, but I pretty much suck at hammering," I said. "I always end up bending the nail before I get it all the way down. I know I'd bend it."

"Aaay. I don't know...ten?" Kenny guessed after thinking about the question a little.

Kurt smiled. He positioned the nail on a spot near the center of the board. It looked like a tiny pin from a new shirt pinched in the long fingers of his giant hand.

"One," he stated confidently.

WHACK!

Holy shit!

Kurt smashed the nail all the way down into the piece of wood with one mighty smash, like John Henry driving a railroad spike into the ground with his steel hammer. Then, to prove this feat was no fluke, he waved another long nail before us and repeated, "One."

WHACK!

He did it again, driving a second long nail completely into the wood with one incredibly fast and powerful swing of his mighty hammer.

Kenny and I both tried the one swing approach. We didn't even come close. We had both known our giant, orange-headed friend a long time, and we both knew he was strong, but we couldn't even begin to imagine how strong. The other thing we didn't know about Kurt was that our happily married buddy was also a master craftsman.

Being the only student in Dagger with a bright red UNSAT tag on my gradebook and my name on the next day's schedule in red ink, I was happy that Kurt had insisted that we accompany him to the wood hobby shop after work to see the furniture he was building in anticipation of the arrival of his new baby. I needed to think about something other than UPT for a little while.

"Guys, this dresser is almost finished. Pull out a drawer, and see how smoothly it opens," Kurt said proudly, as if the dresser was his new baby. Kenny walked over to the dresser and pulled out the top drawer. It made no sound, which was quite different from any dresser I ever had. Also, even though Kenny had pulled the drawer all the way out, it didn't droop at all, staying perfectly parallel to the wood hobby shop floor.

"Aaay. Smooth," Kenny nodded.

"Kurt, did you put the drawers on rollers?" I asked.

"That's right, Ray," Kurt beamed. "If Malia or I need to get some clothes out for the baby or put away laundry while it's asleep, the baby won't hear a sound."

"Aaay, this is, like, better than something from Sears," Kenny complimented Kurt as he tested all of the drawers.

"C'mon over here, and let me show you the baby's crib. The rails on either side can slide down, or you can fold them down in the middle," Kurt said as he led us to another area to demonstrate his high-performance crib.

*

"Tell me something, old buddy." Major Lawson fought back a laugh as he looked over my grade-sheet. "How do you log a 0.3 on a pattern-only flight?"

He was referring to the airborne time I logged for my *Unsat* solo ride. Pilots logged their times in tenths of an hour with every six minutes equaling one-tenth.

"Did you not go around the box more than one time?" he asked, shaking his head while smacking his gum.

"Yes, sir," I admitted. "I only made one trip around the pattern, and the controller made me make a full stop on my first landing."

"You did something stupid, didn't you?" Major Lawson deduced.

"Yes, sir. Pretty stupid," I acknowledged.

"Did I not tell you not to do anything stupid?" he asked.

I didn't know how to answer that.

To clear up the *Unsat* I'd earned on my solo ride, Major Lawson and I planned our mission to fly south from Columbus to Meridian, Mississippi, where we could practice traffic pattern procedures on a little-used Navy runway called Gunshy. Because the traffic pattern at Columbus was always crowded with Tweets, Major Lawson liked to fly to Gunshy, where you usually had the whole traffic pattern to yourself. While this meant I could fly a lot more touch-and-go landings at Gunshy than I probably would fly in the Sunfish pattern, the whole reason for my *Unsat* was the chaos created by multiple jets in the dynamic Sunfish pattern. On a clear day at Gunshy with only one or two jets in the pattern, there wouldn't be the same potential for entropy, but I didn't care. I just wanted to clear up my *Unsat*.

In order to stay below active military operating areas (MOAs), where jets were practicing training maneuvers in the sky, the departure route from Columbus to Gunshy was flown at six thousand feet. It didn't take very long to climb to that altitude. It wouldn't take very long to fly to Gunshy, either.

I really wanted to show Major Lawson that once I got to Gunshy, I knew my traffic pattern procedures. I'd studied my radio calls. I knew the rules for conflicts in the pattern. I wasn't going to do anything stupid.

Leveling off at six thousand feet, I ran my climb and level-off checklists.

"I'm On-Normal-Normal, good pressure, good blinker. How 'bout you?" I asked Major Lawson.

"I'm On-Normal-Normal, good pressure, good blinker," he responded.

As I ran my checks, I noticed the jet seemed to be getting louder. I also noticed that it was becoming more and more difficult to maintain level flight. For some reason, the jet seemed to want to climb, requiring more forward stick pressure on my part to keep the nose down and the picture of half-ground and half-sky in my windscreen. Though the cooler October air meant denser air under my wings to give me more lift and better engine performance than when our class first started flying in the heat of August, our jet seemed to have a mind of its own.

I only had a handful of rides left to fly before I'd be tested with my first of three checkrides in the Tweet, officially called the Mid-Phase Contact check. The Mid-Phase was the gateway to being allowed to fly solo outside of the traffic pattern. Pass the Mid-Phase, and I would be cleared to fly the jet solo to a MOA to practice maneuvers like loops and barrel rolls all by myself. Fail the Mid-Phase, and I wouldn't. And it would be my first of three checkride strikes. At three checkride strikes, students washed out of UPT.

I knew Major Lawson was trying not to give me too much instruction to see if I could fly the jet well enough on my own. Check pilots would not instruct students on checkrides, and if a check pilot needed to take control of the jet from a student on a checkride, it usually meant that the student hooked the ride. *Unsat.* Stee-rike!

I also needed to clear up my *Unsat* without too much help from my instructor.

After finishing my required checklists, I turned my full attention to battling my difficult-to-control aircraft. Louder and louder the engine noise grew. Worse and worse my altitude control became. Up. Down. Up. Down. I pushed the stick. I pulled it. Pushed it. Pulled it.

Down. Up. Down. Up.

"TWEEEEEEEEET!" the engines roared like a boiling teakettle.

Finally, Major Lawson just couldn't take it anymore.

"I GIVE UP!" my Vietnam-era, normally laid back, soon-to-be retired military instructor shouted over the intercom from his seat on my right so that he was sure to be heard over the engine noise. "WHY THE FUCK ARE WE FLYING TO GUNSHY AT MACH-FUCKING-ONE?!"

I clutched and trembled as a lightning bolt of panic, fear, and embarrassment struck my insides. As soon as Major Lawson made his Mach-reference, I knew exactly why the jet was so loud, why I couldn't hold my altitude, and why we seemed to be approaching Gunshy much faster than usual. Overly focused on traffic pattern problems and looking ahead to Gunshy, I'd done something stupid. I had forgotten to pull my throttles back out of MIL power, the 100 percent power setting for takeoffs and climbs.

*

"I GIVE UP! Ha-ha-ha-ha-ha!" Doley gasped for air. "WHY THE FUCK…ha-ha-ha-ha-ha! AH WE FLYING TO GUNSHY…aaah-ha-ha-ha-ha-ha! AT MACH-FUCKING-ONE! Ha! Ha-ha! Ha-ha-ha-ha-ha!"

I should have set 80 percent power once I hit my level-off altitude of 6,000 feet, the setting needed on each of the engines to maintain 200 knots. So of course, instead of maintaining 200 knots en route to Gunshy, the jet continued to accelerate with its engines in MIL. Once Major Lawson yelled at me, I ripped the throttles back, slowed to 200 knots, trimmed the pressure off the control stick, and set the power appropriately. But by then, it was too late.

I had been flying Doley through the story of my post-solo-*Unsat* ride to Gunshy with Major Lawson from the cockpit of a T-37 CFT. The CFTs were mock cockpits in the Student Squadron building in which student pilots could sit and practice chair-flying our missions. Officially, CFT stood for Cockpit Familiarization Trainers, but unofficially Doley called them Crewrest Familiarization Trainers because he found them to be a great place to sneak away from our instructors and knock out an hour of sleep. After I had told Doley what happened on my ride to Gunshy with Major Lawson, we signed out of Dagger to the CFTs so that I could reenact the mission while I told the story.

"Doley, from there...it got worse," I confessed from the student side of the cockpit.

"MACH-FUCKIN'-ONE!" Doley howled from the IP's seat.

"Yeah. So then," I continued as Doley clutched the stitch in his stomach that he'd gotten from laughing, "after Gunshy, we fly to the Southern MOA, and I screwed up my spin recovery."

"Please, stop!" Doley said. "I gotta catch my breath. Aaah. Ow. Ah."

The funniest part about Major Lawson screaming wasn't just how he yelled at me. The funniest part was that with a maximum allowable airspeed of 275 knots, the T-37 couldn't even break Mach One-Half...let alone Mach One. It just wasn't a high performance jet.

"Oh, Mach-fuckin' One," Doley slowly breathed more easily. "That's classic. Okay, what happened next?"

"Next, we leave Gunshy and fly to the Southern MOA to practice a spin recovery," I said.

"Did you screw up the **BOLDFACE**?" Doley asked.

"No, but you know the part of the spin recovery where you throw the control stick full forward to dive at the ground?" I set the picture for Doley: I had already purposely thrown the aircraft into a violent spin at the top of my assigned airspace, had gotten halfway through the steps to recover the jet to controlled flight, and was at the point where the pilot needs to dive at the ground to get air flowing properly under the wings again.

"Lemme guess," Doley said. "You held the stick forwahd too long."

"Yeah, and we nearly went inverted!" I told him.

"My technique is Two Bonks," Doley offered.

"What's Two Bonks?" I asked.

Doley shook the control stick of the CFT. "I have the aircraft," he said.

"Roger, you have the aircraft," I replied, taking my hands off the controls and holding them up.

"I have the aircraft," he repeated, shaking the stick again, and he flew us into a spin to demo his technique for the spin recovery.

"When you hear ya helmet and ya IP's helmet slam against the top of the canopy, that's when you pull back on the stick," Doley said. "Bonk! Bonk! Recovuh from dive."

"I'll keep that in mind," I said.

"Technique only," Doley reminded me.

"Can't be graded," I responded.

"And speaking of grades...Majuh Lawson gave you a Good for the ride?" Doley still couldn't believe it.

"Yeah, I'm no longer *Unsat*," I laughed. "Just Stupid."

*

The IPs at Columbus all said that the reason the best pilots in the Air Force are those who train at Columbus is because the Columbus weather is so bad. As students, we learned to fly around clouds, through clouds, and in clouds except on those occasions when there were too many clouds to perform aerobatics or spins or overhead traffic patterns or practice other required maneuvers.

Lieutenant Wilson explained to Kenny and me that the schedulers wouldn't get in trouble for canceling jets for weather, but he and Lieutenant Prince didn't like to cancel jets if they didn't have to. They needed to keep the class on pace to finish our T-37 training in accordance with the timeline that the computer system had set for our class. Some days, though, the weather was just so bad that no one would crank engines and launch, and flying would be canceled for the whole day. It happened every once in a while, and when it did, Captain Wright was always ready with a classic weather-day speech.

"You might think the instructors in Dagger were assigned to be instructors. You might not. But let me tell you, the pilots in this room have all been hand-picked to be Dagger flight instructors." Captain Wright stood and addressed the class as we listened from our seats in front of our IPs' desks, facing the center of the room. "Dagger flight instructors are the best of the best, and when you combine their knowledge, dedication, and commitment to excellence with the weather conditions in Columbus, the result is the finest training flight in the entire Air Force. And since the United States Air Force is the best Air Force in the world, the IPs in Dagger are the best in the entire world." Classic Captain Wright logic.

"Everybody wants to go to Willie. At Willie, you might see one cloud in the sky in the course of a year. You might not." He paused and smiled. The whole time he spoke, his head scanned the room, sweeping from right-to-left and left-to-right and then back again.

"Phoenix is a beautiful town. The weather is nice, but the pilots at Willie never learn to fly in bad weather conditions. Do you know what happens anytime a cloud appears in the sky at Willie? Training operations shut down for students, and the instructors race to the one cloud in the sky so that they can log some instrument time. About fifteen minutes later, the cloud dissipates. The IPs land, and they get all excited that they can enter 0.3 hours of instrument time in their pilot logbooks." Captain Wright laughed at his joke, a joke that only a Columbus IP could appreciate. Then, he blasted on.

"At Columbus, you'll fly in all kinds of weather. You might be in good weather conditions for a few minutes. A few minutes later, you might not. You'll see thunderstorms pop up all around you as you fly, but you won't fly in a thunderstorm, because no peacetime mission requires thunderstorm penetration. You'll become better instrument pilots than anywhere else in the Air Force. You'll build better decision-making skills than anywhere else in the Air Force. You'll be better formation flight leaders and build better wingman skills than anywhere else in the Air Force, because you'll have to plan for weather, think about weather, and fly in weather constantly, and you'll need to make the best situations out of less than ideal weather," Captain Wright said, pausing to scan the class through his half-closed eyes and shifting his weight from side to side before beginning again.

"Sometimes the weather will cooperate with you, but sometimes it won't. When it doesn't, you will have the knowledge and skills to make the right decisions and moves that will get you home safely. You won't get that at Willie. You won't get that in Texas. I don't know what you get in Enid, Oklahoma, and I never want to know. I don't want to fly there. I don't want to go there. I don't even want to talk about Enid, Oklahoma." He laughed at his own joke and then shifted his stance and scanned the faces of the students.

"After graduating from Columbus, pinning on your silver wings, and arriving at your first operational unit, you'll find yourself flying missions where you won't get to choose the weather conditions," Captain Wright said. "You'll be prepared, you'll be confident, and you'll be successful because you'll have trained on the banks of the Tennessee–Tombigbee River with the Air Force's finest instructors, right here at the best training base in the world in the best training flight in the world: Dagger!"

*

Weather was as much a teacher as any assigned instructor. The skies above Columbus were a bubbling cauldron of atmospheric thermodynamics in which moisture brewed, clouds stewed, and flight plans skewed. A thick layer of haze regularly obscured in-flight visibility to no more than five miles. Growing cotton fields of clouds obstructed maneuvering airspace and cut off ground references. Towering thunderstorms closed off giant sections of sky, forced jets to return to base, and shut down flying operations for hours at a time. You had to adjust as changing weather made sticking to the planned mission more and more difficult. Our instructors helped us build our flying skills. Weather helped us build our decision-making skills.

Except for when the weather was really bad.... On those days, the decision-making might be done for us. Extremely bad weather occasionally resulted in the early cancellation of flying activities. And sometimes, that meant early dismissal!

One afternoon, Doley and I headed downtown to Lenny's Gym to lift after early dismissal. Doley insisted on driving and swung by the playhouse on Azalea Drive right after I'd gotten home and changed. Apparently, he'd just sunk a chunk of his big second-lieutenant paycheck into his car, and he wanted to show off the upgrades—Italian Pirelli racing tires and a radio with a clicker.

Even though we could lift for free at the base gym, now that we lived downtown, ten miles south of the front gate, the base wasn't the most convenient place to lift weights. Traveling back and forth to the base required at least a half hour of driving. With a twelve-hour work day and the need for eight hours of uninterrupted sleep before the next work day, we only had four hours of free time for anything else. Because you needed an hour in the morning to get up, get ready, and get to the base, this left just three hours each evening before you had to be in bed for crew rest. No crew rest...no fly.

That half hour of travel time back and forth to the base to get to the base gym was not an efficient use of free time. So, Doley and I joined a gym downtown, Lenny's Gym, an old auto repair shop comprised of two car bays that had been painted over, lined with mirrors, and filled with workout equipment. Probably from Lenny's basement. We paid ten dollars a month.

Doley and I had begun a new lifting routine. Doley's roommate, the former quarterback on the Air Force football team, started us on a program that followed the Academy strength coach's training regimen. The plan was that you'd find your max weight for a number of different exercises, and then the amount of weight and number of reps you'd lift that month would be based on a percentage of your max. We would do three sets of ten to twelve reps at 50 to 60 percent of our max on Mondays, two to three reps at 80 to 90 percent of our max on Wednesdays, and six to eight reps at 70 to 80 percent of our max on Fridays. In the weeks that followed, we'd build up the weight by a couple of percent each week, and at the end of the month, we'd max out again. If we were good about sticking to the plan, our max should go up each month.

As was usually the case at Lenny's garage-turned-gym, we were the only two guys lifting, which was nice. No pose downs and no waiting for equipment. We finished up our workout in about an hour. Right about the time we finished, the rain lightened up a little. Doley was excited to hop back in the Jeet, his name for his black Volkswagen GTI, and show off his stereo a little more.

As we drove up Highway 45 North, Doley fiddled with his new clicker to play his new favorite Pink Floyd song again. It was still daytime, but the sky was completely overcast. The afternoon's rain wasn't like the typical weather pattern that we'd seen in Columbus over the summer when days would start out clear and hot with hazy blue skies, and by noon, the sky would be spotted with puffy, white clouds. Around three thirty PM, the clouds would have grown and matured into giant, cumulus towers of cotton balls on steroids. You'd get thunderstorms for a half hour to an hour before dinner. Then, the evenings would be nice. No, today was more like a rainy day in Rhode Island — dark, cloudy, and raining on and off all day.

Even though the Mississippi roads were designed to drain quickly into deep ditches that lined the sides of most roads, I noticed a lot of puddles on this particular evening. Highway 45 North was a fairly busy road compared to most other streets in

Columbus. Off to our left, I saw that the Kroger parking lot was packed with cars with lots of traffic driving in and out.

I thought of the time a friend of ours in the UPT class ahead of us had whipped into that lot with a perfect 270-degree *Starsky & Hutch* counterclockwise power-slide before we went to the Mississippi State–Tennessee football game. Kroger was probably a little too busy for a power-slide today.

"HOLD ON, RAY!" Doley ordered out of nowhere, hitting the brakes all of a sudden. The backside of the car in front of us looked like it was about to slam through Doley's windshield.

Luckily, Doley hit the brakes in time, and his new Pirelli tires gripped enough through puddle to pavement to bring the Jeet to an abrupt stop without a collision and only the slightest hint of a fishtail. *Close one!* Doley's upgraded tires had just paid for their four hundred dollar selves.

Observing almost no space between the front of the Jeet and the back of the car in front of us, I invoked my always-sound-cool-on-the-radio voice. "Nice recovery," I said, kind of like one of our instructors might say after practicing a spin or a traffic pattern stall. "Thanks for not waiting until you heard the two bonks," I added.

"Technique only," Doley matter-of-factly replied, like he meant to skid to a stop.

"Can't be graded," I responded mindlessly.

"See the Kroger parking lot over there?" I pointed out to Doley as he clicked. "Saw this guy execute a perfect 270-degree *Starsky & Hutch* power-slide. It was like he was a stunt driver."

"Cool," Doley acknowledged and drove on once the light had turned back to green. He weaved in and out of traffic as we accelerated north on Highway 45, running his new Pirellis through a full road test as if he were now a stunt driver, too. Quite a few big puddles remained in the road, and Doley was enjoying racing through the deepest parts of them with his new tires.

"Nice rooster tail," I commented after one particularly big splash.

"Technique only," Doley acknowledged.

"Can't be graded," I said.

Doley ripped the Jeet hard to the left to turn onto Azalea Drive and drop me off at the house after our workout. As we passed by Kurt and Malia's apartment complex at the top of the street, Doley turned his stereo down and asked me, "How does Kurt do it?"

"Dude, I have no idea. Imagine going from college graduation to wedding to honeymoon to flight school to gonna-be-a-dad all within about ninety days," I answered, shaking my head in amazement and repeated. "I have no idea."

Because Azalea Drive wasn't as well traveled as Highway 45 North, there were huge puddles on both sides of the road. Azalea Drive was a residential, dead-end road, serving as a meandering central artery for about a half-dozen other roads that either ended in cul-de-sacs or shot off of Azalea Drive and circled back to connect up to it again farther down.

After the last of these offshoots, like a waterskier on the Tenn–Tom, Doley slalomed up the long, straight stretch of Azalea Drive, cutting from side to side to splash through every big puddle while Pink Floyd music cranked in the Jeet. Slash to the right. Splash and spray. Slash to the left. Splash and spray.

Never one to miss an opportunity to get in some extra training, Doley turned down his stereo slightly so he could offer instruction on his spraying maneuvers. "Ray, once I turn and set my entry point into the puddle, I accelahrate hahd. Once in the puddle, I turn to parallel the curb, accelahrate, and a final cut away from the curb prior to exiting the puddle to maximize the spray." We might as well have been on a training ride.

"Ray, that was a spray on the right. Now, let me demo a spray to the left," and Doley talked me through his maneuver again, this time on the left-hand side of the road. "Make sure that you mahk this as a demo in your gradebook," he said before turning the music back up.

Doley slalomed and sprayed water all the way up Azalea Drive until we got to the part of the road that made the hook at the top of the question mark. After a right turn into the base of the hook, the 180-degree turn to the left and it legs formed a perfect upside-down letter *U*. On the leg going into the U-turn, one seriously long and very deep-looking puddle presented itself ahead of us.

Doley eyed the giant puddle in the road. As his car sped toward the watery turn, I challenged his driving skills: "I'm thinking...power-slide!"

Never one to pass up a challenge, Doley cranked the Pink Floyd up as loud as he could and laughed. He was going to go for it.

I have no idea how fast we were speeding down the wet, residential Azalea Drive when Doley cut the steering wheel of the Jeet hard to the left and threw us into the power-slide around the big U-turn. Even with my seatbelt fastened, I was thrown up against the inside of the door by the centrifugal force. I felt the back of the Jeet start to fishtail—maybe even hydroplane—as we whipped around the bend.

WHACK!!! BONK! BONK!

We hit something hard and abruptly stopped just off the side of the road. On impact, I was thrown into the side door and window. Luckily, my right shoulder took most of the blow to the window—not my head. I heard a smash and the sound of breaking glass, but I didn't see that any of the windows in the car were broken. Doley looked okay, too. He had shut off the engine right after we'd slammed to a stop, and I was thinking that whatever we'd hit had saved us from tearing up somebody's front yard and had maybe even stopped the Jeet from flipping over.

Doley punched the center of the steering wheel and screamed, "FUUUUUUCCCCCKKKK!!!"

Unbuckling and getting out of the car, we saw that we had hit a telephone pole right at the side of the road as we were coming out of the turn.

The back right-hand side of the Jeet was all smashed in and broken. Red and orange pieces of plastic from what had been the taillights and brake lights were scattered all around the base of the telephone pole. Much of the backside was crumpled. The rear wheel section looked unobstructed, so the car might still be drivable. On first inspection, the new Pirelli looked like it survived unharmed. The telephone pole didn't have a scratch on it. We hadn't left any tire tracks in anyone's yard, either.

Not really knowing what to say, I started with the obvious. "You hit the telephone pole."

"Fuck!" Doley repeated. "This sucks. I just spent all my money on my new ti'as and my stereo. This sucks."

"Don't you have insurance?" I asked.

"Yeah, but I have a deductible. I can't remembah if it's five hundred dollahs or a thousand." Exasperated, Doley put his hands up to his face and repeated one last time, "Fuck!"

"Maybe the power-slide wasn't such a good idea," I suggested, always the master of the inappropriate comment.

"Yaw the one who said powah-slide!" Doley shot back. Then, mocking me, he added, "'I saw a guy execute a perfect 270-degree *Stahsky & Hutch* powah-slide.'"

"Yeah, his was cool," I agreed as if Doley were asking me to respond to the comment. Then, I added, "But yours was better. Except for the telephone pole part. That sucked. Besides, I was thinking that you would do the power-slide in the cul-de-sac at the end of the road." I pointed down to the cul-de-sac at the end of the road.

We had power-slid all the way through the turn and were now looking down the road at the cul-de-sac where my house was. I stopped talking for a moment so that Doley could swear again if he wanted, but he just stared at the back of his car without speaking.

I broke the silence after a moment or two. "Pirelli really does make a good-looking tire."

"Bastid," Doley muttered.

Chapter 11 — "Letdown and Recovery"

"Columbus Approach," I called after I'd finished all my area work. "Tweet 7-6, Area 2, request recovery." It was time to head back to the traffic pattern to demonstrate my proficiency in various types of patterns and landings.

I had put together a pretty good checkride to this point. My takeoff and departure went fine. My aerobatics went pretty well. My spin recovery and traffic pattern stalls were fine. I hadn't pushed the boundaries of my assigned airspace, either laterally or vertically. Most importantly, my check pilot hadn't said a word the whole ride and hadn't had to shake the stick to take control of the jet from me.

During a regular training ride, your instructor pilot might shake the stick and take the jet from you for any numbers of reasons, and you could still pass the ride. But as every student pilot knew, if a check pilot had to take the jet from you on a checkride, you probably were going to hook the ride, get an *Unsat* for a grade, and you could wash out of the program in about two weeks' time.

"Tweet 7-6, Columbus Approach," the controller responded. "You are cleared to Columbus via the Whippet Recovery. Local altimeter is 3-1-1-2."

"Tweet 7-6, cleared Whippet to Columbus; 3-1-1-2," I acknowledged the controller.

The letdown and traffic-entry portion of every ride was usually pretty easy. You pulled the throttles back, let the nose of the jet drop, established a 200-knot glide, ran the necessary checklists, and constantly scanned the sky for air traffic and birds on the way back to Sunfish. The weather was uncharacteristically perfect for flying operations around Columbus Air Force Base. No clouds. No wind. Not even any haze. Usually, even on the clearest days, the sky was so hazy that in-flight visibility was limited to about five miles. Even though the MOAs, the designated airspace where we practiced our maneuvers, were only about fifteen or twenty miles from the base, you usually couldn't see the base from that far away because of the haze of the sweaty Mississippi sky or the building cumulus clouds that popped up in the afternoon and surrounded you while you flew, growing thicker and climbing higher with the day's rising temperature.

Like following a trail of breadcrumbs, you'd use prominent landmarks as you flew the Whippet Recovery to help navigate back to the base. You had to know these if you lost your radio or navigation instruments due to a malfunction. For my checkride, however, the sky was perfectly clear, and I could already see the base from the middle of Area 2, about twenty miles to the northeast of the Sunfish runway. Conditions could not have been more perfect.

The Whippet Recovery had one major altitude restriction that required aircraft fly at or below 7,000 feet by the time they got ten miles northeast of the base. I had attempted to blow through this restriction on a couple of recent rides with Major Lawson. He taught me several techniques to use during my descent to make sure that I'd comply with this altitude restriction. I'd practiced these chair-flying with Kenny, and I was confident that on a clear day, like this one, the Whippet would be no problem. I'd already soloed in the traffic pattern — twice. The hardest part of my checkride was behind me.

"Columbus Approach, Tweet 7-7, Area 5, request recovery." I recognized my classmate Sandy's voice as Tweet 7-7. She was flying her checkride at the same time I was flying mine. Since Area 5 was directly behind Area 2, Sandy was right behind me, and since I was exiting Area 2 from the middle of the MOA, if she was coming out of the front of Area 5, Sandy could literally have been right on my tail.

"Tweet 7-7, Columbus Approach," the controller responded. "You are cleared to Columbus via the Whippet Recovery. Local altimeter is 3–1–1–2."

"Tweet 7-7, cleared Whippet to Columbus; 3–1–1–2," Sandy acknowledged the controller.

"Tweet 7-7, Columbus Approach, be advised traffic at your twelve o'clock low, two miles, T-37 also on the Whippet," the controller told Sandy, referring to me as the traffic in front of her.

"Tweet 7-7, searching," Sandy acknowledged the call, indicating that she hadn't yet seen me.

Trying to help, I rocked my wings a few times to make my jet easier for her to see.

"Tweet 7-6, Columbus Approach, confirm that you can make the altitude restriction at ten miles," the controller reminded me of my restriction on the Whippet as I got closer to Columbus Air Force Base.

"Columbus Approach, Tweet 7-6, we'll make it," I confirmed.

"Tweet 7-6, Columbus Approach, thank you, sir," the controller politely responded.

"Tweet 7-7, Columbus Approach, traffic now at twelve o'clock high, two miles, T-37, also on the Whippet Recovery." The controller was still trying to help Sandy get a visual on me, and if I wasn't mistaken, it sounded like he'd told her that my jet was now higher than her jet. Sandy was now below me even though she was behind me on the Whippet!

"Columbus Approach, Tweet 7-7, searching," Sandy said, still reporting that she couldn't see me.

I rocked my wings several more times while in my gradual descent to try to help her spot me in the perfectly and uncharacteristically clear sky as I passed over the town of Sulligent, Alabama.

"Do you have an altitude restriction on the Whippet Recovery?" my check pilot asked me unexpectedly, like he was going to start testing me on my general knowledge in the jet. This was the first time he opened his mouth on the ride other than when running checklists that required we speak to one another.

"Sir, I need to be at or below 7,000 feet, ten miles northeast of the Caledonia VOR-TAC," I answered correctly. I knew the restriction. I had tried to blow through it enough times with Major Lawson.

"Are you going to make it?" he immediately followed up.

"Yes, sir," I answered incorrectly.

We were still at 9,500 feet and just eleven miles from the base. I pulled the throttles back farther to get the nose of the jet to drop faster, but the throttles didn't have too much farther back to go, and the mileage to the base was decreasing faster than the altitude was dropping on my cockpit instruments. We weren't going to make it!

"I have the aircraft," the check pilot said, shaking the stick to assume control.

No!!!

I didn't let go when he first shook the stick. I held on and resisted his taking control of the jet. If he took the jet, I'd hook. If I hooked, I could wash out.

"I have the aircraft," the check pilot said again, shaking the stick once more.

What was I doing?!

I'd written a haiku about "Transfer of Control" and kept it under the clear plastic in front of my seat at Lieutenant Wilson's desk. If I continued to fight the check pilot for control of the jet, not only would my actions be insubordinate, I could kill us both.

I let go of the stick, showed the check pilot my hands, and said, "Roger, you have the aircraft."

"I have the aircraft," he completed the transfer of control, rolled the jet clockwise into 90 degrees of right bank, and ripped back on the stick bringing on the G-forces along with a rapid descent in altitude. When the check pilot rolled back to wings-level, we were below 7,000 feet, ten miles from the base, and in total compliance with the altitude restriction of the Whippet Recovery. No thanks to me.

"You have the aircraft," the check pilot said once we were appropriately positioned in the sky.

"Roger, sir. I have the aircraft," I said, shaking the control stick.

"You have the aircraft," my check pilot repeated and showed me his hands.

I'd flown us to the area. I'd looped and rolled and kept the jet in the area. I'd stalled and recovered. I'd spun and recovered. I knew I'd be fine in the traffic pattern and that my landings would all be great. But I missed the altitude restriction on the Whippet Recovery!

*

"Aaay! How'd it go?" Kenny asked. He had been waiting for me in the chute shop. In just a few short months at Columbus, Kenny and I had gotten to be pretty good buddies. As tablemates at the same instructor's desk, we briefed and debriefed rides together. We studied together. We even went to the snack bar together. As roommates, we drove into work together. We chair-flew together. We ate together. We partied together—a lot. Kenny was a very fun guy to be around, and he was incredibly loyal to those he considered friends.

"Kenny, I missed the altitude restriction on the Whippet Recovery," I told him.

"Shit! Did the check pilot have to take the jet?" Kenny asked.

"Yeah," I confessed. "He took the jet."

"Shit!" Kenny said again.

We both know that if the check pilot had to take the jet from the student, it was not a good thing. The whole purpose of the Mid-Phase Contact check was for the student to demonstrate that he could leave the Columbus traffic pattern, fly a jet safely to one of the designated practice areas, safely perform basic maneuvers, and safely return to Columbus without presenting a hazard to himself or others in the sky or on the ground. If your check pilot took control of the jet, it probably meant you did not have control and would not pass the ride.

And I did not have control.

*

"So, what happens next, Lieutenant Wilson?" I asked. "Am I on SMS?"

"No," my IP said. "You're on an *Unsat* again, but you're not on SMS."

Just seven days had passed after my surface-to-air *Unsat* from the box. Having hooked my checkride on the Friday before the long Columbus Day weekend, Lieutenant Wilson explained to me what would happen next: I'd have a practice ride on the Tuesday after Columbus Day, and on Wednesday, I'd have a special checkride with one of the squadron's leaders. I wouldn't get a grade for Tuesday's ride, because it would just be practice. Wednesday's special checkride would be the important one. If I passed the special checkride on Wednesday, I'd drop back into the normal flow of training, as if I'd passed my Mid-Phase checkride.

If I failed Wednesday's special checkride, I'd get two more practice rides before a second special checkride. The two additional practice rides would not be graded, because they would just be practice. If I passed the second special checkride, I'd drop back into the normal flow of training as if I'd passed my Mid-Phase checkride. If I failed the second special checkride, I'd go to a Training Review Board, a TRB. The TRB would determine if I could return to pilot training, as if I'd passed my Mid-Phase checkride, or if I'd wash out of UPT and be sent out into the Real Air Force as something other than a pilot.

And I wouldn't be shit.

This sucked!

As Lieutenant Wilson explained the process, Kenny sat with me at the desk. Even though he could be getting ready for his Columbus Day weekend, he was hanging out with me and trying to help me out.

I couldn't have asked for a better flight-study partner.

In between our freshmen and sophomore years at the Academy, Kenny and I were randomly assigned to the same mock compound for prisoner of war training. While most of our classmates fell into line and performed the duties that our mock captors insisted that we do, like digging trenches for their anti-aircraft artillery—Kenny dug a hole under the fence of the POW camp, and when no one was watching him, he escaped. The mock captors rewarded him with a steak dinner and a couple hours of relaxation before making him return to finish his training.

People who didn't know Kenny thought he was kind of crazy. A dive-at-the-ground-while-you-spin-to-your-death kind of guy, you never knew what Kenny might say or even do next, but you did know that whatever it was, you'd want to be around for it, and that everyone would eventually be talking about it.

I was glad that we had become friends, and I was thankful when, on the ride back to our house, he invited me to his parents' house in Atlanta for the Columbus Day weekend.

I probably should have stayed in Columbus and studied, but just like in *Animal House* when everything that could go wrong did go wrong, what was I going to do?

Road trip!

Once we got to Atlanta, smelling Kenny's mom's spaghetti sauce on the stove in the kitchen...having her offer me a *sangwich,* just like my grandmother used to say. Nothing could make an *Unsat* satisfying, but a little Wessels family warmth was just what I needed.

*

After the long weekend, Major Lawson sat in Lieutenant Wilson's chair in the Dagger flight room, looking up and down my grade-sheet at the marks for each of the maneuvers I'd flown on my blown checkride. Kenny and I sat across the desk from him, looking at one another every few moments without speaking. Each time Major Lawson's eyes seemed to travel from the top of the grade-sheet to the bottom and back up to the top again, he'd smack his gum a couple of times. Kenny and I would silently exchange glances and, then, look back at the major.

Unless we were both flying at the same time, Kenny and I sat in on all of the briefings and debriefings for each other's rides. Since the class progressed through the UPT syllabus at relatively the same pace, flying relatively the same rides and maneuvers as each other, you could sit in as an observer on anybody's briefing or debriefing and know exactly what was being discussed, taught, or practiced at any given point in the exchange. Captain Wright encouraged us to listen to as many briefings and debriefings as we could, because it would help us learn faster.

Lieutenant Wilson told Kenny and me that it would also be good practice for when we became FAIPs.

I was one of only three Dagger students to hook the Mid-Phase Contact check. Kenny had passed his. He was moving forward in his training, scheduled to fly solo to an area in one of the MOAs while I'd be flying my do-over checkride.

Meanwhile, on the scheduling board, I'd never seen so many aircraft sorties lined up — about eighteen missions for each of the day's three flying periods. The schedulers were excited, because flying all these missions in one day would move the class ahead of the timeline. Mark Jellicot was super excited, because he was going to be the first Dagger student to *trip-turn,* which is UPT language for flying three times in one day.

Major Lawson placed my grade-sheet flat on the desk, like he was laying down his poker hand for the rest of the table to see.

"Looks like you had a pretty good ride going, old buddy," he said to me. "So, what happened?"

I told him the whole story of the Whippet Recovery, Sandy behind me, her jet below mine, radio calls, wing flashes, and how the check pilot eventually took the jet, because I wasn't going to make my altitude restriction.

"Sir, I'm sorry I let you down," I said, apologizing for screwing up my checkride.

"You didn't let me down, old buddy," Major Lawson shot back, now looking me directly in the eyes from across the desk. "You let yourself down."

I just nodded.

"Lieutenant Wright, I've seen you fly a lot now, and I know what you can do," Major Lawson continued on. "You're a better pilot than this." He picked my grade-sheet back up off the desk and held it out for me to see, even though I already knew what was on it.

"No matter what mission you step to fly, you are going to encounter distractions that can keep you from completing important elements of your job. At 200 knots, you're burning up miles and gas, and that gives you only so much time to handle these other things that may not even be all that important. Once that time, that gas, and those miles are gone, you can't get 'em back." Major Lawson stopped to ensure that I was following along. "Don't waste 'em."

"Yes, sir," I acknowledged.

Lieutenant Wilson had been working on the scheduling board behind Major Lawson, making some changes to the day's third period schedule to fill the last few jets of the day. As soon as Major Lawson and I had a break in our discussion, Lieutenant Wilson jumped in with a question.

"Major Lawson, are you available to fly this afternoon around 1700 hours?" Lieutenant Wilson quickly asked.

"No, old buddy," Major Lawson replied. "I've only got so much energy, myself, each day. As much as I'd like to, I've got other things I need to do this afternoon."

*

I was assigned to fly my do-over checkride with Captain "Turbo" Ted LaGrande, one of the most highly energetic and vocal instructors as any in the T-37 Squadron.

Captain LaGrande was notorious for calling *dead bug!* over the intercom when he was the SOF, which meant that all students had to immediately drop onto their backs, stick their arms and legs up in the air, and shake violently until Turbo Ted commanded us to *recover* to a normal position. According to Air Force doctrine, the last student in each flight room to hit the floor in the dead-bug position was required to buy rounds of beer at the O-Club.

In Dagger, Al, the one guy who was neither an Academy grad nor prior-Air Force, had no idea what *dead bug* was all about, so Al was always the last one to hit the floor, if he even tried to hit the floor at all. Frustrated about not knowing one Air Force tradition or another, Al would protest and storm out of the room. Most of us had no intention of ever showing up at the O-Club to drink the beer Al had to buy, but driving him crazy was fun. Frankly, it wasn't that hard.

Lieutenant Wilson told me to expect to fly a full profile, just like on my first checkride. Since I'd hooked my ride for letdown and traffic entry on the Whippet Recovery, I'd surely be flying the Whippet Recovery from the Northern MOA again. I'd flown well on my practice ride, and with Captain LaGrande, it would probably all come down to the Whippet or whether or not I'd choke flying some other part of my ride.

Just like the Friday before, and very atypical of Columbus, the weather was absolutely perfect for my do-over checkride. What were the odds of that?

"Tweet 4-0, Columbus Departure, turn right, heading one-two-zero. You are cleared direct, Area Red High-Low," the controller said, which I totally didn't expect. If we were cleared into the Southern MOA, which were all named for colors, then I wouldn't have to fly the Whippet Recovery when I returned to the base from my assigned area! I'd get vectors back to Columbus instead. Vectors were easy because instead of having to navigate turns, headings, and altitudes to fly a precisely defined, published procedure, you just flew the headings and altitudes the controller assigned you and repeated them back over the radio.

"Tweet 4-0, heading 1–2–0, cleared direct, Area Red High-Low," I acknowledged.

Yes!

Without shaking the stick to assume control of the jet, Captain LaGrande immediately jumped on the radio.

"Columbus Departure, Tweet 4-0. Request Northern MOA." He was going to force me into a Northern MOA so that I'd have to fly the Whippet.

No!

"Tweet 4-0, Columbus Departure. Negative Northern MOA. Continue heading 1–2–0, direct Area Red High-Low." The controller denied the request.

Yes!

"You keep flying," Captain LaGrande said over the cockpit intercom. "I'm going to talk on the radio." Captain LaGrande wasn't going to let this go so easily.

No!

"Tweet 4-0, Columbus Departure," the controller responded to Captain LaGrande's request. "I'm sorry, sir, the Northern MOA is full. I've got jets in every Area. Unless you want to hold over Tuscaloosa until an Area opens up, I've got to put you in Area Red for now. Say intentions."

Yes!

"Columbus Departure, Tweet 4-0. Proceeding direct Area Red High-Low, heading one-two-zero," Captain LaGrande responded.

We were headed south. Hello, vectors!

"Lieutenant Wright," Captain LaGrande said, "I don't know that this will really help me evaluate what I'm supposed to be testing you on, but today, it will have to do."

Yes!

"Yes, sir," I acknowledged unemotionally, even though I was totally psyched.

In the Southern MOA, I flew all my required maneuvers. On recovery, I complied with all of the controllers' instructions. In the traffic pattern, I safely performed all my patterns and landings. I passed my do-over checkride with Captain LaGrande and returned to the normal flow of training. Another life in the UPT game of energy and entropy! Maybe I could even win.

Chapter 12 — "Continuity"

In an attempt to recreate the success of our Tin Foil Ball Party, Kenny and I tried to repeat its key elements with our Mid-Phase Completion Party. We loaded the fridge and the Pepsi machine with beer. We had Mark Jellicot bring his jam box. Doley brought his newest music, and Kenny got a few dozen goldfish from Kmart for his tank on the mantle. He dumped them into the water right as the first partiers arrived.

"Chuck! Sandy! Where's Marcia?" This had pretty much become my standard off-duty greeting for our female classmates. On duty, the three women usually traveled together, but off-duty, we rarely saw Marcia.

Chuck headed straight for the kitchen with her blender, tequila, and eggs to make her special marguerites. Since I didn't drink anything she'd mixed at our first party, I was going to be sure to drink something she made at this one. By the time she poured her first blended concoction, our rental was full of people, the music was pumping, and an intense evaluation of the Dagger flight instructors had begun.

"Oh, that guy's such a dick!" Doley screamed in response to a name that had just been thrown out.

"What about Lieutenant Wilson?" Chuck asked Kenny and me, putting the pitcher part of her blender back on its base.

"Aaay, he's cool," Kenny said.

"Yeah, very cool," I agreed, clinking my cup to Kenny's and downing half my drink. Even though I was never a big fan of tequila, Chuck's marguerite was pretty good.

"Chuck, how's Lieutenant Peena?" Doley asked her, knowing she'd flown with the Dagger Assistant Flight Commander several times.

"He's a dick," Chuck laughed. "He rips you the whole ride."

"He grabs students by the oxygen mask and jerks their head back and forth when he gets pissed," I added.

"Aaay, he's a total dick!" Kenny declared.

"You should see how Peena treats the crew chiefs," Chuck added. "He's lucky he hasn't found a wrench inside one of his engines at 20,000 feet."

"Aaay, really?" Kenny questioned. "The crew chiefs are awesome! I love how those guys salute you—like on *Top Gun*—when you taxi out for takeoff."

"That is cool!" I agreed.

"Ray, how's Major Lawson?" Sandy asked.

"He's very cool," I said. "And very funny."

"Hold on!" Doley interjected. "Ray, have you flown with Peena?"

"No, not yet," I said.

"Then, how do you know he shakes students' heads by the grabbing their oxygen masks?" he asked.

"Stan Melton told me," I said. "He flies with Peena all the time."

"Chuck, you've flown with Peena, right?" Doley asked her.

"Yeah," she said. "He's a dick!"

"Sandy, have you flown with Peena?" Doley asked.

"Yeah," she said. "He yelled at me, but he didn't grab my oxygen mask."

"Ray, not counting Check Section pilots," Doley clarified, "who have you flown with ova r'ah first thirty rides besides Major Lawson and Lieutenant Wilson?"

"I did a sim with Captain Wright," I answered. "He was awesome."

"I've flown with Captain Wright," Chuck said. "I love flying with him. He's like non-stop motivation." Chuck and I clinked cups, and I finished my first marguerite of the night.

"Hold on!" Doley wasn't going to let the matter drop. I grabbed the blender from its base, topped off Chuck's cup, and refilled mine as Doley spoke. "I've already had to fly with maw than a few guys who ah dicks. How come you haven't?"

"Sorry, Doley," I said. "My IP is one of the schedulers. Lieutenant Wilson takes care of his assigned students."

Kenny and I mashed cups.

"Am I right or wrong?!" I hollered above the din of the party.

"You're right!" everyone but Doley yelled.

"Are we weak or strong?!"

"We're strong!" we finished the Academy cheer.

"That's just bullshit," Doley muttered and shook his head.

Before we finished evaluating all of the Dagger IPs, we were interrupted by screams of horror from the big room where I was playing professional wrestling videos on Kenny's VCR-movie player to the music from Mark Jellicot's jam box.

"Oooh!"

"Ewww!"

"Aaah!"

I hustled over to investigate the disturbance and caught the tail end of the action.

In very rapid succession, our sacrificial goldfish in the tank on the mantle were bubbling up to the surface of the water, like tiny ping pong balls that had been submerged and then released.

Pop-pop-pop-pop-pop-pop! Pop-pop-pop!

Pop-pop-pop-pop-pop-pop-pop-pop-pop!

The goldfish zipped to the surface, bobbed onto their sides, and stopped moving. All three dozen of them died within a couple hundred seconds of one another, and their lifeless little fish bodies floated at the surface of the tank, mouths open and one eye above water.

As I pushed my way closer to the mantle, Kurt's pregnant wife, Malia, who was about a foot and a half shorter than her giant husband, grabbed my arm, and pulled me down to her level so that she could be heard above the moaning crowd and other party noises, now that the loudness had kicked into high gear.

"RAY!" she screamed. "Have you cleaned that fish tank recently?!"

"YES! Of course, Malia! I wouldn't put fish in a dirty tank!" I yelled back, slightly offended. I absolutely cleaned the fish tank, because in just a few short weeks after our last party, both the glass and water had turned cloudier and murkier than the water in Scum Pond, one of our ground references in the Sunfish pattern. I had to clean the tank before we put new fish in, because the water was so disgusting.

I had only met Malia a couple of times before this party...why was she giving me grief about putting fish in a dirty tank? Did she think I was stupid? The store must have sold Kenny a bunch of sick goldfish.

"RAY! What did you use to clean the tank?!" Malia wanted to know.

"MALIA! I used Windex!" I answered. Of course! What else do you use to clean glass? At the Academy, we always used Windex to clean for our Saturday morning inspections. Windex was the best.

"RAY!" Malia hollered again. "Windex has ammonia in it! You poisoned the fish!"

Oh, shit! I poisoned the fish.

Malia was right...I was stupid.

I squeezed my way through the dumbfounded but rowdy crowd to the fish tank on the mantle. I picked up the glass casket of floating goldfish and brought it into the kitchen. I'd killed them. I felt like a jerk, because now, not only had I killed the fish, but how were we going to play Goldfish Frenzy at the party? I needed a Plan B.

I looked around our kitchen for an idea and saw that Kenny had picked up a box of crackers from the store. Moving quickly, I grabbed the crackers, a jar of peanut butter, and a large plate from the cabinet. Within a couple of minutes, I'd made a display on a plate: dead goldfish on Saltines—some plain and some peanut buttered—to serve our guests. Goldfish Frenzy was back on!

"Hors d'oeuvres are served!" I screamed, pushing back into the crowd, holding my tray of ammonia-laced goldfish on crackers. Even though I had to eat about a half dozen of them to entice others to join in the fun, all of the goldfish were devoured by our friends in a matter of moments. This round of Goldfish Frenzy wasn't exactly like the first one we had played, but it was successful, nonetheless.

"This is so gross," Doley said, choking down a PB&fish cracker. "Don't let Sandy see this. It might cause another seizure."

*

Just like on the flight deck in *Top Gun,* the Columbus crew chiefs saluted you and gave you a thumbs up as you left the parking area and headed to the runway for takeoff. You couldn't help but to be filled with pride and confidence. The crew chiefs, who were mostly about the same age as the student pilots, helped us keep our motivation levels high. The crew chiefs kept us safe. These guys were all experts. They were all professionals. They were all proud to serve their country, all proud to serve in the Air Force, and they were all certainly very proud of their jets. They were a great group to work with.

And then, in one swift act of legislation, they were all gone.

In order to save money, at the start of the fiscal year in October, the government instituted some changes to the way it conducted business, and Columbus Air Force Base replaced its highly efficient, highly competent, and highly motivated Air Force flight line personnel with a civilian work force, employed through a government contractor. Student pilots were told that by not having to relocate and reassign Air Force enlisted personnel to new jobs and new bases throughout the world every two to three years, the Air Force would reduce its expenses, and thus reduce its annual operating budget over time. This change was good for the taxpayers and good for the Air Force.

Having heard this rationale explained a few times in almost identical talks by the wing commander, the T-37 squadron commander, and the student squadron commander, I, too, could now convincingly tell the story of how the move would save money over time. What nobody had said, however, was that the immediate impact of the move at Columbus Air Force Base would pretty much result in entropy on the flight line. Did they not know about this? Or was this just something we were not supposed to talk about?

As each October day went by, everyone started to notice that takeoff times scheduled for the later flying periods would get scratched from the scheduling board more and more frequently. The new civilian aircraft maintenance contract personnel couldn't keep up with the required aircraft inspections and minor maintenance issues needed to keep jets flying throughout the days. They weren't prepared to handle the combined demands of moving jets in and out of the parking area every three minutes, handling maintenance issues as they arose, refueling aircraft in a timely manner, and rotating jets that needed inspections into the hangar in a systematic way so as to have enough airworthy jets ready to be flown. The new civilian aircraft maintenance contract personnel just seemed to be running around the flight line and putting out fires, and the preferred method to putting out fires was by grounding jets to buy time to address the problems.

At first, these cancellations were just inconvenient for the aircrews whose jets were scratched from the daily schedule. As October dragged on, however, and the maintenance situation didn't get any better, Columbus Air Force Base was faced with a bigger problem.

Both the T-37 and T-38 squadrons at Columbus had about a hundred jets each, and at any given time, a percentage of these jets required maintenance or scheduled inspections. In order for each squadron to fly more than a hundred missions each day with fewer than a hundred jets on any given day, you needed to have some jets fly one ride after another after another and, sometimes, after another. If a jet wasn't ready to fly at 0800 hours, it was unlikely that the jet could fly at 1100 hours, 1400 hours, or 1700 hours, either. Four missions would be lost—not just one. Beyond merely training rides, the greater UPT timeline was feeling the effect of our new, inefficient civilian aircraft maintenance contract personnel.

The timeline was the official UPT measuring stick. The computerized timeline converted hours logged during jet rides and simulator missions into training days, and the timeline projected whether UPT classes would finish UPT training on their pre-designated graduation dates or not. Dagger flight had fallen behind the timeline. Without enough jets to fly, and add the infamously bad Columbus weather to the mix, all of Columbus Air Force Base was in trouble.

Right after our Mid-Phase Contact checkrides, when the UPT syllabus of instruction called for just about every other ride of ours to be a solo flight, things really got bad. Kenny and I got the whole rundown from Lieutenant Wilson, because he was a scheduler, and schedulers needed to know all about the UPT timeline. According to Lieutenant Wilson, Columbus had fallen more than eleven days behind the timeline. Eleven days behind wasn't necessarily outside of the range of normal for Columbus, but at a recent meeting of the leaders of Air Training Command, our wing commander had been called out in front of his peers. Columbus was behind schedule; the other UPT bases in Texas, Oklahoma, and Arizona were all ahead.

Our wing commander wasn't happy about being called out in front of his peers. Changes were being implemented to the way Columbus conducted its business. He may not have had any authority over the new civilian contractors, but our wing commander sure did have a say in how flight line operations could adapt so that the base wouldn't fall any farther behind the timeline than was necessary.

First, SOFs needed to be less conservative as to how they interpreted the prevailing weather conditions. If the weather was forecast to get worse, assume that it might not, and launch whatever percentage of the fleet could be launched.

Second, flight commanders like Captain Wright needed maximize their allotted number of jet and simulator time slots for upcoming days of training. No assigned takeoff times were to go unfilled. No open simulator times were to go unfilled. All Instructor Pilots were to be available to fill every potential cockpit seat of every single training period—crew rest permitting. If the base couldn't get ahead of the timeline in the jet, it was going to get as far ahead as it could in the simulator.

Third, schedulers like Lieutenants Prince and Wilson needed to find as many guest help instructors as possible. Guest help instructors were pilots like Major Lawson and Class Commander Lieutenant Billy Mike who were not assigned to a specific flight line training flight like Dagger, but they were IPs nonetheless and able to fill jets and sims in order to help get the base back on its timeline. Kenny and I watched Lieutenants Prince and Wilson work the scheduling board and the telephone like a giant puzzle that they couldn't put down until every last problem was solved. No matter how long it took.

According to Lieutenant Wilson, two major factors worked in favor of Dagger flight now that the class had completed its Mid-Phase Contact checkride. One, the class was now eligible to begin the major part of instrument training in the simulator. Two, because we would still need to practice our aerobatic maneuvers, like loops, cloverleaves, and barrel rolls, to prepare for our Final Contact checkride in the jet, just about every other jet ride for us, as listed in the syllabus of instruction, was a solo flight to an area. Schedulers could probably fill as many jets as could be issued to Dagger flight on any particular day.

UPT got a whole lot busier.

*

"Yo! Tur-BIG-lio!" Foghorn Van Dorn bellowed much louder than necessary as he led the class in a review of our academic lesson on instrument flying in the T-37. "What are the six steps you need to take upon reaching the initial approach fix?"

"Sir, the first thing I do is start timing my approach by pressing the second-hand reset button on my clock in the cockpit. Then, I turn the jet to intercept the inbound course." Al was doing okay, so far. "I pull my throttles back to begin my descent. I twist in my course setting, and I track the inbound course." By my count, Al had recited five of the six steps, all of which began with the letter *T*, making it easy for me to keep track. He needed to say one more step, but Al was pausing for such a long time and flipping through his highlighted notes for so long, I didn't think he was going to get the last T-word.

The room got uncomfortably quiet as Al fumbled through his latest stack of index cards. I think Al was the only one who made index cards. While Captain Van Dorn and the rest of the class waited, Al held his study guide up to his face and flipped quickly through his heavily highlighted pages, desperately searching for the last step needed.

From my table, halfway across the classroom, it looked to me like Al may had gotten a little highlighter happy and used fluorescent green to emphasize most of the words in the study guide we'd been issued. Apparently, Doley had observed the same thing.

"Al," Doley broke the classroom silence, "ya' could save a lot of money on highlightahs, if ya' just highlighted the words on the page that ya' thought *weren't* important."

Even Captain Van Dorn laughed at Doley's remark, which only encouraged Doley to continue harassing Al, while Al kept frantically rifling through his papers for the last T-word.

"Al," Doley reloaded and fired again, "why don't ya' just buy a can of fluorescent paint and dip all of ya' study guides into it one page at a time? Ya'd probably save a lot of time, too."

Al was panicking. You could tell. Captain Van Dorn seemed to be enjoying Al's discomfort, and for sure, he was enjoying hearing Doley pick on Al. For his part, Doley was just getting started.

"Al," Doley was firing again, "when ya' pahk ya' cah out in the pahkin' lot, do ya' highlight ya' license plate to make it easiah to find ya' caah at the end of the work day?"

Nice one, Doley!

"I make my radio call!" Al yelled.

"Tur-BIG-lio!" Captain Van Dorn was still laughing. "You got 'em! Finally! You used way too many words, and you'd probably be at your final approach fix by the time you said them all, but you got the steps!" Foghorn clucked proudly, still laughing at Doley's jokes.

The more I observed Captain Van Dorn in action, the more I actually began to think that he liked to pick on Al just for the easy laughs he got from the class.

"Yo, Jellicot! Is there an easier way to remember these steps?" Captain Van Dorn turned to his reliable student with real flight experience.

"Time Turn Throttles Twist Track Talk," Mark answered effortlessly.

"That's right, Jellicot! That's right!" Captain Van Dorn boomed. I don't think Mark ever missed a question in class or on a test. He was definitely Captain Van Dorn's favorite student in both the classroom and the jet.

According to Lieutenant Wilson, even though Captain Van Dorn always made a big deal in the flight room about wanting to fly with Mark and not Al, Captain Van Dorn had become part of Al's IP Continuity, and IP Continuity was an important component in student training. In other words, if a certain phase of training might take fifteen to twenty flights to complete, student pilots should generally fly with only about three or four different instructors over the course of the fifteen to twenty rides in order to optimize instruction and learning. This was especially important for new students.

"Just imagine," Lieutenant Wilson had told Kenny and me, "if a student in danger of washing out of the program went to a review board and had flown ten rides with ten different instructors; no review board would wash that student out because they'd say that the training wasn't consistent." As Lieutenant Wilson explained it, this made sense to me. I understood why the schedulers kept Al flying with Captain Van Dorn a few times a week.

"Yo, Wright!" Captain Van Dorn was ready to have a little fun with me apparently. "What is the mnemonic device...did I get that right, Wright? Mnemonic device? What is the mnemonic device we use to remember those six steps?"

Ah, Captain Van Dorn! Thank you for your generous gift.

I knew he wanted me to say *6Ts* as the way to remember Time Turn Throttles Twist Track Talk. But Captain Van Dorn had also just given me license to say anything I wanted by asking me a question about personal technique. If he was going to have a little fun with me, I thought it only fair that I could have a little fun with him.

"Sir, the mnemonic device I use," I stated simply, as he and the class listened attentively, "is *5Ts and a T.*" Captain Van Dorn's jaw just kind of unhinged and hung open loosely, swinging from side to side, like he was trying to clear his ears.

After the laughter in the room died down, Captain Van Dorn's composure returned. "Yo! Wright! What in *thee* hell?!"

He had clucked probably the best comeback he could manage. "No, that's not right!"

"Sir, that's what I use," I innocently continued. "It stands for Time Turn Throttles Twist Track Talk." As I listed the steps, I held up my hands to count them with my fingers. When I finished my list, I had extended five fingers on one hand and one finger out on the other. "*5Ts and a T,*" I reiterated, showing him one hand with five fingers out and one hand and one finger out to perfectly match my mnemonic device.

While this delighted the rest of the class, Captain Van Dorn clearly wasn't pleased. But how could he possibly say this was wrong? It was technique only.

"Yo! Dolan!" Captain Van Dorn barked, still wanting his preferred phrase: *6Ts.*

Bad move, Captain Van Dorn.

"Dolan! What is the mnemonic device you use to remember the six steps we take once we fly past the initial approach fix?" he asked.

"Sir, the mnemonic device I use," Doley deadpanned, "is *3Ts 2Ts plus.*" Doley was always a step ahead, and his mnemonic device resulted in the class erupting in laughter, louder than before.

"Dolan!" Captain Van Dorn shouted above the classroom howls. "What in *thee* hell?!"

Immediately, Al's hand went up.

"Yo! Tur-BIG-lio! What is it?!" Captain Van Dorn barked disgustedly.

"Sir, is *6Ts* procedure or technique?" Al naively asked his favorite question.

"Shut up, Tur-BIG-lio!" Captain Van Dorn shook his head. He'd had enough of our stupidity for one class. "Just shut up."

*

Now that Columbus Air Force Base was pushing hard to make up time on the flying timeline, instead of flying the usual one mission per day, most Dagger students were flying two.

Flying twice in a day was called *double-turning,* and whether you flew one jet ride and one sim ride, two jet rides with an instructor, or one jet ride with an instructor and one jet ride as a solo mission, double-turning was totally exhausting. In the jet or in the sim, you were always working, concentrating, and making corrections to things you'd screwed up throughout the course of the ride. In the sim, you didn't have the same underlying anxiety and urge to panic that you felt when you flew a real mission in the Tweet, but in the sim, your instructor could secretly hit a fast forward button to accelerate your progress along your flight path or secretly call the sim operator to have him re-program the sim in order to change your surroundings and put you into a new place in your mission. No matter how hard you worked in either the jet or the sim, you were always behind. You were always playing catch up. A constant battle fighting off entropy.

I was never comfortable double-turning. I liked the slower, more manageable pace of flying just once per day. When you double-turned, you had no down time. You had no time to decompress, to review, study, and prepare for your next ride. You just had to do your best to get ready and try somehow to get through the day's second mission. I never liked playing the catch-up game. Over the next eleven flying days, I double-turned seven times.

After a twelve-hour day on the base, I'd use my next three hours for a workout, dinner, and a shower. In the last hour before our mandatory eight-hour period of uninterrupted crew rest, Kenny and I would chair-fly our missions for the next day with each other. Whichever one of us was not practicing his mission would play the role of the IP for the other guy. We usually had a good time practicing and joking around in the comfort of our rental-house-turned-playhouse. Chair-flying wasn't really all that stressful. On the other hand, because Kenny liked to hang out around the house at night in just a white sleeveless undershirt and his tighty-whitey underwear, I was never really all that comfortable chair-flying, either.

Truth be told, I was always anxious about flying solo. Between the maintenance challenges at the base and the pressures brought about by the expectations of my classmates, I started dreading solos.

Prior to taking an aircraft into the sky, Air Force pilots were required to conduct a preflight inspection, known in pilot terms as a *walk-around*. Using your checklist to guide you from one step to the next, you visibly and physically inspected the outside of the jet to ensure that the airframe was in good repair, all maintenance pins and flags were removed, and that the tires had enough tread on them to withstand at least one bad landing during the course of the ride. You also needed to review the maintenance log, the Air Force Technical Order 781, known in pilot terms as *the forms*. The forms were a three-ringed binder of documents specific to each aircraft, a record used to ensure that no required inspections were due, no minor maintenance was necessary, and no pilots who had flown the jet before you had reported any problems that had not been addressed.

As real pilots, instructor pilots could override the need for any required inspection or minor maintenance issue that had been noted in the maintenance logs. Student pilots, however, did not have the authority to override these issues; if a jet required an overdue inspection or had a minor maintenance issue that needed to be addressed, a student could not accept the jet for flight. I understood the concept, but I never really understood how to apply it. That is, I really didn't know how to read the forms.

When we had Air Force crew chiefs on the flight line, most student pilots were confident that these guys had our backs and that our fellow Air Force family members wouldn't let a student accept a jet that might not be ready to launch into the sky. In our first couple of months on the flight line, I grew to trust what crew chiefs told me. I never learned what I needed to know about my jet for myself to review or fill out the forms without worry.

But with the new civilian maintenance personnel, our instructors had become concerned that the civilians might try to pressure solo students to take jets into the air that might not necessarily be suitable for flying. I always felt much more excited about flying solo rides after I had finished them than any time before or during.

Maybe just as nerve-wracking, some guys wanted to use their solo missions to take the jets for a joyride rather than practice the required maneuvers for our Final Contact checkride. They seemed to expect I would want to go joyriding, too. I didn't.

"Aaay," Kenny whispered over my shoulder, "let's meet up on Cheap Suit."

Cheap Suit stood for UHF radio frequency 299.5 MHz, which translated to *two-niner-niner-five* in pilot talk and Cheap Suit in Doley-code, because Doley would tell us that the cost of a cheap suit was $29.95. By giving me the code Cheap Suit, Kenny was suggesting that we should switch from our assigned radio frequency when we were established in an area to an unassigned frequency, like UHF frequency 299.5, so that we could talk to each other—without the controller listening to us. This was totally against the rules, and I didn't want to do it, but every time I flew solo, someone always whispered a secret, meet-up radio frequency in my ear between my locker in the hallway and the flight line van that drove air crews out to the jets.

I only switched over to Cheap Suit one time on a solo, but when I did, I didn't just leave the radio frequency I had been assigned...I changed frequencies by the book. That is, I asked permission from the airspace controller. And when the airspace controller granted me permission, I interpreted my actions as being perfectly legal.

Pilots asked permission from airspace controllers to switch off their assigned frequencies all the time. Sometimes, you requested to go off-frequency to get the numbers from ATIS, the Automated Terminal Information Service, which told a pilot an airport's landing runway, weather conditions, and local altimeter setting. Other times, you may have needed to call the SOF to give a PIREP, a pilot report on weather conditions you encountered during your flight. These were legitimate reasons for which to ask permission to leave your assigned frequency.

Besides, controllers knew that pilots monitored Guard, an emergency frequency on the UHF radio band that pilots listened to in addition to their assigned frequencies — like listening to two radios at once. Controllers had the ability to broadcast on Guard. Controllers knew that if they needed to speak with pilots in an emergency, they could broadcast on the UHF Guard frequency.

After getting the controller's permission, I reached down and changed the numbers of the radio dial on the center console to 2-9-9-5. Then, I switched my radio from preset radio channels to manual frequencies. Like that, I was on Cheap Suit.

I didn't know if I should check in, like pilots were required to do when changing frequencies, or not. But it didn't matter. There were no rules governing radio procedures on Cheap Suit.

"Aaay!!! I'm fuckin' upside down!" I immediately recognized Kenny's voice on Cheap Suit. "I'm fuckin' upside down, lookin' up at some fuckin' piece of shit town in Alabama! I can't believe people live there. Holy shit! What a piece of shit! WUH-HOO! This is awesome!"

Apparently, Kenny was already narrating his joyride while rattling off an anywhere-that-isn't-New York-sucks routine. He sounded like he was having the time of his life, doing doughnuts in the sky, as if he were burning tire track circles, spinning his Mustang in an empty parking lot on Long Island.

"Drop your mask, and watch your face in the mirror when you pull some G's," another voice broadcasted on Cheap Suit. It was another Dagger solo student.

"Hey, guys." I jumped into the Cheap Suit conversation, not really knowing what to say. "Who's on freq?"

I asked this question innocently enough. I wanted to let my friends know I had joined them on the Cheap Suit frequency, but since I wasn't comfortable fooling around in the jet and doing the kind of stuff that they were obviously doing, this was the only thing I could think to say. Nobody answered right away.

"Me," Kenny finally said.

"Me," our other classmate followed right after Kenny in a manner more consistent with the speed at which radio calls were generally exchanged.

"Me," added somebody else whose voice I didn't recognize.

I guess there was at least one rule for radio procedures on Cheap Suit: Don't say your name. This was a good rule, too, because just as soon as we'd finished our little roll call, the voice that I hadn't recognized spoke again and, this time, spoke very sternly through my headset.

"You students need to get off this frequency and stay on your assigned channel. This is a gross breach of radio d—"

I never heard the end of that transmission.

After I caught my breath, I practiced my aerobatic maneuvers and monitored my assigned radio channel. I didn't say another word on the radio until I needed to request clearance back to the base.

*

"Wessels and Wright," Lieutenant Wilson called across the Dagger flight room as we were studying with a group of friends at the center table, "I need to talk to you two at my desk."

Neither Kenny nor I showed any outward indication of guilt. The IP that busted us in the sky must have checked out the daily flight logs to see which students were flying solo. Hopefully, he'd told only Lieutenant Wilson because Lieutenant Wilson wouldn't do anything more than slap us on the wrist. But if our violation had been reported to somebody less forgiving, we could have been in some serious trouble.

Kenny and I sat in our usual seats at Lieutenant Wilson's desk and smiled as if we didn't know what might be coming. I was stupid to have switched over to Cheap Suit. I was one of only three students in Dagger not to have passed the Mid-Phase Contact check, and now, with our accelerated pace of training, I was only about a week away from my Final Contact checkride.

After making a couple of changes to the next day's flying schedule on the white scheduling board behind him, Lieutenant Wilson sat in his chair, spun it around to face us, and pulled himself in close to his desk. By the look on his face, he wasn't about to deliver good news.

"I'm not going to be able to fly with you guys for a while," he said unexpectedly.

Kenny and I were confused.

"I'm scheduled to have surgery on my knee for an old soccer injury from the Academy. I'm going to be DNIF for a couple of months." Heck, Lieutenant Wilson wasn't going to be doing *any* flying.

"Sir, are we going to be assigned to a new IP?" I asked, hoping that we wouldn't.

"Aaay. We're not going to have to fly with a dick, are we?" Kenny and I were thinking the same thing. He just asked it in a more direct manner.

"No," Lieutenant Wilson laughed. "I'll still be your IP. I'm only going to be out of work for about a week. After that, I'll be coming back to the flight line to help Lieutenant Prince with the scheduling duties. I'll be able to brief students for solo rides. I can help you study emergency procedures. But I'll be on crutches for a while; so I won't be able to fly or even sim." Then, he added in a mumble, "Which is actually fine with me, because if I can't fly, I sure as hell don't want to sit in the sim all day."

Back in our study group at the center table, we let everyone in on Lieutenant Wilson's news.

"Who are you guys going to fly with?" Big Kurt asked.

Of course, I assumed that I'd still be flying with Major Lawson, but I had no idea who else would be added to my continuity.

Doley stood up. "Nobody go anywhere. I'll be right back," he announced, stepping back from the table.

Everybody's eyes followed Doley as he quickly walked to the corner of the room where we stored our gradebooks. Doley pulled one of the thin, black three-ring binders from the very end of the row of gradebooks, where both Kenny and I kept ours because our last names were at the end of the alphabet. Then, Doley quickly returned to his seat at the table, carrying my gradebook with him.

"Ray, I don't think that you have evah flown with a dick," Doley declared. "I am going to take a look through ya' gradebook to prove I'm right."

Of course he was right. I never flew with anybody who screamed at me in flight. I never flew with anybody who grabbed me by my oxygen mask and jerked my head around or slammed my head against the canopy with a flick of the control stick, or treated me in a demeaning way of any kind because I wasn't a pilot. I never really considered that when Lieutenant Wilson G-LOC'ed me he did so to be mean. I knew he did it to be funny.

"Just as I thought." Doley nodded his head as he flipped through my gradebook. "Let me share with everybody at this table the instructahs on ya' continuity: Majah Lawson...." Doley smiled and nodded repeatedly, as if he were counting the number of times listed in my gradebook that I'd flown with Major Lawson. "Lieutenant Wilson...." Doley kept smiling and nodding. "Santa Claus," he said next, nodding some more. "Mother Theresa," he announced, and after a brief pause, he said, "and the Easter Bunny."

Doley allowed time for the group at the center table to laugh while he just looked at me, all the while nodding and smiling. When the laughter subsided, he finished making his point. "Not only have you nevah flown with a dick," Doley said, "you only fly with instructahs who give you gifts or bring you candy every time they see you. It's about time you added a dick to ya' continuity."

Chapter 13 — "Downgrades"

First Lieutenant Jeff Prince, the head scheduler in Dagger, was a bulked-up Tom Cruise look-alike who probably spent as much time working on bizarre comedy routines as he did in working out at the gym, and with Al Turbiglio as one of his assigned students, he was never at a loss for new material. Because his desk was right next to Lieutenant Wilson's desk in front of the scheduling board, Kenny and I had interacted with him fairly regularly.

Like Lieutenant Wilson and most of the rest of the other Dagger IPs, Lieutenant Prince was a FAIP, but unlike most of the rest of the IPs and students in the room, Lieutenant Prince was not an Academy grad. He had graduated from Georgia or Georgia Tech and gotten his Air Force commission through ROTC. Maybe that's why he and Al had initially been matched up.

At the end of the flying day, I sat at Lieutenant Wilson's desk and studied for my Final Contact checkride. Even though I was sick of studying, you had to know everything about the operating limits of the Tweet and contact flying for the Final Contact check. I didn't know everything. Not even close.

When the students and IPs started trickling back into Dagger from the last period of flying, however, I stopped reading my flight manuals and impatiently waited for Lieutenant Prince to post the matches for students and check pilots on the schedule for the next day. Luckily, it was the first thing he did when he got back into the room.

"Lieutenant Prince, is that a joke?" I asked as he put my name next to a check pilot.

"Is what a joke?" he asked me back, still writing on the board and not turning around.

"Sir, you've got me up to fly my checkride with Lieutenant Scowcroft," I clarified for him.

"So what?" Lieutenant Prince turned around. "Why would that be a joke?"

"Sir, Lieutenant Scowcroft is the guy who hooked me from the box on my solo," I said. "I don't know that we'd make a good match for my checkride."

"Here, you can read it for yourself," he shot back, dropping some handwritten notes onto the desk in front of me.

This was no joke. Having already failed my first checkride in the T-37, I was going to fly my second one with the IP who hooked me from the box, directed me to make a full-stop landing after one solo traffic pattern, and set me up for my walk of shame.

I fully expected that Lieutenant Scowcroft would grill me on traffic pattern procedures during my hour-long ground evaluation after we'd flown the checkride. I knew I wouldn't miss *Overhead, break departure end. Acknowledge,* like I did the time he hooked me from the box, but I was sure he'd test me on every other potential conflict in Sunfish and probably even ask me to talk him through how I would handle an emergency procedure in a crowded traffic pattern. I felt pretty good about my flying, but I hadn't studied the book part of flying as much some of my classmates did, like Mark or Al or Chuck.

Before my first checkride, I'd learned that students from every UPT class kept books on all of the pilots in Check Section. Students would write notes on the pilot, the type of mission flown, the general knowledge questions and the emergency procedures asked, any pet peeves the check pilot might have, the grade the student earned for the ride, and the number of *downgrades* the check pilot had given the student for each of the evaluable skills on the grade-sheet.

A downgrade meant receiving a grade of *Good* rather than *Excellent* on a certain maneuver, and the total number of downgrades on a checkride was the key indicator for the quality of a student's overall grade. For example, for those students who received grades of *Excellent,* students with a one-downgrade *E* were considered to have flown a better ride than students who earned an *E* with two, three, of four downgrades.

On my first checkride, my *Unsat* Mid-Phase Contact check, I was downgraded for nine of my graded maneuvers on the ride. Having now read through the covert check pilot intel books in every flight in the squadron, I knew that nine downgrades were a lot. I figured that if check pilots knew they were going to hook a student on a checkride, they needed to ensure the *Unsat* was a clean kill and pad the *U* with lots of downgrades. If a student was in danger of washing out of UPT for being graded *Unsat* on multiple checkrides, a student with a record of multiple downgrade *Unsats* would be a lot easier to kick out of UPT than a student with one or two-downgrade *Unsats*. Most students figured that you could get an *E* with up to four downgrades, a *G* with five to eight downgrades, but once you got to nine or more downgrades, you were probably going to hook the ride. Like I did.

Since the student/check pilot match-ups for checkrides were posted the day before these important flights, students could study up on their assigned check pilots to look for clues on the maneuvers they'd be expected to fly or the general knowledge and emergency procedures questions they'd be expected to answer. These covert intel books also revealed the grading patterns of the various check pilots. My first contribution to the secret book in Dagger was that if you didn't comply with published altitude restrictions, you would get an *Unsat*.

After Lieutenant Prince posted my checkride match-up, I dug into the underground intel book in Dagger but found only a couple of write-ups on Lieutenant Scowcroft from past classes. With Captain Wright's permission, I visited our sister flight down the hall in Warhawk to read their secret book, but they didn't have much, either.

Since I had a hall pass, I asked the student Duty Dogs stationed at the doors of Sabre, Thunderbolt, Mustang, and

Excalibur flights if they would get me their secret books, too. Usually, these unmarked binders of underground intelligence were inconspicuously stashed behind the bookshelf that held the student gradebooks in each flight room. But by the time I got to the back of the other flight rooms, I probably spent more time talking to Academy buddies that I didn't get to see that much anymore than I did preparing for my checkride.

Anyway, about the only trend I could spot in all the reports was that Lieutenant Scowcroft liked to fly to Gunshy. And having looked through every secret book in the squadron, it did look like the students were right about the number of downgrades to get an *Excellent,* a *Good,* or an *Unsat.*

*

"Checkride: Final Contact," I wrote at the top of my entry to the Dagger secret book, following the standard format in which all entries had been made.

Checkride:	Final Contact
Check Pilot:	Scowcroft
Student Pilot:	Wright
Profile:	Gun Hi

I was ready when Lieutenant Scowcroft told me we'd be flying to Gunshy. My takeoff and departure were uneventful, and I thought I might be in for a pretty good checkride when I made my first turn two miles past the end of the runway, and my seat stayed in position and didn't slide down its rails to the floor of the Tweet cockpit.

I remembered to set the power on my two throttles at the proper setting when we leveled off at six thousand feet so as not to fly at Mach-fucking-One en route to Gunshy, sixty miles south of Columbus. Still, we got there in less than twenty minutes.

Gun Pattern:	St-in-no flap
Ovhd:	no flap
Ovhd:	S.E.

Major Lawson had made me fly to Gunshy every other ride we flew together. I had no problem finding the airfield and no problem with my straight-in no-flap pattern. I stuck my landing from my no flap overhead pattern, and my single-engine overhead pattern was good, too. When we departed Gunshy for the Southern MOA, I was thinking that the checkride was off to a good start. To that point, Lieutenant Scowcroft hadn't taken control of the jet from me.

Area Hi: T.P. Stalls/slo flight

             P.O. Stalls

             Spin: Pre — LR

                              Rec — HL

I didn't get any downgrades for my work in area White-High. I was pretty good at traffic pattern stalls and slow flight. I nailed my power-on stalls. I did a really good spin prevent with the nose low and the jet turning to the right, and my spin recovery for my high, left-turning spin entry went well, too, having mastered both the spin recovery **BOLDFACE** and Doley's Two Bonks technique. With all the tough stuff done, the easiest parts of my checkride remained.

That's when I started racking up the downgrades, which I noted in my write-up with the letter G for *Good.*

Area Low: Aileron Roll

             Loop — G (pulled off to the right on backside of maneuver)

             Lazy Eight — G (did not finish maneuver in the same direction started)

             Immelmann

             Recoveries: Nose Low — G (did not pull power back quickly enough)

                                     Nose Hi — G (did not

get nose to horizon

quickly enough)

In White-Low, with the exception of my Immelmann, a half-loop where you flip the jet from upside-down to right-side-up just after the apex of the maneuver, and my aileron roll, a move for which nobody ever got downgraded, I got downgrades for all my moves.

And as the downgrade count started creeping up, I started thinking that Lieutenant Scowcroft might be setting me up for another *Unsat*. Especially because of what happened next.

"Columbus Approach, Tweet 7-4, request recovery, Area White," I called over the radio after my nose low recovery.

"Tweet 7-4, Columbus Approach, fly heading 3-0-0, descend and maintain 5,000, Columbus altimeter 3-0-1-5," the controller said.

"Tweet 7-4, heading 3-0-0, down to 5,000, 3-0-1-5," I acknowledged.

I pulled the power, lowered the nose of the jet, turned to a 3-0-0 heading, and set 3-0-1-5 on my altimeter. But when I rolled out of my turn to a wings-level descent, something didn't look right. The sun was in the wrong place, and my flight path was going to take me across the Tombigbee River. The sun was too far to the right in my windscreen, and the river should have been on my left. And I should have been flying on a course that would lead me up the river—not across it. We weren't going the right way.

I checked the magnetic compass at the top of the canopy bow. An unpowered back-up to the primary heading indicator, the mag compass drifted left then right and back again from number to number, like the dial on a scale when you first step on it. I couldn't tell what number it was going to land on, but I did know, however, we weren't headed northeast. It looked like southwest—towards Meridian. We needed to be flying to the northeast...back to Columbus.

If I couldn't fly my jet back to Columbus, I wouldn't pass the ride.

What the hell?!

I knew about a situation in the Tweet where aerobatic maneuvers and spinning the jet on purpose could cause the heading system to get screwed up, its readings becoming unreliable. This wasn't an uncommon occurrence, but because I'd never seen it happen, it was an uncommon occurrence for me. Of course, it had to happen on my checkride!

Follow the river.

I'd read about how to handle the situation, and the checklist strapped to my leg specifically directed me to look for this heading error as part of my descent check. If I confirmed a heading system problem, I needed to *fast slave* the heading system to correct the error by pressing the fast slave switch for no more than two seconds and then maintaining level flight for at least three minutes while the system corrected itself. But now that I was headed to the southwest at 200 knots, if I pushed the switch to correct the problem and then couldn't turn for three minutes, I'd be ten miles off course by the time I'd be able to make a turn to the right course.

I knew I was flying in the wrong direction. I knew I needed to fast slave the heading system, but I also knew that once I did, I'd be locked into flying in the wrong direction for the next ten miles. I had to make a decision.

Follow the river.

Ignoring the information my heading indicator was giving me, I cranked the jet to my right and pointed it up the Tenn-Tom. I knew that as long as I could follow the river, I didn't need navigation equipment to get back to the base. Once I made decision and my turn, I felt like I'd be fine.

"Hey," Lieutenant Scowcroft's voice came through the intercom, "how about we do what the Dash One recommends?" Reaching in front of me from the right seat of the cockpit, he flipped the switch to fast slave the heading system. And just like that, I felt like shit.

Oh, shit! Oh, shit! I just hooked! I just hooked my second checkride.

As soon as Lieutenant Scowcroft fast slaved the system, the aircraft-heading indicator began to correct itself. I knew I needed to keep the wings level after he'd hit the switch, so I didn't try to turn and chase the spinning needle on my instrument panel. I kept the wings level, still pointing the jet up the river, hoping the controller wouldn't give me a new vector for at least another few minutes.

As we descended, I watched the heading indicator, like a gambler watching a roulette wheel. I'd been assigned a vector, which I'd acknowledged. I needed to be flying a heading of 3-0-0. With one failed checkride already, all my chips were on 3-0-0.

C'mon. Three-zero-zero.

It didn't take the full three minutes before the heading indicator stopped...right on 3-0-0! Following the river had worked, and I hadn't lost my all my chips. Yet.

Sunfish: St-in Norm — G (long landing)
               Ovhd: Norm
               Ovhd: -S.E.
Other: Inflight Checks — G (did not fast slave heading system)
               Radio Procedures — G (slow to acknowledge radio calls)
               Airmanship — G (indecisive throughout mission)
               General Knowledge — G (didn't study enough)

I finished my write-up and counted up my downgrades. One, two, three, four, five, six, seven, eight, nine, ten.

"How do you screw up vectors?" Doley asked as I counted the downgrades I'd listed. He'd been sitting next to me, watching and commenting while I made my write-up for the Dagger secret book on student checkrides.

"I didn't screw up vectors!" I protested. "I screwed up by not fast slaving the system when I saw that my heading indicator was out of whack."

Doley was right, though. I did nearly screw up vectors. And that nearly screwed up the whole ride.

In our debriefing, Lieutenant Scowcroft, the guy who hooked me from the box, discussed each maneuver listed on the grade-sheet one item at a time. After more than an hour of feedback on my flying, he asked what felt like hundreds of questions on contact procedures and T-37 systems to test my general knowledge. Then, he had me talk through various emergency procedures from initial identification of unsafe situations to either landing the jet or ejecting and landing in my parachute, reciting all necessary **BOLDFACE** and reading through all necessary checklists.

Can I just have my grade? Did I pass, or did I fail?

Lieutenant Scowcroft made one last mark on the grade-sheet and looked me in the eyes to deliver the verdict.

"You didn't properly correct your heading system in accordance with the T-37 flying manual," he told me. "If this were an Instrument checkride, you would certainly not have passed. But in my judgment, you did show me that you knew how to use ground references to find your way back to Columbus."

Overall: 10 ↓ G

"*G* for *Good*," I said to Doley, closing the secret book. I had passed my second checkride!

"A 10-downgrade *Good!*" Doley said, spinning his pen around in his hand. "Maw like G for *Gift*."

*

"Lieutenant Prince is totally insane!" Kenny proclaimed, sitting down at the center table of the Dagger flight room with Doley, Kurt, Chuck, and me. Kenny and Lieutenant Prince made up the last aircrew to finish their night flying mission. The rest of us were sitting around, eating pizza and drinking beer with our instructors, talking either about the night mission we'd just flown or planning for the cross-country missions we were all scheduled to fly the next day.

This was the most relaxed I think I'd ever felt on the flight line.

Night flying in T-37s was a one-night, one-ride block of instruction that served as an introduction for student pilots to flying in the dark. The mission wasn't complicated, and the expectations for the students were low. The syllabus of instruction mandated that our instructors make a number of demonstrations during the ride, which meant that the IPs got to do a lot of the flying. In my mind, low expectations and lots of IP flying time meant a pretty stress-free ride.

Another reason for beer and pizza in the flight room was that we were all getting out of Columbus for the weekend. Word was that after the Dagger cross-country rides over the weekend, Columbus Air Force Base would actually be ahead of the timeline, like the other UPT bases in Air Training Command. None of this, however, explained what Kenny Wessels meant when he declared Lieutenant Prince totally insane.

Kenny sat at the center table wearing a wide grin. He didn't seem interested in eating or drinking anything. He was happy just to sit and smile.

"Kenny, what happened to your eyes?" I asked. They were totally bloodshot. "I haven't seen eyes that red since the time I was six years old, and I strained so hard on the toilet that I blew out the blood vessels in my eyes."

"Aaay, that's gross! It's from negative Gs," he said, giggling like he was hypoxic. "It was totally sick! We played rollercoaster the whole ride!"

"Wait a second! Wait a second!" Doley interjected. "First of all, Ray, nobody wants to know about ya' bathroom problems. Second of all, Kenny, what's rolluhcoastah?"

"Aaay, Lieutenant Prince kept zooming the jet up to trade airspeed for altitude, which made us slow way down at the top of the altitude block," Kenny explained and zoomed his hand up like a climbing rollercoaster car."As we climbed, he had me make the rollercoaster sound. You know, *Ching. Ching. Ching.* Then, when we ran out of airspeed, he'd unload and push over on the stick, and we'd go totally negative. My hands flew up to the top of the canopy." Kenny acted out his rollercoaster ride as he told us his story.

"I flew up outta my seat because I hadn't strapped in tight enough, and all the pages of the checklists strapped to my legs lifted straight up," he said, standing up out of his seat, flailing his hands over his head. "As we picked up speed on our way to the bottom of the altitude block, we just screamed, like we were on a rollercoaster," and Kenny let out of high-pitched scream, as if someone on *Pee-wee's Playhouse* had just said today's secret word.

Before more stories started rolling, Captain Wright gave Mark Jellicot the signal to wrap things up for the night. Everyone had finished debriefing, the pizza was gone, and even though there was still plenty of beer, we only had another half hour before we would hit the end of our twelve-hour day. By regulation, student pilots couldn't be at work for more than twelve hours.

We cleaned up the flight room and waited for Captain Wright.

"You might have heard that cross-country flying would be one of the high points of your UPT experience," Captain Wright began. "You might not, but if you haven't, I'm here to tell you that it will be. This weekend, when you leave Columbus Air Force Base, flying in your own jet for the first time, you'll come across situations you never expected you'd encounter. You might hear a radio call you've never heard before. You might not. You might be asked to fly an approach that you hadn't planned for. You might not. But you need to be ready for anything, because anything can happen, and if you're ready for anything, you can handle anything, and if you're not ready, you're going to find yourself unprepared and in a whole lot of trouble."

Back and forth, Captain Wright scanned the room as he spoke. Left to right. Right to left. Eyes half-shut as they focused down past the end of his long and slightly sloping nose. He'd shift his weight from his left leg to his right every so often and turn his upper body whenever he did, and he'd begin his scanning again from the new pose.

"Maybe you've picked some fun places to travel to this weekend," he went on. "Then again, maybe not." He paused momentarily to shift and scan. "But let me tell you...wherever you fly, you will get the best training of any pilots in the Air Force with your Dagger IPs and our Dagger flight guest help."

The only thing better than listening to Captain Wright talk in front of the room was listening to him talk after he'd had a couple of beers, and since he'd had a couple of beers, he was going to talk until he ran out our twelve-hour clock.

"Lieutenant Jellicot." Captain Wright scanned the room until his half-closed eyes locked in on Mark. "What have you got planned for the weekend?"

Mark stood up. "Sir, on Friday, I'm going to fly down to Tyndall, home of F-15 Eagle training, because I want to fly the F-15 Eagle after UPT. On Saturday, I'm going to fly to Navy Cecil in Jacksonville, and on the way, I'm going to do a fly-by over the Swamp because the Gators are playing Kentucky, and I'm a University of Florida Gator."

"Sounds like a great cross-country plan, Lieutenant Jellicot," Captain Wright stated proudly. "Have your seat," he said, and Mark sat back down.

"Lieutenant Spranger, where are you headed this weekend?" Captain Wright asked, and big Kurt stood up straight and tall.

"Sir, I'm flying down to MacDill Air Force Base," Kurt beamed. "My family lives in Tampa, and when I first enlisted in the Air Force, I was an F-16 crew chief at MacDill. When I graduate from UPT, that's the jet I want to fly."

"Lieutenant Spranger," Captain Wright proclaimed proudly, "you are going to have a great time. Have your seat. Lieutenant Wessels, where are you off to this weekend?"

Kenny popped up. Still on a high from his rollercoaster ride, Kenny was totally caught up in the moment, as if Captain Wright was the preacher at the Antioch Baptist Church on Highway 45, where you turned 90-to-initial in the Sunfish overhead pattern, and his soul was about to be saved at a tambourine-banging Deep South church revival.

"Aaaay!" Kenny enthusiastically blurted out. "I'm going to HOT-Lanta! My mom and my dad are gonna come out to Dobbins, and they are gonna get to see me flyin' a jet on Friday night and Saturday morning!"

"Outstanding, Lieutenant Wessels!" Captain Wright matched Kenny's enthusiasm and turned to me. But Kenny was so pumped up; he didn't want to sit down. "Then, on Saturday," Kenny continued, "we're gonna fly down to Eglin and get totally trashed in Fort Walton Beach!"

"Have your seat, Lieutenant Wessels," Captain Wright laughed.

"Lieutenant Wright?" Captain Wright said.

Shoot! I was hoping he wouldn't call on me.

Unlike most of the other guys, I didn't really get to make my plan for our weekend cross-country trip. Major Lawson kind of made it for me. Honestly, I wasn't really all that excited about the weekend, but I had to stand up.

"Lieutenant Wright, what will you be doing on your cross-country?" Captain Wright asked.

I know that sometimes it's best to shut up. I had learned that lesson long ago, but maybe because I had had a couple beers, I didn't have my guard up.

"Sir, I will be flying to Knoxville," I began, as if I actually was excited to be flying to Tennessee, while everyone else was either flying home or to a beach party or to a party town, like New Orleans or Houston or HOT-Lanta. "On Friday night, I will be playing Trivial Pursuit™ with Major Lawson and his sister, who—according to Major Lawson—is as big as a barn, cusses like a sailor, and smokes like a chimney."

I could tell that Captain Wright thought this was funny, so like Kenny, I kept talking: "And on Saturday, we'll be flying a low-level mission over Major Lawson's family tobacco farm and landing back in Knoxville again so we can go see his favorite football team, the Tennessee Volunteers, and he and I will sing 'Rocky Top' together all afternoon."

Everybody thought this was great. My classmates were laughing. The IPs were laughing. Even Captain Wright was laughing. Unfortunately, I wasn't joking.

"Lieutenant Wright," Captain Wright smiled after the laughter in the room had subsided, "your plan sounds great, too, and I predict that your T-37 cross-country experience will be an experience that you never forget."

*

"Major Lawson," I nervously confided Sunday morning, "I think I might be having a problem."

I knew nobody wanted to know about my bathroom problems, but I was having a bad one, and things had gotten so bad on my cross-country trip that I had to say something. I was nervous—so much so, I couldn't think clearly.

Normally a wise-cracking, gum-smacking, crusty, old smart aleck, himself, Major Lawson studied my face for a moment before he spoke.

"What's going on, old buddy?" he asked simply.

As anxious as I was about my situation, and as much as I needed help, I was also pretty embarrassed.

"Well, sir, the last two times I've sat down to use the bathroom, I've noticed a lot of blood in the bowl when I'm done with my business," I said.

There! I told him!

Actually, I hadn't told him everything. That morning, it wasn't just some blood in the bowl…it was all blood. The toilet bowl looked like it had been filled with Hawaiian Punch when I stood up.

"You're not on your period, I take it," Major Lawson cracked. He couldn't resist.

When I told him I would try to fly back to Columbus, Major Lawson had me hop in the jet to get my charts and maps organized, and I started running my checklists. But today, even when reading straight from the book in my hand, I couldn't move from one step to the next. Was it the ammonia-laced goldfish? Had I blown a kidney?

Major Lawson hopped in after he'd finished his walk-around. He could tell in an instant that I hadn't finished my checks. "How're you doing there, old buddy?" he asked through the intercom.

I turned my head, and my brain went numb.

Why am I bleeding?

I looked at Major Lawson through my tinted helmet visor and tried to tell him that I was okay, but when I tried to speak, no words came out.

"That's it. Get out," he ordered.

Did I just hook the ride? Am I getting an Unsat *on a cross-country flight because I can't fly the ride? Nobody gets an* Unsat *on a cross-country flight.*

"You're not going to fly today," Major Lawson stated. "I'm fixin' to take you to a doctor. You can do this ride another time."

"Yes, sir," I replied. I could feel my mind and body start to function again. At last, I truly was relieved. I could speak, and I could move, and as I reached for my lap belt, I looked over again and told him, "Thank you."

Major Lawson had me leave all my stuff inside the cockpit—except for my flight cap. After he canceled our flight plan, I followed him to the pick-up truck that his sister had provided for us for the weekend, and off we drove to the doctor's office.

I had no idea what was wrong with me. I wasn't in pain. Maybe my body wasn't able to handle the demands of flying of jets. Maybe I wasn't cut out to be a pilot.

Maybe I ain't shit!

Major Lawson broke the silence as he drove. "How're you feeling, Ray?"

"I'm okay, sir." I said. I didn't know if I was okay, but I suppose I'd felt worse.

"Are you in any pain?" he asked kindly.

"No, sir," I replied. Then, thinking about the situation a little, I added, "I'm just not real excited about having a doctor stick a probe up my ass to find out what's wrong with me."

"Well, old buddy, look at it this way..." Major Lawson thoughtfully offered in his slow country drawl. He tilted his head slightly to the side to look over at me as he drove, and then, he looked back out at the road before he finished his thought. Smacking his gum with a smile, he said, "At least it's not a dick."

*

The doctor's examination didn't take very long. In fact, he spent more time asking me questions than he did looking me over, which was fine with me. Mostly, we talked about my eating habits.

"Usually, I have a couple of Pop-Tarts for breakfast and a Hot Pocket for lunch from the flight line snack bar. In the afternoon, I might have a candy bar or an ice cream." I ate the same thing just about every day. I guess my diet wasn't very good.

"I drink a lot of water, so I am well-hydrated," I added proudly, trying to shake the doctor off his line of questioning. My urine had been exceptionally clear.

"What's a typical dinner?" the doctor asked me.

"I usually eat out. I like Wendy's, but I go to a different place each night—except Tuesdays and Thursdays. On Tuesdays, I eat at the buffet at Pizza Hut, and on Thursdays, I go to the buffet at Quincy's, Home of the Big Fat Yeast Roll," I said.

"I see," said the doctor. "On an average day, how many servings of fruits and vegetables do you think you typically eat?"

I had to think about that. "Maybe one," I guessed. "Sometimes, I have French fries with dinner."

Without saying anything, the doctor started writing in my chart.

I never had to worry about what to eat at the Academy. All our meals were prepared for us in the dining hall. Three square meals each day. Every day. I never had to cook or plan meals. That was somebody else's job. I just had to show up to a table and eat.

In UPT, I was still just showing up and eating. Only, I'd go to the snack bar and buy what I liked to eat. I'd go to a restaurant and order what I liked to eat. I didn't put any thought into what I was eating or how it all fit together. I just showed up and ate.

"I don't think I have to tell you that you're not getting enough fruits and vegetables," the doctor said as he finished writing. "That's what's causing your problem."

So what was my problem? Not enough Vitamin C? Scurvy?

"What you've got, Lieutenant, is an inflamed hemorrhoid," the doctor said.

I didn't respond. I don't think I had any reaction. I was glad that it wasn't a hole in my colon or a bleeding kidney — but hemorrhoids?

"Without enough fruits and vegetables," the doctor continued, "your stool has become too hard. As it passes by a vein that's very close to your rectum, it brushes up against the vein. Each time it does, a little piece of stool rubs off and sticks to the vein. Now, you've formed a clump of hardened stool on the vein, itself." He showed me a picture he had drawn for me in my chart.

Great!

Not only did I have hemorrhoids, I was getting a complete lesson on excretion system malfunctions. Maybe I could sign off *physiological incident* in my gradebook when I got back to Dagger.

"As more pieces of your stool cling to this vein, the clump has grown bigger," the doctor continued. "The vein has been choked off. Blood and pressure builds up at this choke point — just like when you pinch a garden hose. Then, when your hardened stool passes by this inflamed and choked off piece of vein, the site ruptures, and blood squirts out. That's why you've been seeing blood in the toilet bowl."

I wasn't going to die, and I didn't have a life-threatening illness, but this was unbelievably embarrassing. By letting my diet go and eating nothing but junk for the past several months, I had given myself a case of bleeding hemorrhoids that had become so bad I had to cancel a mission. Even though I exercised all the time, dietary entropy had wreaked havoc on my system. Could I repair the damage I had done?

"So, am I in any danger right now? I'm supposed to fly home today. What do I do? Is this a permanent thing?" I asked.

"The good news is that you're not in any danger," the doctor reassured me. "I'm going to write down the name of a stool softener that you can pick up at any drugstore. Just follow the directions on the label." He scribbled something onto his note pad.

"I'm going to give you some information on proper diet and nutrition. My guess is that you probably already know what you should eat. Now, you've got to start practicing it. Every day. Every meal," he said, grabbing a pamphlet about the four basic food groups from a display table in the room.

"Yes, sir," I answered, wondering how I would change my diet when the only thing I knew how to cook was toast. "Doctor, you said that's the good news. Does that mean there's bad news?"

"Well, now that you have this hemorrhoid, you never really can get rid of it. It's there for good. If you keep your stool nice and soft, you'll be fine. The inflammation should go down, and you shouldn't have any bleeding," the doctor told me, trying to speak in a reassuring tone. But is there really a reassuring way to tell someone that they'll have hemorrhoids for life?

"Can I fly today?" I asked, still unsure about that.

"Well, I'm going to recommend that you don't fly for a while," he said. "It's possible that at altitude, with less outside air pressure and your regular blood pressure, you could be more susceptible to spontaneous bleeding. You shouldn't fly until your stool softens and you have a couple of blood-free bowel movements," the doctor told me.

"So, should I stay in Knoxville until I can fly back?" I asked, unsure about what to tell Major Lawson.

"Not necessarily," the doctor said. "If your unit wants you back, you can drive. Columbus, Mississippi, is near Starkvul, isn't it? That's only about an eight-hour drive. I saw the Vols whoop up on Mississippi State the first game of the season in Starkvul, thirty-eight to ten. That was a great game. The Vols looked good that day." All of a sudden, my doctor—like my instructor pilot the day before—had transformed into an orange-wearing, "Rocky Top" singing, Tennessee Volunteers football fanatic.

"I can give you a doughnut to sit on for the drive," he said. "Wait here. The nurse will bring it in and go over my instructions for you."

*

When Class Commander Billy Mike Sims told us, "If you ain't a pilot, you ain't shit," he should have added the corollary: "If you can't shit, you can't be a pilot." This would explain why *Top Gun* never showed Maverick practicing his anti-G straining maneuver on the toilet, farting blood down his flight suit, or sitting on a doughnut in the cockpit of his fighter jet.

Perched on my cushy doughnut seat for the eight-hour drive back from Knoxville, I figured that by the time I returned to Columbus, slept eight hours for my required crew rest, went to the base hospital to see the flight surgeon, and then reported to the flight line, the whole base would know the story of my bleeding hemorrhoids. Major Lawson had called the weekend SOF from Knoxville and told him my story because he needed to get approval to fly our jet back to Columbus without me. I had called Kenny before I left Knoxville in my rental car and asked him to call Mark Jellicot so that Mark could inform Captain Wright and Lieutenant Billy Mike. My classmates might not ask Captain Wright or Billy Mike, but they would ask Kenny — who'd be driving into work that morning without me — and he'd tell them. The whole class — and all of Columbus Air Force Base — would know about my problem.

"Afternoon, everyone!" I called out upon my less-than-triumphant return to Dagger, as if I were Norm walking into Cheers. What other choice did I have?

"Raaaaay!" my classmates sang out in unison, looking up from their briefings.

Everyone watched me walk to Lieutenant Wilson's desk. I waved, like a politician in a hometown parade, as I made my way to my seat. It seemed strange that the IPs didn't care too much that I had interrupted their briefings.

I was glad to see that Lieutenant Wilson had returned to the flight line, though the crutches leaning up against the scheduling board behind his desk indicated that he wouldn't be flying for a while. Of course, I wouldn't be flying for a while, either. As I reached my seat, Captain Wright emerged from his office in the IP briefing room, wearing the same strange smile as the rest of the room.

I wanted to sit down to get all the eyes off me, but because Captain Wright, my superior, was standing, I remained standing.

"Welcome back, Lieutenant Wright," the Dagger flight commander greeted me.

"Thank you, Captain Wright," I acknowledged. "Sorry I'm late...really sorry, sir." I started to pull my chair out from under the front of Lieutenant Wilson's desk so I could duck out of the spotlight, but Captain Wright wasn't done; so, I let go of the chair before I pulled it out very far. Unless he directed me to sit down, I needed to remain standing.

"Lieutenant Wright, did I not tell you that your cross country weekend would be an experience you'd never forget?" Captain Wright asked, as the rest of the room continued to smile giddily.

"Yes, sir," I agreed. "You were right about that."

"Well, Lieutenant Wright, we're glad you made it back. You might have talked about this with Major Lawson — you might not, but go ahead and sign off *physiological incident* on the emergency procedures worksheet in your gradebook," he joked good-naturedly, and the whole room laughed. Then, Captain Wright waved his hand toward my seat, directing me to sit down.

Relieved that he was done, I pulled out my chair, glad to finally be able to sit, but instead, I was treated to the punch line. My concerned classmates had kindly placed a glazed doughnut on a napkin in the center of my seat.

"Lieutenant Wright, your classmates got together and bought you a present," Captain Wright announced before stepping back into his office. "You understand this doughnut is for sitting…not for eating?"

"Yes, sir," I said. "I appreciate that." I turned to the class, offered a polite thank-you wave. Then, I grabbed the napkin Kenny was using with a snack he was eating, placed it on top of the doughnut, and slowly sat down on the now-covered doughnut to more cheers from my classmates.

"Aaay!" Kenny greeted me. This was the first time we'd seen each other since before the weekend. "Talk about a case of Rhoid Rage!"

Chapter 14 — "Cone of Confusion"

"Sir, what about the cone of confusion?" Al asked at the beginning of our academic review session in advance of the big instrument flying exam.

The cone of confusion was a giant, upside-down traffic cone of airspace directly above a VOR navigation tower where the VHF directional signals did not provide reliable instrument readings.

"What *about* the cone of confusion, Turbiglio?" Captain Van Dorn countered.

"Sir, exactly how big is the cone of confusion?" Al re-phrased, now highlighting his workbook with a green marker, because he'd already colored every word and every picture with his yellow highlighter his first fifty times through the pages.

"I'm not sure you can measure the cone of confusion," Captain Van Dorn answered, "because once you're inside the cone, your navigation instruments become unreliable. The upside-down cone is dead airspace above the tower. The higher you are above the tower...the wider the cone gets." Captain Van Dorn paused for a moment to allow Al to keep up with his explanation of the cone of confusion.

Not hearing a follow-up from Al, Captain Van Dorn clucked on, "That's why you either continue flying the heading you were already flying, or if you need to turn to stay on the published course, you turn to a heading you've already calculated in order to establish yourself on the next leg of your route. Once you emerge from the cone of confusion, then you make adjustments."

"Sir, if that procedure or technique?" Al immediately needed to know.

"What about the cone of silence?" I whispered to Doley, sitting next to me.

*

Kurt and Malia invited Kenny and me to dinner. Kurt said they wanted to help me get back to flying status with a good, home-cooked meal. Since my diet had become a sensitive issue, literally, I gladly accepted.

Even though Kurt and Malia's apartment was at the top end of Azalea Drive, the same street where Kenny and I were renting a house at the bottom end, we hadn't made it to their place yet. As students, all we really did every day was go to the base to fly and learn about flying for twelve hours, work out for an hour, eat for an hour, study for two hours, sleep for eight hours, and repeat. In general, we didn't have a lot of time for social calls. Besides, Kurt and Malia were busy enough with a baby on the way.

"Ray!" Kurt shouted from the kitchen while Kenny and I hung out in the living room. "Put the stereo on."

"Sure!" I shot back. To make my way over to the stereo, I had to step over a couple of bean-bag chairs and a pile of neatly folded baby blankets on the floor. "What do you want to hear?" I yelled to back, checking out Kurt's tape collection.

"'Freebird'!" Kurt screamed, walking into the living room, holding his massive hand above his head, as if he were waving a cigarette lighter.

"Kurt, 'Freebird'? Really? Do you want to slow dance?" I asked.

"Ray, I'm from Florida," Kurt reminded me. "If you're from Florida, it doesn't matter if you're at a Kool & the Gang concert. When somebody asks, *What do you want to hear?* you yell 'Freebird'!"

"You got any Kool & the Gang?" I asked, looking again at his tapes.

"Dinner's ready!" Malia called from the kitchen.

"Dinner's ready," Kurt repeated. "Let's 'Get Down on It,'" he joked and waved Kenny and me into the kitchen.

I'd forgotten that food came in so many colors. Most of the stuff I'd eaten since leaving the Academy was some shade of brown. French fries, hamburgers, hamburger buns, fried chicken, chicken strips, Coke, glazed doughnuts, chocolate doughnuts, bread, Snickers ice cream bars, microwavable Hot Pockets. All my dietary staples fell somewhere in the light brown to dark brown color continuum. Even pizza, underneath its red and yellow toppings, was light brown on the bottom.

I didn't want to be rude, but I didn't see anything I wanted to eat. I did see some skinny, egg-roll-looking things that I was willing to try. I liked egg rolls, which are both fried and brown, so I reached across the table to get a couple for my plate.

"Those are called lumpia," Kurt said. "It's a Filipino dish."

"Aaay! Everything looks really good, Malia, and it smells excellent," Kenny complimented. "Thanks for inviting us over."

Kenny, Kurt, and Malia began passing around the dishes, filling their plates with the beautifully prepared foods of all types and colors. I politely passed the dishes with the things I didn't want to eat to the next person without putting anything on my plate.

"Ray," Kurt offered, passing a serving dish back my way, "please have some asparagus."

"Oh, no thank you, Kurt," I replied politely, resisting the dish.

"Ray," Malia jumped in immediately, "I spent over an hour on my feet in the kitchen preparing this meal. You're going to eat all of it."

A little shocked that Malia had just pulled rank on me, I froze for a moment, not sure how to respond. Big Kurt stuck the asparagus dish right in front of my face.

"Ray," Kurt insisted, "isn't someone at the table under doctor's orders to add more vegetables to his diet?" He tilted his monstrous head to the side and glared at me from underneath his furrowed, orange brow.

I didn't know Malia at the Academy, and I hadn't gotten to know her all that well to this point in UPT, but she was very kind to have put together such a large and colorful meal on my behalf. The least I could do was give her asparagus a try. So I took the dish from Kurt and put some asparagus on my plate. Then, I placed the dish in the middle of the table and looked toward Malia, anticipating that she would take the first bite, which would be the signal that we could all start eating. But she just sat there...smiling.

Across the table, Kenny smiled away, too. It was like my return to the flight room from Knoxville all over again.

Kurt stuck another dish of vegetables in my face. This whole dinner was a set-up, a roughage intervention. They weren't going to eat until I filled my plate with vegetables.

Reluctantly, I took a little something from every plate that had been prepared. Once we started eating, I discovered that everything I tasted was delicious.

About the time we finished dinner, Kurt had an announcement to make.

"Guys, Malia and I had a sonogram at the doctor's. We're going to have a little boy," he said proudly, beaming.

"Excellent!" Kenny jumped up from his seat, giving both Kurt and Malia high-fives.

Kurt pulled out a little black-and-white picture that looked like a bad Polaroid of a thunderstorm from an Air Force weather forecaster's radar screen. It had been taken during the ultrasound procedure.

"There's his little pecker," Kurt pointed out.

"Dude! I don't want to see your fetal porn," I protested.

"Aaay! Where? I don't see it," Kenny said, grabbing the sonogram centerfold from Kurt.

"Dude!" I repeated.

*

I'd always thought of myself as being pretty good with numbers. I also knew that I wasn't always the best with words. In trying to memorize our instrument flying lessons to prepare for our exam, the things that I couldn't keep straight weren't so much the numbers we needed to know as they were the words and prepositional phrases that went with the numbers. For example, 10,000 feet, 14,000 feet, and 18,000 feet were all important altitudes to know for things like airspeed restrictions, oxygen requirements, holding pattern timing, flight planning requirements, and altimeter settings, but what I couldn't keep straight were the phrases *at, above, below, at or above,* or *at or below* and when these phrases were to be applied to these important altitudes.

At the end of every mission debrief, whether flown in a sim or a jet, IPs would present student pilots with a hypothetical emergency to hypothetically handle to its hypothetical logical conclusion. Handle the emergency correctly, recite all necessary **BOLDFACE**, and apply all appropriate checklists and the instructor might let the logical conclusion be a safe landing or a safe ejection, resulting in a passing grade for the emergency procedures grade-sheet item. Alternatively, handle the emergency incorrectly, and the logical conclusion would be that you crashed and died, and before your IP recorded your failing grade, you could pretty much guarantee that you'd be grilled on your knowledge of T-37 systems, operations, and procedures, much like an upperclassman back at the Academy might grill a freshman on *Contrails,* that pocket-sized book of Air Force heritage that Air Force Academy freshmen were required to carry at all times.

Even though we were eventually supposed to memorize everything in *Contrails,* I never really learned it that well.

In UPT, a student's knowledge of T-37 systems, operations, and procedures was recorded on the mission grade-sheet under the category of general knowledge. Most student pilots, however, were in agreement that the grade-sheet category of general knowledge was grossly misleading. Knowing that 10,000 feet, 14,000 feet, and 18,000 feet were all important altitudes because of the impact each one had on flying operations, for example, ought to be considered as acceptable "general" knowledge. On the other hand, having to know that standard holding patterns use right-hand turns and one minute inbound legs *at or below* 14,000 feet— unless correcting for wind, in which case corrections need to be made by lengthening the outbound leg to shorten the inbound leg to one minute or shortening the outbound leg to lengthen the inbound leg to one minute, and that one and a half minute legs were required *above* 14,000 feet—unless correcting for winds— went way beyond "general." This type of information needed to be categorized for what it actually was: specific knowledge.

I planned to note this on my course critique at the end of the program, if I were lucky enough to make it that far. But before then, I had a lot to learn.

*

"I missed that stupid question on the test about holding at 14,000 feet," I told Kenny. "I couldn't remember if it was one minute timing *at, above, at or above, below,* or *at or below.* If the question had said 12,000 feet or 15,000 feet, I would have gotten it right."

"Aaay. I guessed lucky on that one," Kenny said back.

We put our flight caps on just as we stepped through the metal door at the back of the Stu-ron, marking our transition from inside to outside. In the sunlight, Kenny's glasses darkened to shades mode.

It was a quick walk across the street from the back door of the Stu-ron building to the center doors of the flight line building. Still seventy degrees in early December, the Columbus weather was so nice that we stopped for a few minutes to watch some Tweets in the Sunfish pattern.

"Looks like Runway 1-3 again today," I stated the obvious.

"Aaay! I think we were on Tree-1 for our first month here, and it's been 1-Tree ever since," Kenny said.

Kenny had suggested a quick trip to the flight line snack bar, but we forgot the time, watching Tweet after Tweet fly over our heads in the Sunfish pattern.

"TWEEEEEEEEEEEEET!" The jet engines screamed as students pushed up the throttles to keep the jet from slowing down to dangerously low airspeeds at which the jets might stall and drop out of the sky, unable to overcome the added drag created by extending the landing gear and wing flaps for the final turn to the runway.

I thought I could wing it!

The warm, rank jet exhaust burned the back of my throat as I pointed my nose to the sky to watch my fellow student pilots struggle to execute their final turns above me. The screeching Tweet engines drilled loudly into my ears, scraping across my brain stem like fingernails on a chalkboard.

"TWEEEEEEEEEEEEEEEEEEEEET!"

But in spite of the smell and the noise, the only thing that really bothered me was my performance on the instrument exam.

Shit!

It squeezed on my insides. I should have been enjoying watching the jets in the pattern, like Kenny, but I wasn't.

Spotting someone in uniform heading our way, I knew a stop and salute were eminent if we didn't get a move on. I opened one of the blue metal doors for Kenny, and we removed our flight caps as we crossed the threshold into the foyer that separated the T-37 training squadron on our left from the T-38 squadron to our right. By the time we'd reached the snack bar, Kenny's glasses had lost their tint.

"I missed two really easy questions on the section about weather symbols," I said, picking up our conversation. "I guessed that the string of semi-circles next to one another on a weather map stood for cold front, because they look like the letter *C*, and I guessed that the string of triangles next to one another stood for warm front, because triangles next to each other look like the letter W. I got both wrong."

"Madonne!" Kenny slapped his palm to his forehead. "Dat's the easiest thing to remember!"

"How's that?" I asked, picking the least rotten apple I could find from the small selection of snack bar fruit.

"Aaay, tits and nipples!" Kenny responded, first cupping his hands in front of his chest and then extending his index fingers to illustrate his mnemonic device. "When it's warm out, chicks' tits are nice and round, like the symbol for a warm front," he explained, once again cupping his hands in front of his chest.

After a dramatic pause, Kenny slid open the glass lid to the ice cream freezer in the snack bar.

"And when it's cold," he continued, "AAAY! The nipples get pointy!" He stuck out his index fingers from his cupped hands. "Like the pointy symbols for a cold front."

Kenny stood and posed with his poking out, cold nipples above the open lid of the freezer so that his mnemonic device would engrave itself into my brain. When he saw that I didn't know how to respond, he closed the sliding lid and pulled in his index fingers.

"Why do you think they use cold water for wet t-shirt contests?!" he asked, and again, he opened the lid to the ice cream freezer, poked out his index fingers from his chest to demonstrate the common attributes of cold fronts and cold nipples.

I'd only failed the test by one wrong answer too many. I would never miss a question on weather symbols again.

*

Lieutenant Wilson sat at his desk to thoroughly test my general knowledge of instrument flying procedures. While I was worried about passing my instrument exam re-take, I think Lieutenant Wilson was focused more on preparing me for possible questions during my Instrument Flying checkride, the third of three flying evaluations in the T-37. Having both recently been reinstated to flying duty, he and I just had our first training mission together in over six weeks.

"When filing a flight plan under instrument flight rules, when do you need to file an alternate?" he asked.

"Sir, if the forecast weather at your destination is less than 3,000 and 3, plus or minus an hour before or after your planned arrival time, you need to file an alternate," I answered.

"Three thousand *what* and 3 *what*?" Lieutenant Wilson wanted more information.

"Sir, if the *ceiling* is less than 3,000 feet above ground level and the *visibility* is less than three miles, you need to file an alternate," I said, providing the labels for the numbers.

"Is that it?" Lieutenant Wilson waited.

"Three thousand and 3..." I thought for a moment, "...or 2 above," I added, remembering that it was *3,000 and 3 or 2 above*.

"Two above what?" Lieutenant Wilson followed up again. Stupid prepositional phrases! I could never keep the prepositional phrases straight, and I really didn't know what he was asking me to say.

"Three thousand and 3 or 2 above...*sir*," I answered.

"Mins," he said.

Mins?

My attempt to distract him by throwing a *sir* his way hadn't work.

I lost my place in the conversation.

Was it my turn to say something?

"Sir, mins are 3,000 and 3," I said, trying to piece together the last couple of things we'd talked about.

"No, 2 *above mins*," Lieutenant Wilson calmly reminded me about how specific I needed to be about general knowledge.

I didn't know what he was talking about.

"Meaning 2 miles visibility above the lowest visibility for landing minimums published for the approach," he clarified for me.

"Oh, 3,000 and 3 or 2 above mins, sir," I repeated, trying to pretend that I knew what he was telling me.

"Is visibility measured in nautical miles or statute miles?" he again asked for a label.

"Yes, sir, they are," I responded, knowing that while this may not be the best answer, it was not incorrect.

"Which are they? Nautical miles or statute miles?" Lieutenant Wilson drilled deeper into the specific.

"Statute miles," I guessed.

"Statute miles?" he called my bluff.

"Yes, sir, visibility is measured in statute miles," I stuck with my answer.

"That's right," he said.

Phew!

I think that was the first question I'd gotten right. As an Academy freshman, this would be the time I'd stick my *Contrails* book in front of my face to pretend like I was studying in an attempt to discourage another question from an upperclassman, but Lieutenant Wilson fired off another immediately.

"Okay, so if you don't have 3,000 and 3 or 2 above at your destination, what weather do you need at an airfield in order to qualify as your alternate?" he asked.

I didn't remember all this. I just knew the numbers for the test. At least, I thought I knew the numbers for the test.

"Sir, you need 3,000 and 3," I tried to say with confidence.

"Three thousand and 3?" Lieutenant Wilson questioned.

"No, sir. It's not 3,000 and 3. It's..." It wasn't 3,000 and 3. *What was it?*

I searched my brain for other numbers I had memorized. "It's...1,000 and 2."

"One thousand and 2?" he asked, as if I needed to tell him more.

"...or 500 and 1," I said, as these numbers popped into my head.

"Which is it?" my IP wanted to know. "One thousand and 2 or 500 and 1?"

"Sir, it's both," I thought I'd remembered. "It's 1,000 and 2 or 500 and 1 above," I said confidently.

"Above what?" he followed up.

Again with the prepositions!

I felt like a boxer being pounded against the ropes. I didn't know how much of a beating I could take, but I knew I couldn't punch back. I didn't have the knowledge; so, I didn't have the power. It was only a matter of time before I dropped.

"Five hundred and 1 above...*sir*," I said.

"No, it's above *mins*," he said. "One thousand and 2 or 500 and 1 above weather minimums for the lowest compatible published approach, whichever is greater."

"Yes, sir, to qualify as an alternate, you need 1,000 and 2 or 500 and 1 above published mins, whichever is greater," I repeated, as if I actually knew it, forgot it, and was now just remembering it.

"That's right. Okay, so what if a published approach is not available?" He began a new line of questioning, letting me off the ropes for a moment.

"Sir, I know this one," I was relieved to say. "You can file using instrument flight rules to a point en route where the forecast weather is supposed to be compatible with visual flight rules at the time of your arrival or to a point served by a published approach procedure where you can descend to VFR conditions and then continue VFR to your destination."

"Wow! How did you know that?" he asked.

"I overheard Lieutenant Turbiglio practicing his flash cards," I joked, though I probably would have been better off if I had made a set of flash cards. I felt my head clear for a moment, and I felt as if maybe I was ready to square up again in the center of the ring.

Then, Lieutenant Wilson punched again. "So, what weather do you need in order to file a flight plan to your destination under visual flight rules?"

Whack!

I answered with the only numbers that I could pull out of my terribly numbed mind. "Three thousand and 3."

"Three thousand and 3?" he jabbed.

"Or 2 above."

"Three thousand and 3 or 2 above?" he jabbed again.

"Yes, sir. Three thousand and 3 or 2 above." I kept my gloves up in front.

"Two above what?" he asked, hitting me square in the face.

"Two above mins." I couldn't think. I couldn't defend myself. I was out.

"You really don't know any of this, do you?" Lieutenant Wilson asked, ready to put me out of my misery.

"Sir, I know 3,000 and 3," I said unconvincingly.

"Do you really? Have you even opened a book in the past month? Do you study on the weekends?" my instructor asked, shaking his head and picking up his pencil to record my grade for our ride, signaling that he was stopping the contest.

"Sir, I've always been pretty good with numbers," I offered. "I'll study, and I'll know this stuff for my checkride."

"You don't just need to know this stuff for your checkride," Lieutenant Wilson countered. "You need to know it to be a pilot."

*

After this failing performance, I shut myself in my room all weekend and studied. Kenny stayed in with me Saturday night to study, too, because even though he passed the instrument test the first time, the bigger challenge still ahead of both of us: the third and final checkride in the T-37: Instrument check.

A weekend of studying and Kenny's mnemonic devices helped me pass my instrument re-test first thing on Monday morning. I flew a few good rides during the early part of the week, and going into my Instrument checkride, I actually felt a little bit of confidence. If I could fly my checkride like I'd flown my last two rides leading up to it, I'd be able to do pretty well.

But the morning of my Instrument check, an unexpected change occurred. Even though I went to MTV's Spring Break at Daytona Beach my junior and senior years at the Academy and may have been present at the kinds of events that inspired Kenny's mnemonic device for cold fronts, I never saw as many pointy nipples at one time as I saw at the morning weather briefing the day of my final T-37 checkride.

"You might have noticed a change in the weather this morning," Captain Wright said at the front of Dagger at the start of the morning's formal report. "You might not."

What happened to seventy degrees?!

"This time of year," Captain Wright said, "when the weather gets a little cooler, the jet stream drops down from the north, bringing all that cold air behind it." Captain Wright scanned back and forth across the room, eyes half-closed, like he was trying to focus on something at the end of his nose, smiling all the while because he was a pilot and was going to get to fly a jet in a couple of hours.

Captain Wright turned on the overhead projector and put the slide for the weather report back on the screen for the second time that morning. "When a cold front like this one meets up with the nice warm weather we've enjoyed for the past several weeks, the cold air pushes the warm air up, and we can get some very extreme winds. At Willie in Arizona, when the wind blows, flying shuts down for the day, but here at Columbus, it's just another day, which is why we train the world's best pilots."

As clichéd as any of Captain Wright's soapbox speeches were, I loved his passion; his words never failed to inspire. While the constant studying and the everyday evaluating and the pressure of fail-and-you-ain't-shit totally sucked, listening to Captain Wright talk about why we did these things always made me feel good.

"You might know that colder, thicker air means that your jet will perform better and be more responsive to your inputs closer to the ground. You might know that higher winds at altitude mean that you'll need to constantly make corrections to your headings in order to stay on course and that you'll need to calculate the effects of extreme winds as you fly your fix-to-fixes on your Instrument rides," he said. "Then again, you might not know what to expect."

Okay, so I didn't feel quite so good after hearing him say these things.

"Lieutenant Wright," the Dagger flight commander called me out. I stood up from my seat immediately. "You might have thought that after a month of flying in near-perfect weather and seventy-degree temperatures, being on Runway 1-3 for the past month and a half, and practicing your approaches and landings in virtually calm winds for as long as you can remember that you'd have the same conditions today. Isn't that right, Lieutenant Wright?"

"Yes, sir!"

"You might not have thought that on the day of your checkride, you'd have a runway change, and you'd have to takeoff, fly your departure, and land in directions opposite to those you'd been practicing for so long. Isn't that right, Lieutenant Wright?" the Flight Commander asked.

"Yes, sir!"

"But did you ever expect, Lieutenant Wright, that you'd have a forty-degree temperature drop, thick, dense, thirty-degree air under your wings at ground level, and 80-knot winds from the northwest to slap your tail around at altitude on the day you had to fly your Instrument checkride?" he asked.

"No, sir!" I responded with as much fake confidence and enthusiasm as I could manage.

"That's why Columbus trains the best pilots in the Air Force!" Captain Wright exclaimed. "Isn't that right, Lieutenant Wright?"

"Yes, sir!" I acknowledged, still standing. But it sure would have been a lot easier if things had just stayed the same one more day...or at least until I'd flown my Instrument check.

*

Because of the strong headwind on Runway 3-1, my takeoff roll was a little shorter. Because of the cold, dense air flowing into the engines and around the aircraft, my jet accelerated a little faster and climbed a little steeper. Because I wasn't paying attention to the effects the changes in weather conditions were having on my flying, I didn't notice that I nearly exceeded the Tweet's maximum airspeed while the landing gear were still in transition from hanging below the jet to being fully tucked into the jet's underbelly after takeoff.

"Don't do this," Captain Folsom, the check pilot assigned to me for my Instrument checkride, said, shaking the stick, taking control, and ensuring that I did not overspeed the landing gear while they still dangled under the jet.

"You have the aircraft," he said after he'd prevented the unsafe situation I'd created and was ready to let me fly again.

"Roger, I have the aircraft," I said, shaking the stick to acknowledge that I had control.

"You have the aircraft," he acknowledged.

"I have the aircraft," I repeated and rolled into thirty degrees of left bank to fly my departure to Meridian, where I'd have to fly the VOR-Alpha penetration. As soon as I rolled into my turn, my seat dropped all the way to the floor of the cockpit because I hadn't properly adjusted it to a locked position when I ran my checklists on the ground—just as my seat had on my first ride with Major Lawson.

I'd flown over fifty times since my dollar ride, performed more than a hundred and fifty takeoffs, if you include takeoffs after touch-and-go landings. After my very first takeoff roll, when I zigzagged down the runway and nearly ran the jet into the grass off to the side of it, I'd never botched a takeoff as badly as the one I'd just flown. Heading down to Meridian, I couldn't help but wonder if I'd just set the Air Force record for fastest checkride *Unsat*, having been airborne less than a minute before my check pilot had to assume control of the jet.

The morning's 80-knot wind from the northwest blew the giant tail of my Tweet across the sky like a kite in an open field. It kept knocking me to the left of my course as I flew south from Columbus to Meridian, Mississippi. The time I needed to make corrections back to my course took time away from being able to prepare for the next leg of the ride. In addition to knocking me off my route, the northern component of the northwest wind was adding about a mile per minute to my ground speed. The ground was racing under my wings faster than the time that I'd leveled off at altitude without remembering to pull back my power, and Major Lawson yelled at me for flying to Gunshy at Mach-fucking-One.

This left me with even less time to run my checklists, make my course corrections, and review the VOR-Alpha procedure, which was now strapped to my right leg on top of my in-flight guide. Instead of having about twenty-five calm minutes for the ninety-mile flight from Columbus to Meridian, I barely had twenty, and I spent most of them fighting the wind. Before I was ready, it was show time.

I knew about the tricks to the VOR-Alpha penetration. I had flown it on a couple of training rides, and practiced it in the sim. I knew that the VOR broadcast beacon, itself, was both the initial approach fix and the final approach fix, which meant that at both important points in the approach to the runway from my cruising altitude, I'd be in the epicenter of the cone of confusion. Once I'd hit the cone, my navigational information would become unreliable. The needle on my instrument panel that was supposed to guide me to the proper course would spin without purpose. I'd need to turn to headings that would help me stay close to my courses, but being in the cone, I wouldn't know if I was on course until I'd flown far enough away from the VOR to escape the confusion.

At the final approach fix, the point at which I needed to have the landing gear extended for landing, the cone of confusion wouldn't be so much of a problem because the cone was skinniest near the ground. I wouldn't be in it very long, but having the VOR as the final approach fix did present another trick.

At most airfields the navigational aids guided aircraft right to the runway, and the mileage indicator counted backwards to zero as the jet got nearer to the airport. Like a countdown, this was easy to visualize. But at Meridian, because the VOR was more than three miles away from the runway, the mileage marker on the instrument panel increased the closer you got to the airfield. Instead of mileage ticking down to zero for landing, mileage ticked down to zero upon passing over the final approach fix and ticked back up to three the closer the jet got to the runway. And this just didn't look right.

I'd been able to fly this VOR-Alpha approach a couple of the few times I'd tried it, but those were under normal conditions and calm winds. On this day, the weather was anything but normal, and because this was my Instrument checkride, I was under the hood, meaning my check pilot made me jam a folded up map into the front of my helmet across the top part of my sun visor to prevent me from looking outside the cockpit. My field of vision was confined to the instrument panel in front of me and the books I had strapped to my legs. I couldn't peek outside for a glimpse of the ground or sky even if I'd wanted to.

I reviewed the rest of the approach. *Descend from 6,000 to no less than 2,100 feet while flying northwest. Then, reverse course so as to remain within 10 miles of the VOR. Fly southeast. Cross the final approach fix with landing gear down at no less than 1,600 feet. Then, begin final descent to the runway.*

At the initial approach fix, I reported leaving 6,000 feet for the approach. The headwind was so strong that after only flying a few miles to the northwest, I'd dropped down to 2,100 feet. I was well within the 10 miles allotted to complete my turn for reversing course.

With an 80-knot wind on my nose, my mileage indicator wasn't moving very quickly.

Three.

I was already at the proper altitude.

Four.

I grew impatient.

Five

I decided to begin reversing course and went for it.

"Not yet," my Check pilot, Captain Folsom, offered a not-so-subtle clue.

Foolishly, I ignored him.

Because I'd gotten down to 2,100 feet so quickly, I turned inbound, back toward the VOR, my final approach fix on the next part of the approach. I needed to get the jet slowed down, descending to no lower than 1,600 feet, with the landing gear and flaps lowered for final approach to the runway. But with the wind at my back, now pushing me along my path, I couldn't slow the jet down fast enough, and the mileage marker was almost down to zero. I was flying much too fast. The cone of confusion hadn't confused me, but the wind sure did.

With the jet's throttles all the way back, I was hoping we'd slow down enough so that I could drop the gear before we crossed the VOR. I knew I'd hook the ride for sure if I reached the final approach fix without having the landing gear down.

In anticipation of the jet slowing itself down, I reached up and grabbed for the gear handle on my side of the cockpit.

"Gear clear, sir," I said as we got to the final approach fix, still keeping an eye on the airspeed indicator because I had not sufficiently slowed down to safely lower the landing gear and flaps.

Please! Slow down!

"No," Captain Folsom said forcefully, "the gear are not clear." Not so subtly this time, my check pilot reached up to the handle on his side of the cockpit and blocked me from lowering the landing gear.

I hadn't adjusted enough for the wind!

Flying into an 80-knot headwind when I started my approach, I didn't cover the amount of ground I would have travelled if the winds had been calm. Once I reversed course, flying with an 80-knot tailwind, I cover a lot more ground than I would have travelled without winds and was pushed from behind toward my final approach fix.

Because I couldn't slow down the jet in time, I blew past the final approach fix without having lowered my landing gear. Because I could not report *final approach fix, gear down* to Meridian Tower, Meridian Tower would not clear me to land. Because I had not made the proper adjustments for the conditions of the day, I did not successfully fly the approach. Because I did not successfully fly the approach, I did not pass my Instrument checkride.

Back at Captain Folsom's desk in Check Section, he summed things up perfectly as he handed me my grade-sheet.

"Today just wasn't your day," he said.

The big, red *U* at the top confirmed that I'd just failed my second checkride.

Chapter 15 — "Don't Act a Fool"

"I ain't never unbuckled a dead man," said Sergeant Bubba Rollins of the Mississippi State Highway Patrol to begin his safety presentation in the base theater just before the holidays. Attendance was mandatory.

"If you is out carousin' and havin' a good time this Christmas…maybe you is out havin' you some drinks. One. Two. Three. Four. Maybe you have five drinks. Six drinks. Don't get behind the wheel. If you get behind the wheel and drive after you been drinkin', that's drinkin' and drivin', and drinkin' and drivin' is actin' a fool," he said. He walked to the front of the stage and stared into the crowd momentarily for added effect.

"Don't act a fool," Sergeant Rollins warned.

Decked out in his smartly pressed Mississippi State Highway Patrol uniform, Sergeant Rollins walked and stared his way back to the center of the stage. "I'll never forget the time I had to tell a boy's parents, his momma and his daddy, that their boy was dead," he recollected. "This boy had been out carousin', drinkin' and drivin', not wearin' his seatbelt, and actin' a fool."

The Highway Patrolman squatted down, pretending he was sitting in his squad car to set the scene for this part of his story. "I'll never forget one Christmas on our state highways," our guest speaker went on, "a one, two, three, four-car accident."

"Four! Ah-ah-ah-ah," I whispered as the Count from *Sesame Street*.

Doley made the sound of thunder.

Sergeant Rollins had been introduced as a master storyteller and entertainer who would spin yarns that would indelibly etch life lessons into our brains. We were told that he would entertain and educate us like a uniformed mix between humorist Mark Twain and Mississippi's own Jerry Clower. He was in uniform, but I wasn't hearing anything that reminded me of Twain, Clower, or humor.

"The red car was a fancy sports car, and the driver had been out drinkin' with the driver of the blue one, which was a pick-up truck. After these two boys had been out drinkin' — and probably carousin' — they went drivin'. Neither boy was buckled. And then, these boys thought it would be a good idea to commence to havin' themselves a drag race." Sergeant Rollins walked to the front of the stage again and briefly lowered his microphone for his dramatic pause and stare into the audience. "Drinkin' and drivin' and bein' unbuckled is bad enough, but now you throw on drag racin', and these boys was actin' a-fool. These boys was racin' about fifty, sixty, seventy, eighty — we figure about ninety miles per hour."

Kenny took a turn as the Count. "Ninety! Ah-ah-ah-ah," he laughed, and I did the thunderclap.

I know the stories were sad, but the storyteller was terrible. Every anecdote seemed to follow the same pattern of carousin', actin' a-fool, counting, and maybe some color for the purpose of description. Besides, even though Christmas was less than two weeks away, I once again found myself only two rides from washing out of UPT. I wasn't in the mood for a lecture on DUIs and seatbelts.

"These two boys, out drinkin', probably carousin', actin' a fool on our highways…before they could hit the brakes, these two boys had crossed into the lane of some oncomin' traffic, and when the four vehicles involved all came together, they all crashed and tangled and tumbled off the road," Sergeant Rollins shared, re-enacting the four vehicles tumbling off the road with spellbindingly vivid description. "One. Two. Three. Four."

Right on cue, Count Doley took his turn, "Four! Four crashed cars! Ah-ah-ah-ah."

Kenny made the thunderclap, and then we all feigned attentiveness so as to fool the aisle patrol, who stopped at the end of our row of seats to investigate the noises coming from our area of the dark theater.

"Now here's why I say, *Don't act a fool,*" Sergeant Rollins dramatically returned to the front of the stage to put his microphone down by his side and stare into the crowd for a moment. "Because wouldn't you know that in one of them cars was a momma and that momma's baby, and when I came upon that momma, she was dead, because she had been throwed five, ten, fifteen, twenty feet from the car and killed."

We were all thinking the same thing when we heard *five, ten, fifteen, twenty.* I knew it was my turn to be the Count, but I couldn't say anything. Not only was the momma dead, but the aisle patrol was again suspiciously close to the end of our row, so I held my tongue.

"Killled because two boys was actin' a fool. And killed because that momma wasn't wearin' her seatbelt. I said, *I ain't never unbuckled a dead man,* and I'll tell y'all now that I ain't never unstrapped a dead baby from a car seat, neither. But on this night, one Christmastime, that momma's baby wasn't strapped into a car seat," Sergeant Rollins sadly reported. "Now, at the time, I didn't know that that dead momma was a momma, and I didn't know that that dead momma had a baby, but I was the one who got to go into the woods at the side of the road to find if any others had been throwed from that wreck."

For a few minutes Sergeant Rollins told about his search, counting the steps he'd taken into the woods, counting the trees he'd passed along the way, and naming the colors of the things he could see with his flashlight...all of this leading to his grand finale.

"When I finally found that dead momma's baby, face-down in the mud that was brown, I picked up that dead momma's baby and turned her little mud-face to mine so I could get a look into her brown, mud-covered eyes," Sergeant Rollins stated. This had to have been his cue to himself to return to the front of the stage and pause his story for another admonishing stare into the crowd.

Then, he lowered his voice to a whisper, but by sticking his microphone right up against his mouth, his words got louder. I was sure he'd rehearsed this part of his talk.

"And when I looked into that dead momma's baby's two brown, mud-covered eyes..." He paused yet again at the front of the stage for one more dramatic moment to build to his crescendo...

"SHE," he sighed.

"WAS," he barked.

"TRINGLIN'!" he screamed.

And at the front of the stage, screaming at the top of his lungs, Sergeant Rollins clenched his fists up by his shoulders, squinted his eyes, stretched back his lips, gritted his teeth, and shook himself violently.

I was pretty sure that *tringlin'* was not a word, but when Sergeant Rollins screamed it and clenched up his fists, squinted his eyes, stretched back his lips, gritted his teeth, and shook himself violently, I had a pretty good idea what tringlin' meant. Like the rest of the audience, I stood up and applauded as Sergeant Rollins performed his tringle for us, because even though his storytelling sucked, I had never seen a more well-executed tringle.

*

Just like when I hooked my Mid-Phase Contact check, my next ride after hooking my Instrument check would be a practice ride, and then I'd have a special checkride with one of the squadron's leaders. I wouldn't get a grade for my next ride, because it would just be practice. My special checkride would be the important one. If I passed the special checkride, I'd drop back into the normal flow of training, which meant that I'd essentially be done with T-37s.

If I failed my special checkride, I'd get two more practice rides before a second special checkride. The two additional practice rides would not be graded, because they would just be practice. If I passed the second special checkride, I'd drop back into the normal flow of training, which meant that I'd essentially be done with T-37s. If I failed the second special checkride, I'd go to a Training Review Board. The TRB would determine if I could return to pilot training after now having failed two out of three checkrides and one of three academic exams, or if I'd wash out of UPT and be sent out into the Real Air Force as something other than a pilot.

And I wouldn't be shit.

Lieutenant Wilson told me to expect to fly a full profile, just like my checkride. Since I'd hooked the ride for three things—Takeoff/Transition to Instruments, Low Altitude VOR, and VOR Final Approach—I'd surely be flying these portions again.

Lieutenant Wilson flew my practice ride with me the day after I'd hooked. Rather than redo the VOR-Alpha approach down at Meridian, Lieutenant Wilson had me fly a similar VOR penetration to Runway 4 at Tuscaloosa Regional Airport, which was only about sixty miles southeast of Columbus Air Force Base and thirty miles closer to Columbus than Meridian, so I didn't have a lot of time to prepare for my penetration to the airport from altitude. Things happened quickly because there wasn't a whole lot of distance to travel—but thankfully, because the cold front had worked its way down over the Columbus area, the winds were back to normal. I didn't have to deal with making major corrections for the winds.

Being less than a twenty-minute trip from Columbus to Tuscaloosa in the Tweet, we were able to plan a lot of extra practice into the ride. For an hour and a half, Lieutenant Wilson worked me through aerial calisthenics like I was a basic cadet at the Air Force Academy back on the parade field for morning physical training. In addition to working on those things I'd screwed up on my checkride, Lieutenant Wilson had me fly multiple instrument approaches, a couple of fix-to-fixes, and we even dropped into the Southern MOA on the way back from Tuscaloosa to use the maneuvering freedom within Area Blue to practice some things that might come up on my checkride redo. With the cold air, calm winds, and the short trip to Tuscaloosa, our fuel seemed to last forever, and I was hit with just about every maneuver on the grade-sheet. We even practiced the widely misunderstood 30-45-180 maneuver a couple of times on the ride.

In a car, you reverse direction with a U-turn—or maybe a power-slide—but when flying a standard instrument turn at thirty degrees of bank in a jet, because your turn radius is so big, by the time you turned around to the opposite direction, the U-turn would have brought you at least two miles to the side of the course on which you were flying before you tried to reverse direction. Why not cut it? Because the goal of instrument flying is to handle the jet more like an airline pilot than a fighter pilot—you can't whip a U-turn. (Too many passengers would spill their drinks.)

So, as a way of reversing direction and lining the jet up over the exact same path it had just flown, the 30-45-180 maneuver allowed pilots to turn to a dogleg heading, fly their U-turn, and then undo the dogleg to reverse the original course. Instead of looking like the letter *U*, the ground track for this maneuver looked more like a lowercase *b* or *d*, depending on the direction of the dogleg. You'd start at the top of the letter, turn out to fly the rounded part, and reverse direction to fly back up the stem of the letter in the opposite direction to fly back over your original ground track heading the other way.

The *30* in the 30-45-180 maneuver came from the part of the rule that allowed the U-turn to be performed when angling into a published approach from within 30 degrees of the outbound course. This meant that even if a pilot weren't exactly lined up with the right path, he could still turn to a heading 45 degrees away from the published course to start the dogleg.

In his classic, crazy way, Kenny liked to offer instruction by demonstrating his own take on the 30–45–180 maneuver driving on Highway 45 North. But Kenny didn't use his version of the maneuver to reverse directions. He used it to avoid red lights — especially after a night of carousing.

"Aaay, if you're less than thirty yards from the light, and it's yellow or red, whip it hard, forty-five degrees to da right, into the turnin' lane." Kenny coached me through his maneuver each time he performed it, as if he were my instructor pilot demonstrating this move to me for the first time.

"Keep up ya speed, and look for cars coming down the other road," he continued, "and if it's clear, floor it." Kenny would gun the gas on his Mustang, race across multiple lanes of oncoming traffic of the intersecting road, and whip his car hard into the right-turns-only lane to bypass the intersection.

"Finish da merge back ta da original road, and da 30–45–180 maneuver is complete wit'out ever havin' ta stop for da red light," Kenny explained.

Sometimes I was more nervous riding in a turbo-charged convertible with Kenny than I was flying in a jet with a check pilot.

But with Kenny's instruction in mind during my review ride the next day, I flew the best ride I'd ever flown in the T-37…daily ride, practice ride, or checkride. I returned to the normal flow of training. I'd failed two-thirds of my checkrides and one third of my academic exams the first time around, but I'd made it halfway through the program.

*

A couple days later, the student pilots of Columbus Air Force Base were surprised with yet another mandatory meeting in the base theater. Nobody in our half of the class's telephone chain knew why. It couldn't be the DUI tote board; based on it, we were looking pretty good at just over eighty days since the last student DUI and circumcision.

"ROOM, TEN HUT!" somebody commanded, and in unison, the audience of student pilots in the theater stood and snapped to the position of attention.

Student Squadron Commander Lieutenant Colonel Stewart walked out onto the center of the theater stage. As Stu-ron commander, he was in charge of class commanders like First Lieutenant Billy Mike, academic instructors like Captain Van Dorn, and all of the student pilots, like us. But because we spent most of our time on the flight line in Dagger, we hardly ever saw him.

Lieutenant Colonel Stewart was flanked by two student pilots marching rigidly behind him. The students stopped their march and stood at attention when Lieutenant Colonel Stewart turned to face the audience. One of the students was from the 88-07 class, but he was in Warhawks—not Dagger. The other guy, someone I recognized from the Academy, was in the 88-08 class, a month behind us. They'd become known as the Orange Pumpkins for the most prominent color of their class patch and scarves.

Even after Lieutenant Colonel Stewart commanded, "At ease," and the rest of the theater sat down, the two students on stage remained at attention, standing straight and tall, hands by their sides, and eyes focused on a distant target in front of them.

"My Pink Flamingooooooooes, my Orange Pumpkiiiiiiiiiiiiiiins, my Nightmaaaaares, and all of my UPT studeeeeents, when you first arriiiiiiiiiived at Columbus Air Force Baaaaaaaase, I cheeallenged youuuuuuuuuu to conduct yourselves with Columbus Cleeaaaaaaaaass," Lieutenant Colonel Stewart whined in his annoying, high-pitched, sing-songy voice from the front of the stage.

I couldn't stand his whiny voice, and he had that awful upstate New York way of sticking extraneous long *e* sounds in front of his short *a* sounds. *I cheeallenge you.* Lieutenant Colonel Stewart always cheeallenged the students.

"Just a couple of days agooooooooo," he whined on, "we heard Sergeeant Rolliiiiiiiiins of the Mississippi State Highway Patrooool tell us not to *ee*act a fooooooool. Well, let me tell youuuuuuu theeat these two fooooooools behind me do not heeave Columbus Cleeaaaaaaaass!"

Lieutenant Colonel Stewart stopped for a moment to contemptuously drill his stare into the faces of the students behind him. The student squadron commander's move looked as awkwardly rehearsed as one of the Mississippi State Highway patrolman's dramatic moves from the same stage earlier in the week.

"Leeast niiiiiiiight, my wiiiiiife *ee*and my two beauuuuuutiful daughters were almost kiiiiiiiilled by these two fooooooools," Lieutenant Colonel Stewart bemoaned after he'd turned back toward the audience. "*Ee*as my wife *ee*and my two beauuuuuutiful daughters were driving home *ee*after shopping *ee*at the Kroooooger, these two fooooooools nearly hit my feeamily by using the right-heeand turn lanes to speed around a red liiiiiight."

"Aaay, dat's my move," Kenny whispered.

With the two student offenders still standing rigidly at attention behind him, Lieutenant Colonel Stewart dramatically detailed how his wife saw one of the students' cars performing Kenny's 30–45–180 maneuver near the Kroger.

"My Pink Flamingoooooooooes, my Orange Pumpkiiiiiiiiiiiiins, all of my UPT students, when you first arriiiiiiiiived at Columbus *Ee*air Force Baaaaaaaaase, I cheeallenged youuuuuuuuuu to conduct yourselves with Columbus Cleeaaaaaaaaass," Lieutenant Colonel Stewart repeated his opening whine.

"These two fooooooools *ee*acted a fooooool. These two fooooools do not heeave Columbus Cleeaaaaaaaass!" he yelled.

"Effective immediately, I *ee*am placing these two foooooools on milit*ee*ary SMS, *ee*and if I hear of other episoooodes like this, I will not hesitaaaaate to put *ee*anyone in this buildiiiiiiing on milit*ee*ary SMS."

I half-expected him to tringle at that point, but Lieutenant Colonel Stewart was too original for that. He just turned and stormed off the stage. The theater was called to attention, and the student pilots were dismissed.

*

I didn't care all that much about formation flying in the T-37, though I knew I would eventually have to learn the material for T-38s. At this point, we were now the senior class on the Tweet side of the flight line. There were no more academic tests. There were no more checkrides. We'd have to fly a formation solo, but we'd fly it on the wing of one of our Dagger IPs—not a check pilot. We didn't have to worry about failure anymore—only death. We were almost done with T-37s.

Captain Wright had praised Sandy one afternoon during the formal release for being the first Dagger student to fly a formation solo—two months before we were scheduled to fly formation rides. That was cool. Flying a solo mission in the Sunfish pattern, Sandy reported an unsafe landing gear indication in the cockpit and requested a chase ship. Within a minute Lieutenant Prince and Chuck appeared on Sandy's wing to inspect her landing gear and escort her around the pattern for a safe landing. She'd handled her emergency like a champ.

During the first formal report of the formation flying block of instruction, Chuck and Sandy again proved themselves to be the class experts on formation flying procedures when they were called to stand up and handle a radio-out emergency. With only three feet of sky between the wingtip of the formation leader— *Lead*—and the wingtip of the wingman—*Two*—pilots used hand signals to communicate with one another as much as possible so as not to clutter up the radio for the rest of the pilots in the sky.

Going beyond the standard hand signals we were learning, Chuck and Sandy carried on a complete conversation using sign language to successfully handle their emergency, stunning our IPs and amazing the rest of our class. Sometimes, our IPs tried to pick on the women in our class, but with Sandy, Chuck, and Marcia, we had three pretty tough women.

Other than them, aside from Mark Jellicot, the only thing the rest of us knew about formation flying came from *Top Gun*.

You never leave your wingman.

Knowing I needed to eventually learn the formation hand signals, seeing our Class Leader Mark Jellicot and our Class Highlighter Al Turbiglio practicing their formation signals at the center table of the Dagger flight room, I sat down and joined them.

Mark Jellicot pointed to the sky and twirled his finger round and round.

"Pitchout!" Al said, and Mark nodded.

Mark made a fist with an extended thumb, tilted his head back, touched his thumb to his mouth, and made a drinking motion.

"Fuel check!" Al said.

"Chugalug!" I said.

"Fuel check," Mark corrected me.

Doley came over to the center table. He had seen the hand signals flying and wanted to get in on the action, too.

"Let's review," Doley said. Beginning with his index and pinky fingers extended and his middle and ring fingers touching his thumb, he ran me through his full repertoire of hand signals. "This is Little Bunny Foo Foo. This is Hook'em Horns. This is Hang Loose Hawaii. This is the Secret Devil Sign. And none of these should be confused with the signal for an echelon turn," Doley said.

"I thought that last sign meant Bon Jovi," I offered.

"Actually, it means I love you in sign language," Chuck said, joining the growing crowd at the center table.

"In F-4s in the Philippines, we never flew echelon turns," Mark Jellicot reminisced, putting his hands out in front of him, palms down to represent two jets in fingertip formation and then rotating them at the same time into sixty degrees of bank so that the top of his left hand paralleled the bottom of his right hand.

Mark moved his angled, parallel hands slowly to his right in perfect formation, maintaining sixty degrees of bank throughout his maneuver, to illustrate an echelon turn with two jets in formation. "On my first formation ride, I didn't feel comfortable pulling up that close to that big belly," Mark said, referring to Two's proximity to the underside of Lead's jet.

"Hey, that's what your wife said," I quipped, referring to the belly of Mark's flight suit.

Big Kurt was next to join the party at the center table, holding two plates of breakfast food, a half-pint carton of skim milk, and a Styrofoam cup of water in his oversized hands. "Guys, Chuck," he greeted everyone, "I have an announcement."

Kurt placed his all-I-could-eat-in-a-day-sized breakfast on the table at the open seat next to me. "Malia and I have picked out a name for our son."

"Let me guess: Kurt," I said.

"Ray, don't interrupt," Kurt warned. "He's going to be...Kurt II."

"Isn't that what I said?" I asked. "So isn't he going to be Kurt, Junior?"

"No, Ray," Big Kurt shook his giant head. "Not *Kurt, too,* as in *Kurt, also...Kurt II,* as in *Kurt, Roman numeral two.*"

"Kurt, the Roman numeral two suffix is typically used when a boy is named after his uncle," I argued. "If you name your son Kurt, he's Kurt, Junior."

"Ray, shut up," Kurt shook his giant head again. "He's my kid. I can name him anything I want, and I'm going to name him

Kurt II, and it will be spelled with the Roman numeral two, and I'm going to tell you why right after I have a bite of this breakfast burrito."

Everybody around the table waited and watched in awe as Big Kurt destroyed about half of the first of his two breakfast burritos with one mighty bite. A couple of chews later, he continued.

"Just like when you fly in formation, Lead says, *Tweet 2-7, Check,* on the radio, and Two says, *Two,* to let Lead know he's there, I'll say, *Kurt, Check,* and my son will say, *Two,*" Kurt explained. "I will be Lead, and my son will be Two...just like a two-ship formation." Then, he all but finished his first breakfast burrito with a second bite.

I got it...and I kind of liked it. Kurt was right. He could name his kid anything he wanted. I never really thought that much about peoples' names before, but I guess they're kind of like class patches. If we could have a pink flamingo for our class's official flight school patch, why did Kurt have to conform to conventional naming mores for his kid?

"See," Kurt said, now remarkably done with both of the breakfast burritos that had been on his plates, "my boy and I are going to be close. It's going to be like we're a two-ship formation. Lead and Two." Kurt reached around me with his extra-long arm and crushed me with a massive hug, pretending I was his son.

"We'll be together all the time." Kurt continued to squeeze me excitedly, transitioning to his funny *Where's Mr. Square?* voice. "There won't be anything we can't do together, and nothing will ever break us apart." He wrapped his other arm around me and squeezed me so hard that he pinned my arms to my side and nearly cracked my ribs.

*

Much like changes in atmospheric pressures affected how jets behaved in the sky, changes in the various pressures on the flight line affected the way people behaved at work. As the senior class on the T-37 side of the flight line building with no more checkrides until T-38s, the pressure had eased substantially since we'd first reported to Dagger. In this environment, the general attitude of our class had devolved from one of *work hard and have fun* to simply *have fun*. Sometimes, that fun came at the expense of others. Mostly, we had fun with our own classmates, but by pure accident, one of our instructors, Lieutenant Peena, got caught in the line of fire.

For the second time in the same week, Doley began to laugh so hard that he absolutely lost all ability to function. Unlike the Tringlin' Incident at the base theater, however, I had no idea what Doley was laughing at this time.

"Lieutenant Dolan." Lieutenant Prince stopped his pre-flight briefing while Doley continued to laugh and wheeze and gasp for air. "Did you have something you wanted to say?"

Doley tried to say something but couldn't.

"I'm sorry, Lieutenant Dolan," Lieutenant Prince said. "Could you say that again?"

Nothing.

Lieutenant Prince closed his checklist but kept a hand inside it so as not to lose his place in his formation briefing.

"Lieutenant Dolan," Lieutenant Prince said calmly, "if my formation is to make its assigned takeoff time, we need to finish our briefing and leave in the next five minutes."

He smiled and stared at Doley. "I order you to stop laughing."

At first, this made things worse, but eventually, Doley stopped laughing long enough to blurt out one thing.

"Peena fuel!" Doley screamed. Again, he burst into another fit of laughter.

Lieutenant Prince contorted his face with a mock sneer. "I didn't say *Peena fuel*," Lieutenant Prince rebutted. "I said *bingo fuel is five hundred pounds.*"

Bingo fuel was a phrase a pilot used to describe when the fuel in the jet's gas tanks reached a low enough level that if he didn't fly home, he might run out of gas. Like most of our stupid jokes, we had a little fun with Peena fuel, but unlike most of our stupid jokes, Captain Wright's assistant was the punch line.

"So, what is Peena fuel, anyway?" Lieutenant Wilson asked me as I looked past him in the right seat of the cockpit in order to concentrate on Kenny's jet. Kenny was flying his formation solo and leading us into the Southern MOA. We were supposed to be in fingertip formation—only I was bouncing up and down, struggling to maintain the proper position on Kenny's wing.

"Sir, Peena fuel is five hundred pounds," I deadpanned.

"I'm not talking about bingo fuel," Lieutenant Wilson said. "Why do you call it Peena fuel?"

"Sir, I don't know," I answered—even though I knew. "We use *Peena* for any word: Peena fuel...Peena butter and jelly...takin' a Peena.... It's kind of like *smurf*."

"Aaay, Tweet 2-7, go channel 1-9," Kenny's voice came over the radio.

"Two," I acknowledged, immediately switching my radio from channel 18 to 19.

Kenny checked me in on our new frequency and led us through the maneuvers we'd briefed for our mission: wingwork, echelon turns, pitchouts and rejoins, and trail.

As the wingman, I jerked the throttles and control stick wildly, struggling to keep my jet in the proper position for each maneuver. Formation flying was a serious workout.

"Tweet 2-4, Check," I heard Chuck's radio call to check in her formation on channel 19, the channel all jets assigned to the Southern MOA monitored when maneuvering in the areas.

"Two," Al called in immediate response to Chuck. He was solo on her wing.

"Columbus Approach, Tweet 2-4, flight of two, established Area Red," Chuck reported.

"Tweet 2-4, Columbus Approach, maintain Area Red until ready for recovery. Request recovery on channel 1-8," Columbus Approach directed.

"Aaay, Tweet 2-7, go trail," Kenny commanded when he was ready to lead me through some of the T-37's more complex tricks.

"Two," Al replied from Area Red, inappropriately responding to Kenny's call before I could answer it.

"Two," I said, acknowledging Kenny's command and then added, "Tweet 2-7, two's in," to let him know I was in position and that he could begin leading me through his tricks.

"Two," Al said again on channel 19.

"Tweet 2-4, Two, this is Lead," Lieutenant Prince's voice came over the radio. "The radio call you just responded to was meant for another formation out here in the Southern MOA. Please remember that we are Tweet 2-4."

"Two," Al said, acknowledging Lieutenant Prince.

"I think Turbiglio is so nervous about his solo," Lieutenant Wilson observed, "he's answering any radio call he hears."

"Yes, sir. That dumb Peena," I joked, yanking and banking to keep up with Kenny.

"I don't think Lieutenant Peena is all too happy about you guys using his name as a joke," Lieutenant Wilson said. I clumsily shook the jet up and down, back and forth, and side to side, getting farther and farther out of position the more Kenny pulled his maneuvers.

"Sir, nobody says Peena over the radio," I replied, trying to downplay how often people in our class actually used his name in vain.

Once Kenny finished his profile as the formation leader, he waggled me out to route position by shaking his rudder back-and-forth. He flashed me the position change hand signal, and I became the flight leader.

After a little bit of wingwork, I commanded, "Tweet 2-7, go trail."

"Two," Kenny called, sliding back into position.

"Two," Al called from his formation.

"Tweet 2-4, Two, this is Lead." Again, Lieutenant Prince reminded Al that our radio call was not meant for him.

"Lieutenant Turbiglio sure has that Two call down, doesn't he?" Lieutenant Wilson remarked as I banked up our Tweet with Kenny following at my tail.

"Yes, sir," I agreed. "He knows it like the back of his Peena."

As the formation leader, I took Kenny through the same series of maneuvers he'd performed for me. After a bunch of pitchouts and rejoins, echelon turns, and a little more wingwork, I was getting close to having only five hundred pounds of fuel left in my tanks. We were near our bingo fuel, and it was almost time to be heading back to base.

"Aaay, Tweet 2-7, Lead. Two is Peena," Kenny called over the radio.

Time to go home.

"Two," Al said yet again.

"Tweet 2-7 Lead copies," I called over the radio, ignoring Al's call, and waggling my rudder to direct Kenny to move out to the route position so he wouldn't have to change radio frequencies while flying right on my wing.

"Tweet 2-7, go channel 1-8," I said to Kenny, directing him to flip to the frequency over which we needed to request our recovery instructions from Columbus Approach, and as soon as I heard his "Two," I clicked my radio to channel 18.

I waited a few moments to give Kenny a chance to change channels and give me a head nod, which let me know he was on the new frequency. Before I could check him in over the radio, however, somebody else transmitted a call on channel 18.

"Tweet 2-4 Lead." It was Al.

Why was he on channel 18?

Neither Chuck nor Lieutenant Prince answered.

As a courtesy, since Al had beat me to his radio call on channel 18 and he was in a formation, I waited for his wingman, Chuck or Lieutenant Prince, to reply. Because I still hadn't checked Kenny in on our new frequency and hadn't requested recovery to Columbus, I turned the formation to keep our jets within the boundaries of Area Blue and waited for Al's formation to complete their series of radio calls.

"Tweet 2-4 Lead," Al called again after a brief pause.

Nothing.

Again, neither Chuck nor Lieutenant Prince answered.

"Tweet 2-4 Lead. Tweet 2-4 Lead!" he called twice.

Silence.

"Tweet 2-4 Lead! Tweet 2-4 Lead! Tweet 2-4 Lead! Tweet 2-4 Lead! Tweet 2-4 Lead! Tweet 2-4 Lead! Tweet 2-4 Lead! Tweet 2-4 Lead!" Al went totally nuts. "Tweet 2-4 Lead! Tweet 2-4 Lead!"

"Shut the fuck up, Turbiglio!" Lieutenant Wilson screamed. "Give them a chance to respond!"

Lieutenant Wilson hadn't keyed up his microphone when he yelled this, but even if he had, Al wouldn't have heard him. Transmitting his radio calls with non-stop panic, Al's broadcast blitz blocked all other calls on channel 18.

"Tweet 2-4 Lead, Columbus Approach on Guard," the controller called, using the emergency radio frequency that all aircraft monitor at all times. *Guard* was essentially a second radio that stayed on in the background. Guard allowed pilots and controllers to send emergency messages over the airwaves without having to wait for a break in the regular chatter taking place on the non-emergency frequencies, like channel 18. Whoever this controller was, he was a genius.

"Tweet 2-4 Two is on channel 1-9," the controller continued, broadcasting on Guard. "Turn to channel 1-9, and you'll find your wingman."

"Tweet 2-4 Lead, channel 1-9," Al acknowledged the controller.

"I hope you and Wessels never do anything that stupid," Lieutenant Wilson said.

"Sir, don't worry," I answered. "We both saw *Top Gun.*"

"What's that supposed to mean?" my IP asked.

"You never Peena your wingman."

*

As soon as I got back in the flight room after our ride, I told Doley about Al's Tweet 2-4 Lead meltdown and how he was actin' a fool in Area Red. Doley went right to the dry erase board at the front of the Dagger flight room and wrote *Tweet 2-4 Lead! Tweet 2-4 Lead!* over and over again, hoping to fill the entire board before Al got back to the room.

Kenny and I took our seats at Lieutenant Wilson's desk, where we'd debrief our ride and get our grades. Doley sat down next to Kenny as if to listen to our debrief, but I knew he was more interested in listening to what Lieutenant Prince would say during Al and Chuck's debrief at the desk next to us.

We sat and watched the entryway to the Dagger flight room, waiting to see Al's reaction to the board at the front of the room. Unfortunately, I never got the chance to see it.

Stan Melton burst through the Dagger entryway in a state of complete panic.

"Peena is pissed!" Stan warned. "He's really pissed!" Then, Stan left, probably to drop off his flight gear in his locker…or maybe to grab a bag of pork rinds from the snack bar.

Lieutenant Peena was the next one to walk through the Dagger door. Two steps into the room, he stopped, put his hands on his hips, and glared at the white board filled with *Tweet 2-4 Lead!* His face turned bright red, and after a moment or two, he stormed behind Doley, Kenny, and me toward the door to the IPs' briefing room. As he crossed the threshold, he took his T-37 checklist book and fired it into the back wall of the IP room. I heard the book hit the wall before he slammed the door shut.

"THESE GUYS AREN'T PILOTS!" Lieutenant Peena screamed in the IP room. "THESE GUYS ARE CIRCUS PILOTS! WHEN THEY LAUNCH, WE MIGHT AS WELL START THE CIRCUS MUSIC FOR THESE CLOWNS!"

"Aaay, he throws like a girl," Kenny whispered.

"Lieutenant Wright!" I stood up as soon as I heard Captain Wright call. "Report to me in my office."

"Yes, sir," I barked.

"Looks like you've been S'Peena'ed," Doley joked quietly.

Captain Wright was the only instructor in the room when I saluted him at his desk. Lieutenant Peena must have left through the door to the hallway. Captain Wright didn't invite me to sit or stand at ease, so after he returned my salute, I remained standing at attention in front of his desk.

"Lieutenant Wright, I do not want to hear the phrase *Peena fuel* ever again," Captain Wright plainly stated.

"Sir, I have never used that phrase on the radio," I protested.

"Lieutenant Wright, you are not listening. I did not say that you have ever used this phrase on the radio. I do not care if you have ever used this phrase. I said that I do not ever want to hear it again." Captain Wright paused for a moment so that what he had just told me could sink in.

It sank in.

"Lieutenant Wright, I know that Lieutenant Jellicot is your class leader, but I see what goes on in that flight room, and I know what role you play. I don't care if you've ever said Peena fuel at all," he said. "I just know that you have the power to stop it, and it stops now. Understood?"

"Yes, sir." I understood.

"Dismissed," Captain Wright ordered.

I took a step back, left foot first, and saluted. "Good afternoon, sir," I said. I had some work to do out in the flight room.

Everyone was staring at me — students and IPs alike — when I opened the door back to the main briefing room of Dagger. Thankfully, the white board at the front of the room had already been erased. Everybody knew what was going on, but I had my orders. I walked around the room and made sure I told every student, "No more Peena fuel." They all got the message.

Lieutenant Wilson and Kenny waited patiently for me to make my way around the room before beginning our formation debriefing. For Kenny, his formation solo was his last ride in the T-37, and he could not have cared less about getting his grades. Because of my bleeding hemorrhoids and I-check failure, I had fallen a few rides behind Kenny, and I still had several more rides to go before I'd be finishing with my solo. The grades weren't all that important to me, but having failed two out of three checkrides, I didn't think I could afford to fail any formation rides in the Tweet.

"Since you two are both probably going to come back as instructors," Lieutenant Wilson began, "I'm going to let you grade each other. It will be good practice for when you're FAIPs."

Just like that, entropy had been neutralized and order had been restored to the Dagger flight room.

Students could not make jokes at the expense of instructors. Instructors were pilots. And students weren't shit.

"Lieutenant Wessels, how would you grade Lieutenant Wright's fingertip flying?" Lieutenant Wilson asked Kenny. "And can you characterize his fingertip flying with only one word?"

Kenny thought for a moment. He knew that in order for me to be cleared to fly my formation solo, I'd need a grade of at least a *Fair* for each category, which meant that even though I sucked, I was at least safe.

"Aaaay, I'd give Ray a *Fair* for his fingertip flying," he said, "and if I had to describe his fingertip flying with one word, hmmmm...." Kenny smiled widely and checked to make sure Doley was listening.

Please don't say Peena!

Kenny clenched his fists up by his shoulders, squinted his eyes, stretched back his lips, gritted his teeth, and shook himself violently.

"Tringlin'!"

Chapter 16 — "Crossing the Hall"

Kenny surprised me with a flawless formation rejoin on my left. Not that I hadn't seen him fly good rejoins before the two-week Christmas break...I just didn't expect to see his car pull up next to mine as we cruised back to Columbus on I-20 West, just east of Tuscaloosa. I had flown into Birmingham after spending the holidays in Rhode Island, and Kenny was racing back from Atlanta. We hadn't planned to meet up on our return, but because the Isuzu P'Up, Winner of the Baja 1,000, couldn't go much faster than sixty-five miles per hour and Kenny rarely drove his Mustang convertible less than eighty-five mph, he caught me on the highway as we traveled back to resume our UPT training.

As the impromptu formation leader, my job was to clear and plan, which on I-20 West meant to stay in my lane, maintain a constant speed, and not drive Kenny into the back of a car in front of him in his lane. As number two in our formation, Kenny's job was to *be there,* and in spite of the two columns of cars that quickly formed behind us because our formation didn't allow other vehicles to pass us on the two-lane section of highway, Kenny maintained perfect, three-foot fingertip spacing between the passenger door of his Mustang and the driver's side door of the P'Up.

Typically, a formation flight leader didn't need to spend much time looking over at his wingman, but on this occasion, Kenny's car, loaded with his Christmas presents and holiday purchases, required the same kind of study as a What's Wrong with This Picture? game.

The first wrong thing was quite obvious: Kenny's spiky, jet-black hair had been changed to a tint of orange that was brighter than the spray paint we'd used on our vintage 1950s refrigerator. In a new twist to an old episode of *The Brady Bunch,*

Kenny's Mom must have finally opened up her hair salon and experimented with her new hair tonic on Kenny.

The second wrong thing was so wrong for so many reasons: Belted into the passenger seat next to Kenny was a full-sized, full-figured female mannequin. While she didn't have any hair, she was completely dressed in Kenny's dark-blue cadet athletic jacket and dark-blue Academy uniform pants. Kenny probably buckled her into the seat to prevent her from flying out of the convertible onto I-20 West at eighty-five miles per hour.

Sergeant Rollins probably ain't never unbuckled a dead mannequin, neither.

Before I got to pick out the next wrong thing in Kenny's car, I glanced up at my rearview mirror and noticed that our impromptu two-ship formation had caused such a bottleneck of traffic that I-20 West looked like a professional stock car race under the yellow caution flag. Two columns of slow-moving cars were packed tightly together behind us, unable to pass or change positions until the track was cleared and the green flag was waved. As much as I was enjoying finding things that didn't belong in Kenny's car, I didn't enjoy being the pace car on the highway.

I gave Kenny the hand signal for a position change and combined it with a goodbye wave. I'd learn all about his new stuff and his Christmas vacation back in Columbus.

*

Kenny's hair color wasn't the only thing that changed over the Christmas break. Class Commander Lieutenant Billy Mike had been promoted to Captain Billy Mike. Mark Jellicot, our class leader, and Val Martelli, the Warhawk section leader, were also promoted to captain, but because Billy Mike was a pilot, and Mark and Val were students, Billy Mike wore shiny, silver, metal captain's bars on his flight suit, and our classmates were issued blue and white cloth rank insignia that looked like they had been colored with fat tipped magic markers to sew onto their flight suits. After all, students weren't shit.

The airspace changed over Christmas break, too. Well, the military operating areas were still the same, but the airspace that the T-37s used for training in the Northern and Western MOAs was reassigned to the T-38s, and the airspace that the T-38s had been using was reassigned to the T-37s. The exception was the Southern MOA, Areas Red, White, and Blue, which remained T-37 training airspace. Student pilots were prepared for this change, having made our new T-37 area maps before we'd left for Christmas. Everybody had to have the right maps—even though much of the class, including Kenny, had finished all of their T-37 training rides.

Most of the guys thought the new airspace configuration would work to our advantage when we crossed the hall to the T-38 squadron a couple of weeks down the road. Since the ground references in the MOAs above northwest Alabama were the ones we'd been using for our T-37 training, we wouldn't have to learn new ground references for T-38s while struggling to learn the new systems and new procedures for our new jet. I agreed this was good, but I still had several formation rides left in the T-37—including my solo.

I had to learn the new T-37 airspace anyway—and all the new ground references below our classrooms in the sky. Kenny tried to convince me that the best way to learn these references would be to drive to these remote places and experience them firsthand. But he was done with his T-37 training—Tweet complete! He no longer needed eight hours of crew rest—not until we crossed the hall to fly T-38s. I couldn't go out during the week...unless I wasn't on the flying schedule for the next day. I needed to behave myself.

But when one evening's weather report predicted bad weather the next day, I went out anyway. We hit Mack's Western Supper Club in Crawford, forty minutes southwest of Columbus, where the owner sang strange X-rated songs from behind a chicken-wire fence. Another night, I made Kenny stay local, and we went to Classix, the Class Club of Columbus, for Comedy Night, which wasn't that funny. We tried to find a good bar in Starkville, a college town thirty minutes to the west on another night, but we couldn't. On our first Friday back, we made a pilgrimage to Elvis's birthplace in Tupelo, an hour to the north, for Elvis's birthday, but that place pretty much sucked, too.

The biggest disappointment came over the weekend. We ventured to a public high school on the outskirts of Columbus named after the great General Stephen D. Lee of the Confederate States of America to see rapper Kool Moe Dee perform his hit single "Wild, Wild West" in the gymnasium. The show was supposed to start at nine o'clock. At eleven PM, Mr. Dee still hadn't taken the stage. We tried to get our tickets refunded.

Outside, at the ticket office of the Lee High gym, I pushed our three tickets through the small opening in the window to the girl on the other side of the Plexiglas. "We'd like our money back, please," I said. "We came to see Kool Moe Dee, and it's been two hours, and we haven't seen Kool Moe Dee."

"Tix a' non-a'funnaba," the girl replied, pushing them back.

I hadn't seen that posted anywhere, not even on the tickets. So, I tried again.

"Miss, I'm sorry. These tickets do not say non-refundable. These tickets say *Kool Moe Dee* and *9:00 PM*. It's eleven, and I haven't seen or heard from Mr. Dee. I don't think he's even here. Please give us back our money."

"Non-a'funnaba," the girl said shaking her head and looking over my shoulder, as if looking at something in the distance. Then, she flicked the lights in the ticket booth on and off a couple of times, put a hand up over her head, and with one finger pointing up, she waved her hand around and around in big circles.

"What's going on?" Doley asked, coming up from behind me where he had been talking with Kenny.

"This girl won't give us our money back, and I think she's trying to distract me with a pitchout signal," I said, characterizing both our conversation and her formation hand signal.

"Aaay, dat's bullshit!" Kenny said.

"Total bullshit," I agreed. "She hasn't completed the prereqs to fly a pitchout."

Just then, a Columbus Police Department squad car pulled forward in the parking lot with its roof lights flashing—no sirens…just lights. The car stopped in front us, and a cop got out. The flashing lights stayed on. I was kind of glad. Maybe, the cop could help us with our dilemma.

"Is there a problem here, boys?" the policeman said loudly.

I looked back at the girl in the ticket booth, only to see that she had locked eyes with the cop and was pointing at me. Fine. I had no problem telling the officer what was happening.

"Yes, sir," I began. "We each paid fifteen dollars to see the Kool Moe Dee concert here at nine o'clock. It's after eleven, and the performer hasn't shown up. We'd like to get our money back."

"Y'all from the Arr Base?" the policeman asked.

"Sir, we're stationed at Columbus Air Force Base," I started my usual reply to this stupid question, but before I got to tell him that I was from Rhode Island, Kenny was from Long Island, and Doley was from Massachusetts, he cut me off.

"Then, what are y'all doin' here?" he asked what I'd already answered.

"Sir, we came to see the Kool Moe Dee concert," I repeated smartly, showing that maybe I was little bit annoyed. "It's been two hours, and the guy whose name is on the ticket hasn't even shown up yet. We'd just like to get our money back."

"Y'all don't need to be here," the policeman said, ignoring my explanation completely.

Kenny jumped in impatiently. "This is bullshit!"

"What did y'all say?!" The cop turned from me and got up in Kenny's face.

"Aaay!" Kenny wasn't about to back down. "I said..."

"He said, *We're leaving, Officer*," Doley interrupted, uncharacteristically pronouncing the *R* sounds at the end of his words, like he wasn't from New England.

"I ought to take y'all three *boys* to jail right now for cussin' a policeman," the cop said. "Y'all understand?"

No, actually, I didn't understand. Kenny didn't swear *at* the policeman. He was describing our circumstance. We were the ones who were right. This *was* total bullshit, and the girl in the ticket booth *should be* giving us back our money. Why wouldn't this cop help us?

"Sir, we're leaving now," Doley insisted, and without any hesitation or discussion, he forcefully put one hand on my back, slapped the other on Kenny's back, pushed us toward the parking lot, and made us leave.

*

Most cadets at the Academy didn't get to downtown Colorado Springs too much until we were seniors. Freshmen got one weekend pass per month to go off-base. Sophomores got two, and juniors got three. But you couldn't have a car until you were a junior, and you couldn't get a car loan until you were a senior. Because I spent part of my sophomore year on Academic Probation, I forfeited those weekend passes. So, it wasn't until my senior year, after I'd committed to giving a large percentage of my future pay to a local bank to buy the Isuzu P'up, Winner of the Baja 1,000, that I got into the habit of going downtown and hanging out at bars.

Seniors who weren't in trouble for bad grades or bad behavior could use off-base passes nearly every weekend. And when I got to be a cadet squadron commander during my senior year, I earned extra privileges of being able to leave the campus every night of the week if I wanted to. And I wanted to. But not wanting to go out alone, which was no fun, I needed a wingman. Someone, like me, who could leave campus during the week—and there were only a few dozen of us with this privilege. Someone, like me, that liked to share stories...that didn't care all that much about stupid stuff...that liked to laugh. And enjoy a beer. Or six. Someone who had my back...and someone whose back I had.

And I found someone. A perfect someone. We weren't best friends, but we were great friends. When I wanted to go out, he'd go, and when he wanted to go out, I'd go. And now, he had come to Columbus for UPT. While he wasn't in my UPT class, he was in the class behind me, the Orange Pumpkins, and he'd moved into my neighborhood—off Azalea Drive just a short walk away from the house Kenny and I were renting. And I needed to talk to him. I needed his counsel.

"Smart thenkin' by Dolan," Jimmy Joe said, when I finished telling my senior-year wingman the story of the Kool Moe Dee concert the next day at his rental house in our neighborhood. Because he was in the Orange Pumpkin class, I didn't get to see him much, but every once in a while, we'd hang out together on weekends and drink beer and tell stories.

For all the time we spent together, I still couldn't really understand much of what Jimmy Joe ever said. I never had much trouble understanding most people from the South, but Jimmy Joe, a native Deep South, Auburn War–Damn Eagle Alabamian, mixed up not only his vowel sounds but his word phrasings so much differently than I was used to...sometimes, I had no idea what he was saying! We communicated more on a conceptual than a verbal level. And after my experience at the concert, I needed the help of a true Southerner to understand a couple of concepts.

"So, what'd y'all do after y'all left?" Jimmy Joe asked, knowing that my classmates and I couldn't let the night end without drinking.

"Well," I began, "we figured that if we went to the Club, we'd maximize our drinking time. So we ended up at the Club."

The Club, a smoke-filled, drinking and dancing dump, had to stop serving alcohol at midnight on Saturdays in order to comply with local blue laws that prohibited the sale of alcohol on Sundays, but it could stay open until one AM because the Club was outside of the city limits of Columbus. So that its patrons could continue to drink until closing time, the Club would sell six packs of beer in buckets of ice right up until midnight. If we'd gone to any of the bars within the city limits, we probably would have had only enough time for one or two drinks after the Kool Moe Dee non-concert before closing time at midnight, but by going to the Club and getting two buckets of beer, we each got to throw down four beers before we had to head home.

"Smart thenkin', Rye," Jimmy Joe said to me, pronouncing my name with a long *I* sound instead of a long *A* sound.

We each drank a little from our long neck beer bottles, reclining in his lawn chairs. I wasn't too hungover from the night before, but my eyes were burning from being exposed to all the cigarette smoke at the Club. I put my thumb over the opening of my beer and turned the bottle upside down so that I could wet my thumb to rub beer on my eyes for relief.

"Why does every bar in town have the word club in its name?" I asked once I'd given my eyes a cool rinsing. "Have you noticed the places around Columbus? There's the Club, the 45 Club, Classix–The Class Club of Columbus, Mack's Western Supper Club..."

Before he answered, I added, "In Colorado, we hung out at Cowboys, Studebakers, Meadow Muffins.... None of them had *club* in their names. Why is everything around here a club?"

My Alabamian buddy smiled at me and took a long swig from his long neck bottle, but he just shook his head.

"I am a member of only two clubs: the stupid Officers' Club—to help pay off the ten thousand dollar chandelier in the lobby—and the Columbia Record and Tape Club," I continued. "But I'm only a member of the O-Club until I leave Columbus, and I'm only a member of the Tape Club until I buy four more tapes at twelve bucks each, plus shipping, to make up for the thirteen cassettes that I bought for a penny. I'd show you my collection, but all my tapes melted last summer in the Stu-ron parking lot after baking in the cab of the Isuzu P'Up, Winner of the Baja 1,000."

I took a drink from my beer. "And I even have membership cards for my clubs! I don't have a membership card for the Club or the 45 Club or Mack's Western Supper Club."

Jimmy Joe drank a sip.

"Yep. You do," he said.

What was he talking about?

"I do not," I rebutted.

Jimmy Joe took another long drink of his beer.

"Look at your hand," he directed me.

I still had a stamp on the back of my hand from the Club the night before. I had taken a shower to get the smoke off of me, but I hadn't scrubbed my hands very well.

"That's just the stamp I got on my hand for paying the cover charge at the door. Everybody who paid the cover charge got a stamp," I said.

"Wrong side," Jimmy Joe said, shaking his head.

And when he could tell I had no idea what he was talking about, he added, "Look atcho palm."

I flipped my hand over and looked at my palm. I still couldn't figure out what he was trying to tell me. "Jimmy Joe, what in *thee* hell are you talking about?" I asked, using the Southern version of the expression, hoping to make a connection.

Jimmy Joe sat up in his lawn chair, leaned over toward me, and spoke about as clearly as I had ever heard him speak. "Yo' membership card! Yo' palm!" He held up his own hand and tapped on his palm a couple of times.

I couldn't figure out what he was saying.

"You is white, ayn't you?" Jimmy Joe said, getting to his point.

What?!

"Tha's yo' membership card," Jimmy Joe tapped on his palm some more, making sure I understood. "You is in the club!"

"No way," was all I could come up with.

"Wye!" my friend shot back, pronouncing the word with a long *I* sound again instead of a long *A* sound. "Thenk about it. How many black people you ever seen at these clubs around town?"

"I guess I never really thought about that," I said.

So, I thought about it.

"I don't think I've ever seen any black people in the clubs," I acknowledged. "But I just figured that maybe they didn't want to go to these clubs."

"Tha's right," Jimmy Joe said. "Tha's wha' you jus' figured." He took another long drink from his beer before he finished his point. "But did you ever stop and thenk that maybe what you jus' figured jus' ayn't the wye thengs is?"

I had to think about that.

"No," I admitted. "I didn't."

"Tha's right, Yankee Boy," Jimmy Joe agreed, downing the rest of his beer. "Columbus ayn't no Rhode Island town."

He grabbed two more beers from the cooler next to his chair, opened them, and handed me one.

"Lemme as' you this," he continued. "Why do you thenk that Columbus cop was fixin' to tyke y'all downtown to have y'all spend a night in jyle?"

"I told you," I said, "because Kenny said bullshit!"

"Wrong!" Jimmy Joe shot back, burying his head in his non-drinking hand. "Tell me a'gin what was wrong with that picture las' night."

We had already covered this, but I'd tell him again, if he wanted to hear it. "We each paid fifteen bucks to see Kool Moe Dee at Lee High at nine o'clock—"

"Wrong!" Jimmy Joe cut me off. "Lemme he'p you out. If you was that cop, what was wrong with tha' picture las' night?"

"Kenny said bullshit to the cop," I repeated.

"You really don't git it, do ya?" Jimmy Joe just laughed.

I guess I didn't.

"Lemme he'p you." He took three big gulps from the beer he'd just opened, and after he lowered his bottle, he again sat up on the edge of his lawn chair. His smile was gone. Jimmy Joe got serious.

"Rye, besides you and Dolan and Wessels, how many white people was at tha' rap concert las' night?" he asked.

I didn't have to think about that. All three of us had said something about it to each other at one point or another during the night.

"None," I said. "We were the only three white people there."

"Ez'actly!" Jimmy Joe nodded. "Y'all three was someplyce y'all dedn't belong."

What?!

All we wanted to do was have a good time listening to Kool Moe Dee.

"In that cop's mind, tha's wha' was wrong with tha' picture las' night," my friend said.

*

I was the last student in Dagger to finish T-37 training, so my last student ride in the Tweet was as a formation solo on the wing of two instructors flying together, Lieutenant Wilson and Lieutenant Prince. Even though Lieutenant Prince was the formation commander as the highest-ranking instructor, he allowed Lieutenant Wilson to grade me. I got an *Excellent* for my last ride.

That same afternoon, Class 88-07 officially crossed the hall.

A tall, lanky, balding guy, T-38 Class Commander Captain Halliwell didn't greet our class with the same threats of failure that we'd heard from Captain Billy Mike when we first began our UPT training. Quite the opposite, he told our class that he'd heard nothing but good things about us. He liked our pink scarves. He liked the whole pink flamingo concept. He liked the design of our class patch, even though he couldn't figure out its hidden meaning.

Captain Halliwell seemed like a pretty laid-back guy, yet a wave of anxiety came over me, and my mind started to race. What if there were people who perceived our use of the word *club* was done with the intent to exclude certain groups? I was the one who had suggested the phrase *Columbus Beach Club,* thinking that clubs are formed around a common interest, like the beach—not for building fences to keep out people who are different. I had intended for Columbus Beach Club to be an antiestablishment statement; I never realized that some people might take it for exactly the opposite.

Soon after, we had a three-day weekend in January because of the new Martin Luther King, Jr. Day holiday. That Friday morning, Doley let me know he was flying to his roommate's home in Naples, Florida, for the long weekend, round-trip tickets were just ninety-nine dollars out of Birmingham, and that I was invited.

Over the Christmas Break a few weeks earlier, I had realized that if I was going to do better in UPT and stop failing checkrides and academic exams, I'd need to come up with a better system for getting through the program rather than trying to do just enough. Now, here I was about to jump on a flight to Florida for the weekend! But we had just finished T-37 training, and it happened to be my twenty-third birthday, and tickets were just ninety-nine dollars.

Doley had me meet him at his house. On my way there, I passed by the car dealership on Highway 45 with the sign that flashed the time, temperature, and brief message. In honor of the special, three-day weekend, a new message flashed prominently.

Happy Birthday
Robert E. Lee

Chapter 17 — "We Paint the Mother Pink"

"New jet. New day."

Our T-37 instructors would say this to us over and over again when we practiced emergencies in the simulator to deal with minor malfunctions and execute **BOLDFACE** for major problems. After landing, ejecting, or crashing at the conclusion of each emergency situation, the IP would spin his magic dials to reset the sim, restore order to the universe, and say, "New jet. New day," as a quick way of saying, "You're alive, and the entropy you'd just experienced with your previous aircraft has gone away."

Crossing the hall that separated the two different flying training squadrons in the flight line building at Columbus Air Force Base was a new-jet–new-day experience. Our new jet was the Northrop T-38A Talon, a twin engine, afterburner-equipped, supersonic sports car. Nicknamed The White Rocket, this jet had once been the ride of choice for the Air Force Thunderbirds and was still used by NASA astronauts for flying practice and chasing down the Space Shuttle. It was longer and sleeker than the Tweet, could fly more than twice as fast and twice as high, and the single-seat version of the aircraft, a fighter jet designated the F-5, was used in *Top Gun* as the MiG-28s flown by the bad guys.

Going from the T-37 to the T-38 side of the flight line felt like going from the bike I rode as a little kid, a three-speed Huffy with a banana seat, sissy bar, and colorful plastic straws on my wheel spokes, to the ten-speed Schwinn racing bike I got for my thirteen birthday that all the teenagers rode. Sleek. Fast. Powerful. Now, we were the big kids in UPT.

Crossing the hall also meant that we'd left Dagger behind. I had enjoyed getting to know my T-37 instructors. Lieutenant Wilson was cool, Major Lawson was a riot, and Flight

Commander Captain Wright was my hero. Having failed two out of three checkrides in Tweets, I was probably ranked last in my class at this point in our training. But I kind of felt lucky, because I knew that not all of my classmates had the same kind of experience with IPs that I'd had in the Tweet squadron.

As students, we were still assigned to the 14th Student Squadron. That didn't change. But to learn to fly our new jet, our class reported to the instructors of the T-38 squadron. Our half of Class 88-07 reported to Eagle flight, and the Warhawks half now reported to Scorpio flight for their T-38 training.

The first thing we all did when we walked into the T-38 Eagle flight room was find our gradebooks. The gradebooks had been laid flat on the tops of the desks of the instructor pilots, two or three per desk, all around the room. Find your gradebook, and you'd found your instructor. Though there were no instructors in the room at the time, their names were painted in large black letters on white wooden nametags cut in the shape of a T-38's profile, hanging from the ceiling above their desks. We still had about ten minutes before the start of the formal briefing, and our new Eagle flight instructors were all behind the closed door of their private IP briefing room, adjacent to the main flight room. I didn't necessarily care to be best friends with my new IP, but I hoped he wasn't the type of guy that treated student pilots like they ain't shit.

"Ray! You're over here with me!" Brendan Sweet called out from back by the schedulers' desks, though not too loudly so as not to disturb our new instructors in their room as they prepared our day one. Brendan was a blond-headed, soft-spoken, short-statured Florida beach bum who took his boat out waterskiing on the Tennessee–Tombigbee Waterway any weekend the weather was warm. He'd taken Kenny and me out waterskiing and kneeboarding a bunch of times during the summer and fall, and we always had a good time.

"Looks like we're both assigned to Lieutenant Baiber," Brendan said as he offered me a handshake.

"All right, B!" I said, shaking his hand, slightly disappointed not to have Kenny as my partner again. "Let's have a look at the pictures on the desk and see if we can figure out what our Lieutenant Baiber is all about."

Since Mark Jellicot, as class leader, would call the students to attention when the IPs entered the room, we'd only get to see those instructors who would pass through our field of vision while we stared straight ahead, standing in front of our assigned seats. Because our own instructor, Lieutenant Baiber, would be sitting at the desk behind us, Brendan and I wouldn't get to see him until after the morning's formal briefing had ended, which could take as long as another hour. The pictures that IPs kept under the clear plastic desktop protector on top of their desks usually gave some clues about the instructor. If the instructor pilot had been part of an operational Air Force unit, he'd have pictures of the aircraft he'd flown and maybe some squadron patches that he'd worn. If the IP were a FAIP and Columbus were his first assignment, he'd probably have pictures of the jet he'd like to fly next and maybe some of the dollar-ride dollars he'd been given by his students since he'd been an IP.

The chairs on our side of Lieutenant Baiber's desk were facing into the center of the room for the formal briefing, and rather than turn mine around, I knelt backwards in it to look at my new instructor's pictures. Brendan knelt too.

"Aaay," Kenny said, coming up from behind me. Over the long weekend, he had gone home and had his mother return what remained of his spiky orange hair to its natural jet-black color. "You guys look like you're in church."

"Well, I think we might be," I said, pointing to Lieutenant Baiber's desk. "Look. Pocket cards for 'The Lord's Prayer,' 'Lord, Guard and Guide the Men Who Fly,' 'The Ten Commandments,' and a bumper sticker that says, 'God is my co-pilot.'"

"Aaay —" Kenny pointed at the bumper sticker — "does dat mean God *is* shit?"

"Kenny," I said, thinking through his logic, "I think that's exactly what that means because if you ain't a pilot, you ain't shit, but if God is a co-pilot, then He must be a pilot, meaning He's clearly not *ain't shit,* and that would mean He *is* shit."

I grabbed Kenny and Brendan's hands. "Let us pray," I said, but they both pulled away from me as fast as they could.

"Aaay! Get outta here," Kenny laughed.

I realized I had no idea where Kenny's seat was in our new flight room. "Where are you sitting? Who's your IP?"

"Aaay, I'm right next to you. This is my IP's desk right here," he said, showing me his gradebook at the desk in the seat right next to mine. Then, pointing up at the nametag hanging from the ceiling, he tried to pronounce the name painted on it.

"Captain Stiger? Stigger? Steeger? I don't know how to say it," he admitted.

It didn't matter. We'd find out soon enough.

"Room! TEN-HUT!" Mark Jellicot commanded, and in unison, my classmates and I snapped to attention.

Our new Eagle instructors filed into the flight briefing room and took their spots at their desks. I kept my eyes fixed on a spot on the white dry erase board at the front of the room. Not knowing if we were in for six months with another great flight commander or six months with a dick, I didn't want to take any chances on giving our new leader a reason to scream at me.

Eagle Flight Commander Major Carrington looked older than any of the flight line instructors we'd had to this point in our training. I don't think he was as old as Major Lawson, but Major Lawson didn't work on the flight line. Whereas Dagger's Captain Wright could have been my older brother, Eagle's Major Carrington had at least a decade on me…maybe more. Unusually skinny for a major, I figured him to either be a long-distance runner or suffering with an eating disorder.

His high and tight haircut indicated a more militant approach to the military than I cared for, but Eagle was his flight. He set the example, and he laid down the law. My first impression was that our Eagle experience might not be the same as the good times we'd had in Dagger. And this was confirmed when Major Carrington welcomed our class with his major admonition: "Don't get my Irish up."

We sat and listened to our new leader with rigid attention. We were the new kids, we weren't pilots, and we weren't shit. Nobody dared be the first one to twitch a muscle or get caught gazing around the room while we were supposed to be focused on the Eagle flight commander. Or so I thought...because when Major Carrington told us that he'd been an RF-4 pilot before being assigned to Columbus, Mark Jellicot nearly jumped out of his seat and his flight suit.

The RF-4 was a modified version of the F-4, the jet Mark had flown in the Philippines with the Fiends, but instead of weapons for combat, the RF-4 was equipped with cameras and sensors for reconnaissance. This didn't matter to Mark, however, because after six months with the FAIPs and a couple former cargo pilots in Dagger, Mark was finally back in the company of a fighter pilot!

*

After our first Eagle flight formal briefing had concluded, and we finally got to turn around, I greeted my new instructor, offering my hand: "Hi, Lieutenant Baiber, I'm Lieutenant Ray Wright."

A massively large paw reached across the desk to shake and effortlessly crush my hand. "Nice to meet you," my new IP said softly with a kind smile.

If my big buddy Kurt was the Hulk Hogan of UPT, my new instructor pilot for the T-38 was Andre the Giant. He was taller and heavier than Kurt, and like the Giant to the Hulkster, he was thicker, not as athletic-looking, and not nearly as muscular. I hadn't seen the inside of a T-38 yet, but I couldn't imagine how my new IP crammed his oversized body into the cockpit.

"Hey, Lieutenant Baiber," Brendan said on his turn to shake. "Nice to see you again."

If Brendan knew First Lieutenant Baiber from the Academy, that meant our new IP was a First Assignment Instructor Pilot, still another FAIP from the class of 1985.

"Why didn't you tell me you know him?" I whispered to my new tablemate while our new IP attended to some scheduling business.

"My bad," Brendan said simply, shaking his head and shrugging his shoulders. As dynamic as Brendan was on the water, when tethered to the back of a speeding motorboat, he was usually quiet and reserved around people, even his friends. He was one of those guys that could have a good time at a party by just watching everybody else have a good time without having to say a word to anyone all night. He'd talk to you if you talked first, but if you didn't talk, Brendan might not say anything at all.

"Lieutenant Baiber," I pointed to his wife's picture in the wallet-sized family portrait under the protective plastic top of his desk, "is this Babe Baiber?"

My massive new IP politely smiled and quietly replied, "That's my wife."

Without paying any attention to how he annoyed he might be by me calling his wife, *Babe Baiber,* I pointed to the picture of the child for my next icebreaker.

"Lieutenant Baiber," I asked, "is this Baby Baiber?"

Again, my massive new IP politely smiled and quietly replied, "That's my daughter."

As if we'd rehearsed for this moment like we'd rehearsed for the "Captain Wright Rap," Doley, who happened to have just walked up to Lieutenant Baiber's desk behind Brendan and me, elevated my stupid line of questioning to an even greater level of stupidity with a special song just for the occasion.

Oooh, Baby, Baiber
Baby, Baiber
Oooh, Baby, Baiber
Baby, Baiber!

Doley belted out the Salt-n-Pepa and performed his dance moves as the students and instructors of Eagle laughed at the show. Seemingly not annoyed at all, my new IP smiled widely and softly laughed along with everyone else. Somehow, I don't think this was the first impression that Class Leader Mark Jellicot wanted us to make with our new T-38 IPs, but it made me think that Eagle might not be that bad after all.

*

"Ray, I'm going to paint Kurt II's room blue this weekend. He'll be here in less than a month," my big buddy Kurt said as we studied our T-38 Contact flying procedures together at the table in the center of the Eagle flight room.

"Kurt, I hate to say this, but when I looked at that ultrasound picture, I wasn't so sure that baby was a boy," I teased. "I wouldn't be so quick to paint the room blue. I don't think you can cover blue paint with pink paint...it wouldn't match our class patch and flying scarves. What do you think about the name Kurtina?"

Of course, I had no idea what I was looking at when he and Malia showed me the ultrasound picture, which looked like a bad, black-and-white negative of a scratched-up record album.

"Ray, we're having a boy, his name will be Kurt II, and this weekend, I am going to paint his bedroom blue," my friend countered.

"All right. Fine. What do I know about ultrasounds, anyway?" I conceded. "Can I come over and help?"

"No, actually," Kurt answered. "I do need you to help me, but I don't need you to help paint."

"What do you need, big buddy?"

"Well, Malia can't be around paint fumes. Can I bring her down to your house on Sunday afternoon for a few hours?" he asked. "That's the only time I'm going to be able to paint. She can bring dinner," he added.

"Kurt, of course she can come over on Sunday," I said. "And don't worry about dinner. We'll be watching the Super Bowl. All she needs to bring is a six pack of long necks for the Pepsi machine."

I didn't know how Kurt did it. How did he manage to be a successful student pilot, a new husband, and do all his furniture building, too? I had none of the responsibilities that Kurt had, and in three T-37 checkrides, I had two *Unsats* and a *Good* for grades; I was one more checkride *Unsat* from being kicked out of the program. Kurt had all this other stuff going on in his life, and for his three checkrides, he had scored three *Excellents*. He had to have been ranked up at the top of the class, which was great, because if anyone deserved it, Kurt did.

As we sat next to one another at the table in the center of the room and I pretended to study, I wondered what the first wallet-sized photo of Kurt and Malia's baby might look like. Lieutenant Baiber was bigger than Kurt, but his baby looked too normal. With Kurt's giant head and hands and Malia's petite frame, however, this baby had the potential to look like a real freak. Rather than study, I thought it would be more fun to put together some caricatures of possible body types for Kurt and Malia's soon-to-arrive son.

"Kurt, I've made some rudimentary sketches of what your child might look like, based on a mixture of your physical characteristics and your wife's physical characteristics." I opened my workbook to the "Notes" pages where I'd put together my collection of drawings.

"As you know, all babies have big heads," I sighed. "And unfortunately for Malia in this first scenario, even though the baby will not be tall like you, Kurt, he will inherit Malia's tiny body but your head and hands." I revealed my first baby drawing to Kurt, who buried his face in his large hand and shook his supremely large head back and forth.

"Malia's going to kill me," he said.

"Hold on a minute! There are other possibilities!" I said, pretending to offer some hope, even though I knew the pictures only got more and more extreme, depicting babies with bigger and bigger heads.

"Give me that book," Kurt said, pinching both of my forearms in one of his powerful hands and pulling my workbook away from me.

He studied my sketches for a few moments before releasing my arms from his grip.

"Dude, you're a dick," he said. "My head is not that big."

"Not that big?!" I exclaimed. "Then why did the NFL just announce that your flight helmet will be the site for Super Bowl XXV?"

Kurt flipped my workbook at me like a Frisbee.

"Ooooooh!" I said, pointing at him and standing up from my seat.

From the other side of the room, Doley started to sing.

Oooh, Baby, Baiber
Baby, Baiber
Oooh, Baby, Baiber
Baby, Baiber!

*

"I want my MTV." I wrote it in the lower left-hand memo section of every monthly check I disgustedly wrote to Columbus TV Cable. Cable sucked in Columbus.

Kenny and I watched the Weather Channel a lot. Probably too much. Learning to fly was a lot easier on a clear day.

Unfortunately for student pilots at Columbus Air Force Base, as terrible as the cable TV company was, the weather was worse.

The night before our T-38 dollar rides, Kenny and I had the Weather Channel on as we worked our bills.

I knew the dollar I'd created for T-37s would not be appropriate for my new IP, Lieutenant "Ooh Baby" Baiber. For sure, he wouldn't want to show a dollar-ride dollar like the last one I'd made to his co-pilot. Or his wife. Or someday his daughter. So, instead of buying ten dollars worth of porno mags and spending all night not studying, I'd picked up a copy of *Muscle & Fitness* magazine at the base exchange. Rather than cover the back of my dollar with naked ladies being intimate with aircraft parts, I planned to cover the back of it with female bodybuilders using aircraft parts for barbells, not sexual gratification.

Despite the grainy quality of the television picture, the next day's forecast on the Weather Channel was looking pretty good: clear skies, calm winds, and temperature in the fifties. After about an hour of work, my dollar was looking pretty good, too — full of steroid-injected, pectoralis-nippled, horse-jawed, female bodybuilders. In a way, it was more disturbing than my T-37 porno collage.

*

As soon as we'd finished up the morning's briefing and the flight room doors were opened, Lieutenant Carmody, one of the eight FAIPs in Eagle, walked in with his G-suit draped over his shoulder. He had been outside the doors, waiting for the formal report to end. In addition to the G-suit on his shoulder, his disheveled hair and severe case of mask-face indicated he had been flying already. Since we were one of the earliest flights to have reported to the flight line, Lieutenant Carmody must have been flying the weather ship.

The weather ship was the name given to the first T-38 to fly every day. Only instructors were allowed to fly the weather ship. The job of the weather ship was to check out the weather conditions in the local flying area, the traffic pattern, and to make a recommendation for the flying status to the SOF.

On the T-38 side of the hall, the SOF's call sign was "Janitor." In order to determine the proper flight status for flying operations, Janitor needed to know more than the radar picture from the Weather Channel, and what better way to know then to have a jet with two IPs fly around the base and the MOAs and report exactly what they saw. Where were the clouds? Could aircraft perform over-the-top aerobatics in the MOAs without going into clouds? Was the weather good enough for students to fly solo? Those were the types of questions the weather ship needed to answer in order to help Janitor determine the flight status.

Before he walked back into the IPs' private flight room, the portly Lieutenant Carmody took a few steps into the room, sunk his fists into his gooey sides and made a general announcement to the enthusiastic new students of Eagle.

"Well, 88-07, we had heard so many good things about your class from your Tweet IPs in Dagger, and the Stu-ron told us that you were one of the top classes on this base," he announced in his deep voice that always sounded as if he were gargling while he spoke. I thought he sounded like Marvin the Martian from *Bugs Bunny*.

Looking around the room to be sure he had most students' attention, he continued, "But from what I saw this morning while I was out in the weather ship, there's a new top class on this base, and it's not yours. You guys look bad."

Lieutenant Carmody stood for a moment, shaking his head, and then turned toward the door of the IP room. I really didn't care all that much about which class was the top class in UPT, but Mark Jellicot wasn't about to let Lieutenant Carmody's challenge go.

"Lieutenant Carmody, what did we do that is making us look bad?" Mark asked.

"You didn't do anything," Lieutenant Carmody gargled, "but someone else did, and that's what looks so bad. You must be embarrassed."

"I don't understand what you're saying," our confused class leader replied.

"You will after your class flies today," Lieutenant Carmody cryptically croaked. He walked away from Mark, ducked into the IP room, and immediately closed the door behind him.

"Mark, I need to talk to you!" Scorpio Section Leader Val Martelli said, walking through the Eagle doorway from the hall. Val made a quick look around the room to make sure he wasn't interrupting anyone's flight briefings.

"Hey, Everybody! Val's here!" Kenny called out so that we could show him the proper respect. "Valsalva!"

Everyone pinched their nose and nodded, performing our mock-Valsalva ritual as Mark made his way over to Val. Even Mark Valsalvaed. The T-38 IPs hadn't seen our tribute to Val yet, so most looked around with a quizzical *What's that about?* look on their faces.

The two section leaders ducked out into the hall, leaving the rest of us to sit around and wonder what was happening.

After about a minute of cluelessness, those of us with flights in the first flying period got our gradebooks to prepare for our rides, and the rest of the class made plans to chair-fly, study, or hide from instructors for the next couple of hours. I was scheduled for my dollar ride with Lieutenant Baiber, so I started looking over the profile he had given me. Kenny sat down to listen to my pre-brief and mission plan.

"We've got trouble!" Mark Jellicot stormed back into the room in a panic, making his announcement to no one in particular, as Lieutenant Carmody had done a few minutes earlier. Every student turned toward Mark.

"The Nightmares have painted the roof to the VFR entry point for the T-38 traffic pattern," Mark declared.

Who cares?!

The Nightmares were a class of non-Academy graduates, four classes behind ours. They had been trying to make a good impression on the wing commander and other leaders at the base through a series of weekly spirit missions. At the Academy, cadet squadrons and each class demonstrated *esprit de corps* by decorating prominent landmarks with meaningful numbers, colors, and mottos under the cloak of darkness for the rest of the Academy to see the next day. Though on any given night, most cadets would rather sleep than conduct a spirit mission, some guys were just into that type of thing, and if someone didn't respond appropriately to another group's spirit mission, you never heard the end of what great spirit these nocturnal idiots had.

"The roof of the T-38 VFR entry point is now painted with a black and yellow checkerboard pattern to match the Nightmares' flying scarves!" Mark looked all around, making sure he was addressing all the Eagle students, but as he relayed his news to the room, he walked straight over to Kenny and me.

"The Nightmares are still in T-37s! They haven't even crossed the hall! We're the freshman class in T-38s! We're flying our dollar rides today! This makes us look really bad. They had no right to paint the VFR entry point. I'm going to light up that class leader. I've really got the beak," he ranted.

Mark loved to use the phrase *the beak*. It was a uniquely UPT phrase meaning one was extremely agitated. I avoided using it because I thought it was stupid, like a lot of other UPT sayings.

Doley, Kurt, and most of the rest of the class circled in behind Mark. "We need to come up with a plan," Mark declared. He paused to see if anyone would volunteer a plan.

No one offered anything. Mark asked more directly, "What are we going to do?"

First of all, there was nothing we could do at this moment. I had to fly in a little over an hour, and I needed to start briefing up my dollar ride with Lieutenant Baiber in another couple of minutes. I didn't have time to worry about the color of the roof of the VFR entry point. Secondly, I didn't think this was such a big deal. The Nightmares had obviously executed a well-planned spirit mission. They were showing some pride and doing a little self-promotion. Good for them.

I didn't want to make eye contact with Mark. But then, he leaned down on Lieutenant Baiber's desk to speak right to Kenny and me.

"Guys, what do you think we should do?" he asked, trying to force Kenny or me to respond.

Fine!

This was ridiculous. I closed my gradebook and got up to face the mini-mob now gathered behind Mark. The way I saw the situation, whining to the Nightmares or to anybody else wouldn't solve anything. We had to one-up them. With something bigger and even stupider.

"Here's what we're gonna do," I said, and in my best John "Cougar" Mellencamp impersonation, I laid out the plan of action to Mark and our incensed classmates behind him. "I give you the deeds, and the keys, and then WE PAINT THE MOTHER PENK!"

Even though I couldn't watch MTV in Columbus, I had memorized these lines from John "Cougar" Mellencamp's classic commercial for MTV's Little Pink Houses contest a few years earlier. The contest winner would become the owner of the MTV Party House in Indiana and would paint it pink with John "Cougar" Mellencamp. The contest ran the first summer I got to go home from the Academy, which was when my parents got cable. That commercial played after every three or four videos.

Since our class's flying scarves were pink, this seemed to me the most appropriately stupid course of action. I think the mini-mob thought so, too. I don't know that anyone recognized that I was trying to sound like John "Cougar" Mellencamp, but after I'd said, *We paint the mother pink,* everybody repeated it, like the Munchkins when Glinda the Good Witch first told Dorothy, *Follow the yellow brick road.*

Reassured that painting the roof of the VFR entry point pink, the color of *our* class scarves, would make all things right with the world again by covering up the colors of the Nightmares' scarves, the mini-mob dispersed. Students went back to briefing up their dollar rides, studying their flight procedures, and general time-wasting.

While I was on my dollar ride, Kenny was going to rally support for the paint-the-mother-pink work ahead of us, and when Kenny was flying during the second period, I'd try to get guys to go with us. Doley would probably help. I didn't know about Kurt because his wife was due with the baby any day. I wasn't too sure about anyone else.

*

"Aaay! Dat's it!" Kenny yelled and pointed, holding his T-38 area map that we'd used to find our way out to the VFR entry point.

The barn sat at the back, left side of a dirt parking area. It looked a lot bigger from the ground than it did from the air, traveling at three hundred knots earlier in the day. It wasn't an animal barn, as I had envisioned it to be; it was a storage barn for hay and large farm equipment. The side facing the parking area had no wall, and if we wanted, we could have driven right in. In fact, we could have driven a cargo plane in, because this thing was more like an aircraft hangar than a barn.

There wasn't much to the structure, itself. It was framed with steel I-beams, had three aluminum walls, an aluminum roof, and looked to be about forty feet tall. Tractors and farm

322

equipment were parked in the middle of the barn. Giant bales of hay were stacked up against the wall on the right. I didn't see any lights or any windows or, more importantly, any ladders.

In the bed of the P'Up were the six gallons of pink paint that I'd picked up at Sears. Doley pulled up as Kenny and I leaned up against my tailgate, surveying the landscape. Doley stuck his head out of his window.

"Doley-mania Zero-One, Bahn with the numbuhs," he said.

"Do you really have the numbers?" I asked.

"What numbuhs?" Doley laughed at his own joke and got out of the Jeet.

Kurt and Malia came up the dirt road next. Kurt had to bring Malia, now in her ninth month of pregnancy, because if she went into labor while he was on the roof of a barn thirty miles from their apartment, he wouldn't be able to get her to the hospital, and he might miss the baby's arrival. They couldn't take that chance.

Doley marshaled Kurt into a parking spot, just as a crew chief on the flight line directed a jet into a parking spot upon return from a mission. After exchanging thumbs ups, Doley gave Kurt the signal to cut off his engine, and the five of us gathered at the back of the P'up to discuss our next move.

Nobody else came.

"So how are you guys planning to get up on that roof?" Malia challenged us.

"I've got a fifty-foot ladduh," Doley said, "but I left it back at the house."

"You dumb bastid!" Kenny reprimanded him.

"We don't have a lot of sunlight left," I said, pointing west. "We've got to come up with something soon."

Kenny, Doley, Kurt, and I walked over to the barn. Knowing she was unable to paint, Malia brought a camera, and she snapped pictures of the cotton fields that surrounded us.

Approaching the huge barn, I looked for a way up to a loft or for a ladder or just for an idea, but I couldn't see a thing. I had no clue how we could get on the barn roof.

"Kurt, you got anything?" I hopefully asked my handyman friend.

"Yes, Ray, I *got* something. I've got a wife who's due with our first child any minute, thirty miles from the nearest hospital, taking pictures of cotton fields. That's what I've got," Kurt stated.

"Doley," I said and turned toward Doley, "you got..."

"All right Kenny!" Doley shouted out, cutting me off before I could finish my question.

Kurt and I looked where Doley was pointing. Kenny was shinnying along the underside of the I-beam that ran along the ceiling on the right of the barn where the wall and roof met. His back was parallel to the ground. His head moved toward us at the front of the barn as he worked his way across the beam.

When Kenny got to the corner at the open front of the structure, he threw his left arm up to the roof, grabbed the wall with his right hand, and let his legs drop. With a move that was part pull-up and part press-up, he swung, lifted, and willed himself from under the roof to a point where his waist met the roof line. Then, he whipped his legs over the roof's edge and rolled on top.

Totally fearless! Totally amazing! Kenny did it! He'd scaled the walls of the barn and climbed onto the roof!

Kurt, Doley, and I stood at the opening of the enormous barn, looking forty feet up at Kenny. He leaned over the edge and waved us up.

"How did he do that?" I asked my friends.

"I saw the whole thing," Doley said. "He climbed up those hay bales—" Doley pointed to the right side of the barn to some hay bales piled up against the wall. "Then, he climbed that beam in the middle of the bahn to the othuh beam that runs along the top of the wall. He crawled upside-down on that beam to the cornuh, and five seconds latuh, he was on the roof."

"Kenny," I yelled up, "you forgot the paint!"

"T'row it up!" he shot back. "I'll catch it!"

"Why don't we make a supply line and hand the paint up, station-to-station?" Kurt suggested, obviously thinking that throwing the paint cans might result in either a mess or an injury.

"I'll get the cawnuh," Doley offered.

"I'll get the hay bales," Kurt called.

"I'll get the paint," I said, turning back to the P'up, realizing I should have parked closer to the barn.

As I went to get the paint cans, Malia was walking around the edge of the vast cotton field. Now nine months pregnant, she kind of waddled when she walked, not because she seemed to be struggling with her weight, but because her belly was so big, and she was so small, that walking normally was impossible. Malia stopped every so often to evaluate the landscape for her next picture. Whenever she stopped moving, she leaned backwards a little to keep her balance.

I passed the paint cans up to Kurt on the hay bales, and so started the chain. Once all six paint cans were on the roof, Kenny helped Doley climb up on top. Kurt reminded me that I had forgotten the brushes and rollers, so I went back to get those, while Kurt made his way to the roof.

Malia must have snapped a full roll of film or gotten tired, because when I got back to the P'up, she had climbed into the bed of the truck and stretched out. She sat with her back against the cab and her belly and legs out in front of her. Because I had parked facing away from the barn, Malia had a perfect vantage point from which to watch all the paint-passing and beam-climbing action.

"I don't believe this," she said just loudly enough so that I heard.

Grabbing the bag of painting supplies, I looked up to the roof at Kurt. Malia could not have described the situation any better.

Forty feet above the ground, Kurt dangled from roof's edge, while his legs crazily appeared to be pedaling an invisible bicycle. Every few pedals, he tried to swing his legs from one side to the other, in an attempt to get a foot up onto the roof. Like a pedaling pendulum, Kurt's legs rocked back and forth between the four o'clock and eight o'clock positions but never high enough to be able to catch the edge of the roof with one of his feet. Adding to the comedy of this dangerous situation was that with each flailing swing of his legs, Kurt's pants dropped a little lower down his butt.

From Kenny and Doley's perspective on top of the roof, Kurt must have looked completely calm and not in need of any assistance. His head and shoulders were above the roofline, and his outstretched arms clutched the rooftop; so Kenny and Doley couldn't see what was happening below the roofline. From my perspective on the ground, Kurt's pedaling and flailing legs, pumping forty feet in the air, looked like Wile E. Coyote running in mid-air, after just having been fooled into stepping off the side of a cliff by the Roadrunner.

Everyone knew what would happen next: The coyote would keep running for a couple of seconds in mid-air, look into the camera, and then fall to the ground, resulting in a big cloud of dust. Then, a rock would fall on him and crush him. The only thing missing from this scene was the rock.

"Kurt Spranger!" Malia shouted to her husband. "If you fall and get hurt, and I have to take care of this baby by myself, I will kill you!" There was the rock.

Hearing Malia scream, Kenny and Doley immediately appeared at the edge of the roof. Each of them grabbed one of Kurt's arms, and they helped pull him up.

Before I could join them, Malia locked her stare on me. I was still standing next to her at the back of the P'up. I interpreted her stare to mean that she would kill me, too, if anything happened to Kurt. I couldn't just walk away without acknowledging her scowl and her displeasure. I innocently stared back at her for a moment, trying to think of something to say.

Finally, I decided to match her sternness with my own. "Malia," I said, dropping my eyebrows low without breaking her eye-lock, "if you're going to let Kurt out of the house in pants that don't fit, you really need to get him a belt." Before she could respond, I jogged to the barn with the brushes and rollers and climbed to the roof to join the others.

From the roof, we could see that there were still a bunch of T-38s in the traffic pattern, but we couldn't really see the runway or the base. As I had noticed during my ride earlier in the morning, the Nightmares hadn't painted the whole roof; they had only painted the back half of it with the black-and-yellow checkerboard pattern they had on their flying scarves and class patch. The rest of the huge roof was still unpainted aluminum.

We'd gotten ourselves and our stuff onto the roof, but we still faced a few challenges. For one, the roof was quite large. I had never painted anything like a house or a roof before, and I was pretty confident that we didn't have enough paint. Sunset posed another challenge and an even bigger concern for us. The problem wasn't so much darkness, but if we didn't get this job done and get back home quickly, we were in danger of violating our crew rest requirement for eight hours of uninterrupted sleep.

Once we started painting, Kurt soon found another problem. "Guys," he said, "this pink paint isn't thick enough to cover up the black. It will cover up the yellow, but the black is going to show. What do we do?"

Kenny knew. "I give you the deeds, and the keys, and then WE PAINT THE MOTHER PENK!" he said.

Doley and I joined in when Kenny got to the *we paint the mother pink* part. While this suggestion didn't solve the problem, it *was* funny.

"How about we just leave the black, paint the yellow, and if we have anything left, we paint what they didn't paint?" Doley offered. "We'll turn this into a black and pink checkuhboahd with as much pink unduh'neath as we can."

The pink paint covered the Nightmares's yellow squares quite nicely, and because each brightly painted pink square was surrounded by dark black squares, the pink really popped out. I thought this would look really cool from the sky, and in thinking that, I became aware that I hadn't heard any jet engines in the last few minutes.

"Official sunset has occurred," Doley announced, just as the RSU controller would announce from the box, known as "Live Oak," in the T-38 traffic pattern—the equivalent of what we'd called Sunfish in the T-37 pattern. Sunset marked the end of normal flying operations each day, and because it was nearly sunset, all the jets that had been in the Live Oak pattern had landed. We had about fifteen minutes of light left.

As my friends and I finished up work on the roof of the VFR entry point, I looked across the big, metal roof with its now black-and-pink checkerboard pattern and broad band of pink paint underneath the checkerboard for my inspiration. I wasn't as quick as Doley at creating song parodies, but after running through some lyrics a couple of times in my head, I belted out my own version of "Pink Houses" for my buddies on the roof.

> *There's a black man from Columbus*
> *He stays in his black part of town*
> *He's got 38s*
> *Flying through his front yard*
> *But they land at official sundown*

And there's a woman nine months pregnant
In the back of a pick-up bed
And she looks at her husband and says, "Hey darlin'
I sure hope our son doesn't have your...giant head"

I didn't have any other verses in mind. I was just going to sing the chorus. I should have known, after having spent a little more than half a year around Doley, that he'd be ready to take my song to the next level:

Oh but ain't that Columbus
And U-P-T
Ain't that Columbus
No sweat for me, baby
Ain't that Columbus
Runway 1-3
Little pink houses
For you and me
Oooh, yeah
For you and me

By the time we used up all our paint, it was too dark to see the finished product. None of us really cared at that point. We just wanted to get the job done, get home, and get ready to fly again the next day.

Chapter 18 — "Energy Losses and Gains"

After confessing to Lieutenant Baiber that I had not slept for eight uninterrupted hours, my penance was that, in addition to being grounded for the day, I had to serve as Duty Dog for the morning's flying period and Snacko in the afternoon. Both sucked, but this served me right for staying out too late to paint the mother pink and violating crew rest. Besides, working the duty desk at the entrance to Eagle flight, I had the perfect vantage point for when the class leader of the Nightmares stormed into Eagle and demanded that Mark Jellicot meet him out in the hallway.

"I've the beak out to here!" the Nightmares' class leader screamed, his open hand about an arm's length in front of his face to mime his beak's growth to an extreme size.

"You painted over our class colors!" he whined, and then he tugged on the black-and-yellow checkerboard-patterned scarf. "You had no right to paint over our roof!"

"Hey, when I heard that your class painted the T-38 VFR entry point with your class colors, I had the Mo-Zam-Beak!" Mark fired right back at the guy, throwing in his own twist on the expression. "Your class hasn't even finished T-37s! What the fuck, over!"

Another UPT expression.

"Your class's stupid pink lawn flamingos are everywhere on this base! We're sick of you Pink Flamingos!" Nightmare Dude whined some more. "We paid that farmer one thousand dollars to let us paint his roof. And we bought four hundred dollars worth of ladders! It took us half the day on Sunday to paint the roof of that barn, and now, after just one day, our yellow paint is covered with pink."

The longer he rambled, the more this guy looked like an idiot.

"What about all that money we spent? What about having the farmer's permission? You didn't have the farmer's permission!"

Nightmare Dude was self-destructing, and Mark could not have cared less.

From day one of UPT, Mark totally bought into the whole If You Ain't a Pilot, You Ain't Shit game at Columbus because that's the game that he played as an F-4 back-seater in the Philippines. For class leaders, this mythology was extrapolated to the seniority of the training classes in the program—the farther a class was from graduating from UPT, the more shit-like its students were compared to the classes in front of it. Mark had no time for the guy, because he wasn't shit.

"How about this? When your class finally makes it to this side of the hall, you pay the farmer another thousand dollars, and you can paint his roof again," Mark suggested dismissively.

The class leader of the Nightmares had no comeback.

Mark proudly walked to his locker, like he was shit, to get his G-suit and other flying gear.

As we began our training in T-38s, Mark had to be the top student in the class. He had earned grades of *Excellent* on nearly every daily ride he flew in T-37s and, more importantly, on all three of his T-37 checkrides. He had done pretty well in academics, and as class leader, Mark would get extra credit toward his class ranking. To make things even more exciting for Mark, our flight commander in Eagle, Major Carrington, had been an RF-4 pilot in the reconnaissance version of Mark's jet, and Mark was getting to fly with him.

Before picking up his flight helmet and parachute in the chute shop, Mark came back into Eagle to give me instructions in case the class leader from the Nightmares returned. But as he stood next to me in all his UPT glory, with his protective green anti-G chaps resting on his big, soft belly and the foot-and-a-half-long air attachment hose dangling from his shoulder by his left arm, I pictured him more as a Scottish bagpiper than anything else.

*

"Lieutenant Baiber, how come I get *Goods* on all my rides, and Lieutenant Sweet gets *Excellents* on all of his rides?" I asked after about my fifth ride in the T-38, all of which had been with him.

Lieutenant Baiber looked across his desk at me for a moment before he replied in his usual deep and quiet voice.

"That's because your flying is good," he said, "and Lieutenant Sweet's flying is excellent."

No doubt, champion waterskier Brendan was as smooth in the jet as he was behind a boat on the Tombigbee River.

"Excuse me, Lieutenant Baibuh," Doley said, pulling up a chair next to me at Lieutenant Baiber's desk, "I'd like to listen in on this discussion."

"Sure," Lieutenant Baiber nodded. "Have a seat." He pointed his model T-38-on-a-stick at the empty chair next to mine. Most times, the jet-on-a-stick was an instructor's puppet, used to illustrate a story; other times, it was a teacher's pointer, used to direct a student's attention to something or to invite a nosy friend to sit down.

"Sir, I don't think I phrased my question properly," I said as Doley made himself comfortable at Lieutenant Baiber's desk. "What does Lieutenant Sweet do that makes his flying excellent?" I asked, approaching my IP from a different angle.

"For one thing, he's got hands of gold," Lieutenant Baiber answered.

"Would you call him 'Golden Hands' Sweet?" Doley interrupted, spinning his pen every few seconds and definitely enjoying the direction of the conversation.

"Yes," Lieutenant Baiber smiled. "Golden Hands Sweet. I think that's appropriate."

"How much bettuh is Golden Hands than Lieutenant Wright?" Doley butted in before I could rephrase my question again.

"Well, obviously, it's the difference between being good and being excellent," Lieutenant Baiber said, perhaps enjoying the opportunity to give me a taste of my own medicine.

"In that case," Doley continued on, "would you considuh Lieutenant Wright to have hands of lead or hands of iron?" He gave his pen a couple of consecutive spins after that one.

"Doley, please!" I said. "I'm trying to have a serious discussion with *my* assigned instructor."

"Nickel?" Doley kept after my IP, spinning his pen around in his hand again. "Coppuh?"

"I would say that Lieutenant Wright has been flying a good aircraft to this point, as reflected by his daily grades," Lieutenant Baiber answered Doley's question.

"Thank you, sir." I said, ready to rephrase my original question yet another time. I hadn't meant to make this a discussion about how excellent a pilot Brendan was or how average a pilot I was. For once, I was actually asking a question so that I might be able to do better in UPT.

"Lieutenant Baiber," I began again, "in order to take my flying from good to excellent, what do I need to do differently?"

Pretending like he finally understood what I was trying to ask, my oversized instructor asked, "Are you familiar with the First Law of Thermodynamics?"

"Yes, sir," I said, "Energy cannot be created or destroyed."

"That's part of it," Lieutenant Baiber acknowledged. "What's the other part?"

I had no idea. My major at the Academy was humanities. I just shook my head.

"Lieutenant Dolan, do you know?" Lieutenant Baiber asked Doley.

"Sir, I don't think Lieutenant Wright will learn anything if I give him the ansahs," Doley said, spinning his pen to punctuate his point.

"Lieutenant Dolan, I can tell that you are going to make an excellent FAIP," Lieutenant Baiber said, twirling his jet-on-a-stick to punctuate *his* point.

Lieutenant Baiber pulled a computer printout of my daily grades from my gradebook. He flipped it upside down to the blank side of the paper and began to draw.

"Energy cannot be created or destroyed. That is correct," he said, "but the First Law also states that energy can be transformed from one form to another."

Like most of our IPs, Lieutenant Baiber drew his pictures and wrote his words upside-down so that they'd be right-side-up to the students on the other side of his desk. After drawing the upside-down axes for a simple graph, he labeled the *x*-axis *Airspeed* and the *y*-axis *Altitude*.

"Lieutenant Wright, what is the total energy of a system?" he asked me as he drew a diagonal line through the center of his graph.

"Sir, the total energy of a system is equal to the sum of the potential energy plus the kinetic energy in a system," I said. I did pick up a few things in school. After all, even a humanities major had to have aerodynamics, thermodynamics, and a bunch of engineering and physics classes.

"That's right," he acknowledged, plotting a point in the middle of his diagonal line and labeling it: *15,000 ft, 300 knots*.

"Lieutenant Dolan, when you are practicing maneuvers in your assigned block of airspace, what variable that you control best determines your potential energy?" he softly asked, drawing a second diagonal line, parallel to the first one he'd drawn, but about an inch to the right of it...from our side of the desk.

"Altitude," Doley said.

"Correct," Lieutenant Baiber stated, plotting a point on the second line at the same height as the first. He labeled the center point on the second line: *15,000 ft., 400 knots*.

"Lieutenant Wright," my IP continued, "when you are practicing maneuvers in your assigned block of airspace, your kinetic energy is primarily a function of what variable that you control?" he quietly asked, drawing a third diagonal line parallel to the other two he'd drawn but about an inch to the left of the first one.

"Airspeed, sir," I answered.

"Correct," Lieutenant Baiber said, plotting a point on the third diagonal line at the same height as the first two points. He labeled the center point on the third line: *15,000 ft., 200 knots*.

His upside-down drawing complete, Lieutenant Baiber looked up from the paper. "To go from good to excellent, you need to do a better job managing energy," he said. "You're not doing a good job managing energy."

"Lieutenant Wright wastes a lot of energy," Doley said, adding his own observation in support of my instructor.

I looked over at Doley with my *please shut up* face, and in return, he spun his pen one turn around his hand.

Lieutenant Baiber picked up his T-38-on-a-stick and used the nose of his model as a pointer to direct our attention to the diagonal line in the center of his graph.

"In the T-38 at a 1G load, you can exchange 1,000 feet of altitude for 50 knots of airspeed in MIL power," he said, pointing to the center of the diagonal line where he had written: *15,000 ft., 300 knots*.

"The total energy of your jet at 15,000 feet and 300 knots equals the same total energy at 11,000 feet and 500 knots," Lieutenant Baiber said, sliding his jet-on-a-stick down the diagonal line in the middle of the graph. "It's also the same energy level at 21,000 feet and no airspeed," he added, bringing the nose of his jet-on-a-stick back to the top of the same diagonal line in the middle of his graph.

"On this particular energy level, the one that passes through 15,000 feet and 300 knots, you can hit the parameters for any aerobatic maneuver we fly and stay within the vertical limits of your area," Lieutenant Baiber said. He flew a loop with his toy jet. A loop required 8,000 to 10,000 feet of vertical airspeed and an entry airspeed of 500 knots.

"For contact flying, this diagonal line is the ideal energy level for your maneuvers. Whenever you pass through 15,000 feet, check your airspeed; it should be 300 knots. Whenever you pass through 300 knots, check your altitude; it should be 15,000 feet. If one of these two numbers is higher than fifteen-and-three, your energy level is higher than the ideal contact level, and you're over here...right of center. If one of these two numbers is lower than fifteen-and-three, your energy level is too low, and you're over here...at the left."

Lieutenant Baiber flew his jet-on-a-stick through a series of aerobatic maneuvers at his desk, and at some point during each trick, he'd softly say, "Fifteen thousand feet...I check my airspeed," or "Three hundred knots...I check my altitude."

When he finished his mini-aerobatic profile, he rolled his jet-on-a-stick back to wings-level and held it out over the middle of his desk.

"If your energy level is too high, G-up the jet a little, or turn in the horizontal plane with your power slightly back," he said, weaving his model back and forth with its wings at 60 degrees of bank. "If your energy level is too low, zoom the jet by trading airspeed for altitude. Unload to zero-Gs. Or light the afterburners, if you're really low on energy."

Lieutenant Baiber looked across his desk to check in with Doley and me. "Are you following me so far?" he asked.

For the most part, I followed what he was saying, but if Doley wasn't going to ask any questions, I wasn't going to say anything until Lieutenant Baiber had finished or until Doley got up and left.

Seeing that we had no questions, my massive instructor leaned over his desk and looked around, like he was about to tell us a secret. "This is what Golden Hands does well," he said quietly. "He manages his energy level and executes his maneuvers at the right parameters, and when he's not flying at the right energy level...." He looked around again and leaned over his desk even more for emphasis and whispered, "He fixes it."

Lieutenant Baiber then gave a number of examples from my handful of rides with him of how I'd adversely impacted my energy level while maneuvering in my assigned airspace. Not only was I wasting energy with my power-slides, I was subsequently wasting gas having to re-build my energy level.

"Ya' lucky to even be getting *Goods* for grades," Doley offered, spinning his pen.

"Thanks, Doley," I sarcastically acknowledged.

Turning back to my IP and our energy conservation conversation, I asked, "So, if my energy's bad, I either need to zoom or light the afterburners?"

"No, not necessarily. Check your energy as you go. Stay on top of it. Make corrections as appropriate," Lieutenant Baiber said, swishing his jet-on-a-stick through a series of maneuvers, like an orchestra conductor directing an aerial masterpiece.

"Let me give you another example," he said. "Here's why you're having trouble with your loops."

I thought my loops were fine, but Lieutenant Baiber was right. Every time I tried to fly a loop, I'd either try to bust through the top of my assigned altitude block at the apex of my maneuver or drop through the bottom of my block and break a major rule of engagement. I always started at the right place, but I always just hoped that I'd finish at the right place.

"You do a good job of hitting your entry speed of 500 knots," my IP said. "But instead of pulling right to 5Gs, you barely pull 4Gs."

Because I wasn't introducing the G-forces fast enough, I was carrying too much airspeed in my climb. On his graph of diagonal energy lines, I was zooming the jet to the diagonal line on the right, increasing my energy level too much. By not getting to 5Gs, I kept bumping against the top of my area and coming out of the bottom of my loops with too much airspeed.

"I bet Golden Hands pulls 5Gs," Doley said.

"Every time!" Lieutenant Baiber smiled upon hearing the nickname of his star pupil.

As Lieutenant Baiber demonstrated the proper way to fly a loop with his jet-on-a-stick, Mark Jellicot paraded by the desk with his G-suit draped over his shoulder Scottish-bagpiper style.

"Lieutenant Baiber, I have an idea," I said. "We could cross a G-suit with a set of bagpipes, and depending upon the G-forces on the jet, the air that flowed through the suit would play a different song. At 4Gs, the suit could play 'Auld Lang Syne,' and at 5Gs, it could play 'Amazing Grace.'"

Lieutenant Baiber broke off the loop at his desk and stopped flying his jet-on-a-stick altogether to give some thought to the idea of a bagpiping G-suit.

"I think you'd need a pretty good tailor to put a suit like that together," Lieutenant Baiber replied.

"Sir," I said, "our class leader knows a place in the Philippines..."

*

"Not many people are going to see the sun today," Lieutenant Baiber's voice hit my ears through the speakers in my flight helmet as we punched through the thick, gray, endless quilt of clouds that blanketed the sky.

"Feels good, sir," I said, soaking in the warmth of the bright sun through my canopy in the perfectly clear blue airspace above the bad weather. I headed to the center of my assigned area. Until I reported that we were established in the sector, however, I had to maintain my 300-knot climb. Since Sector 3 was so close to the base, I'd be there in no time—probably before I'd climbed to 15,000 feet. A less than ideal energy level.

My plan had been to establish a good energy level before I started any of my area work. Moreover, I needed to stay within the boundaries of my area today without the benefit of ground references—using what IPs call the pie-in-the-sky method with navigation instruments, but I hadn't figured out exactly how to do that yet. Instead, my plan was to use the method students called center radial, where I'd use my navigation equipment to line up on an electronic beam that originated at Columbus Air Force base and shot through the center of my area, like the spoke of a bicycle wheel shot out from its axle. I would fly away from Columbus Air Force Base on the center radial, the spoke through the middle of Sector 3, and before I hit the outer rim, I'd turn around and follow the center radial back to the front.

Once established in our assigned airspace, I leveled off at 15,000 feet and 300 knots and performed the required checks before starting my maneuvers. In between each checklist item, I looked up into one of my rearview mirrors on either side of the canopy bow to see if I could catch a glimpse of Lieutenant Baiber. Sometimes, I could see his gray helmet, dark visor, and olive oxygen mask just fine, but other times, I couldn't see him at all, as he was always moving around, checking outside for other air traffic.

Lieutenant Baiber didn't talk too much when we flew. He communicated his messages with an economy of sound and words that forced me to pay attention to what he was saying, but I wasn't always the best at paying attention to what he was saying.

"At what altitude did you break out of the clouds?" Lieutenant Baiber asked as I set 95 percent power on both engines, put the nose down, and began to accelerate to 350 knots for my first move: a lazy eight.

"Sir, I didn't notice the altitude when we broke out of the clouds," I answered.

"Those clouds below us may affect your ability to fly over-the-tops. Depending on where they are, you may not have established the right energy level," he said, forcing me to realize that I needed to know the altitude of the clouds.

Even though the top of my assigned airspace was 22,000 feet and the bottom was 8,000, that space might include the cloud bank. If the clouds reached as high as 12,000 feet, I wouldn't be able to fly any over-the-top maneuvers like the loop or the Immelmann, which may take up to 10,000 feet of vertical airspace. I needed to know where the clouds were.

I broke off my entry into the lazy eight, and descended to investigate the cloud tops, which I found right around 10,000 feet. I leveled off at 300 knots to make some quick calculations.

"Sir, with the cloud tops at 10,000, I can fly over-the-tops, but I'll need to set my energy level at sixteen-and-three instead of fifteen-and-three," I proudly reported to my instructor, having calculated and adjusted for the loss of two thousand feet of cloud-covered airspace at the bottom of my altitude block and the need for 10,000 feet of vertical maneuvering room to fly over-the-tops.

"How's your energy level?" Lieutenant Baiber asked.

No! How stupid!

"Ten thousand and three, sir. It's not good," I acknowledged...kind of. The truth, however, was that my energy level could not have been worse. Flying along the very bottom of my area at 10,000 feet and 300 knots, I was in no position to fly any maneuver I'd planned for my profile. To complicate matters, I was approaching the back of the sector. I turned around to stay in my assigned airspace.

"What's your plan?" Lieutenant Baiber asked.

"Sir, I'm going for the zoom," I said, pushing the throttles from MIL to MAX to light the afterburners by dumping fuel directly into the tailpipes.

With the extra thrust, the T-38 raced across the tops of the clouds faster and faster. I kept the jet at 10,000 feet to let it accelerate, and even though it was fine for me to cut through the cloud tops with an instructor in the jet as long as I wasn't flying acrobatics, I dodged in and out of the puffy bumps like Luke Skywalker racing along the surface of the Death Star. Maybe the ride hadn't started out all too well, but this was awesome!

Three hundred and fifty knots...400...450. If 16,000 feet and 300 knots put me on the right energy level for the weather conditions, then using Lieutenant Baiber's equation for altitude and airspeed, at 10,000 feet, I ought to be at 600 knots. I needed more speed.

Though the T-38 traveled about twice as fast as the T-37, I never really felt the sensation of its speed until I'd zoomed along the tops of the clouds.

Passing 500 knots, I dropped out of MAX power, and once I'd confirmed the shutdown of the afterburners, I pulled the nose of the jet up to about 60 degrees above the horizon. I pushed forward on my control stick and unloaded to zero Gs, and we rocketed up away from the clouds. Now weightless, I floated above my seat, held only by my lap belt and shoulder harness. The pages of the checklist I had strapped to my right thigh floated up. The jet was screaming higher and higher into the sky, and I sensations of speed and power were so awesome, I couldn't help but scream, too.

"YAAAAAAAAAAA HOOOOOOOOOOOOOOOO!" I shouted out loud as we shot to the top of the altitude block.

I knew I had wasted a lot of gas with my acceleration maneuver, but it worked, and it was unbelievably fun. As my airspeed bled off and my scream tapered off, I transitioned to a turn and established the proper energy level from which to start my aerobatics.

First, I started with the tricks that required lower airspeeds and power settings. As I flew my lazy eight, each time I passed through 16,000 feet, I checked my airspeed, and each time I passed through 300 knots, I checked my altitude. I did the same as I executed my barrel roll, and through my first two maneuvers, my energy level was looking good.

I turned to stay in my area and lined up for my last two moves, a loop followed by an Immelmann, both of which were over-the-tops with an entry speed of 500 knots. Because I would be starting these last two tricks around 12,000 feet, slightly higher than usual, I knew I'd need to get right into a good 5G pull-up to keep the jet under 22,000 feet, the top of Sector 3.

Lieutenant Baiber had told me in the flight room that I had a habit of only pulling to 4Gs. I had already wasted too much gas on this ride to earn my first *Excellent,* but I wanted to show him I could fly a proper loop.

I hit 500 knots just below 12,000 feet, threw my head back to check for traffic, and smoothly pulled back on the stick. The bladders of my G-suit filled with air and pushed against my legs and stomach. I tightened my abdominal muscles and strained against a closed glottis, forcefully breathing every two to three seconds, as I'd been taught, to keep my blood from pooling in the lower parts of my body away from my brain, which could cause me to G-LOC. I was going to nail this loop.

"Pull," I heard Lieutenant Baiber's calm voice in my helmet as the jet rumbled through my high-G pull-up.

"Pull," he repeated.

I was going to nail this loop.

"5Gs," I heard him say softly as I fought off the G-forces and we arched up into the sky.

"5Gs," he repeated.

I was going to nail this loop.

"Your G-suit is playing the wrong song!"

I looked at my accelerometer. I had barely pulled 4Gs.

*

"How do you think you did managing your energy level today?" Lieutenant Baiber asked as he checked over the grade-sheet one final time.

"Sir, I think I did a pretty good job with that," Brendan answered as he and Lieutenant Baiber were debriefing their ride, which they'd flown after Lieutenant Baiber and I had flown my ride earlier in the day. Lieutenant Baiber had asked me the same question. I couldn't answer it like Brendan did.

"Me, too," Lieutenant Baiber agreed. "I'll give you an *Excellent* for today's ride."

As had become the daily norm at Lieutenant Baiber's desk in Eagle flight, Golden Hands had been graded *Excellent,* and I had barely squeaked by with another *Good.* It's not like I was in a contest with Brendan, but just one time before I soloed, I'd like to get an *Excellent,* too.

Back in Dagger flight, Kenny and I always seemed to get about the same daily grades...mostly *Goods* and every once in awhile an *E.* Maybe this was because we studied the same things at home together every night. Then again, maybe it was because we didn't study as much as everyone else did every night, and *Good* was about as good as we deserved. I didn't know the reason, but after being one checkride *Unsat* from being removed from the program, the way I looked at it was this: On any given ride, a *Good* was a good enough.

"Eagle flight!" the SOF's voice came over the intercom.

"Yes, sir," the Duty Dog responded.

"Send Lieutenant Spranger to the TOC," the SOF ordered.

"He's not back from flying," answered Lieutenant Baiber, who was now working on building the next day's schedule. The SOF did not acknowledge Lieutenant Baiber's reply.

"Lieutenant Wright, would you please go down to the TOC, and tell the SOF that Lieutenant Spranger is still flying?" Lieutenant Baiber asked.

"Yes, sir," I said. As I got up from my seat, Lieutenant Baiber pulled Kurt's magnet off the next day's flying schedule.

Why did he do that?

I wondered if Kurt was about to get an *Unsat* for his ride.

The TOC—Training Operations Center—was a short walk down the hall to the left—just past the men's room and across from the chute shop. After telling the SOF that Kurt was still flying, I took the hall pass just given me and headed to the snack bar. Even though I wasn't hungry, I could kill some time before the formal release.

I hadn't expected to see Kenny on my way down the hall. He was supposed to be in the sim building to test his knowledge of **BOLDFACE** and emergency procedures before being cleared to fly solo. As the last scheduled mission, Kenny ought to have been the last student to return. All sim rides lasted an hour and fifteen minutes. Something happened.

"Aaay," Kenny approached me with unusual restraint, "what are you doing right now?"

"Nothing," I said. "Why? What's up?"

"I need to know what you think about something," my roommate said.

"Do you want to go with me to the snack bar?" I asked.

"Nah," he shook his head. "Let's go outside."

I turned around and walked back up the hall with Kenny, past the TOC, past the men's room, and past Eagle. I had to stop at my locker to get my flight cap, because the only outside place you go could without wearing a hat was the flight line. Kenny already had his hat, having just come from the sim building. We walked out the door at the end of the long hallway, the one that we used to exit to the parking lot at the end of the day.

"What's up?" I asked again.

"Aaay, I need to know what you think," Kenny repeated what he'd said in the hallway. "My EP sim was going really bad. I was fuckin' up **BOLDFACE** left and right, and I was flyin' like shit..."

"Oh, that sucks." I didn't know what else to say.

"Aaay! Yeah, it sucked," Kenny agreed.

"Was this your first or your second EP sim?" I was thinking that maybe if it was his first EP sim, his IP might let him get by with messing up a few times and crashing once or twice, but if it was his second EP sim, he was probably screwed and would get an *Unsat*.

"Aaay, this was my first," Kenny said, which made me think he'd be okay.... But there was more.

"But we didn't finish," Kenny confessed. I waited, but he didn't give more information.

"How come?" The only time I'd ever heard of anybody not finishing a sim ride was when lightning was within three miles of the sim building, and all rides would stop until the storm passed. The day had been totally cloudy, but we hadn't had any thunderstorms.

"Aaay. Dat's what I gotta ask you about," he said. Then, he looked around to make sure nobody was watching or listening to us, and even though nobody was, Kenny still leaned in close to my face to be absolutely sure that no one could catch what he was about to say.

"Aaay, I was fuckin' up so bad...I knew I was going to hook," Kenny started. "The longer the ride went, the worse I was doin'. I don't know what it was. I just couldn't think straight. Finally, I thought that if maybe I got an *Incomplete*, the ride wouldn't count, and I might get a fresh start another time."

"Is that why you're back early?" I asked, still not quite grasping what happened.

"Aaay. Yeah. Dat's what I need to ask you about." Kenny looked around yet again to make sure no one had sneaked up on us to eavesdrop.

"Do you think my IP would know if I hit the red button?" he asked.

"Did you hit the red button?" I asked back.

"Aaay. I'm not sayin' I did," Kenny replied, "but if I did, do you think my IP would know?"

I had no idea. Oh, I knew what the red button was. The red button was the kill switch in the sim. If you had a fire, or if you had a body part caught between moving components of the simulator, those would be the times you hit the kill switch, and the power would be shut down. But if you were having a bad ride, that wasn't a reason to hit the red button.

"Did the power shut off just in your sim, or in both of the sims in the little sim bay?" I needed to understand. If the red button turned off the power to only Kenny's sim, either his IP or the Sim Operator would probably figure it out, but if it turned off the power to both sims in the same corner of the building, Kenny might be okay.

"No," Kenny said, getting even closer to my face. "The power shut off in the whole fuckin' building. Everything. It was pitch black. We had to feel our way out by using our hands to find the fuckin' walls. From the walls, we had to find the fuckin' doors."

In my mind, I pictured the events in the sim building like a scene from *The Poseidon Adventure*, where instructors, students, sim operators, and Major Lawson, whose office was in the sim building, blindly tried to find their way out of the shipwreck. I wish I could have seen it happen, but then again, in the dark nobody saw it happen.

"Well, there are eight simulators in the building," I reasoned after I'd stopped laughing. "Every sim has a kill switch, but they might be able to rule out the T-37s, because students and

IPs sit side-by-side, and if they were paying attention to one another, they might know if the other guy did it, but in T-38s, since the instructor can't see the student, and since you said all the power in the building went out, which includes the computers and any recording equipment, I don't think anyone would be able to know which sim hit the red button."

Of course, I really didn't know.

"I think you might be okay," I bluffed.

"Aaay," Kenny nodded, finally backing up out of my personal space. "Dat's exactly what I thought. Don't tell anyone."

I never got to the snack bar. Curious to know what was going to happen to Kenny, I followed him back to Eagle and took my seat at Lieutenant Baiber's desk, right next to Kenny's seat at Captain Steiger's desk.

As I sat down, Golden Hands Brendan, to my left, whispered some potentially bad news.

"Ooh Baby took all of Kurt's magnets off the scheduling board," he said. "Do you think maybe he hooked his ride today?"

"I don't know," I whispered back, "but Kenny might have hooked his EP sim." We were about to find out.

"Wessels, grab a grade-sheet and a Form 803," Captain Steiger said to Kenny as he circled around to the back of his desk. When an instructor told a student to get an Air Training Command Form 803, the Air Force equivalent of white lined paper, it was never a good sign. It meant that the instructor would be making a gradebook write-up, a handwritten entry into the gradebook about something in the student's training that couldn't be told simply by the letter marks recorded for individual flying maneuvers.

In my T-37 gradebook, for example, I had 803 write-ups for *Unsat* checkrides, for the *Unsat* solo when I got hooked from the box, and for not flying for an extended period of time due to inflamed hemorrhoids. Of course, there were other—mostly administrative—reasons that an instructor might make an 803 write-up, but having heard Kenny's story, this didn't bode well for him.

"Let me see those papers," Captain Steiger said, reaching out to Kenny, who had returned to his seat after getting the forms.

Would Kenny get hammered with an Unsat *or escape with an* Incomplete?

"Things weren't going very well for you today," Captain Steiger began. Kenny sat innocently and listened attentively.

"Oh?" Kenny prepared to take some notes.

"It was probably a good thing that the power went out," Captain Steiger said as he quickly composed a brief essay on the Form 803. "I'm not going to grade this ride. I'm going to give you an Incomplete."

The expression on Kenny's face didn't change, but I knew relief was washing over him.

"I hadn't told you this yet," Captain Steiger continued as he spun the Form 803 around for Kenny to read and initial. "Friday is my last day as your instructor."

"Aaay, why's that, sir?" Kenny replied, stunned.

"I'm going to be the assistant flight commander in Falcon flight. You'll be assigned to a new IP," Captain Steiger told him. Then, he got up.

"Congrats," Kenny told his soon-to-be-former IP as Captain Steiger left the flight room.

"Holy shit!" Kenny said after Captain Steiger was gone. "It worked!"

As he and I laughed and told each other about our respective rides, Kurt finally returned to the flight room. Still wearing his G-suit and carrying his checklist and in-flight guide, Kurt took a couple steps through the Eagle doorway and waved his free hand up over his head to get everyone's attention. Not everyone had seen him, and because some aircrews were busy debriefing their rides, there was still a lot of chatter in the flight room.

"Hey! Quiet!" Eagle Flight Commander Major Carrington called, putting a stop to the noise. He directed everyone's attention to Kurt. "Lieutenant Spranger, what did the SOF tell you?!"

With the eyes and ears of Eagle now focused his way, Big Kurt stood proudly in flight room doorway with a smile that could not possibly have been pulled back any farther on either side of his face.

Why were his magnets pulled off the schedule? Why did the SOF need to speak to Kurt?

Kurt stretched his extra-long arms up over his head and squeezed his massive fists.

"It's a boy!" he proudly proclaimed.

The students and IPs of Eagle erupted with cheers and applause.

Chapter 19 — "Crude Encounters"

"I'm going to demonstrate this first one for you," Kurt said, sounding very much like one of our instructor pilots. "Just like you would do before any maneuver, make sure the area is clear. Then, gently lay the baby down on the changing table."

"Is that procedure or technique?" I asked the new father.

"That would be procedure," Kurt answered.

"Got it," I said.

"Kurt!" Malia yelled from the other side of their apartment, "Hurry up, and change the baby!"

"Yes, Malia!" Kurt called back. "But remember, Uncle Ray needs to learn how to change a poopy, so he can babysit for us when we want to go out!"

Kurt had to talk me through every step of the baby's diaper change: undoing the dirty diaper, removing the FOD, cleaning, and drying the baby. While he worked and instructed, I put my pinky against the baby's hand. He squeezed me firmly with his little fingers. Unlike the pictures I'd drawn for Kurt showing the possible combinations of Malia's petite body and Kurt's elongated extremities, their baby was perfectly proportioned.

"Would you look at the size of that pecker!" Kurt proudly declared. "Ray, you were absolutely right in predicting Kurt II would inherit my best qualities."

"Kurt!" Malia yelled from the other side of the apartment again. "Stop playing with the baby's penis, and bring him to me!"

"She wants to breastfeed the baby," Kurt whispered as he finished with the new diaper. "You know, after a woman has a baby, her boobs fill with milk. They get really huge, and—"

"Kurt, c'mon! Enough with the penis and boobs!" I pleaded. "'Please, please, can we call it a tallywhacker?'" I threw in a line from *Porky's*, hoping to get Kurt onto another subject.

"Penis is so personal," Kurt recited the next line.

"We should have you and Kenny over for that movie," he said.

"That's okay, man." I shook Kurt off like a pitcher shaking off a catcher's sign for a certain pitch. "I've seen it…the movie, I'm talking about."

"Check to see that both sides of the diaper are secure," Kurt coached, transitioning back to his diaper change instruction, "and return to Mommy."

I waited for Kurt in the living room of the apartment while he brought his son back to Malia. I didn't want to give him the opportunity to instruct me through the proper steps for breastfeeding a newborn as his wife demonstrated. I was very happy for my friends, but I was happier to let them keep their family business within the family.

"Ray-bonus, I am so proud of Malia," Kurt said upon returning to the room. "She is such a great mom, and she did such a great job during the delivery! It was amazing."

Wait a second…?

"Kurt, I thought you were flying when the baby was born," I said. "How do you know about how Malia handled the delivery?"

"It's all right here," Kurt answered, grabbing a videotape from inside the glass-doored stereo cabinet on which his TV sat. "Malia set up our camcorder on a tripod, and she videotaped the whole birth. Have a seat, and we'll watch it. I'll talk you through the different stages of the labor and delivery."

"Hey, I would love to," I tactfully replied, "but I told Kenny that I would be his designated driver for Comedy Night tonight. I've got to get back to the house to get ready."

"Okay," Kurt said. "But take this videotape. You and Kenny watch it. You need to see what a great job Malia did at the hospital. Just bring the tape back when you're done."

Kurt stuck the videotape of the birth of Kurt II in my hand and then wrapped his giant hand around mine and held it there so that I had to take the tape. As happy as I was for my friends and their newborn child, I really didn't feel comfortable watching a video about their family business. But Kurt was so proud—and so strong—I couldn't say no.

*

I had all my cadet uniforms tucked away in my class-colored footlocker. I was pretty sure Kenny had all his cadet uniforms in his footlocker, too. At the Academy, we had uniforms for all occasions. We had tuxedo uniforms for formal occasions, dress uniforms for Saturday morning inspections, and parade uniforms for parades. We had workout uniforms for working out, swim trunk uniforms for swimming, pajama uniforms for sleeping, and bathrobe uniforms to cover our pajama uniforms if we had to go to the bathroom.

We had uniform raincoats for days when it rained, uniform parkas for days when it was cold, and uniform light-weight jackets, called athletic jackets, for days when we didn't have a clean uniform shirt and needed to cover up a dirty one. We had long-sleeve and short-sleeve fatigue uniforms for field activities. During the school year, we'd wear our fatigues as the UOD, uniform of the day, once a month on Fatigue Day.

Ever since Kenny had set up his mannequin in the big room after Christmas break, her UOD had been Kenny's dark blue cadet pants, his athletic jacket, a cadet flight cap, and his Air Force-issue sunglasses. We'd talked about dressing the mannequin up in different outfits for different occasions, but we never changed her. Every so often, we might add an accessory, like Kenny's sunglasses or the multi-colored whistle chain that I had made out of strands of gimp I'd bought at one of the local malls, but whatever accessories we may have added, we hadn't changed the basic outfit on Kenny's mannequin.

"Bra and panties!" Kenny yelled and danced gleefully as I stepped into the big room through the front door.

"Bra and panties!" I cheered upon seeing the lacy bra and silky flowered underwear, now the only items of clothing on the mannequin— except for her flight cap and sunglasses.

This had certainly been an eventful day. Kenny had flown his first T-38 solo. I had earned my first *Excellent* grade from Lieutenant Baiber. And perhaps most significantly, for the first time since our return from Christmas break, Kenny's female mannequin was dressed in something other than the Air Force Academy UOD.

"And just where did our houseguest get her new bra and panties?" I asked.

"Bra and panties!" Kenny yelled throwing his hands into the air. He danced giddily around again.

"Bra and panties!" I cheered triumphantly, lifting my arms and pointing my index fingers to the ceiling.

Kenny laughed and smiled slyly.

Still dressed in my uniform, I started for the bathroom to take a shower to get cleaned up for Comedy Night.

Kenny and I hadn't been going out as much since we'd started T-38 training. For one thing, we had a lot to learn: new terms, new **BOLDFACE**, new procedures, new parameters, new instructors, new systems, and so much more than could possibly be jammed into the human brain. We had been spending a lot of time studying and chair-flying together after work. For another thing, Doley had convinced me to join him in giving up drinking for Lent, and if we weren't going out to get drunk, what was the point in going out?

We hadn't been to Comedy Night in over a month...ever since we were in T-37s. It was usually good for a few laughs, but we mostly went for the free buffet that came with the five-dollar cover charge—not so much for the comedy or for getting drunk.

The Comedy Night buffet usually looked pretty good. The problem, however, was cigarette smoke.

The dense cloud of cigarette smoke trapped up against the ceiling burned your eyes, choked your throat, and seeped into the taste of the food. Everything pretty much tasted like a cigarette butt. Still, because we didn't have to cook or spend much, we went.

Kenny had two theories about people who lived in Columbus. The first was *everybody knows everybody*. The second was *everybody smokes*. I had a hard time disproving either theory. I didn't care if people who wanted to smoke smoked, but why did I need to smell it? Why did I need to breathe it? Why did I need to taste it?

Taking a shower before going to Comedy Night was kind of a waste, but as I crossed the hallway from the bathroom back to my bedroom, I did feel refreshed and looked forward to blowing off some steam.

I hadn't told Kenny about the birthing video, smuggled into the house in the side pocket of my helmet bag just in case he'd actually want to watch it. Before I got dressed, I opened my footlocker and buried the video underneath the neatly folded stacks of cadet uniforms I'd probably never wear again.

*

The dense cloud of cigarette smoke trapped against the dimly lit ceiling had already started to creep down toward the buffet stations by the time we arrived. Kenny and I went straight for the nearest food cart and filled our plates with a bunch of over-steamed and soggy food. As long as we could eat it before the smoke reached our eyes, nose, and throat, we didn't care. We did need a place to sit, however, and most of the tables around the club were either taken or saved for friends.

"Aaay! There's Saeed!" Kenny yelled above the noise— pointing to a small and very dark-skinned man sitting at a table all by himself.

Blowing his own contribution to the thickening cloud of cigarette smoke meandering along the ceiling was our newest classmate, Saeed, a Kuwaiti exchange student who had just washed back into our class from 88-06 about a week earlier.

Washing back wasn't very common. It happened only when the TRB determined that the student's training did not follow the proper procedures or that the student did not receive fair treatment. In those cases, the board might allow the student to return to the normal flow of training, and the reinstated student would resume his or her training with a class that wasn't quite as far along in the syllabus. This was called washing back.

For Saeed, his washing back wasn't handled by the Training Review Board. It was handled by the Embassy of the State of Kuwait. He had some challenges with UPT and hadn't been ready to solo in the T-38 when the rest of Class 88-06 soloed. While most of that class moved on to the next phase of their training, preparing for the T-38 Contact checkride, Saeed needed more time. And because our class, 88-07, was just beginning to work our way up to our initial solo rides, his embassy bought him a few extra rides outside of the syllabus of instruction, and Saeed washed back into our class.

"Aaay, Saeed! Can we sit wit' you?" Kenny asked. In Eagle, Kenny and Chuck befriended Saeed immediately. Because the instructors had called him "Al" for the hyphenated prefix of his last name, I had initially called him "Al," too. Once I got to know him through Kenny, however, I called him by his first name.

"Yes, please...please sit." Saeed smiled and gestured regally with the hand that held his cigarette. Kenny and I both shook hands with him and sat at his table.

Easily the best-dressed man in the nightclub, Saeed also sported the best mustache of any man in Columbus. He took great personal pride in the thick, bushy hairs of his upper lip and looked very much like a darker skinned, better mustached version of Omar Sharif. In the size department, however, Saeed was shorter and smaller framed than even my pocket-sized T-38 tablemate, Golden Hands Sweet.

Until I saw him smoking at the table, I didn't know that Saeed smoked.

"Saeed, those things will stunt your growth," I said, pointing toward his cigarette.

"Shut up," Saeed responded to my cigarette remark. "You are stupid."

Whenever I teased Al Turbiglio or somebody else in our class, Saeed would say, "You are Crazy Man," but whenever I joked at his expense, he would always strike back at me with the more insulting, "You are stupid."

Having to learn English to be able to come halfway around the world to train to fly in America had to have been tough. Having to learn to speak like a pilot with all of the technical words, acronyms, **BOLDFACE**, and mnemonic devices in a language that wasn't his native tongue had to have been incredibly difficult. Having to trade a life of wealth, privilege, and luxury in one of the world's richest countries to live in the roach-infested visiting officers' quarters at Columbus Air Force Base, where student pilots ain't shit, had to have totally sucked. And having to leave his wife and family for the anachronistic gentility of Columbus, Mississippi, where not only being from the Arr Base but also being dark-skinned made him a *persona non grata* must have been the most difficult of all.

"So, you want to fly fighter?" Saeed asked as we began to eat our soggy food.

"Aaay, yeah!" Kenny answered first. "I want an F-15, but I'll take whatever fighter they wanna give me."

"What about you, Crazy Man?" Saeed asked me.

"Nah," I said. "I'd like to fly a C-141 out of Charleston, South Carolina, but I'd take any cargo jet on a base near a beach."

"You do not want to fly fighter?" Saeed asked incredulously.

"No, not really," I answered, shaking my head. "I just want to be stationed in a nice place and be able to travel around the world."

"Aaay, Saeed," Kenny said. "What about you? What do you wanna get when you graduate?"

"That is easy," Saeed said. "When I graduate...in my Air Force I will fly F-1 Mirage."

"Whoa! Cool!" Kenny reacted like he knew what an F-1 Mirage was. I knew it was a fighter made by the French, but I had no idea what it looked like. I didn't think that Kenny really knew, either.

"Yes, very good jet. Very hot," Saeed acknowledged. "Also, when I graduate...grandfather will give me two more wives."

"Aaay! Two more wives! Dat's even better than a fighter!" Kenny yelled.

"Follow me," Saeed ordered, pointing to the dessert table, "heading 2–7–0."

*

Over the next couple of weeks, all Eagle students soloed for the first time in the T-38, including Saeed. In a tedious, mob-rule ritual pushed onto all of us by Mark Jellicot, student pilots returning from initial solos were involuntarily baptized in the dunk tank, a Petri dish of dirty swill, culturing next to the chute shop.

After our initial solo rides in the T-38, our focus shifted to the next major milestone, the T-38 Contact checkride. The first of three checkrides in the T-38, the grade we earned for this evaluation would play a major role in determining class rank, whether we'd be rated as FAR or TTB, and ultimately the aircraft we'd be assigned to fly after we graduated from UPT. For those students who wanted to fly a fighter, an *Excellent* grade on the T-

38 Contact checkride was the key to earning a FAR rating. For me, having already failed two checkrides, passing the T-38 Contact checkride was my key to staying in the program, and because I had no interest in flying a fighter, just passing was my focus.

On my second-to-last ride before my checkride, however, I couldn't put the wheels of the jet on the ground within the first quarter mile of the runway without the wing flaps extended.

The wing flaps, when extended, added both lift and drag to the airfoil, allowing for the jet to approach the runway more steeply and at a higher power setting, where the engines operated more effectively. In a no-flap landing configuration, which we practiced for emergency situations that would preclude the flaps from extending, the jet didn't generate as much lift. A no-flap landing necessitated a flatter approach to the runway. Since the stall speed of the jet was also higher without the wing flaps extended, no-flap approaches and landings required faster airspeeds than normal landings.

In the traffic pattern, I kept making the same mistake on my no-flap patterns and landings over and over again. While my approaches were nice and flat, by carrying a little too much airspeed and by not reducing my power at the proper point, I was carrying too much horizontal momentum as I crossed the runway threshold. And even when I pulled my power all the way back to idle, I just floated down the runway. And I floated. And I floated. And I floated.

Captain Wright always said that one of the three most useless things for a pilot was runway behind you. By not planting the main landing gear on the ground until well beyond two thousand feet down an eight thousand-foot runway, approach after approach, I created a whole lot of uselessness on my ride. This point was not lost upon Lieutenant Baiber, and for my performance, I earned the grade of *Unsat* for the ride and a giant red tag on my gradebook.

Two rides before the most critical checkride in my training to date, I hooked.

*

I brooded at the center table of the Eagle flight room, contemplating my fate in the program and in the Air Force. I knew I probably should have been preparing for my next ride with Lieutenant Baiber to clear up my *Unsat*, like my classmates were preparing for their Contact checkrides by studying and quizzing one another, but I'd already read up a little on the check pilots and didn't feel like studying.

"Aaay, Kurt! How'd it go?" Kenny called out from the center table when Kurt hustled back into Eagle all pumped up and fired up to take to the skies.

Kurt flashed Kenny a huge thumbs up.

Right after the formal report, Kurt had gone down the hall to Check Section to brief up his flight profile. Kurt was stopping back in Eagle to tell his IP about his mission and maneuvers before heading out to fly.

Everybody was rooting for Kurt. Even though we all were competing against one another for class rank in order to be assigned the most sought after aircraft and locations, UPT never felt like student versus student. It felt more like student versus instructor. And it felt most like student versus check pilot.

And of all the potential student versus check pilot match-ups Kurt could have drawn for his Contact checkride, he'd drawn the toughest grader. According to the secret student intel books around the T-38 squadron, this check pilot had given out more *Unsat* grades than nearly the rest of the check pilots combined, and he almost never gave *Excellents*. None of the students wanted to fly with him, and without even knowing the guy, every student hated him—though surely, Kurt didn't show it.

While a number of IPs were known to be tougher graders than others, Doley had his own explanation as to why this one particular pilot was so hated by the students of Columbus Air Force Base.

"It's the Ugly Rule," Doley explained one afternoon at the center table of the Eagle flight room.

"Doley, what is the Ugly Rule?" I'd never heard this maxim.

"The Ugly Rule: If someone's ugly and you don't know him, you automatically hate him," Doley stated like this was a universal truth that everybody should have known.

To Doley's point, this particular guy was one ugly dude. A spindly-framed pilot who wore tight, form-fitting flight suits, his face was so gaunt that his cheeks and eyes sunk down into his elongated face. Pulled in by the gravity of his eyeballs at the bottom of his deeply laden eye sockets, his eyebrows crimped together and highlighted what looked like a permanent scowl that glared angrily beneath a thick tuft of dark brown hair that he wore parted down the middle of his head.

Based primarily on looks, though more appropriately aligned with his reputation, the students of Columbus Air Force Base had tagged the hated check pilot with a perfect, villainous nickname: Skeletor, the ultimate enemy of both student pilots and the Masters of the Universe!

"Aaay! Go kick some ass, Kurt!" Kenny shouted as Kurt headed back out of the flight room to go fly.

Kurt turned back to face the students and IPs in Eagle. Placing his flying checklist and in-flight guide on the duty desk, Kurt unzipped the front of his flight suit, spreading the sides of his uniform apart like Clark Kent changing into Superman. Revealing a poorly fitting He-Man t-shirt and an inadvertent flash of underwear, Kurt blasted, "BY THE POWER OF GRAYSKULL!"

The whole room roared with laughter. Kurt zipped up his flight suit, picked up his books, and marched out to the flight line to kick some Skeletor ass.

Kenny was the first one to catch his breath after Kurt left the room.

"Aaay! Dat was awesome!" he said.

"I can't believe he still wears Underoos," I added, once I stopped laughing.

*

"Have you been to an Assignment Night yet?" I asked Doley as we met in the O-Club lobby underneath the ten thousand-dollar chandelier. There was an Assignment Night nearly once a month at Columbus Air Force Base, as class after class progressed to this milestone in the UPT program.

"Nah, no reason...b'faw tonight," Doley replied. On this Friday night, Doley's two roommates were in the class getting assignments, 88-04—and I'd become friends with both of them over the past eight months. I wanted to see what assignments they'd get.

"You been to one?" Doley asked me.

"No, this is my first," I said, tucking my flight cap into the pocket at the bottom of my right leg. "I'm not really into hanging out at the O-Club."

"The O-Club is a Blow-Club," Doley attested. He was bound to say this sooner or later.

As a student, I never felt like I could relax at the O-Club. It was just another element of the UPT game. For one thing, too many instructors hung out at the O-Club. A lot of the married IPs lived in base housing, and the O-Club was a place they could take their families for a meal and a swim in the club pool, or they might just hang at the bar for a night of drinking and a few rounds of Crud, a full-contact bar game that pilots played on a pool table. The commanders on the base were often spotted at the O-Club, too. I wasn't into hanging with instructors, swimming with their families, rubbing elbows with the colonels, or playing Crud.

For another thing, to discourage drunk driving on weekend nights, the Columbus gate guards would set up mini-obstacle courses using orange safety cones at the two exits from the base that led back to town. After I'd heard some of the war stories about having to navigate these minefields, I didn't know if I could drive through them sober — never mind after a few hours of drinking beer! I had no interest in taking any chances of getting a DUI on base, but since I'd given up drinking for Lent and wouldn't have any alcohol in my system, this wouldn't be a problem.

There was also the FAIP Mafia. What if I did or said something stupid at the O-Club? Should I expect retribution from the FAIP Mafia? Downtown, I could act a fool, and as long as I didn't get a DUI, end up in jail, or violate crew rest, I didn't have to worry about any potential consequences on the base. But if I pissed off a member of the FAIP Mafia at the O-Club, would I make myself a marked man?

I don't know if my FAIP Mafia paranoia came more from being a student apprehensive around instructor pilots or from being a Rhode Islander apprehensive of the Mafia, but I didn't want to cross this group…if, in fact, it did exist. Still, I was ready for some fun. After clearing up my *Unsat* and getting through my own Contact checkride by the skin of my teeth, the week had ended a whole lot better than it had started.

"Doley, do you think there really is such a thing as the FAIP Mafia?" I asked as we walked toward the O-Club ballroom, where Assignment Night ceremonies were held.

"Fuck yeah!" Doley confidently replied. "Ray, at least two-thirds of the IPs ah FAIPs, and if the FAIPs want you out of UPT…you ah gone."

"Hang on a sec," I said, grabbing Doley's arm before he went through the door to the ballroom and the Assignment Night festivities taking place on the other side. This didn't make sense.

FAIPs were lieutenants and captains, the bottom of the pilot rank structure on the base. How could FAIPs control a student's fate?

"Doley, FAIPs can't control review boards. Those are lieutenant colonels," I said. "And they don't control assignments. Those are done in Texas for the students that aren't going to be FAIPs."

"Ray, think about it," Doley said matter-of-factly, like I should have known without him having to spell things out. "At any given time, every student is three rides away from washing out of UPT. If the FAIP Mafia is connected to the IP, the schedulah, or the check pilot, they can easily *Unsat* a student for one or maybe even two of the three strikes."

I hadn't thought about that.

"Then, even if the FAIP Mafia can't control the IP in the final review ride, think about how nervous the student is at his last chance to stay in the program, and by that time, the FAIP Mafia could have created a gradebook full of Unsats b'faw the student evah got to that point," Doley said, painting the picture for me of how a group of instructors could potentially screw over a student.

"Fuck!" That was about all I could say.

Maybe there was a FAIP Mafia.

"Doley, what if the FAIP Mafia doesn't like a student, but they can't wash him out because he passes his final review ride? How can they screw with his assignment?" I asked.

"Ray," Doley replied immediately, like I should have known this answer already. "By that time, ya r'already screwed! If you get bad grades on y'aw daily rides, and you don't pass y'aw checkrides, y'aw not gonna get FAH'ed, and if you ahn't FAH'ed, and you've got a gradebook full of *Unsats*, y'aw probably going to end up with a suck-ass plane at some shit-hole base."

"Fuck!" That was about all I could say. If Doley was right, it didn't matter how well I flew or how badly I sucked. If the

FAIP Mafia didn't like me, I was screwed and would have no chance at being assigned to a cargo jet at a base near a beach.

But...

"Doley, what if the FAIP Mafia likes you?" I wondered.

"Why? Do you think that's why you passed y'aw Contact check yestahday?" Doley asked.

"Hey, c'mon now!" I responded to this cheap shot. "I didn't suck that bad. I was no Golden Hands, but I earned my *Good*."

Doley laughed, because I'd told him the story of how I got disoriented in my cloverleaf, and instead of turning the same direction at the top of each loop in the maneuver, I turned right, then left, then left, then right.

"What did y'aw check pilot say about y'aw clovahleaf?" Doley asked.

"He said it looked more like a broken slinky than a four-leaf clover," I told him yet again.

Doley loved that line.

"And you still got a *Good!*" He laughed some more. "You don't think someone was taking care of you?!" he added.

No. I thought I flew a pretty good ride — except for the cloverleaf. I was glad to still be moving through the program, but I didn't know what to think about assignments anymore. Our Assignment Night was still three months away...for those of us lucky enough to get that far. I hoped Doley's roommates were about to get good news.

We walked into the main ballroom, which was also the O-Club dining room, but for Assignment Night it had been converted into a small theater. Rows of chairs were lined up to face a podium and a giant movie screen at the front of the room. Nobody in the gathering crowd of both student pilots and IPs was sitting yet, though, as the festivities weren't scheduled to start for another twenty minutes.

"Hey, there's Chuck and Sandy!" Doley called out. The O-Club ballroom was way louder than the lobby, and we headed over to our classmates.

"Guys, where's your beer?" Sandy asked. Everybody was drinking.

"I'll go out to the bar and get us a pitcher," Chuck said.

"Chuck, I'll go to the bar with you, but I gave up drinking for Lent," I confessed.

I followed Chuck through the noisy crowd in the ballroom, out through the quiet lobby, and over to the extremely loud and full bar.

"A pitcher of Bud and a Coke for my designated driver!" Chuck screamed to the bartender over the din of the partying bar crowd and the guys at the pool table playing Crud. I needed to get Doley a Coke, too, so I pushed my way up to the bar behind Chuck. Before I got to her, however, I accidentally bumped into a short but rugged IP who was one of the more rowdy guys at the bar.

I didn't recognize him from the flight line, but by the wings on his chest, the patch on his arm, and the rank on his shoulder, I knew he was a Check Section IP, and because he was a young captain, he was probably a FAIP. I certainly didn't want to piss him off.

"Sir, please excuse me," I said politely. "I didn't mean to bump into you."

"Hey! Lieutenant Wright!" he shouted at me, getting up on his toes to get in my face, slurring his words, and treating me to a splash of spittle. "Did I just hear that you're the designated driver?!"

"Yes, sir," I responded with the minimum words allowed. I couldn't see anything good coming out of this.

"Good, Lieutenant Wright!" he said, treating me to a second spraying, and obviously having read my cloth rank and nametag. "Everyone should have a designated driver!"

"Yes, sir," I answered. Luckily, he turned away and headed for the Crud game.

"Ray, do you know who that was?" Chuck yelled in my ear when I reached her at the bar to get Doley's Coke.

"No, but I saw that he's a check pilot. I just wanted to get away from him," I replied.

"Ray, he's not just a check pilot. I've heard he's the Godfather of the FAIP Mafia!" Chuck said. "Congrats! I think you're *in* with the Godfather of the FAIP Mafia."

What did it mean to be *in* with the Godfather of the FAIP Mafia? Did that mean he'd help me pass my checkrides? Or did that mean that I was a made man?

"Fuck!" That was about all I could say.

"What?" Chuck asked. "What's the matter with that?"

"Chuck," I hypothesized, "do you think the Godfather of the FAIP Mafia has the final say on which students are going to be FAIPs?"

Chapter 20 — "Tone Deaf"

"I need to get FAR'ed," Al Turbiglio said as a group of us sat at the center table in Eagle, quizzing each other on formation procedures. After moving through our T-38 Contact checkrides, we moved into the next phase of training, formation flying.

"Al, what the hell ah you talkin' about?" Doley blurted, shaking his head.

"The guys in my unit back in Pittsburgh told me I need to get FAR'ed. I need to prove to them that they made the right choice. If I don't get FAR'ed, they might take away my spot," Al nervously replied.

For those students wanting to fly a fighter, a strong performance throughout the formation phase of training meant a strong possibility that they might be FAR'ed, thus deemed qualified to fly fighter, attack, or reconnaissance aircraft. For students like Al, none of that mattered.

"Al, y'aw gonna fly a C-130!" Doley yelled. "It's a cahgo plane. With a big crew to keep an eye on you! It's not even a jet! You don't need to get FAH'ed!"

"You don't understand, *Doiley!*" Al tried to insult Doley by mispronouncing his nickname with a strange accent. "You think you're so great because you went to the Academy! The Academy grads around here take care of you! The FAIP Mafia takes care of you! I need to get FAR'ed! You don't understand!" And Al stood up from the table and stomped out of the room.

Some eyebrows went up.

I really had no idea why Al always seemed to be under so much pressure. Of all the students in Eagle, only Al and Saeed already knew what aircraft they'd be flying and where they'd be stationed after graduation. The rest of us competed for class ranking and our assignments, and we were totally at the mercy of the needs of the Air Force.

"I don't want to be FAR'ed," I said after Al stormed out of the room. "I'd be very happy to be rated TTB." My closest friends, like Kenny, Doley, and Kurt, knew this already, but those that didn't were relieved to hear me say it; I was one less person with whom they'd have to compete.

"Well, I want to get FAR'ed, because I want to fly the F-15 Eagle," Mark Jellicot volunteered, as if telling us this for the first time. This triggered an obligatory chain reaction of admissions at the center table of students saying how badly they, too, wanted to be FAR'ed.

"I'd like to get FAR'ed," confessed Chuck, one of the three women students in Eagle.

That surprised me. I didn't expect any women to say this.

It didn't matter that Chuck's checkride scores or academic test scores put her near the top of our class and way ahead of me. Women could not fly fighters. By saying that she wanted to be FAR'ed, Chuck was pretty much saying that she wanted to be an instructor. She wanted to be a FAIP!

"Chuck, if you get FAR'ed," I said, "you'll automatically be FAIP'ed. The girl from 88-04 who got FAR'ed got FAIP'ed on their Assignment Night. Do you really want to be a FAIP?"

"Ray, I wouldn't mind being a FAIP," Chuck confirmed. "As a matter of fact, I think it'd be pretty cool."

The guys around the center table sat dumbfounded. Chuck was probably the smartest person in our class, but what the hell was she thinking?

"Chuck, I'm intrigued," I said. "Why would you not mind being a FAIP? Do you want to stay in Columbus?"

"Ray, c'mon," she laughed. "I enjoy flying aerobatics. I enjoy formation flying. Since Congress and the Air Force say that I can't fly fighters, where else could I do these things if not as a FAIP? The only option for a chick pilot to do that type of flying is to be an instructor."

"I never thought about it like that, Chuck," I said. I truly hadn't.

For me, being a FAIP was about as bad an assignment as I could possibly get, but for Chuck, because she liked aerobatics and formation flying, being a FAIP was about as good an assignment as she could possibly get. Because Chuck wasn't a dude, she wasn't shit. And unfortunately for her and other women pilots in the Air Force, that was the way the system worked.

*

A third of the way through the T-38 phase of training, I hadn't quite figured out our Eagle flight commander. Back in Dagger, Captain Wright addressed our class like an enthusiastic high-school coach delivering a rousing pep talk before a big game. But in Eagle, the authoritarian Major Carrington always sounded to me like a dad...a little anxious about letting us kids drive the family car for the first time. In Dagger flight, I didn't want to disappoint Captain Wright. In Eagle, I didn't want to piss off Major Carrington.

"We won't be launching any solos today. PIREPS are calling the ceiling at 1,400 broken, 2,500 overcast, and crews are breaking out of the weather at about 8,000 feet. It's a thick deck. Formation missions need to be sure to clearly review the Lost Wingman procedures prior to flying," Major Carrington cautioned the aircrews of Eagle.

Before he concluded the morning's formal briefing, he paused at the front of the room to display his well-shined flight boots and the white walls around each of his freshly lowered ears, the weekly work of Three-Fingered Wayne, the base barber.

"Fly safe," he ordered.

This was Mark Jellicot's cue to snap to attention and call, "Room! Ten-hut!"

An hour and thirty minutes later, almost immediately after takeoff, our two-ship formation was enveloped in thick, opaque,

Columbus clouds. Using the skills I'd developed to this point in my training, I was able to stay in position, three feet off of Kurt's left wing, for all of about seven seconds before Lieutenant Baiber took control of the T-38 from the back seat to save us from losing Kurt in the surrounding cloud soup and having to call Lost Wingman.

"I have the aircraft," Lieutenant Baiber said, shaking the stick from the rear cockpit.

"Roger, sir, you have the aircraft," I said, taking my hands off the stick and holding them up for Lieutenant Baiber to see.

"I have the aircraft," he said, shaking the stick.

As soon as Lieutenant Baiber assumed control, our jet stopped its jerking convulsions of pitch and power and settled back into three-foot wingtip-to-wingtip spacing with our formation leader. While the short wingspan of the T-38 meant that Kurt's giant head was less than thirty feet from mine when we were in the proper position on the wing, the clouds were so thick that sometimes, I couldn't see him, and I certainly couldn't see his instructor in Kurt's rear cockpit.

"Maintain your references," Lieutenant Baiber instructed. "You've got to work to stay in position." Then he offered some pointers on how to fix my deviations.

I could barely see the references on Kurt's jet that I was supposed to use to fly three-foot wingtip spacing— never mind maintain them! Every once in awhile, we could catch a glimpse of Kurt's massive, white helmet through the clouds. I was absolutely terrified and relieved Lieutenant Baiber was doing the flying.

On a clear day, thousands of feet above the ground, flying three feet off your flight leader's wing at three hundred knots, wasn't quite so scary. Too high in the sky to get any real sensation of our true speed, I could concentrate on my fingertip position without worrying about getting lost in clouds. And the smoother my leader flew, the easier I found it to stay in position.

In a thick bank of Columbus clouds, however, not only was I worried about losing sight of my leader and potentially banging into him, but the clouds racing between our jets at three hundred knots forced me to appreciate that we were screaming through the sky, burning ozone holes strapped to a couple of very powerful machines that with one wrong move by any of the four of us could have sent us tumbling toward the ground.

"Ready to fly?" Lieutenant Baiber asked.

"Yes, sir," I lied nervously.

"You have the aircraft," he said.

"Roger, sir. I have the aircraft," I said, shaking the stick with my tringlin' hand.

"You have the aircraft," he repeated.

"Roger, sir. I have the aircraft," I answered back, probably one too many times.

With my right hand jerking the stick and my left hand jolting the throttles, I bounced up and down on Kurt's wing again like I was riding a mechanical bull, struggling to stay in the proper fingertip position, the way Lieutenant Baiber had so easily done both in and out of the clouds.

"Don't accept deviations," Lieutenant Baiber coached. "Make corrections expeditiously. Small corrections...."

*

Kenny invited Doley, Saeed, and me to his parents' house in Atlanta for Easter— not that Saeed had any interest in celebrating Easter, but he was willing to go along with us for the adventure. For Easter dinner, Kenny's mom had prepared a huge spread of food, and since I hadn't eaten a home-cooked meal since Christmas break, I was really looking forward to Mrs. Wessels's cooking. I also liked checking out Kenny's dad's collection of Coca-Cola memorabilia from his years of driving the Coke truck. They reminded me of things my mom collected and displayed around our house in Rhode Island.

I always felt at home at Kenny's parents' house. I think Saeed may have had a slightly different experience.

"THIS IS OUR EASTER HAM!" Kenny's mom yelled to Saeed at the far end of the table, as if he were hard of hearing. "ON EASTER WE EAT HAM!"

"No thank you," Saeed politely declined.

"WHAT?! YOUS DON'T LIKE HAM?!" she screamed.

"Aaay, Ma! If he doesn't want ham, he doesn't have to eat ham!" Kenny jumped in. "Don't make him eat ham."

"Alright, Kenny!" Kenny's mom yelled back. "He doesn't want ham…he doesn't have to eat the ham." She looked down the table and saw that Saeed didn't really have much food on his plate other than some plain spaghetti. "Pass him the calamari," she told Kenny.

"SAEED, HAVE SOME CALAMARI!" Kenny's mom yelled down the table as Kenny attempted to hand him the serving plate.

"No thank you," Saeed declined again.

"WHAT?! YOUS DON'T LIKE CALAMARI?!" she shouted with disbelief.

"AAAAY! MA! He doesn't want calamari!" Kenny interjected.

"Look at his plate, Kenny," she said in a more conversational tone, as if Saeed wouldn't be able to understand her because she wasn't speaking loudly anymore. "He isn't eating. No wonder he's so thin. He needs to eat."

Mrs. Wessels surveyed the feast on the table, trying to figure out how she might be able to entice Saeed into eating something she'd prepared other than the small pile of noodles he'd taken.

"HOW ABOUT SOME GRAVY FOR YOUR PASTA?!" she offered. I loved how she called spaghetti sauce *gravy*, like my own grandmother.

"No, thank you," Saeed politely declined once more.

"Aaaay, Ma!" Kenny was trying to get her to stop pushing food and just let Saeed eat what he'd taken. But because his plate wasn't filled like the rest of our plates were, I think Mrs. Wessels—like my own grandmother—was worried that he would go hungry, and that was not acceptable at her table.

"WHAT DO YOUS EAT FOR EASTER, ANYWAY?!" she tried a different approach.

"MADONNE, MA! He's fine. Please, let him eat what he wants," Kenny pleaded.

Then, after a quick staring contest that his mom won, Kenny tried a different approach and changed the subject.

"Aaay, Dad, I picked up a ceiling fan for my room at the mall yesterday. Can you drive over next week and help me install it?" Kenny asked his father. "I want to put it up in my room before it gets hot again."

"Yes, Kenneth," Kenny's dad replied. "I'd be happy to drive over and help you install a ceiling fan. How about Tuesday?"

"Aaay, Tuesday's perfect, Dad. *Tanks*. I'll leave you a house key," Kenny said.

*

After Easter, we were back on early week, reporting for duty two hours before sunrise in order to have an hour for the formal report and an hour to brief up the first missions of the day so that the first flights could take off right as the sun rose. Kenny and I had gotten to like early weeks better than late weeks because we'd started riding bicycles together on the weekends, and on early week, we'd have enough daylight after work to go for long rides.

When training for tactical formation flying began, one of the Eagle IPs suggested that students practice maneuvers with one another while riding bikes in a parking lot. Kenny and I took our tactical maneuvering to the back of the University Mall. It was actually a fun way to practice, and maneuvering in the parking lot really did help us understand the timing of our tactical turns. A lot of guys were having problems with this. Problems with tactical turns led to problems staying in the proper position. Plus, when Lead didn't plan properly, or Two wasn't in the proper position, it created problems for the formation. And this seemed to happen a lot. Lead would need to come up with a new plan, and of course, Two would need to be there.

"Aw shit!" Kenny screamed across the parking lot in the middle a tactical turn. "My dad is coming over tonight! I forgot!" We were only about a mile away from our rental house, but we'd been riding for more than an hour.

Kenny raced off through the parking lot. We'd talked about putting extra clothes on the mannequin to cover up the bra and panties before his dad showed up, but we'd forgotten.

We didn't get back in time. When we entered into the big room, Kenny's dad was waiting for us. He looked agitated, and he cut right into Kenny as soon as we stepped in the room.

"Kenneth!" his dad reprimanded. "WHAT THE HELL IS THIS?!"

Obviously, Mr. Wessels wasn't very pleased with what he saw, and for the first time since I'd met Kenny, I don't think he knew what to say or do.

"Aaay, Dad! It's not what you're thinking..." he began, still fighting to catch his breath after racing back on our bikes.

"NOT WHAT I'M THINKING!" his dad screamed. "WHAT THE HELL ARE YOU THINKING?"

Kenny tried a staring contest with his father, but he lost this one, too, when he broke eyelock and looked around the room, trying to come up with a way to calm down his father. I stayed next to my friend to support him, but I had no idea what I could do. I didn't think he appreciated the mannequin's UOD the way Kenny and I did.

Just as the silence approached a level that was almost too uncomfortable to bear, Kenny's dad screamed, "WHAT THE HELL ARE YOU DOING WITH A PEPSI MACHINE IN YOUR HOUSE?"

*

I knew that keeping the formation in Sectors 6 and 7 would be easy because of Grenada Lake. Of all the ground references we used when flying around Columbus Air Force Base, Grenada Lake may have been the easiest to identify and use. Shaped like a giant pair of pants, there was no mistaking its distinct shape and size for any other body of water within a three hundred-mile radius.

The other great thing about Grenada Lake was that it was centrally positioned within Sectors 6 and 7.

Stay over the lake... stay in my area.

"What's your plaaan?" my guest-help instructor for the day, Captain Morawski, cawed through the intercom from the back seat. Like Major Lawson, Captain Morawski was not assigned to our flight as a full-time flight line IP. I think he worked with the support squadron trying to integrate computers into UPT. Not just for our gradebook records...but for optimizing training, scheduling takeoff times, monitoring the timeline...all kinds of stuff I didn't really care about. A former tanker pilot, he flew with Eagle students once a day.

Captain Morawski was a pretty likable character. He spoke in a raspy, high-pitched voice that sounded like he always had a stuffed-up nose because his sinuses never drained properly. To alleviate the pain caused by this condition, crackerjack Air Force doctors drilled holes just below his eyes into his sinuses to unclog the blockage. The scars on his face under both eyes made him look like he was wearing sad clown face makeup all the time.

During our contact phase of training, Captain Morawski flew with Al Turbiglio a lot. In the formation phase of training, he'd been added to my continuity. On this particular ride, he alone had to deal with us both — Al was flying solo on our wing.

"Let's start him off with an echelon turn," I said over the intercom to Captain Morawski to signal the start of the maneuvers once we were established in Sectors 6 and 7.

"Alright, that sounds like a pretty good plaaan," Captain Morawski cawed. "Let's hope Turbiglio haaas a clue."

I checked Al in on channel 19, the discrete frequency that jets in the Western MOAs were assigned to monitor. I flashed Al the secret devil sign with my left hand, and rolling into 60 degrees of right bank, I pulled back on the control stick to bring the nose of the jet across the horizon. Because 2Gs of force were needed to maintain level altitude in a 60-degree bank turn, I pushed my power up a little. This offset the loss of lift brought about by the increased bank angle and the loss of energy brought about by the increased G-load.

Since Al was right underneath the belly of our aircraft throughout the turn, I wouldn't be able to see him until I rolled back to wings-level. I had to trust that he was in the proper echelon position. The best way for me to ensure this would be easy for Al was to fly a nice, smooth turn as Lead. When I rolled out of my turn, Al was right there!

"Aaalright, Turbiglio!" Captain Morawski cawed through the intercom. "Maaaybe Turbiglio's got a clue today."

I gave Al a quick thumbs up, and then, I pointed my index finger up and spun it in a circle. Pitchout. Though I didn't have to wait for Al's head nod, I did, and once he nodded, I pushed my throttles to MIL and ripped a 180-degree power-slide away from his jet at 300 knots to reverse direction and keep the formation over Grenada Lake at 20,000 feet.

As Two for the pitchout maneuver, Al's job was to wait four seconds before initiating his power-slide to reverse his direction. By waiting four seconds, Al would create about a mile spacing between our jet and his. After I had turned 180 degrees, I would fly straight ahead for the same four seconds, which would allow Al to finish his turn. Then, after I'd counted off four seconds, I'd rock my wings to signal our rejoin. More simply put: I turn, he waits; he turns, I wait. Then, we turn into one another to get back together.

"One thousand one, 1002, 1003, 1004," I counted for Captain Morawski after rolling out of my power-slide. I rocked my wings, and set up a 30-degree banked turn to my left at 300 knots to keep us over Grenada Lake. Then, I started looking back for Al.

"Do you see him?" Captain Morawski asked after I'd established my left-hand turn.

"No, sir. I don't see him," I said, scanning the sky over my left shoulder. "Do you see him?"

"No, I don't see him. I can't imaaagine he's—" But Captain Morawski didn't get to finish his thought.

"Hang 2-1! Two is Lost Wingman!" Al called. This was strange because Lost Wingman was something that happened when you were in bad weather. There wasn't a cloud in the sky.

"I haaave the aircraft," Captain Morawski said immediately, shaking the stick.

"Roger, you have the aircraft," I said, releasing my grip.

"I haaave the aircraft," Captain Morawski repeated.

"Haaang 2-1, Two, Lead copies you haaave lost sight, aaand you have broken out of formation. Maintain aaat or below 1-niner thousand until visual contaaact re-established. Lead is in 30 degrees of left bank over the southern paaant leg of Grenada Laaake," Captain Morawski called over the radio to Al. I still couldn't see him.

Since we were both at 20,000 feet, by directing Al to stay at or below 19,000 feet, Captain Morawski created a vertical separation between our jets so that if we didn't regain visual contact, there was no danger of a collision.

"Hang 2-1, Lead, Two is out of 2-1 thousand for 1-niner thousand." Al acknowledged over the radio. Al must have inadvertently climbed a thousand feet in his power-slide, and

Captain Morawski had actually just directed him to fly through our altitude, which is exactly what we didn't want him to do.

"Hang 2-1, Two, disregard. Maaaintaaain 2-1 thousand until visual contact. Lead is now over the kneecaaap of the lower paaant leg of Grenada Laaake," Captain Morawski called, wanting to prevent Al from shooting through our flight path without us seeing one another.

"Hang 2-1, Lead, Two is out of 1-niner thousand for 2-1 thousand. Searching," Al called back. He had already descended. Still not seeing us, he was about to fly through our altitude again!

That dumb bastid!

"Hang 2-1, Two. NEGATIVE!" Captain Morawski ordered with a high-pitched squeak. "Stay at 1-niner thousand until visual contaaact is reestablished."

"Hang 2-1, Lead, Two; 2-1 to 1-niner thousand," Al acknowledged. "Hang 2-1, Two, searching."

Beep.

We weren't alone on channel 19. Someone else was on our frequency, listening to our drama unfold, and had just hit the tone button on the radio to send Al the secret pilot message: "You dumb bastid!"

Captain Morawski was getting frustrated. "Find him! Find him!" he yelled over the intercom. "We're a sitting duck being hunted by a clue-seeking missile. The laaast thing I need right now is to have Turbiglio raaam his pitot tube through my sinus cavities!"

I was looking up, down, right, left, above us, next to us, in front of us, and everywhere else trying to find Al. I was also trying to do all I could to keep from laughing over the intercom at Captain Morawski's *clue-seeking missile*. It was good enough to become the title of my next UPT Haiku.

"Hang 2-1, Columbus Approach, sounds like your formation may have come apart. Would you like some help getting back together, sir?" the controller had called us on channel 19 with an offer to help.

Beep.

Another *You dumb bastid!* message.

"Negative!" Captain Morawski said over the radio. "Columbus Approach, Hang 2-1, thanks for the offer, but we'll get our own formation baaack together."

Even a former tanker pilot had more pride than to agree to let a Controller vector our two jets back together on a perfectly clear day. "We're going to do this ourselves...using ground references. Getting vectored back together in VFR weather—we wouldn't be able to set foot in the flight room," Captain Morawski told me over the intercom.

"Hang 2-1, Two, Lead is in a left-hand turn, flashing our wings, and our position is..." he paused his radio call for a second and rolled the jet up into 90 degrees of left bank in order to get a clear look at the ground below us.

"We are over the crotch of Grenada Laaake," he said. "Repeat, we are over the crotch of Grenada Laaake."

Beep. Beep. Beep. Beep.

*

Back in Eagle, Doley captivated the masses.

"We're over the crotch of Grenada Laaake," Doley cawed, imitating Captain Morawski's raspy, high-pitched voice to a tee. "We're just underneath the scrotum of the laaake. If you're in the taint, you're in the wrong plaaace. You definitely don't want to be in the taaaint. Taint a good place to be."

"Shut up, *Doiley!*" Al screamed over the din of howls and laughter.

"BEEP!" Somebody made a sound like they were hitting the tone button in the jet.

Al threw up his hands and stomped out of the room.

"What's going on in here?" Major Carrington asked, emerging from the IP briefing room.

I think we'd gotten his Irish up.

"It doesn't sound like much studying," he said, which resulted in the students scurrying back to our desks.

Having restored order to the flight room, Major Carrington walked over to Lieutenant Baiber's desk to get a look at the scheduling board.

"What are you two studying?" he asked with his back to Brendan and me while checking Lieutenant Baiber's latest arrangement of magnetic nametags. Golden Hands gave me a look and a head shake that told me he couldn't come up with anything to say.

"Well, sir...," I started, trying to buy time, "we were just talking about something that doesn't seem to make a whole lot of sense to us."

"What's that?" Major Carrington sat in Lieutenant Baiber's seat. B and I stood up to show proper military courtesy but mostly to buy more time to think.

"Sit down. Sit down," the Eagle flight commander ordered. "Let me hear your question."

"Well, sir...," I started again, and thankfully something came to me. "Sir, all our IPs say that the best formation rides are the ones that are best briefed before the flight, but it seems to me like our flights are never flown the way they are briefed."

I hadn't gotten to my question yet, but Major Carrington already had an answer:

"And they never will," he stated plainly.

"Sir, to me, that's what doesn't make any sense. Why—" I started, but again, he had an answer for me before I got to my question.

"Second Law of Thermodynamics," he said.

I thought about this for a moment without responding.

"What is the Second Law of Thermodynamics?" Major Carrington asked before I spoke again.

"Sir, it's entropy," I said. "Things move from a state of order to disorder."

"There's your answer," Major Carrington stated. "Entropy. There is no such thing as a perfect ride. No matter how good you are, no matter how good the weather is, no matter how shit-hot the jet you fly is, something is going to happen during the course of every mission that you don't want to happen."

"Yes, sir. I pretty much experience that every time I fly," I agreed.

"And you always will," Major Carrington predicted confidently, "and that's why we say the best flown formation rides are the ones that are the best briefed. When those unexpected events begin to happen, you've already discussed them. You're prepared for them. You know what to do to fix them. And you take the proper course of action to put things back in order."

Chapter 21 — "When Explanations Make No Sense"

The upkeep of our rental house had evolved toward a state of maximum entropy. We had rotten food in our caution orange fridge. Our freezer had crystallized into a frost cave with ice walls so thick they could only be chipped away with a hammer and screwdriver. The air conditioner sprayed water onto the hall carpet through a vent when it was on, but we hadn't gotten around to calling a repairman.

So, after a long week during which I'd flown seven times, four of them solo, with two of my rides having been flown that very Friday, Kenny and I cleaned the house for a big party. Doley's roommates had graduated from UPT and needed to report to their first assignments in the Real Air Force. Doley was moving in with us over the weekend, as the lease on his rental house had expired.

"Aaay, I'm showerin' before people start showin' up," Kenny said, standing in the doorway of my bedroom as I opened my footlocker.

"I wasn't even paying attention to the time," I replied.

"Aaay!" Kenny responded with his unique version of *you're welcome*. Then, before he headed down the hall to his room, he asked, "Aaay, you didn't happen to pick up one of those wrestling tapes from the video store that we usually show at our parties, did you?"

"Shit!" I shook my head. "I forgot. Do you have any good movies?"

"Naah, I don't got any movies. I just rent 'em," Kenny answered. "Do you got any movies or videos?"

I turned my hands up and waved my head around trying to get Kenny to appreciate that other than comic books, cadet uniforms, and some civilian clothes, I didn't have a whole lot of worldly possessions.

Why would I have movies if I didn't have a VCR?

Kenny headed off to his room. I was just about finished cleaning for the party, and then I'd jump in the shower. I folded up the winter blanket I hadn't used all winter to stash in the open footlocker. Sliding over a folded up pile of cadet uniforms to make room, I suddenly realized that I did have a videotape that we could play at the party after all.

"Kenny!" I screamed down the hall having just come up with the dumbest idea of my life. "I have a video for the party!"

*

"Dude, you're an asshole!" Kurt yelled at me as he entered the Eagle flight room on Monday. Everyone was hunched over their desks, preparing for our upcoming T-38 night flights. My giant friend stomped over to my seat and angrily stabbed my chest with his powerful index and middle fingers pressed together.

"Kurt, I'm sorry! Really, I shouldn't have done it! I know. I'm sorry!" I pleaded, recoiling from his two-fingered stab, thankful that he held back his true strength and didn't jab his fingers right through my rib cage and rip out my heart and hold it in front of my face so I could see it beat a couple times before I died.

"What the fuck were you thinking?!" he screamed in my face.

"Kurt, I wasn't thinking! I was stupid. I know! I'm sorry. Kurt, I'm sorry," I groveled. I didn't know what to say...other than I'm sorry." And I really was sorry.

"What in *thee* hell made you think that showing the videotape of my wife giving birth was appropriate entertainment for a UPT party?"

"Kurt, it was stupid. I'm sorry," I said. I felt like shit. If he wanted to kick my ass, I would have let him beat me to a pulp right there in the flight room without resistance. I had played the videotape of his wife giving birth to Kurt II to a mix-tape that included songs like "I Want Your Sex," "Dirty Diana," and of course, "Push It."

For a few minutes at the party, the combination of video and music catalyzed the bizarre and chaotic atmosphere Kenny and I always liked to encourage at our parties until the joke — and the delivery — went on too long. Then, the whole scene just got really weird and really uncomfortable. A crowd of guys gathered around the TV, chanting, "Push! Push! Push!" and singing, "Ooh Baby Spranger. Baby Spranger," over and over again, and the girls at our party all left the big room to hide in the kitchen.

Finally, Chuck, the voice of reason, pulled me aside and convinced me that showing Malia's birthing video wasn't right. I turned off the tape, ejected it from the VCR, and stashed it back in my room at the bottom of my footlocker. But by that time, it was too late. The damage had been done, and I had no way to put the lid back on Pandora's box — so to speak.

"One minute!" Mark Jellicot announced, letting us know that in just sixty seconds the IPs would file out of the IP briefing room into the main room of Eagle, and we'd be called to attention for the evening's formal briefing.

We were flying our nighttime formation rides. I was nervous enough flying during the day, but this night, knowing that Kurt was angry with me, I wasn't feeling all that nervous about flying in the dark. I had betrayed my friend's trust.

Malia had helped nurse my bleeding hemorrhoids back to health by forcing me to eat vegetables. She'd taught me proper aquarium cleaning techniques so as not to poison goldfish. She'd welcomed me into her apartment and shared her husband while she was pregnant and planning her baby's arrival. We'd watched a Super Bowl together and watched her husband dangle from a barn roof forty feet above the ground — though his pants were just thirty-nine feet above the ground.

"Thirty seconds!" Mark Jellicot called. We needed to take our places at our instructors' desks with our seats facing outward and our gradebooks behind us, ready to be called to attention when our IPs entered the room for the formal report.

"You're lucky my wife is so cool," Kurt said with his giant finger pointed in my face. "Because she thinks what you did was funny." Kurt held his mad face momentarily, and then he started laughing.

He wasn't mad!

"You dumb ass," he said, once he knew I realized he wasn't pissed off at me. When I smiled, however, he punched me so hard in my chest that I fell back into my chair behind me.

I deserved that.

Kurt offered me his giant hand and pulled me back to my feet.

"Ten seconds!" Mark Jellicot called.

I pointed toward Kurt's seat. "Time to make like a baby..." I told him.

"...And head out?" Kurt finished. "You're a dick," he said and went back to his chair in front of his instructor's desk. My chest hurt where he'd punched me.

"Room, Ten Hut!"

Snapping to attention, my classmates all waited for Mark Jellicot to salute Major Carrington at the front of the room for our first night of T-38 night flying. I tried to drop the smile from my face to display the proper military bearing for the position of attention. But I couldn't.

*

We sat around the center table in Eagle, quizzing each other on T-38 formation procedures, waiting for a break in the weather so that we could launch our night missions. We'd canceled night flying on Monday due to bad weather and again on Tuesday, but because Columbus Air Force Base was once again falling behind the training timeline and, even worse, falling behind the other training bases, the SOF was going to make us wait until our crew rest expired before he'd let us go home for a third night in a row.

"When do you break out of formation?" Mark Jellicot threw out another question.

"In front of Lead," Chuck answered.

"Under Lead," Kurt added.

"If you lose sight of Lead," Al Turbiglio replied, referring to one of his highlighted flash cards.

"If Lead tells you to," I answered.

"If you're a hazard in the formation," said Golden Hands.

"That's all of them," Mark Jellicot declared. "If you're in front of Lead or under Lead, if you lose sight of Lead, if you're a hazard in the formation, if Lead tells you to do so...you break out. Does anybody have an acronym for that?" he asked, looking to help us remember the answer for a test or if we were asked this question on our checkride.

"Or a mnemonic device?" I added.

"I bet Doley has one, and I bet he's probably got a song," George Biezinger offered.

"Beez with Guarantees!" I interjected.

George Biezinger's name was Jonathan. He went by George. But everyone called him "Beez." Able to blend into any group of friends or environment, Beez seemed to be described or defined by circumstance and surroundings more often than for being George, Jonathan, or Beez. For example, when he showed up in Dagger one day with a curl in his normally straight blond hair, he was "Beez with a Tease." When he returned from Thanksgiving break sporting a cheesy moustache, he was "Beez with a Cheese." When he had an allergy attack in Eagle, he was "Beez with a Sneeze." Once spotted with a girl at a party, he was "Beez with a Squeeze," but when he became single again, we joked that he was "Beez with Disease."

"As a mattah-a-fact, Beez, I *do* have a song for that." Doley said and stood. He never turned down a chance to be in the spotlight.

All eyes and ears tuned into Doley, the undisputed master of UPT song parodies.

When situations quickly change
Position seems unsure
You're in front of or under lead
What are you waiting for?
Lost in the crotch above the lake
Breakout
Don't start to ask
And when Lead tells you, then you do it fast
So if you're in his wake
With too much overtake
Breakout
'Fess up your flaw
Do not ignaw
Breakout and shout,
"It's Two; I'm out"
Breakout

We all clapped and cheered. Yet another classic Doley song parody to a top pop song!

"Don't you think that's a lot to remember for a test or a checkride?" Mark Jellicot unenthusiastically responded. "I don't picture myself singing answers to general knowledge questions from Skeletor."

Everybody at the center table grew quiet at the mention of Skeletor's name. For most students, a strong performance on the T-38 Formation checkride meant the difference between being FAR'ed or TTB'ed—fighter pilot or tanker co-pilot—and as history had demonstrated, flying a checkride with Skeletor didn't often result in grades that reflected strong performances.

"Doesn't anybody have anything easier to remember?" Mark Jellicot asked the group.

Seeing that no one else was about to step forward, Kenny volunteered. "Aaay! I got something. SHIT! S-H-I-T," Kenny said, spelling it out for those of us unfamiliar with the word. "'Cause if you end up in a position where you gotta say, *Shit!*, you definitely gotta break outta formation."

Some of the students around the table laughed nervously.

"S—*Lose sight*," Kenny said, emphasizing the "s" in "sight."

"H," he said next. "*Hazard.*" He looked around the table, nodding at everyone to be sure they were following along.

"I—*In front of or under*," Kenny said next.

"T—*Told to*," he finished, looking all around the table to make sure everyone understood.

"Aaay! S-H-I-T, SHIT!" Kenny said one more time for emphasis, nodding to acknowledge his good work.

"SHIT," I agreed. This worked for me.

"Shit," Doley whispered, his attention focused elsewhere. "This doesn't look good."

I followed the direction of Doley's gaze to the duty desk of the Eagle flight room. Sandy had just appeared in the doorway.

Sandy had been having trouble in the formation phase of flying. Having hooked three rides in a row, she'd been sent to a review board, convened to determine whether she would remain a student pilot or be washed out of the program.

The room turned instantly quiet.

Sandy wasn't wearing her olive green flight suit, instead standing in her dress blues. Mark Jellicot got up and started to say something, but Chuck grabbed him from behind and pulled him back. "I got it," she told him.

Marcia, the other woman in our class, stood up, too, to make sure none of the rest of us made a move toward Sandy.

Nobody moved.

Everybody watched.

Like the time Chuck and Sandy carried on a complete conversation using sign language to successfully handle a formation emergency during a Dagger formal report, they communicated across the room without talking. This time, however, everyone understood exactly what was being said.

Chuck and Marcia then walked over to their friend — our friend — and each put a hand on her back. Together, the three women turned, left the Eagle flight room, and disappeared down the hall.

Several awful minutes later, Chuck and Marcia returned.

Sandy did not.

*

Leading up to our Formation checkrides, student pilots were paired up with a classmate in preparation. Being paired up with another student meant that you'd fly your last half dozen formation rides against your partner so that you'd learn each other's moves, begin to function as a team, and then when you'd fly your Formation checkrides against one another, there wouldn't be any surprises.

Once paired up, student pilots would alternate roles as Lead and Two. On one ride, I would lead the formation out from the base, and my formation partner would lead the formation back. On the next ride, the roles would be reversed, and my formation buddy would lead the departure from Columbus, and I would lead the formation back to the base. Neither the students nor our instructors had any way of knowing if we'd fly the departure as the leader or as the wingman on our checkrides. By alternating our positions on each ride, we'd maximize our practice as both Lead and Two.

Formation partners reserved different blocks of airspace at the TOC desk for each mission to practice the different checkride profiles we might be assigned. The easiest block of airspace was Echo, just behind the Northern MOA, northeast of Columbus Air Force Base over Alabama. The biggest block of airspace with the best ground references was the Pickwicks up in Tennessee. Even though it was easy to keep within the area boundaries in the Pickwicks, you had to be a lot more efficient with your energy management and use of fuel because the drive to Tennessee and back took so much gas.

If you weren't given one of these big sectors, you flew a High-Low profile in the local airspace sectors also being used by students flying contact missions. To use these sectors, however, formations needed two adjacent sectors for maneuvering, and the lower portions of these sectors, 8,000 to 22,000 feet, were usually occupied.

As you waited for the lower airspace to open up, you'd fly your tactical maneuvers in the High block of the assigned airspace, 24,000 to 29,000 feet. Then, when the Low airspace opened up, the formation could drop down into the lower altitude block to fly its other maneuvers. A High-Low profile required two lead changes, one in the high block and one in the low block, and sometimes, you got stuck waiting in the high block for airspace to open up below you. I didn't like the High-Low profile that much.

Once the formation reached its assigned airspace during these final training rides, students would practice full profiles to demonstrate mastery of all formation maneuvers: pitchout and rejoins, echelon turns, wingwork, close trail, extended trail, and tactical formation. Lead would clear and plan, and as Two, the wingman's job was to be there. Halfway through the ride, students would change positions, and the new Lead would lead the new Two through the same series of maneuvers, clearing and planning to stay within the assigned airspace and working to manage proper energy levels and maximize fuel efficiency for the mission.

"Lieutenant Wright, let's talk about your extended trail out in Echo," Lieutenant Baiber said, holding up two T-38 model jets-on-sticks, one in each hand. "Where was your wingman when you sent him extended trail?"

"Sir, he was one my right wing on the outside of my turn," I answered.

Like a master puppeteer, Lieutenant Baiber positioned his jets-on-a-stick in a left-hand turn with Lead on the inside of the turn and Two to the right and slightly behind Lead.

"Lieutenant Biezinger," Lieutenant Baiber asked Beez, my checkride partner-to-be, "you called *in* pretty quickly. Was it easy to get into position from where Lieutenant Wright had you on the outside of his turn?"

"Oh, yes, sir. Getting into the right extended trail position is usually pretty easy for me," Beez answered. "I was happy to get off Ray's wing, too, because I had been staring into the sun so long that my eyes were starting to burn."

"Interesting!" Lieutenant Baiber nodded, looking at me to see if I'd react to Beez's insinuation that I had screwed him over as the formation leader by keeping him in a position that forced him to stare into the sun.

Lieutenant Baiber spun his chair around to the white scheduling board behind him and drew a large, circular, orange sun with lines radiating outward, like the kind of sun kids make when they learn to draw with crayons. Then, Lieutenant Baiber picked up his jets-on-a-stick and reset his T-38 puppets back in fingertip formation position in a left-hand turn so that my jet lined up directly between Beez's jet and the sun.

"Lieutenant Wright," my instructor said, "did you realize that you'd done this?"

"No, sir, I didn't realize this. I wanted Lieutenant Biezinger on the outside of my turn, because if I sent him to extended trail from the inside of my turn, as soon as he cracked his wings to pull away, he'd be in front of me," I answered. I held my hands up to illustrate our jets with Beez on the inside of my left-hand turn and pivoted my hands left to demonstrate how doing so would have caused Beez to shoot in front of me.

"That's what I was thinking, Beez," I said. "I wasn't trying to drag you through the sun. I was trying to put you in the right position for our next set of maneuvers. My bad."

Lieutenant Baiber turned back to Beez.

"Lieutenant Biezinger," he said, "what did you think about Lieutenant Wright's aerobatics as he led you through extended trail?" Rather than give me direct feedback on my flying, he let Beez offer his personal critique.

"Well, I wasn't going to say anything, sir, but since you asked...Lieutenant Wright totally screwed me," Beez replied. "When I called in, he turned into me and nearly spit me out of the cone. I probably got as close as five hundred feet before I made an aggressive move to his six and put myself back into proper position. I don't know if Lieutenant Wright saw that."

"Aggressive!" Lieutenant Baiber echoed.

"Yes, sir," Beez smiled. *"Aggressiveness is a state of mind..."*

"Not to be confused with reckless abandon." Lieutenant Baiber completed the quote from our flying manual.

Aggressiveness was meant to describe good formation wingman habits of making proper adjustments and timely corrections to maintain the correct position. Students had so overused this quote, however, that it had become clichéd. In our debrief, Beez aggressively positioned his flying skills as superior to mine, talking some serious smack.

What the fuck, over!

I knew I'd flown okay. I hadn't done anything dangerous or stupid enough to have Lieutenant Baiber give me an *Unsat*. Of course, I could have done better, but even Major Carrington said there's no such thing as the perfect ride. I'd flown okay.

Lieutenant Baiber loved to joke with me, and he was such a good-natured person that I never minded his ribbing. But I was starting to get pissed that my partner for my upcoming checkride kept trashing my flying to make himself look good. We were supposed to be a team.

I should rip his shit right back!

But I didn't say anything.

Sometimes, it was best to shut up.

*

"He was Beez with Insensitivities!" I summed up my debrief for Kenny and our new roommate Doley as we relaxed with a few beers after work on the brown velour sectional couch in the big room of our playhouse.

"That sucks," Doley said. "But Beez with Insensitivities is a fawced rhyme. That sucks maw."

"It didn't really roll off the tongue, did it?" I admitted. I thought for a moment. "How about Beez with Scrutinies?"

"Fawced rhyme," Doley repeated, shaking his head.

"Beez with Expertise?" I tried again.

"Naah," Kenny didn't like that one, but I felt like I was getting closer.

"Beez with No Fleas!" Doley declared.

"Yes! That was exactly his attitude!" I agreed, pointing at Doley. "It was almost like he had turned into one of our IPs."

"Aaay, what's up with dat?!" Kenny asked.

"He had turned into an IP!" Doley confirmed. "In a group, Beez becomes the people around him. He's a social chameleon! He turned into an IP because two IPs were at the debrief. He's like Zelig." Doley made reference to one of our recent movie rentals. "You shouldn't have put up with his shit. You shoulda called him out on *his* flying."

"I was tempted," I admitted. "But what good would that have done? I have to fly a checkride with the guy. I don't think it does me any good to fight with him. I need to work with him so I can pass my Formation checkride, 'cause if I don't, it's strike three for me, and I wash out of UPT, and I ain't a pilot. And if I ain't a pilot, I ain't shit."

"Aaay, if anybody ever says Sandy ain't shit, I'd punch 'im in da mout'!" Kenny declared.

The three of us tapped our beers together and toasted our friend Sandy.

Having failed two checkrides in T-37s, washing out of UPT for failing a third checkride was always in the back of my mind. Luckily, I'd managed to survive each time I got into trouble. Two-thirds of the way through flight school, our class seemed to be beating the odds quoted to us so many times during our first week on the base. Losing Sandy came out of nowhere.

For a military training program that so strictly adhered to the course's syllabus of instruction, UPT had turned out to be more unpredictably difficult than I ever could have imagined. At the Academy, even though we worked hard and cadets never had enough time to get everything done, we learned to rely on one another to pull everyone through to the end. *Cooperate and graduate.* That was the motto that kept us working together.

In UPT, however, things were different. It wasn't enough just to get most of your work done. While most of your classmates in UPT were great about helping you when they could, they were all working hard to survive the program, too. And not only did you need to learn a lot to fly a supersonic jet aircraft, you needed to learn how to deal with a constantly changing environment.

The weather at Columbus was always changing. The maintenance personnel on the flight line kept changing. Friends were graduating, moving out, and washing out. IPs moved in and out of Eagle flight like passengers on *The Love Boat*. Kenny was on his second IP. Lieutenant Carmody, the IP who teased us about the Nightmares painting the roof of the VFR entry point, moved out to Check Section after a month. We'd had two different assistant flight commanders in Eagle. And in a nightmare to end all nightmares for Kurt, his air officer commanding for three years at the Academy appeared in Eagle flight one day to reprise his Academy role of Kurt's tormenter — only now as his Eagle IP. As cadets, we had nicknamed this senior officer "Tennis Ball Head" for his coarse, pubescent, blondish-gray head of hair. And Tennis Ball Head was a total dick.

*

Beez and I walked side-by-side as we headed to the chute shop on the way to fly our Formation checkride. Though we'd practiced the High-Low mission profile several times, I was noticeably nervous because I'd been assigned to fly with Lieutenant Carmody as my check pilot. Other than the time he teased our class about the roof of the VFR entry point and my first emergency procedures sim ride, I'd luckily avoided working with him closely. I couldn't have hidden all the laughter his frog-like voice generated — Doley called him Lieutenant "Kermitty" to hammer home his point.

But even worse — Beez was flying with Skeletor.

A Master-Distracter of the Universe, himself, Doley caught me on my way into the chute shop to give me some parting words of wisdom. In his best Kermit the Frog voice, he said, "Hi-Lo, Kermit the check pilot here reporting to you live from the Castle Grayskull."

I wished I'd had a comeback for him with some kind of Marvin the Martian joke, but I couldn't think of anything quickly enough. I wasn't as quick-witted as Doley.

Throughout the checkride, Beez and I worked well together. The weather was near perfect, winds were fairly calm, and the visibility was seven miles into the distance, which was great for Columbus. We flew our tactical maneuvers in the High MOA, and Beez led me in close trail, maneuvering at a low power setting to drop down into the Low MOAs, Sectors 6 and 7 over

Grenada Lake, which we both knew quite well. We didn't have any surprises, and the mission was going exactly how we'd briefed.

Right up to the part where...

Beez was leading me through some wingwork, doing a good job of hitting the parameters of ninety degrees of bank and 3Gs of backstick pressure while I flew just off his wing, keeping three feet between the edge of my wingtip and his.

I had come to envision wingwork as a series of sine waves. Lead would pull the nose of his jet up to climb to the peak of the sine wave, and at the peak, he'd roll the jet into 90 degrees of bank. Because the wings did not produce any lift at 90 degrees of bank, the nose of Lead's jet would drop down below the horizon, and the jet would descend and accelerate. At the bottom of the sine wave, Lead would roll back the speeding jet to wings-level and initiate a 3G pull back through the horizon and up towards the peak of the sine wave once again. And back at the top, the jet slowed down again, and Lead would roll back into 90 degrees of bank to repeat the oscillation.

Our check pilots wanted us to show them four oscillations—or pulls—of wingwork, hitting 90 degrees of bank at the top of each wave and pulling 3Gs at the bottom of each wave. Lead needed to ensure that Two was properly positioned for two pulls on each wing. Two's job was to be there.

As the formation leader, wingwork was a great time to evaluate and adjust the energy level of the formation. Each time the nose of the jet passed through the horizon, you could see if the energy level of the aircraft was increasing, decreasing, or remaining the same by looking at your airspeed and your altitude and comparing it to the previous pass through the horizon. Since the only thing Beez needed to fly after wingwork was one set of extended trail where we'd need to fly over-the-top maneuvers, I knew he was aiming for the classic contact energy level of 15,000 feet and 300 knots.

We'd done this together so many times by this point in our training, I thought I knew what Beez would do next. He had my jet on his right wing, and in 90 degrees of right bank, we were accelerating back up to about 450 knots, where he'd roll out of his bank, make a smooth 3G pull back to the horizon, and roll away from me into some left bank so that I'd be positioned on the outside of his turn. Once he had me on the outside of his turn, he'd direct me to move to the extended trail position.

I'd acknowledge Beez's radio call, move into extended trail, and we'd both use MIL power, full throttle on both engines without engaging the afterburners. I'd vector away from his jet to drop from three-foot wingtip spacing back to a range of 500 to 1,000 feet behind him. When I had maneuvered into the proper position, I'd call *in* over the radio. Then, so as to ensure our jets' engines were set to the same performance levels, we'd both set our throttles so that the temperature of the exhaust gas shooting out of the backs of our engines was 600 degrees Celsius. Beez would then lead me through the extended trail aerobatics for that part of our evaluation. To me, this seemed like a good plan.

Unfortunately, this wasn't Beez's plan. Instead of pulling back to the horizon and rolling away from me, Beez tried something we'd never practiced before. With our noses pointed down at the ground, our jets accelerating through 400 knots, and Beez's jet banking into mine with me on the inside—not the outside—of his turn, Beez directed me to move to the extended trail position.

As soon as I acknowledged his order, I was in trouble.

"Hang 7-1, go extended trail," Beez called.

"Two," I replied over the radio.

I pushed my power to MIL, as we'd briefed, and instantly, my jet was even with his. I looked for a way to turn so that I could create some space between our two jets. I had to get to the outside of his turn in order to move away from him, but because

Beez had me positioned on the inside of his turn and he was already turning into me, if I turned into him, I'd hit him.

Since I was about to move ahead of him, I had to try something else. Having never seen this situation before on any training ride and never having discussed it with any of my instructors, I analyzed angles, options and alternatives in a fraction of a second.

Turn left into Beez — I hit him. Death!

Stay on my current path — we hit each other. Death!

Roll away from Beez... I move in front of him, and he might smash into me. Possible death!

Possible death is better than death!

I rolled away from Beez, and as soon as I cracked my wings away from him, I shot in front of him.

SHIT!

Not only was I in front of Beez, I lost sight of him, and I was definitely a hazard to the formation. By turning away from him while on the inside of his turn, I flew directly across Beez's flight path.

Shit! Shit! Shit! Shit! Shit!

"Hang 7-1, two is breaking out," I rapidly called out over the radio, hoping that instead of driving the nose of his jet through the floor of my jet, Beez would alter his flight path once he saw me in front of him and know that I was breaking out of formation.

At this point, I was no longer focused on passing my checkride. I just wanted to finish the ride alive! Knowing I had neither the skill nor the experience to extricate myself from my position in front of Lead, I did the only thing I could think of and screamed like a baby!

"Aaaaaaaaaaaaah!" I involuntarily blurted over the intercom.

"I have the aircraft," Lieutenant Carmody gargled, shaking the control stick.

"Roger, you have the aircraft," I acknowledged thankfully, throwing my hands over my head to the top of the canopy.

"I have the aircraft," Lieutenant Carmody repeated.

Immediately, he banked the jet further away from Beez's jet and rolled our aircraft totally upside down. He pulled the stick back to pull us toward the ground. Then, he continued his roll another 90 degrees to point our wings back in the direction of Beez's jet, which I still couldn't see. Then, he pulled back on the stick again, ripping the nose of the jet across the horizon.

This was not a move that we'd been taught at any point during our formation training, and there was no way I could even have imagined it—let alone fly it. In the front cockpit, one thought kept passing through my mind.

Please save us. Please save us. Please save us.

After his quick pull across the horizon, Lieutenant Carmody flipped the jet from 90 degrees of left bank to 90 degrees of right bank, and looking up and to my right, I saw Beez at my two o'clock high. I had no idea how he'd done it, but Lieutenant Carmody had not only gotten us out of danger, he put our jet into the proper position behind our formation leader from which to fly extended trail.

"You have the aircraft," Lieutenant Carmody gargled after rejoining the formation.

"Roger, sir, I have the aircraft," I said, shaking the stick.

"You have the aircraft," my Check pilot repeated.

"Hang 7-1, Two's in," I called to Beez over the radio, and he started his aerobatic maneuvering with me giving chase at a distance of 500 to 1,000 feet behind him.

The whole sequence of events, from the time Beez called, "Go extended trail," to the time I'd called, "Two's in," couldn't have lasted more than ten seconds. Ten terribly terrifying seconds. Now that Lieutenant Carmody had taken the jet from me on my checkride, I didn't know if I would pass the ride, but at least I was alive. For now, there was nothing left to do but fly and complete the mission.

When I got back to Eagle to grab my gradebook for the debrief in Check Section, Major Carrington and Lieutenant Baiber already seemed to know what had just transpired in the sky, but Major Carrington wanted me to tell him the story in my own words.

"Lieutenant Wright, did you initiate the break out, or were you directed to break out?" Major Carrington asked after I'd given him my version of what happened.

"Sir, I broke out," I said. "I was in front of Lead."

"Stay right here," he ordered. "I don't want you to go down to Check Section until I come back."

"Yes, sir," I answered as Major Carrington left the flight room and headed down the hall.

"Ray, you had to break out?" Doley asked, approaching me as I stood next to Lieutenant Baiber. "Did Kermitty take the jet?"

It was a logical next question. But, really, Doley was trying to figure out if I'd hooked my checkride.

"Yes, Doley, he took the jet," I said. Then, I added, "And I'm pretty sure if he didn't, I wouldn't be here right now to tell you about it."

"Shit!" Doley said shaking his head.

"You did the right thing by breaking out," Lieutenant Baiber offered. "The ride is behind you now. Forget about it. Concentrate on your ground evaluation, and do as well as you can. Control what you can control."

"Yes, sir," I replied.

"Ray," Doley jumped in again, still trying to figure out if I had a shot at passing the ride. "After he took the jet, did he say anything to you?"

I appreciated that Doley was trying to give me support. He knew that if I didn't pass the ride, I would probably be removed from the normal flow of the UPT syllabus of instruction for having failed my third checkride, and a sequence of events would begin that would lead to my reporting to a special review board and possibly ending my flying career. And I wouldn't be shit.

"As a matter of fact, he did, Doley," I said. "After he took the jet, Lieutenant Carmody said, *Where's the kaboom? There was supposed to be an earth-shattering kaboom!"*

I said it in my best Marvin the Martian voice, and I thought both my timing and delivery were excellent. For the first time in our UPT experience, Doley was the one at a loss for words.

*

"Sir, Second Lieutenant Wright, R.J., reports as ordered," I announced as I saluted Major Carrington, who sat at his desk with my gradebook and another report opened in front of him.

I had no idea how this was going to go.

"How do you think you did?" Major Carrington asked after saying to stand easy. He smiled up at me from his seat at his desk. He was talking about the course overall. This was the day we'd learn our general standing in the class.

"Sir, I don't think I did very well," I answered honestly, knowing I should have done better.

"Well, there's always room for improvement," he said, still smiling at me as I stood before him.

That was an understatement! I had failed two out of three checkrides in the T-37, and while I'd flown well enough to earn a *Good* on my T-38 Contact check, I'd had the jet ripped out of my hands on my Formation checkride because I found myself in a very dangerous position from which I didn't have the skill to recover. Remarkably, I earned a passing grade of *Good* from Lieutenant Carmody for that ride.

The official reason that I'd been given that grade, according to Lieutenant Carmody, was even though he'd taken the jet and set me up in the proper position from which to fly extended trail as the wingman, I had properly handled a very dangerous situation that had been created when my formation leader had directed me to assume the extended trail position from the inside of his turn at a very high airspeed with our noses below the horizon. Since I'd flown all of my required maneuvers well and recognized the need to break out when the situation call for it, I had been awarded a passing grade. I couldn't believe it, and some of my classmates couldn't believe it, either, but I'd passed my Formation checkride. I don't know how, but Beez had passed, too.

"Yes, sir," I finally acknowledged Major Carrington, not knowing what else he might be expecting me to say.

As the lowest-ranking student in the class, simply due to alphabet, I was the last student pilot to find out if I'd been ranked in the top half of the class with a FAR rating or the bottom half of the class as TTB. Kenny had just come out of Major Carrington's office before me, and he'd been FAR'ed. Of course, Mark Jellicot had been FAR'ed. Kurt had been FAR'ed. Doley had been FAR'ed. Golden Hands Brendan had been FAR'ed. Chuck had been FAR'ed. Even Beez had been FAR'ed.

"So, Lieutenant Wright," Major Carrington softly said, "do you think you are FAR or TTB?"

"Sir, I think I'm probably TTB," I answered.

"Well, congratulations," he said, and he told me how I'd been ranked. I stepped back, saluted, and walked back out into the main Eagle flight room.

The entire room was staring at me, IPs and students alike, as I emerged from the IP briefing room.

"Well?" Mark Jellicot asked.

"FAR!" I answered, loudly enough for everyone in the room to hear.

Most of the class congratulated me. Some of the guys that wanted to fly fighters but didn't get FAR'ed did not. They grumbled under their breath at their seats. I was okay with that; I knew they were disappointed.

Meanwhile, *I* was disappointed. By not being rated TTB, I seriously doubted I'd be assigned to fly that cargo jet in South Carolina.

"Congratulations, Lieutenant Wright," my IP Lieutenant Baiber said. "Have you given any thought to buying a boat?"

*

Mark Jellicot's van showed up in our driveway that night. Mark couldn't have been more excited. He was one step closer to his F-15 Eagle, where fellow fighter pilots might actually call him Gator or Fiend (and not Ho-Ho). He had picked up Kurt at the top of Azalea Drive, and the two of them came to our rental house with a bottle of tequila. Stupidly, we all did shots before heading to the Club for Thursday night Ladies' Night.

Since our class was scheduled for T-38 cross-country missions the next day, our jets had been assigned the last takeoff times on Friday afternoon. We figured we had enough time to get crew rest and sober up before having to fly our missions. I didn't know if this was the best plan, but I didn't care; I was ready to have a good time with my good friends, and Kurt very rarely came out with us.

"Who are you flying cross-country with, Kurt?" I asked from the back seat of Mark's van.

"Fuckin' Tennis Ball Head!" Kurt answered from the front passenger seat, turning around. Kenny held out the tequila bottle.

"I have the tequila," Kurt said, shaking the bottle back-and-forth.

"Roger, you have the tequila," Kenny said, letting go and showing Kurt his hands.

"I have the tequila," Kurt repeated. Kurt downed a double-shot straight from the bottle.

"Can you believe that shit?" Kurt lamented. "I had to put up with that fucker at the Academy for three years! He did everything he could to make my life miserable. Now, he shows up at UPT, and not only is he my IP, but I have to go cross-country with him, and he acts like we're best buddies."

"Kurt, the next time you're building some furniture in the wood hobby shop, maybe you could sneak out some spackle and help Tennis Ball Head putty up the holes in his face," I suggested.

"How does that happen, anyway?" Doley chimed in. "It looks like somebody lit a fiya on his face and stomped it out with a golf shoe."

"Aaay, how about that other major's face — the new guy in the Stu-ron?" Kenny asked, referring to Major Patterson, whose upper lip had a split under his nose that resembled curtains being spread apart from the center. Like our class commanders and academic instructors, he was assigned to the Student Squadron — not the flight line. But because he was going to be the SOF in the T-38 squadron for our cross-country weekend, he had come into Eagle flight that day, angrily dictating the Dos and Don'ts of cross-country decorum interspersed with a list of his personal pet peeves.

"You mean Smudgie?" Doley asked. "His face looks like somebody tried to hit a golf ball off his lips with a nine iyin and fuhgot to replace the divot."

"I think he should grow a mustache and grow it long on one side so that he can do a mustache comb-over, like bald guys try to cover up their bald spots," I said.

"Aaay, you might wanna start thinking about that," Kenny said. "I'll book you an appointment at my mom's hair salon."

"Who are you...? Beez with No Fleas?" I responded, reaching for the tequila while the others laughed more at Kenny's joke than mine. I shook the bottle to ensure positive transfer of tequila control.

"A mustache wouldn't work," Doley said. "He couldn't pull it off. The only guys who have mustaches around the flight line ah the enlisted guys and the Kuwaitis."

"Why is that?" I asked. "According to regulations, officers can have mustaches. I saw a guy at the Assignment Night party at the O-Club with a mustache. Why don't more guys on the flight line have mustaches?"

Nobody had an answer.

Thinking I'd killed the conversation, I brought the discussion back to Smudgie, as there were more things we needed to cover other than the ravine in his upper lip.

"How about Smudgie saying there's nothing more embarrassing than seeing cross-country student pilots in an O-Club wearing jeans and no belt! I never wear a belt with jeans," I said. "He made a huge deal about belts! Who wears a belt with jeans?"

"I don't wear a belt," Doley said. "I wear suspenduhs."

"Like Rerun?" I asked.

"Hey hey hey!" Kurt turned around, grabbed, and shook the tequila bottle. I showed him my hands, acknowledging he had control.

"Aaay, where's everybody going tomorrow?" Kenny asked. "I'm going to Hot-lanta. My parents are going to meet us at Dobbins."

"I'm going to Tampa," Kurt said. "My family is going to meet us, too."

"I'm going to Panama City," Mark Jellicot said. "I'm going to catch up with some buddies from college, and I want to check out the F-15 Eagles at Tyndall."

"Dude," Kurt said to Mark before taking one more shot of tequila and passing it on, "you're so lucky you don't have to worry about being FAIP'ed."

Having been part of the Fiends in the Philippines, Mark was almost guaranteed a fighter.

"We're screwed," Doley said. "How could we not be FAIPed? I just hope I get a T-38 and not a T-37."

"What if our instructors don't want us to be FAIPs?" I asked. "What if they thought we might not make good IPs?"

"If we don't get picked as FAIPs, we'll get scum-fightahs," Doley speculated. "Like an F-4 or an F-111."

"Do you think I have any shot at a C-141 to Charleston?" I asked.

"Not a chance," Doley said.

I didn't want to believe that. I didn't want to believe that I had no control over my destiny. I didn't want to believe that I'd survived UPT only to be FAR'ed and subsequently FAIP'ed. I wanted a say in my assignment, assuming I passed my last checkride.

"Ooh Baby Baiber wants to go to cross country to Wright–Patt," I bemoaned.

"Ohio?!" Doley questioned. "You have the keys to a supersonic jet! You can go anywhere in the country! Y'aw goin' to Ohio?! What the hell ah you thinking?"

I grabbed the tequila bottle, which had made its way back to Kenny, and shook it to let Kenny know I had control. I gulped down a double-shot.

"Ooh Baby says Wright-Patt is one of the bases that check pilots like to make students fly to for Navigation checkrides. He says it will be good practice," I explained, holding the bottle out for somebody else to take. I didn't like tequila.

"That right?" Doley considered. "Maybe I'll go, too."

"Well…don't forget your suspenders," I said.

"Hey hey hey," Kurt turned around again, shaking-and-taking the tequila as we pulled into the parking lot of the Club. By the time I'd unbuckled, he'd downed the bottle.

Chapter 22 — "If I Leave Here Tomorrow"

Though only the beginning on June, the temperature consistently hit ninety-five degrees during the day. Unless you were in an air-conditioned environment, you were sweating from the time you woke up until the time you went to bed. As with the previous summer when we'd arrived in Mississippi, the clouds would build throughout the morning, and an earth-rattling thunderstorm would strike between three thirty and four PM, shutting down flying operations until the lightning show passed and no longer presented a threat to aircrews. After four years on the side of a frigid mountain in Colorado, I loved the sun and the heat and the thunderstorms. The lawn around our rental house flourished in this weather pattern, too.

Because we didn't own a lawn mower, if we didn't borrow one from our friends on the weekend or have some kids knock on our door offering to mow the lawn for a few bucks, the grass didn't get cut. By early June, we hadn't done much borrowing, and there hadn't been much door knocking, and without any mowing, the grass had grown to well over a foot high in the front yard. Kenny, Doley, and I knew we needed to mow, but none of us ever made time to take care of it, which is why it wasn't getting done. The grass was taking over the property.

One Saturday, as Doley and I were getting ready to head downtown to Lenny's Gym for a workout and Kenny was out on a long bike ride, training for a triathlon, the knock we'd been waiting for finally came. Only, it wasn't a teenaged kid looking to mow our lawn for a few bucks...it was an eighty-year-old man dressed more for Sunday afternoon brunch than for mowing a lawn in ninety-five-degree heat.

"Tell me about this guy that's mowin' ah lawn, again," Doley said as we were driving back from the gym. Doley hadn't met the guy because I'd answered the front door and talked to him, and when we left for the gym, we left through the garage so as not to have to talk to him. I think Doley had only a glimpse of the old man.

"Doley, he's an octogenarian," I said, "dressed for Sunday brunch at Quincy's—"

"Home of the Big, Fat Yeast Roll," Doley interrupted.

"Home of the Big, Fat Yeast Roll," I affirmed. "He's wearing a button-down shirt, corduroy pants, a giant silver chuck wagon belt buckle, and a tube sock on his right hand."

"I'm glad he's wearing a belt," Doley said, "but the paht I don't get is why the tube sock on his hand?"

"Because of the salve!" I said for the fourth or fifth time. I'd had to tell this story on the car ride to the gym and a couple of times in the gym. "His doctor gave him some salve to grow his fingers back. When he'd reached under the lawn mower last month, a couple fingers got cut off, and the doctor told him the salve would help grow them back."

"And he believes his fingahs ah gonna grow back," Doley said.

"Yes, if he uses the salve the doctor gave him and keeps the tube sock on his hand, his fingers will grow back," I said.

"How much ah we paying this guy?" Doley asked.

"Ten bucks," I answered.

"You shoulda said five. Old Man Tube Sock Hand wouldn'ta known the diff'rence," Doley said.

We'd been at the gym well over an hour, but as we approached the house at the end of Azalea Drive, we both could see that the lawn had not been mowed. Well, half of one row had been mowed, but the mower sat in the middle of the front yard at the end of the half-mowed row. The octogenarian's truck was still parked in front of the house, but the old guy was nowhere to be seen.

We found Old Man Tube Sock Hand on the comfortable brown velour sectional sofa. He had helped himself to a large cup of lemonade from the fridge, made himself at home, and was watching CNN.

"Hey, sir," I said to the old guy, "is everything okay?"

"Hey there, young feller. My lawn mower got stuck in yer grass. Then, I thought I might've heard a razorback," he said. "Since I was stuck and hot, I came in and got me a drink. I thought I might could cool down, but it's hot in here. I think yer air conditioner's broke."

"You only mowed half-a-row of grass in an owah and a half?" Doley asked incredulously.

"Well, young feller, after my mower got stuck, I didn't want to reach up under it. Last time I did," the old guy said, "I cut off a couple of fingers." He held up the hand covered by the tube sock. "I got some salve on it. If I keep the salve on it, my fingers will grow back. Besides, I heard a razorback."

Doley threw up his hands and headed down the hall.

"Who do y'all think's gonna win, young feller?" the old guy asked me, pointing at the TV with his tube sock and sipping his drink. CNN was running a story about the Democrat presidential primaries.

"Sir, I don't think it matters. None of them are going to beat the vice president," I answered.

"I don't know much about this young feller from Massa-tu-setts," the old guy said, "prob'ly a educated man. His momma saw to that. I'm sure he loves his momma. Of course, Gore is from Tennessee, but he seems like a phony, even though he's a educated man. His momma made sure he had a education. I'm sure he loves his momma."

I found myself uncomfortably comfortable with Old Man Tube Sock Hand. I had already worked out and watched *Pee-wee's Playhouse*. That's about all I had on my list of things to do for the morning. Later, Kenny, Doley, and I were planning to go to a big party that the instructors were throwing at a lake. The FAIP Mafia Party.

"This is Jassie's second time," Old Man Tube Sock Hand carried on. "He's a educated man. His momma saw to that. I'm sure he loves his momma. He's a godly man, too. I know he loves God, and I don't know if I can say that about these other fellers. Of course, Jassie's a Neegra. There ain't never been a Neegra that's been president. Do you think he can win, young feller?" he asked me.

"Sir, I don't think he can win," I answered. "But I think that has more to do with his politics than his skin color."

"I don't know 'bout that, young feller. Sometimes, people think more about a man for what he is than for who he is," the old guy said.

He took another sip of lemonade. "Been that way a long time."

I had a pretty good idea Old Man Tube Sock Hand was not an educated man, but I didn't doubt he'd seen a lot over the course of his long life. In America, there never had been a black president. In Columbus, black people didn't go to white clubs, and white people didn't go to black concerts. In the Air Force, student pilots didn't wear the same uniforms as rated pilots. And real pilots didn't wear pink. And women pilots didn't fly fighters. And Columbus leaders walked around saying that if you ain't a pilot, you ain't shit. Things had been this way a long time. And these mores were manifestations of the same attitude. I didn't think his thinking was right. But was he wrong?

*

I felt like I'd replayed the whole year of flight school on fast forward in my mind while I tried to rest in Kenny's hammock. I don't know if half the images that had flashed through my head made any sense, but then again, I don't know that half the stupid stuff I'd done in the past year made any sense. After talking with

Kenny and Doley, both of whom had gone back inside, I was even more convinced that it didn't matter.

Mountains or beach? Not likely.

Fighter or tanker? Doubtful.

T-37 or T-38? Probably.

UPT was pretty efficient. For an Academy class, the combination of Academy grad plus FAR rating usually resulted in a FAIP. History had proven this.

History had also proven that one out of every three UPT students who started the program would wash out; however, for our class, the washout rate was only about one student in five. As a student pilot, I couldn't change the system. But as a class, could we change the norm?

I didn't feel any less hungover than I did when I woke up. Now that our next-door neighbors had fired up their power tools to give their perfectly groomed property its weekly manicure, I knew I wouldn't get any more sleep. I rolled out of the hammock and headed inside.

I checked the freezer to see if we had any frozen juice concentrate that Doley bought every once in a while. We didn't. We had a tray of ice cubes.

I wanted to use the ice for a nice, cold glass of water, but as hard as I tried to pull the metal tray out of the dense frost that grew from the bottom of the freezer, I couldn't budge it. The ice cube tray was stuck.

Absolute zero...the Third Law of Thermodynamics!

I wouldn't be able to move the ice tray without unplugging the fridge to melt the frost.

Unless I melted down on my Navigation checkride, which I was projected to fly by midweek, I'd likely be stuck in Columbus for the next couple of years. Kenny? Doley? Kurt? Chuck? Golden Hands? Beez? The other FAR'ed students? How many of us would be stuck? Were we all destined to be FAIPs? What did it take to escape an efficient system? What did it take to change one? We'd know in less than a week. Friday was Assignment Night.

*

Eagle had been incredibly busy in the month since I'd flown my Formation checkride. I'd flown over twenty instrument and navigation missions as a combination of local rides, out-and-backs, and weekend cross-country flights to prepare for my Nav check. I'd also flown a half-dozen sim missions.

One day, Lieutenant Baiber and I flew to New Orleans Naval Air Station with a drop down from altitude along the way to fly an instrument approach at Meridian Naval Air Station. We got gas in New Orleans, checked the weather, used the bathroom, and then flew back to Columbus with an instrument penetration and runway approach at Birmingham International Airport for extra practice. We flew to Eglin Air Force Base in Fort Walton Beach, Florida, and dropped into Montgomery, Alabama, to fly an approach along our route. At Eglin, we got gas, checked the weather, used the bathroom, and then flew back to Columbus.

Student pilots even got to fly solo out-and-back missions one afternoon. Two instructors in a T-38 led a long convoy of solo students to Fort Campbell, Kentucky, like a momma duck leading her babies, single file behind her, on a long journey. At Fort Campbell, we got gas, checked the weather, used the bathroom, and because the flight line operations center had a great snack bar, we also got to drink a delicious chocolate milkshake in between flights.

While every T-38 had its own government-issued fuel card to pay for gas to fill its tanks at all these bases, student pilots were expected to carry an additional form of currency for the crew chiefs who assisted us away from Columbus: class patches. And the way the chiefs asked always seemed the same.

"Say, Lieutenant, I've never seen one of those pink flamingo patches," a crew chief would say.

"Yeah, this is our class patch," I'd respond innocently.

"I collect patches. You don't happen to have an extra one?" the crew chief would ask. To conclude this ritual, I'd give the crew chief a patch.

A lot of IPs collected patches. Some displayed them on their desktops. Others kept them in a desk drawer. As a kid, I collected baseball cards; these days, I collected comic books – but I liked to read comics. I didn't want a patch collection. But there was a patch I wanted.

Besides Babe Baiber, Baby Baiber, and all the God paraphernalia displayed on Ooh Baby's desktop, my instructor did have a patch I thought was pretty awesome.

A red ring wrapped a sky blue circle. Both were outlined in black. At the top of the red ring, SHUTTLE was printed with white stitching. CHASE TEAM was printed at the bottom. In the blue circle in the middle of the patch, the Space Shuttle and a T-38 flew in formation.

I didn't think I'd ever get to be an astronaut, but it was cool to know I was flying the same jet the guys at NASA flew. I wanted a SHUTTLE CHASE TEAM patch.

I let Lieutenant Baiber know this. He was the head scheduler in Eagle, and one day, he made it possible. When the time was right, Lieutenant Baiber scheduled an out-and-back so that he and I could take a field trip to the Johnson Space Center at Ellington Field in Houston, Texas.

*

"Houston, Cuddy 4-8 here. The Eagles have landed," Lieutenant Baiber reported to Houston Ground Control once he'd taxied us clear of the runway. Based on his corny radio call, I knew my instructor was just as excited to visit the Johnson Space Center as I was.

Lieutenant Baiber handled the landing and ground operations because I'd flown the instrument ride under the bag in the back seat. *The bag* was a grunge-gray curtain that hung from bungee cords stretched along the length of the rear canopy. The bag forced students to fly the jet using only cockpit instruments with no outside references. Students weren't allowed to taxi from the back seat. While my IP taxied, I marveled at the wonders of the NASA flight line.

In some ways, Ellington Field at the Johnson Space Center was the Australia of military airfields. NASA aircraft followed a different evolutionary path than those at other bases around the world. Some planes were distant cousins of more traditional aircraft designs with elongated wings or oddly placed humps along the fuselage. Others were truly different species of flying machine with the strangest airfoil shapes I'd ever seen, either on a flight line or in a comic book.

In other ways, the airfield was like a high-end sports car dealership. NASA had painted its aircraft, including its fleet of T-38s, with the glossiest, brightest, whitest paint I'd ever seen. Each of these sleek NASA pearls had one Crayola blue racing stripe painted on its sides with a thin, lighter blue pinstripe above and below. For me, the coolest part of seeing these T-38s was *NASA* written in large red letters on tail of each jet.

Of course, we weren't allowed to park our T-38 anywhere near the NASA jets. Houston Ground Control gave Lieutenant Baiber instructions to drive to the transient aircraft parking area for visitors. We cut off our engines, grounded our jet so it could be refueled, and went in search of a Shuttle Chase Team patch.

Lieutenant Baiber had told me of a good Mexican restaurant just outside the NASA gate. I dubbed it Casa NASA. Time permitting, we'd grab a quick Pollo Apollo or Burrito Orbito, but if early afternoon thunderstorms popped up, we'd cut our field trip short, and get back to Columbus ahead of any bad weather.

Without a doubt, flight planning rooms were pretty cool places with all their maps, charts, and high-tech weather equipment. Most had pictures and memorabilia from past aircraft and squadrons stationed at the base through the years. Nearly all of them displayed the patches of visiting pilots. The shield or crest of the home base was usually carved out of wood, painted nicely, and mounted prominently on one of the walls.

With such close ties to the space program in Houston, this particular flight planning room had far better memorabilia than most. Astronauts spent a lot of time coming in and out of Ellington Field, and the pictures and patches displayed in this flight planning room made it a veritable astronaut hall of fame.

Everywhere you looked, there was a space mission patch or a team photo of an astronaut crew. Every mission into space had its own patch. I didn't see any with a double entendre or hidden meaning. On the other hand, I didn't see any NASA Beach Clubs.

The walls around the room were covered with pictures from space and portraits of astronauts. Most of the pictures were signed and had brief notes. Some had astronauts in their spacesuits; others, in their flight suits. I knew many of the astronauts' names from watching Apollo and Space Shuttle missions on TV and from studying aerodynamics, astrodynamics, thermodynamics, and Air Force heritage. They'd all been in this very room, and all had probably eaten at Casa NASA.

While Lieutenant Baiber was busy talking to the weather forecaster at one end of the building, I checked out a couple of Apollo models on a coffee table. I built the same models of a Saturn rocket and the lunar landing module when I was a kid. Nostalgically lost in NASA memorabilia and memories of childhood dreams, I didn't notice someone behind me.

"Say, Lieutenant, I've never seen one of those pink flamingo patches," a voice said over my shoulder, snapping me back from my childhood.

"Oh, yes, sir. This is our class patch," I responded automatically. I got up from the seat in case the voice came from a senior officer. I was hoping I wasn't going to be asked to surrender another of my dwindling supply of class patches.

At the big table behind me, looking over aeronautical maps and charts, stood a modern-day astronaut. I didn't recognize his name or his face from pictures on the walls, but I certainly knew his blue crayon-colored flight suit, the NASA patch, and the pilot wings on his chest.

"Is that your T-38 out back, Lieutenant?" the astronaut asked.

"Yes, sir. Well, it's not really mine," I said, pointing to the other end of the building where Lieutenant Baiber was now on the phone near the weather forecaster's desk. "I'm here with my instructor."

"How much longer do you have in training?" the astronaut asked.

"Sir, I've got about a month left," I said.

"Have you been given your first flying assignment?"

"No, sir, but I'll find out Friday," I answered.

"That should be pretty exciting, Lieutenant," the astronaut said, smiling, looking up from his charts. I imagined he was thinking back to when he learned his first assignment.

"Yes sir," I agreed, even though I wasn't too confident. But the astronaut didn't have to know that.

"Sir, have you been to space?" I asked him before he asked me if I wanted to fly a fighter.

"No, not yet, Lieutenant," he said, still smiling. Then he added, "I was supposed to go up this summer, but our missions are still suspended. Now, I'm on the schedule for 1991." The astronaut looked back down and jotted some notes on his flight planning card.

He was going to have to wait three more years before he got his outer-space dollar ride!

Would he have to give his spacecraft mission commander a dollar bill with naked ladies on the back after he returned to Earth?

"Wow, sir, that should be pretty exciting for you," I said. Then, I added, "That gives you a lot of preparation time for your mission."

"You bet," the astronaut said proudly, looking over at me again. "And that's what makes a successful mission, Lieutenant. We always know what we want to happen, but we don't always know what's going to happen. If we take control of the things we can control, and prepare for that things we can't control, when unplanned events occur, we empower ourselves to keep control. But if we're not prepared to keep control when unplanned events occur, entropy will work its chaos as fast as our lack of preparation will allow it."

I struggled to follow his logic.

"And we lose control?"

"That depends upon the constraints we have in place, Lieutenant," the astronaut corrected me. He folded up the chart he'd been using to plan flight and make his calculations. He picked up his mission planning card and slid it onto the blue crayon-colored NASA clipboard that he would strap around his thigh in flight. And when he'd gathered all his stuff and was ready to head to the flight line, he walked over to me and offered me some final words of wisdom: "But without constraints, we do — *very rapidly* — lose control."

Thinking there was a hidden meaning in what he was saying, I had to ask him what he meant before he left.

"Sir, are you talking about Challenger?"

"No, Lieutenant," the astronaut replied, "I'm talking about everything."

*

During my Nav Check, the check pilot never had to take the jet. He let me fly in the front seat on the ride back from Navy Cecil in Jacksonville to Columbus, a good sign that I hadn't hooked. He hadn't yelled at me and hadn't even really spoken to me on either the out-ride or the back-ride of the out-and-back.

Passing or failing my Navigation checkride, the last of the six UPT checkrides, was going to come down to my performance on the ground evaluation.

If my check pilot wanted to make things extra tough, he could grill me for the next two hours to see how much I knew or — more accurately — how much I didn't. Check pilots were like dentists, nonchalantly rubbing that pointy, curved instrument over your teeth until they found a cavity or tartar patch, and then they'd pick, pick, pick until they'd either dug the cavity to the nerve or scraped away the tartar from your teeth along with your top layers of gums.

On the other hand, if my check pilot thought my flying was pretty decent, he might be satisfied with asking me only an hour's worth of emergency procedures and general knowledge questions that represented a reasonable cross-section of systems and topics covering various degrees of difficulty. Maybe, he'd include just a few challenging situations or questions, but he'd do so only to be able to say that he treated all checkride students fairly.

I'd read the intel books on my check pilot. I had an idea of the general knowledge and emergency procedures questions I'd be expected to answer. I expected the worst. I knew I was in for the toughest evaluation of my UPT experience.

From the depths of his cavernous eye sockets, beneath the crimped-together eyebrows of his elongated face with its permanent scowl, Skeletor locked his gaze on me, ready to pick, dig, and scrape at the cavities and tartar in my brain.

"Let's see how much you know," he sneered.

"Yes, sir," I responded innocently, trying hard not to reveal how confident I felt sitting across from the toughest grader in Check Section. He had given out more *Unsat* grades than nearly the rest of the check pilots combined! Every student hated him...Doley's Ugly Rule.

But I had done my homework. I was prepared.

*

"Ray, tell us again what Skeletaw said when he gave you ya' grade," Doley asked for the third time since we'd arrived at the O-Club, downing his third cup of beer.

I crimped my eyebrows and sucked in my cheeks to hollow my face. "Do yourself a favor," I said in my most evil cartoon character voice, "learn how to do a fix-to-fix." Then, to keep up with Doley, I downed my third cup of beer, too.

"What a dick!" Doley laughed, pouring us both more beer from one of the many pitchers being passed around the Daedalian room where both sections of our class were being held before we'd be led into the main ballroom of the O-Club for the Assignment Night ceremony.

"Hey, man," I laughed, "he gave me a *Good*. Who cares if he's a dick?"

"Do you think I might be assigned to an F-15E? The Strike Eagle?" Mark Jellicot worried out loud. "I like the air-to-air mission...not air-to-mud. The Strike Eagle is a hot jet, but I'd rather fly the regular F-15 Eagle."

"I don't know if I'm even going to get an assignment tonight!" Al Turbiglio lamented. "My C-130 unit wanted me to get FAR'ed. I didn't get FAR'ed! What if they don't want me now?"

"Ray, you know I want to fly F-16s, but I'd be okay being a FAIP," big Kurt confided, tapping his cup of beer to mine as if offering a toast. "Malia's already stationed here, and with a baby now, I could be home every night. Instead of deploying all over the world, I'd rather be home with my wife and son."

"Kurtie, if we both get FAIP'ed," Chuck offered, coming over with her beer and tapping our cups, "we'll have good times together."

"Aaay, just get me the fuck outta Columbus!" Kenny interjected.

"Do you think we'll get outta here?" Doley asked.

"We'll know soon enough," I said, holding my cup out in the center of our little group for yet another team toast.

"ROOM! A-TEN-SHUN!" Al Turbiglio barked his strange-sounding, non-Academy-trained command just as we all were about to drink.

"Y'all, relax, y'all," the familiar voice of our short and portly class commander from T-37s, Captain Billy Mike Sims, called as he entered the room. He was immediately followed by his tall and lanky counterpart, T-38 Class Commander Captain Will Halliwell, who'd told us six months ago how much he liked our pink scarves.

"Class 88-07! Welcome to your Assignment Night!" the affable Captain Halliwell called out, which drew enthusiastic cheers from our class. "Captain Sims and I congratulate you, and we'd like to set some expectations for tonight's ceremony."

"Y'all, don't screw it up! Don't get a DUI!" Captain Sims warned.

"Once we move you into the main ballroom, make sure you fill in all the seats in front," Captain Halliwell said. "One of us will call the room to attention when the wing commander arrives. After he says *take seats*, he knows students want to hear how many fighters will be given out, and he likes to have a little fun with that."

"Y'all, be sure y'all play along with the wing commander," Captain Billy Mike warned. "Y'all, show some damn Columbus Class. Don't piss him off!"

"The wing commander will give out the first assignment of the night to the top performing student. That's usually the first fighter of the night," Captain Halliwell stated, and the class cheered again at the mention of the word *fighter*.

When the cheering died down, Captain Billy Mike added, "Y'all! If y'all get a fighter, and then y'all go out and get a DUI, y'all will lose y'all's fighter."

"After the wing commander gives out the first assignment to the top performing student," Captain Halliwell continued, "Base Operations Officer Colonel Ginsberg will give out the next assignment. This will be the first instructor pilot assignment of the night."

"Booooooooooo! Booooooooooo!" we all responded.

"Y'all, listen!" Captain Billy Mike yelled. "Y'all, listen!" he yelled again as we quieted down. "Some of y'all will be assigned to be instructors tonight. Y'all need to appreciate that the people who chose y'all are not only in the audience, but that we're instructors, too. Y'all need to show some respect."

"Captain Sims is right," Captain Halliwell added. "Those of you selected to be FAIPs tonight will be congratulated by your new squadron commander for either the T-37s or T-38s. You'll be given a flying scarf for your new squadron and a bottle of champagne. Please remember that this person will be your new boss."

"Y'all, don't screw up y'all's first official time y'all meet y'all's commander by doing something stupid," Captain Billy Mike admonished.

"Guys," I whispered to Kenny and Doley, "if we get FAIP'ed and then get a DUI, do you think they'll take away our IP assignments?"

"Aaay! Pour me a beer," Kenny said, holding out his plastic cup. I grabbed another pitcher as it passed through the crowd. Doley held out his cup as I refilled Kenny's. After refilling Doley's beer, too, I topped off my own.

"Ray, how does it feel to be done with all ya' checkrides?" Doley asked me as the three of us brought our cups together.

"Aaay! You're done!" Kenny screamed. He popped me with a head butt to my eyebrow.

"Ow! You bastid!" I grimaced. "I guess I'll finish UPT," I said, laughing nervously.

"Now, let's go see if we get out of Columbus."

*

Like the night I attended the Assignment Night ceremony for Doley's former roommates, the O-Club was packed with students and IPs alike. I saw Captain Wright from Dagger flight and most of his Dagger instructors. Major Carrington and most of our Eagle IPs were in the crowd, too. I saw Lieutenant Holtzmann, my fellow Rhode Islander, with his fake teeth firmly in place. I saw Captain Morawski, our guest-help T-38 instructor with whom I'd rubbed the crotch of Grenada Lake. The guy Chuck had called the Godfather of the FAIP Mafia was there again, too.

For the Assignment Night ceremony, the main ballroom of the O-Club was set up like a theater. At the front of the room, the small stage area had a podium at the left and a giant square movie screen that was probably ten feet by ten feet at the back right corner. Throughout the night, a slide projector behind the screen would display the mug shot of student pilots as we were called up to the stage, and as our assignments were announced, a picture of our newly assigned aircraft would be projected onto the screen.

In order for the slides to be seen by all the rows of folding chairs set out to fill the big room, the room needed to be dark. There were a couple of stage lights by the podium, which allowed the audience to see the speaker, but with the stage lights in his face, I doubted the speaker could see the audience except for those times that someone opened a door at the back of the room and let in some light from the ten thousand-dollar chandelier hanging in the lobby.

With these bright lights shining in his eyes, our steely-eyed wing commander paced back and forth on the stage, sweeping the seats in front of him with the antenna of his black walkie-talkie — as if it had the power to detect which of us might be thinking about getting a DUI. While he might like to have a little fun with the students, he looked more annoyed to me.

After pacing the stage and scanning the class with his stupid antenna, the orange-headed, red-freckled, steely-eyed wing commander pulled the microphone out of its holder at the podium and barked in his Texas twang: "Class 88-07, we all know why we're here tonight."

The whole class screamed wildly. The audience that filled the room—our instructors, fellow students, and other guests—politely applauded. The wing commander paced the stage, allowing our class to enjoy the moment.

"We're here tonight to give away some airplanes!" he gruffly barked to more cheers and applause.

"I know that classes like to hear how many fighter jets will be given on Assignment Night," the wing commander continued. "I know students like to hear which of you have been selected to be fighter pilots." He paused for more cheers and applause.

"Now let me ask you, Class 88-07," he said, squinting his steely eyes into the light that shined in his fair freckled face, and holding the microphone to his mouth, he called out, "what do you want to hear?!"

There was only one answer to this question.

"FREEBIRD!!!" Kurt and I both stood up at the same time and screamed as loudly as possible. Kenny and Doley each held up an arm with a bent thumb atop a closed fist, as if holding up cigarette lighters at a rock concert. The rest of the class followed suit, lifting imaginary cigarette lighters above their heads, too. Billy Mike was probably feeling for his own lighter right about now.

Momentarily stunned, the wing commander lowered his microphone and looked completely confused. Then, thinking he understood what we'd said, he held up the microphone and barked, "You want some birds? Well, we're going to give you some birds!"

"That was completely ridiculous," Doley leaned over and whispered loudly through the darkness over more cheering.

"Lord, help me," I prayed out loud, "I can't change."

"Where's Captain Jellicot?!" the wing commander called out. "Jellicot, get up here!"

"HO HO! HO HO! HO HO!" the whole class chanted as Mark Jellicot's mug shot was projected onto the movie screen. Mark excitedly jumped up from his seat and ran to the stage faster than the most enthusiastic contestant on *The Price is Right.* This meant only one thing: Mark was ranked as the number one student pilot in the class.

"Congratulations, Captain Jellicot!" the wing commander barked out like a Texas-version of Bob Barker. "You will be flying the F-15 Eagle in Bitburg, Germany!"

The entire class went absolutely nuts—clapping, cheering, screaming, and chanting, "HO HO!" Mark had worked extremely hard the whole year, and he certainly had earned the number-one ranking.

The next assignment, however, would not be quite as exciting. The next assignment was the one where the wing operations officer would name the first FAIP from our class, and as much fun as Assignment Night would be for those of us assigned to desired jets and locations, like Mark Jellicot, it would suck for others of us who might end up being stuck with planes that no one wanted to fly in places where no one wanted to live. It would be nice if everyone was about to get their first choice for assignments, but everyone knew that assignments like Mark's would be the exception and not the rule.

I hoped the first FAIP would be Chuck, and I hoped that she'd be assigned to fly a T-38. Chuck wanted to be an instructor, and while the T-37 was a fun jet to fly, the T-38 was faster, more comfortable, had a much greater range for cross-country weekends, and flew more formation missions, which I considered the most fun. T-38 instructors also flew with students who had six months of training under their belts, rather than with students brand new to jet flying.

After taking the microphone from the wing commander, the wing operations officer, a shorter, grayer, balder, crustier-looking man, pulled out a 3-by-5 index card from a zippered pocket on the chest of his flight suit. With the exception of Mark Jellicot, Valsalva, and maybe Chuck, those of us who had been FAR'ed held our collective breath while the ops officer put on his glasses to read from his index card. Nobody felt safe.

"Who's the funniest guy in the class?" the ops officer read from his card.

SHIT!

"DOLEY!" I screamed and looked toward my friend's seat through the darkness. It didn't matter what we answered—all that mattered was what was written on the index card.

I tried to start a chant: "DOLEY! DOLEY! DOLEY!"

Some of the class joined in, but knowing exactly what I was up to, Doley countered with a chant of his own. "RAY! RAY! RAY!" he yelled. But his chant didn't seem to resonate through the room as loudly as mine.

Once again, the officer at the front of the room had no idea what was going on. The student pilots of UPT Class 88-07 weren't following the script he'd been handed.

"Doley?" the ops officer said.

"DOLEY! DOLEY! DOLEY!" the chant grew louder.

"Well, listen up!" the ops officer yelled, quieting the crowd. "I said listen up!" he yelled a second time, like an order, and we all shut up.

"I don't know how funny Doley is," the wing ops officer grunted, "but my index card here says Ray Wright is the funniest. So, Ray Wright, you've got a T-38 to Columbus."

And just like that, all of the potential outcomes I'd dared to envision for my first flying assignment—cargo jets, beaches, mountains, travel, fun—were gone. I was a FAIP, a T-38 FAIP. Now, I was the one who was stunned.

My giant mug shot flashed up on the movie screen, followed by a beautiful picture of two T-38s flying in formation above the crotch of Grenada Lake. And when I saw that beautiful crotch shot, I couldn't fight it any longer. The T-38 was a great jet to fly! I knew I'd have a lot of fun teaching others to fly it. In my heart and my stomach, I didn't feel badly about this assignment, not at all. I smiled strongly and pumped my fist in the air.

Proudly, though not as enthusiastically as Mark Jellicot, I reported to the stage to accept my first assignment, my T-38 flying scarf, and my bottle of champagne from my future squadron commander, who had joined the operations officer on stage. My classmates applauded and congratulated me upon return to my seat—in part, happy for me that I'd been assigned to the T-38 and, in part, happy for themselves that they hadn't been named the first FAIP. But the night was still very young.

*

When the last aircraft had been assigned, ten of us would be remaining at Columbus as instructors, six of the ten coming from Eagle flight, including Kurt and Chuck. Most were assigned to T-37s, and Beez with me in T-38s.

Overall, our drop wasn't too bad. Nine guys got fighters. Valsalva and Golden Hands both were protected and got F-16s. Of course, Saeed got his F-1 Mirage. At the other end of the FAR spectrum, Kenny and Doley—who were what Doley had called *scum FAHs*—both were assigned a prop plane called the OV-10.

"HOLY SHIT! I GOT A OV-10!" Kenny had screamed back in his seat after learning his assignment. "WHAT THE FUCK IS A OV-10?!"

"Who cares!" Doley answered. "They're paht of Tactical Air Command, and that means one day, we'll be flying fighters!"

Four of our classmates were assigned to the C-141. But none of these were stationed in Charleston, South Carolina. Of course, Al Turbiglio was assigned a C-130 to his National Guard unit in Pittsburgh.

After the show was over, I took a fully clothed plunge into the O-Club pool before being kicked out of the building at midnight. I had to drive Kenny and Doley home in the Isuzu P'Up, Winner of the Baja 1,000, and I needed to sober up a little bit. Struggling to keep from dropping my champagne bottle while I pulled myself out of the water, I grabbed for the offering hand in front of my face.

"Lieutenant Wright, congratulations on your T-38," the Godfather of the FAIP Mafia said, giving me a handshake after he'd pulled me from the water.

"Thanks, sir," I said, shaking his hand.

"I happened to learn my next assignment this week, too," the Godfather continued the conversation.

"Congratulations, sir," I said. "I hadn't heard that." Truthfully, I hadn't. I didn't even know this guy.

"How would you like to buy my boat?" he asked out of nowhere. "I'll make you a deal."

For the past year, every time I had heard an IP make this joke, I thought it was stupid. And I kind of hated it. And I never took it seriously.

Until now.

"How much?" I asked.

"Let's talk," the Godfather said.

Chapter 23 — "Souls of Men"

The students crowded around Lieutenant Baiber's desk, admiring the Monday morning flying schedule as if it were a masterpiece on loan from the Mississippi Museum of Art. With a simple grid of magnetic tiles arranged on a white dry erase board, the schedulers had created a modern mosaic marvel. To the untrained eye, the little rectangles merely listed the takeoff times, mission numbers, IP names, and student names that would be flying in the last four jets of the morning. But because our PQ vision was now nearly fully pilot-trained, all the students of Eagle truly appreciated that the schedulers had created a tiled magnum opus in celebration of our long year of hard work and good times shared with the greatest of friends. In the last four jets of the first flying period of the morning, Kurt, Kenny, Doley, and I, had been grouped together to fly in a T-38 four-ship formation ride.

What made the masterpiece even more masterful was that we'd each paired to fly with the coolest FAIPs in Eagle flight. It was as if the four of us were about to go play Thunderbirds in the northeast Mississippi sky.

In my mind, however, I envisioned not only the wild excitement of being able to match my nearly fully trained flying skills against those of my best friends, but I also pictured the side-splitting laughs we'd have goofing on one another's mistakes in the ensuing debrief upon our return to the flight room following our mission. For as fun as flying jets could be at times, the best part of the past year in UPT had been the times that I'd spent hanging out and laughing with these three guys.

Without Kenny, my balls-to-the-wall roommate who loved cutting loose with good buddies, UPT would not have been the crazy adventure on the banks of the Tombigbee that it had become over the past twelve months. Though Kenny might appear to be the most non-traditional of military officers with his Fonzie sounding, order confounding, goldfish buying, orange hair dying, tin foil balling, catch Sandy falling, answer guessing, mannequin dressing, barn roof climbing, party fun priming, movie renting, moonshine fermenting, friends-first thinking, candlewax drinking, darkness making, lacrosse stick shaking, Mustang racing, and chaos-embracing antics, he was the most loyal and caring friend that any person could ever hope to know in a lifetime. Kenny relentlessly delivered unconstrained fun with unconditional commitment to everyone he knew.

When Sandy fainted in Dagger during Lieutenant Holtzmann's safety briefing on the dangers of drinking and driving, Kenny was the only person to jump out of his seat to catch her before she hit the floor. When Saeed washed back from 88-06 to our class, Kenny was the first to befriend our new Kuwaiti classmate, include him in our off-base activities, and welcome him to his own home and family in Atlanta. When I failed my T-37 Contact and Instrument checkrides, Kenny was there to chair-fly with me, study with me, and rent his favorite movie comedies to watch with me to help me get through my toughest times. In solidarity, he even changed his diet after I'd blown a bloody hemorrhoid!

Kenny made his own path, and that's what made him non-traditional. Yet while some may have regarded his conduct with uncertainty, Kenny certainly never hesitated to alter his course to help others. He turned bad times to good and ordinary times to great. Kenny made things happen, and to me, he was the best possible kind of officer and the best possible friend.

In Doley, I'd found the childhood best friend I never got to meet as a kid. Growing up in New England, we'd been weaned on the same TV stations, memorizing the same favorite shows. We listened to the same music and parodied song lyrics to make stupid situations even stupider. We followed the same sports teams, were crushed by the same World Series and Super Bowl losses and overjoyed by the same NBA and NHL championships. We probably even had the same posters of Larry Bird and Bobby Orr hanging in our bedrooms as kids.

To our classmates, Doley and I had a Pierce and McIntyre kind of relationship, and we played these roles throughout the UPT year, entertaining our friends in the flight room—with the possible exception of Al Turbiglio, our Frank Burns. I enjoyed Doley's razor sharp wit, and he never ceased to impress me with how he could take a funny subject and exploit it until he'd squeezed every last possible laugh out of his audience.

To me, however, our friendship was much more than laughs. I admired the confident persona Doley always projected. I knew I needed to be more like him. Sometimes I let my troubles in UPT get me down. Even if Doley had his own challenges to deal with over the course of the year, I never knew him to get bummed out by things. Our regular workout hours in the gym after a day on the flight line were as good for my mental fitness as they were for my physical fitness. For as out of place and out of sorts as I often felt in Columbus, Mississippi, Doley's perspective on events and his confident attitude reassured me that I, too, could persevere. And just listening to Doley's accent when he spoke or sang one of his original songs or picked on Al Turbiglio always took me back to a happy and comforting place.

I'd known big Kurt the longest. Ever since we'd played baseball together as freshmen at the Academy, we'd been pretty good friends. But as we began UPT, Kurt and his new wife Malia were in a different place in their lives than the rest of us. Not only were they married, they were preparing to be parents—and then they were parents. And though Kurt worked and studied as hard during UPT as even our class leader Mark Jellicot did, Kurt dedicated even more of his time and energy to his family. More than merely a giant among men, Kurt was a man among boys.

Sure, he enjoyed sharing laughs and good times in the flight room, in the classroom, and on an occasional night out, and he had earned top grades on all his checkrides and academic exams, but the times that I heard true love and passion in Kurt's voice were when I listened to him demonstrate the workings of the dresser or crib he'd built for his son in the wood hobby shop, or when he tried to teach me how to change a poopy diaper, or when he'd beam with pride about his wife's breast-feeding skills or the size of his baby's penis. Big Kurt inspired me to reach for more in life than just being a pilot, and the more time I spent with Kurt the family man, the more I didn't mind spending less time with Kurt my baseball buddy.

Along with his wife Malia, who welcomed me into her home, taught me to eat vegetables, and quickly forgave me after I'd publicly aired her childbirth video like a National Geographic TV special, Kurt consistently demonstrated to me that it's not what you are but who you are that matters most in life. While I often heard the stupid saying *If you ain't a pilot, you ain't shit* at Columbus Air Force Base, I don't think I ever heard it from anybody I respected, and Kurt and Malia debunked this myth every time I had the pleasure of being in their company.

When I looked at the morning's schedule, these were the images I saw. Like a truly great work of art, this tiled mosaic elicited a deep personal and emotional response. I was moved by this beautiful, year-end homage to friendship and good times, as told by little rectangular magnets on a white, dry-erase board by the simple, perfect order in which they were arranged.

0803	MOORE	WESSELS	F5801
0806	BAIBER	WRIGHT	F5802
0809	KUDYM	DOLAN	F5803
0812	FREEMAN	SPRANGER	F5802

An absolute masterpiece!

"Okay," Major Carrington broke the museum-like quiet of the crowd admiring the schedule, "who authorized this gaggle?"

After stewing for a moment to the point where he'd gotten his Irish up, Major Carrington called out, "SCHEDULERS! Where are my schedulers?!" And this signaled to the students gathered around Lieutenant Baiber's desk to scatter.

Since Kenny's name was at the top of the grid of magnets, he headed to the TOC to get the tail numbers and parking row positions for the jets we'd be assigned to fly for our four-ship mission.

I hustled down the hallway to the snack bar for some breakfast. Kurt and Doley caught me between the T-37 and T-38 squadrons.

"Guys, we've got to hurry," Kurt said conscious of time.

"Wait a second," Doley said, stopping short of the snack bar doorway. "We're not in that much of a hurry. Look at this," and Doley pointed to a thin-waisted, muscular-looking man paying the Snacko at the cash register.

I couldn't believe my PQ eyes!

Dressed in a starched, white, short-sleeved shirt, sharply pressed dark pants, shiny black shoes, and the dark, hard-brimmed hat of a commercial airline pilot, stood a remarkably slim, fit, and professional-looking civilian.

"Major Lawson?" I called out loud. "How have you been, sir?"

"Mighty fine! Mighty fine, old buddy!" Major Lawson smiled widely and reached over to put his left hand on my shoulder as we greeted one another with a handshake. "But I'm First Officer Lawson now — not Major. How's the hemorrhoid?"

"It's mighty fine, thanks," I said.

First Officer Lawson slapped me on the back and laughed. Then, he turned to shake hands with Doley and Kurt.

"Have you been hitting the gym?" Doley asked him. "You look pretty fit."

First Officer Lawson chuckled. "Well, Doley, old buddy, I have been doing a little running and attempting a few push-ups every now and then, but mostly you're seeing the results of a little less beer at night and the girdle I'm wearing under my new uniform." Doley, Kurt, and I looked him up and down to try to detect evidence of the girdle.

"Kind of sexy, don't y'all think?" he said as we studied his transformed physique. Then, First Officer Lawson lifted his right leg and blew a loud, nasty fart. He hadn't transformed too much.

"I got a T-38 for my assignment," I told him, backing away to avoid the blast cone and to grab some breakfast stuff for Kenny and me.

"That's mighty fine, Ray," the new airline pilot said, and before he turned to head out of the snack bar, he added, "I have no doubt you are going to make a mighty fine instructor."

"You might say that about Lieutenant Spranger, here, too," a familiar voice added, coming through the snack bar doorway behind Major Lawson. "Lieutenant Spranger, you might be up for this…you might not, but I've got a desk for you in Dagger flight when you return from instructor school."

"Captain Wright from Dagger flight, I would be honored to be one of your instructors," Kurt enthusiastically accepted Captain Wright's offer.

And all my IPs are picked by hand!

After saying our goodbyes and checking out with the Snacko, Doley, Kurt, and I hustled back to Eagle with food and drinks in hand.

"Why is it that guys like Major Lawson get out of the Air Force, and dicks like Smudgie stay in the Air Force?" I asked my buddies as we quickly walked up the long hallway. "Do you guys think that will ever change?"

"It won't ev'a change until people who wear jeans without belts ah r'accepted in the O-Club," Doley said.

"On that day, the O-Club won't be a Blow Club," I added.

Big Kurtie leaned down and whispered in my ear. "Don't worry, Ray. We can change it. But right now, we've got skies to conquer."

Back in Eagle, the students had once again crowded around Lieutenant Baiber's desk. This time, they were staring at the Monday morning flying schedule as if it were a car wreck in a ditch off the side of Highway 45 North.

Kenny, Doley, Kurt, and I were still up for a four-ship mission, but two of the FAIPs had been taken out of the formation. Kurt would be flying with Tennis Ball Head, and I would be flying with Smudgie! This totally sucked!

What had started off as potentially the greatest ride in UPT history now had the potential to end up as the all-time worst. I looked around the room for Lieutenant Baiber.

"Why aren't we briefing up this four-ship right now?!" Smudgie's whiny voice screeched from the IP briefing room. "Aren't we supposed to be briefing the four-ship right now?! We're supposed to brief a four-ship an hour and a half prior to the first takeoff time. Where is Wright?! Where is Spranger?! Where is Dolan?! I don't want to cancel this mission!"

Shut up!

I grabbed my checklist, my in-flight guide, my drink, and Kenny's drink. I left our food on Lieutenant Baiber's desk.

Smudgie met me as I crossed the threshold to the doorway of the Eagle IP briefing room. As the highest ranking officer in the formation, he was the formation commander, and he had taken charge. Hands on hips, feet slightly wider than shoulder width, he annoyingly whined out questions to which I knew he didn't want answers.

"Wright, Dolan, Spranger, where have you been? Getting snacks? GET IN HERE!" he whine-screamed in my face. "We need an hour and a half to brief up this ride! Wessels and the instructors are already in here! Let's go! We've only got an hour and a half before our takeoff time!"

"Yes, sir!"

"A four-ship is a high-visibility mission," Smudgie whined and squeaked as we took our seats. "Because our call sign identifies us as a four-ship, we will have the attention of everyone in the sky, on the ground, and on the radio. We look good by being in position in the sky and on the ramp. We sound good when our radio calls are sharP and crisP."

Smudgie emphasized the *P* sound at the end of the words *sharp* and *crisp,* just like I'd learned to call out marching cadences at the Academy:

Hup! Toop! Threep! Fourp!

"So, we all need to sound sharP and crisP by adding the *P* sound to our call signs, and everybody says it the same way. Is that clear?"

All four crews, students and instructors, alike, acknowledged that we would add the *P* sound to our call signs. Doley shot me a look and half a smirk, as if to say both good luck and "It's about time you had to fly with a total dick like this guy."

When we were done briefing up the objectives for our mission, I headed out to my locker to put away my scarf and get my G-suit, flight gloves, and water bottle. Kurt and Doley caught up to me in the hall, and together, we walked to the chute shop to inspect our parachutes and helmets before stepping into the heat of the Mississippi morning to get to our jets.

"Ray, you're number two in the formation," Kurt said. "If you don't sound good, the whole formation doesn't sound good. Don't forget to add the *P* sound to your radio calls."

"Ray, if ya' radio calls don't sound shahP and crisP, you'll ruin the ride for the rest of us," Doley warned. "Don't forget to add the *P* sound to ya' radio calls."

Just then, Kenny stepped out of the bathroom, directly across the hallway from the parachute shop, in time to overhear what the other two were telling me.

"Aaaaaay!" Kenny called out, like the Fonz, "unless you want to have an accident when you fly," he laughed, "don't forget to pee."

Kenny was an absolute genius! I don't know if he realized the gift he'd just given me, but it was Perfect, and once again our best buddy four-shiP had become the masterPiece I had originally envisioned.

Soaked in sweat after only fifteen minutes in the oppressive early morning heat of the Mississippi summer sun, Smudgie and I strapped into our jet after completing our pre-flight checks. With our helmets now on and our comm-jacks plugged in and powered up, his whiny voice rattled my brain stem in earsplitting stereophonic clarity: "Lieutenant Wright, are you ready? Don't forget to add the P sound to your call sign. Do you understand me?"

"Yes, sir," I said into my mask, smiling. I understood perfectly. I understood that to this point, we had talked about the P sound and adding it to our call signs, but we hadn't really practiced. That left the door nicely open.

All four crews gave a visual thumbs up to Kenny, our flight lead, to indicate we were finished with pre-flight checks, had our engines cranked, and were ready to taxi to the runway. Kenny knocked his helmet with his fist and flashed a couple of numbers for the radio channel.

Listening for the click of Kenny's microphone on the radio, I was ready with my radio call. And as good wingmen, Doley and Kurt, I knew, would be doing exactly the same thing I did. In fact, Smudgie, himself, had made the point in the mission briefing that everybody needed to say the same thing at the same pace in the same way.

Here it comes, I thought. *Kenny, then me, then Doley, then Kurt.*

Click—

"Fang 6-1, check."

"Two Pee!" I said.

"Three Pee!" Doley said.

"Four Pee!" Kurt said.

Perfect! Perfect! Perfect!

"Noooooooooooooooo!" Smudgie cried over the intercom. I could feel his fist banging on the instrument panel behind me. "Noooooooooooooooo! Noooooooooooooooo!"

Who ain't shit now, asshole!

"Columbus Clearance Delivery, Fang 6-1, flight of four, request clearance," Kenny called requesting our departure and altitude instructions after takeoff.

"No! No! Nooooooo!" Smudgie kept screaming and screeching through my headset all during Kenny's radio call to clearance delivery.

Oh, this was so good!

"No! No! No! Not 2 *Pee!* Not 2 *Pee!* It's *TooP!* Not 2 *Pee!* You were supposed to say, *TooP!* I told you to add the *P* sound…not to say, *Pee!* I have the aircraft! I have the aircraft!" Smudgie whined and vigorously shook the stick, taking control of the jet.

*

According to the T-38 Syllabus of Instruction, my only remaining ride in UPT was my *zoom-and-boom*. A special, one-ride block of Contact instruction, the zoom-and-boom introduced student pilots to the realm of supersonic flight.

Lieutenant Baiber had told Brendan and me that the zoom-and-boom used to be flown as a student's T-38 dollar ride. The syllabus had been changed, however, because instructors felt that students could only appreciate how differently the T-38 handled at supersonic speeds after having become proficient in handling the jet at subsonic speeds.

"Why is Lieutenant Wright on the schedule to fly twice?" Major Carrington asked Lieutenant Baiber about ten minutes before my IP and I needed to begin our flight briefing.

"Sir, Lieutenant Wright needs another 1.4 hours of flying time to meet the minimum time needed to graduate," Lieutenant Baiber said, standing up to speak. "Most zoom-and-booms don't even last a full hour. He's going to need an extra ride in order to have enough flying time to meet the graduation requirements."

"Lieutenant Wright can fly a 1.4 on his zoom-and-boom," Major Carrington stated, looking up about a foot to meet the eyes of my gigantic instructor. "That will save the taxpayers about ten grand in jet fuel, and it will free up that afternoon jet for someone else to fly."

Lieutenant Baiber turned around and looked at the scheduling board. I don't know that he liked Major Carrington making changes to his schedule, but I never heard him complain. For such a big guy, Lieutenant Baiber was the most soft-spoken and mild-mannered person I'd met at Columbus Air Force Base.

Initially, when I'd seen all of his God memorabilia displayed on his desk on our first day in Eagle, I thought I'd been assigned to someone who would want to have God talks with me all the time to convert me to his interpretation of religion. But Lieutenant Baiber was a teacher, not a preacher. In the jet, he taught with precision coaching. He might ask me a timely question, like: "How does this look?" He might say one word, like *pull*. He might make a brief statement like: "Your G-suit is playing the wrong song." And that would be enough to get me make corrections to set things right.

In the way Lieutenant Baiber approached life, he taught by example. Whereas many pilots at Columbus liked to elevate their sense of self-importance by saying, *If you ain't a pilot, you ain't shit*, Lieutenant Baiber treated everyone, including non-pilots, like students, enlisted personnel, and civilian maintenance workers, with dignity and respect.

Although I may not have been as openly religious as Ooh Baby, I would follow his example as an instructor and an officer, and if my personal system were efficient enough, maybe I could contribute to changing bigger systems.

"The only way to log a 1-4 on a zoom-and-boom," Lieutenant Baiber said to Major Carrington, "would be to zoom, boom, and hold. You'd have to enter a holding pattern up at altitude with no other maneuvering and then fly one overhead pattern to a full-stop landing. That's about the only way to even come close to having enough gas for a 1-4."

"That's exactly what I was thinking," Major Carrington agreed. "Stick me in the zoom-and-boom with Lieutenant Wright. You can use this period to find a mission for the jet we're freeing up for next period. I'll make sure Lieutenant Wright logs a 1-4, and he can be done with the program."

Lieutenant Baiber rearranged the magnets on the scheduling board as ordered. Instead of finishing UPT with some awesome, high-G maneuvering, I was about to end the program in a holding pattern.

In our mission briefing, Major Carrington gave me very clear expectations of things I would observe in and around the aircraft when we ripped through the sound barrier somewhere over Tupelo, birthplace of Elvis. And though I wish I could say that the sky turned purple, and I saw Elvis dancing on the wing, all that really happened inside the aircraft was some instrument needles bounced up and down momentarily, just as Major Carrington had foretold.

I did notice that the controls were a little sluggish inside our pressure wave. That is, it took more control stick deflection to get the jet to behave how I wanted it to behave—kind of like I'd lost my power steering fluid. Other than that, and the Mach Meter hitting Mach 1.1, I didn't feel much like Chuck Yeager.

Once we transitioned back to subsonic flight, Major Carrington took control of the jet and established our holding pattern about twenty-five miles northeast of the base at twenty-nine thousand feet to maximize our time in the sky. We flew oval after oval, trying to use the least possible amounts of energy and fuel. I don't know which was more uneventful, breaking the sound barrier or spending forty-five minutes in a holding pattern.

"So, Ray," Major Carrington surprisingly addressed me by my first name over the intercom as we entered our second holding turn, "now that you're done with UPT, what did you think about it?"

I didn't know if he was asking me for a critique of the program or my reaction to the program. So, considering he might possibly be my new boss after I'd been trained to be an instructor, I thought the better way to answer would be to give him my reaction to my personal UPT experience.

"Sir, it was a year of hard work. I certainly felt my fair share of stress. But it was also a lot of fun," I answered. Then, after a brief moment of reflection, I added, "And to this point in my life, it was the greatest, most thrilling adventure I've ever experienced."

Major Carrington laughed through the intercom...a happy laugh.

"That's great, Ray," he said, still half-chuckling. "Overall, how do you think you did in UPT?"

How did I think I did?

This was a loaded question. I thought I sucked, but I couldn't say that I sucked because Major Carrington and his fellow instructors had just chosen me to become one of them!

Out of six checkrides, I'd failed two and had no *Excellents*. I'd failed an academic exam in T-37s and had a *Marginal* room-inspection grade while I'd lived on base. For most of the year, I just tried to survive and stick around to fly another day. Relative to a lot of my classmates, I didn't think I did too well.

"Sir, I wish I'd done better," I admitted.

"Oh?" he replied.

Shit!

I realized that my answer sounded like I wasn't happy with my assignment.

"Sir, it's not that I'm not happy with my assignment," I backtracked. This was the truth. Although I might not yet have been too keen on Columbus, I had just bought a boat and was looking forward to having fun on the river. I liked flying the T-38, and I'd be working with a lot of good people. And lately, I'd been thinking a lot what the astronaut had told me just before my delicious Burrito Orbito at Casa NASA.

As an element or a component of a system, I'd always be bound by the limits and constraints of the system. But if I built my own system, like Kurt and Malia or Mark Jellicot or UPT, I could define my own limits and constraints. I could take control of what I could control. I could prepare for things I couldn't control. I could empower myself to keep control. And when unplanned events occurred, I'd know how to handle them. Like executing **BOLDFACE** for emergency procedures.

"Major Carrington, what I meant to say was that I didn't perform as well as I think I should have," I said. "Sir, I think I was capable of more."

"I see," said Major Carrington rolling the jet into thirty degrees of right bank to begin another inbound leg of our holding pattern. "Why do you think that is, Ray? Why do you think that maybe you didn't perform as well as you should have?"

I looked at the clock on my instrument panel. Maybe I had been prepared to fly my final rides in the program, but I was not prepared for another hour's worth of questions, pneumatically sealed under a cone of silence with Major Carrington. He would keep us airborne until he was sure we could record a flight time of 1.4 hours. I couldn't duck his questions. He had control of the jet.

"Sir, I should have taken UPT more seriously and approached it like a challenge, where every day provided another opportunity to excel. Instead, I played within the UPT system, like it was a game. I could have used more of my free time to be better prepared, and had I been better prepared, I have no doubt that I would have performed better," I told him.

"I see," Major Carrington said again, rolling again into thirty degrees of right bank. He executed his holding pattern turns flawlessly. I had been timing his inbound and outbound legs, to make sure they were both a minute and a half long. After our first turn in holding, I thought he'd been messing up the times, but I didn't say anything. It wasn't until our third trip around the big oval in the sky that I realized he'd been adjusting his timing to correct for the winds at altitude, which is what he should be doing, according to the books. I should have known that sooner. When I came back to Columbus as a FAIP, I'd know that's what I needed to do.

"Ray, what would you like to fly after you serve your time as an instructor?" Major Carrington asked, rolling out of his turn.

"Sir, as much as I had wanted to fly a C-141 at Charleston Air Force Base after UPT, I'm really not thinking about my next assignment anymore," I said. "I'm actually more focused on being a FAIP. I enjoy flying, I enjoy working with people, and I'd like to be a really good teacher."

"Ray, that's great. With that attitude, you will be an excellent instructor," Major Carrington said. "Have you calculated how long we need to remain in this pattern to ensure that we log a one-four?" he asked.

"Yes, sir. I have," I replied confidently.

"Excellent!" Major Carrington said. "Then, please let me know when you are ready to take control."

I was ready to take control. It had been a long time since I had been in control.

"Sir, I have the aircraft," I said, shaking the stick.

"Roger, you have the aircraft," Major Carrington responded. Glancing in my rearview mirrors, I could see that he was holding up his hands.

I shook the stick from side-to-side one more time.

"I have the aircraft."

Made in the USA
Middletown, DE
24 March 2018